P17

BOSTON
ACCESS ®

D0539693

Orientation

Although Boston is only the 20th-largest city in the country, its grandeur—based on more than 350 years of history—is genuinely impressive. The **Freedom Trail** alone connects 13 historical sites from colonial and Revolutionary days, including the **Old State House, Paul Revere's House,** and the **Old North Church.** Such events as the Boston Massacre, the Boston Tea Party, Paul Revere's midnight ride, and Samuel Adams's impassioned protests against taxation without representation have all left their mark on the city and its residents.

Despite its historic ambience, Boston's student population—about 100,000 a year who flock to the city and nearby **Cambridge**—keep the spirit young and constantly in flux. Many are tempted to stay on, and do. "It's so livable," they marvel, meaning walkable and packed with odd pleasures—not that the shortest distance between two points is ever a straight line here. The older parts of the city, particularly **Beacon Hill** ("the Hill") with its Brahmin residents, the **North End,** and Cambridge (across the **Charles River**), were laid out helter-skelter along cow paths, Native American trails, and the ghosts of long-gone shorelines (from the very start, the city has stretched its limits with infusions of landfill). Logic is useless in assailing the maze, but getting "lost" is half the fun. You could spend a day wandering the narrow cobblestoned streets of the Hill and never run out of charming 18th- and 19th-century town houses with interior lives you can only guess at. Furnish your own dream abode out of the grab bag of **Charles Street** antiques stores in Beacon Hill, or while away a lazy afternoon sampling the market wares in the North End— here a nibble of fresh mozzarella, there a briny olive, and virtually everywhere a cappuccino topped with lively conversation. Eventually you'll gravitate, as the natives do, to the banks of the Charles River, where runners, walkers, bicyclists, and skaters whip by on their invigorating rounds.

Though the climate is trying at times (the seaborne weather can be quite capricious), it's certainly never boring. Summer's lush abandon cedes gradually to bracing autumns and bitter-cold Decembers, but greenery and sanity reemerge with the magnolias abloom along magnificent **Commonwealth Avenue** and the willows weeping around the **Public Garden** lagoon.

After a day on your feet, you'll be anxious to dive into a seafood feast (one of Boston's trademarks) or perhaps a gourmet meal. As recently as a dozen years ago, you might have had trouble coming up with more than a handful of interesting restaurants in Boston; now the problem is choosing among them— a number of talented chefs have sprung forth in an atmosphere of camaraderie rather than competition. Literature likewise provides rich repasts. **Harvard**

Rowes Wharf

Square is said to boast the largest per-capita concentration of bookstores in the country, and readings often draw crowds in the hundreds. And finally there are the Boston sports teams. As frustrated as they may get with the players, **Red Sox** fans are inevitably caught up in the romance of tiny **Fenway Park**, a classic dating from the golden age of ballpark design. But this should come as no surprise to anyone who knows a born-and-bred Bostonian. They are a people who savor the intimacy, the authenticity, and, above all, the history of their lovely city—and rightly so.

How To Read This Guide

BOSTON ACCESS® is arranged by neighborhood so you can see at a glance where you are and what is around you. The numbers next to the entries in the following chapters correspond to the numbers on the maps. The type is color-coded according to the kind of place described:

Restaurants/Clubs: Red   **Hotels:** Blue

Shops/ 🍃 Outdoors: Green   **Sights/Culture:** Black
& Wheelchair accessible

Rating the Restaurants and Hotels

The restaurant ratings take into account the quality, service, atmosphere, and uniqueness of the restaurant. An expensive restaurant doesn't necessarily ensure an enjoyable evening; however, a small, relatively unknown spot could have good food, professional service, and a lovely atmosphere. Therefore, on a purely subjective basis, stars are used to judge the overall dining value (see the star ratings at right). Keep in mind that chefs and owners often change, which sometimes drastically affects the quality of a restaurant. The ratings in this guidebook are based on information available at press time.

The price ratings, as categorized at right, apply to restaurants and hotels. These figures describe general price-range relationships among other restaurants and hotels in the area. The restaurant price ratings are based on the average cost of an entrée for one person, excluding tax and tip. Hotel price ratings reflect the base price of a standard room for two people for one night during the peak season.

Restaurants

★	Good	
★★	Very Good	
★★★	Excellent	
★★★★	An Extraordinary Experience	
$	The Price Is Right	(less than $10)
$$	Reasonable	($10-$15)
$$$	Expensive	($15-$20)
$$$$	Big Bucks	($20 and up)

Hotels

$	The Price Is Right	(less than $100)
$$	Reasonable	($100-$175)
$$$	Expensive	($175-$250)
$$$$	Big Bucks	($250 and up)

Map Key

1 Entry Number   **Freeway**

City/Town ●   Highway   ⊏ Tunnel

Ⓣ = subway stop

Point of ■   Tertiary Road
Interest

Logan International Airport (BOS)

Gate Locations for Major Airlines

A Colgan Airways
Continental Airlines
USAir Shuttle
(to LaGuardia
in NY only)

B American Airlines
American Eagle
America West
Cape Air
Delta Shuttle
Midwest Express
Mohawk Airlines
Quantas Airways
Sabena World Airlines
(departures only)
USAir/USAir Express
Virgin Atlantic Airways
(departures only)

C Delta Air Lines
Delta Connection
Skymaster
TWA (domestic)
TW Express
United Airlines
United Express

D Charter Flights
Alitalia Airlines
(departures only)

E International Flights
Northwest Airlines
(domestic)

Car-rental counters and baggage claim are located on the lower level.

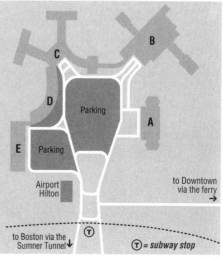

B

C

D   Parking

A

E   Parking

Airport
Hilton

to Downtown
via the ferry
→

to Boston via the
Sumner Tunnel ↓

Ⓣ

Ⓣ = subway stop

Area code 617 unless otherwise noted.

Getting to Boston

Airport

Located three miles east of downtown Boston on a peninsula across the harbor from the city, **Logan International Airport (BOS)** services more than 50 domestic and international airlines in its five terminals. The airport is fully accessible to people with disabilities.

Airport Emergencies	561.1919
Currency Exchange	567.2313
Customs and Immigration	565.4658
Ground Transportation Hotline	800/235.6426
Information	561.1806
Lost and Found	561.1714
Medical Clinic	569.8652
Paging	Terminal A: 561.1940,
Terminal C: 561.1806,	Terminal E: 561.1804
Parking	800/235.6426
Police	561.1700
Traveler's Aid	542.7286

Airlines

American	800/433.7300
Air Canada	800/776.3000
British Airways	800/247.9297
Continental	800/525.0280
Delta	800/221.1212
TWA	800/221.2000
United	800/241.6522
USAir	800/428.4322

Getting to and from the Airport

By Car

Legendary traffic snarls can make the trip via the **Callahan Tunnel** (to Logan) or the **Sumner Tunnel** (out of the airport) as long as 30 minutes, sometimes even more. And it's best to plan not to arrive at or leave from Boston's busy air terminal between 4PM and 6PM on a weekday—especially a Friday.

To get to Boston from **Logan,** bear left on the first ramp coming out of the airport, and follow the signs to Sumner Tunnel (there's a $1 toll). At the end of the tunnel are signs for the **Central Artery.** For the North End, take the Central Artery North exit; for downtown, head in the direction of Central Artery South.

To get to the airport from downtown, follow the Central Artery ramp signposted "Airport" to the Callahan Tunnel (there's no toll in this direction). A large horseshoe-shaped road takes you past all five terminals. There is long-term parking in the middle of the horseshoe and short-term parking at each terminal.

The first long-distance telephone call was made from Boston to New York City on 27 March 1884

Shuttle buses will transport you from outside the terminals' baggage-claim areas to car-rental counters (they are all open 24 hours).

Avis	561.3500, 800/331.1212
Budget	787.8200, 800/527.0700
Hertz	569.7272, 800/654.3131
National	569.6700, 800/227.7368
Thrifty	569.6500, 800/367.2277

By Limousine

Though car services are the most expensive choices, they are a comfortable way to travel. **Boston Coach** (387.7676), **Leros Point to Point** (848.6803), and **A&A Carey** (623.8700) are three good limousine companies.

By Subway

The **Massachusetts Bay Transportation Authority (MBTA**; 722.3200, 800/392.6100) is the least expensive way to travel to and from the airport, and takes the shortest amount of time. Take the *Blue Line* to the **Airport** station (a 10-minute ride from the **Aquarium** or **Government Center** stops in downtown) and connect with free **Massport** shuttle buses that make stops throughout the airport (look for sign on each bus indicating which terminal). Travel time to the airport from the **MBTA** station is about ten minutes.

By Taxi

Cab stands are located at all airport terminals; the common practice is to share a ride with others headed your way, as traffic congestion can easily run up the cost of the trip. Fares can skyrocket during peak travel times and can be almost as high as the cost of a limousine.

By Water Shuttle

A free shuttle bus runs between the airline terminals and the **Logan Boat Dock.** At the pier, passengers take the **Airport Water Shuttle** (recorded information 330.8680, 439.3131) across **Boston Harbor** to **Rowes Wharf** (at **Atlantic Avenue**) on the edge of downtown Boston (and back). A seven-minute ride (including the bus), this is a favorite way to travel among seasoned visitors (and residents) for three good reasons: the ferry charges a moderate fare, takes a scenic route, and avoids traffic entirely.

Getting Around Boston

Bicycles

Bikers have several scenic options in Boston. Two particularly appealing paths are the **Greenbelt Bikeway** and the **Dr. Paul Dudley White Bikeway.** The Greenbelt outlines the entire perimeter of Boston's famous **Emerald Necklace,** an 8-mile chain of parkland extending from the **Boston Common** to **Franklin Park.** The Dudley starts along the Charles River, then traverses several sections of town. You can rent mountain bikes, touring bicycles, or a cross betweeen the two at **Community Bike Shop** (496 Tremont St, between Arlington and Berkeley Sts,

542.8623) or **Back Bay Bicycles** (333 Newbury St, between Hereford and Massachusetts Aves, 247.2336). Maps of local trails are available at the bike shops or from the **Department of Public Works** (State Transportation Building, 10 Park Plaza, 973.8000). See also "Boston by Bike: Plum Paths for Pedal Pushers" on page 170.

Boats and Ferries

As Boston is embraced by the Boston Harbor and the Charles River, traveling by water is an enjoyable, convenient way to get around the city. **Community Boating** (21 Embankment Road, 523.1038; TTY 523.7406 ♿) provides tours of the Charles River, as well as small sailboats for rent. **Bay State Cruise Company** (723.7800) offers cruises from **Long Wharf** and **Commonwealth Pier** around the Boston Harbor, to the USS *Constitution,* and to **Georges Island,** as well as ferries to **Provincetown** in the summer. **Boston Harbor Cruises** (227.4320) features 90-minute historical sight-seeing cruises.

Buses

The **MBTA** (722.3200, 800/392.6100) operates the city's buses, as well as the subways, streetcar lines, commuter trains and boats, and vans for riders with special needs. Crosstown and local buses travel throughout greater Boston and **Cambridge.** Tokens (available at any subway station), exact fare, or **MBTA** passes (see Subway below) are required.

There are two terminals for commuter and long-distance buses: the **Greyhound Terminal** (10 St. James Ave, Back Bay, 800/231.2222) and the **Peter Pan Terminal** (555 Atlantic Ave, 800/343.9999) near **South Station** on the waterfront. The following bus lines service the Boston area and beyond:

Bonanza ....423.5810 (northeast US)

Concord Trailways ....426.7838 (New Hampshire)

Greyhound.............................423.5810 (nationwide)

Peter Pan Bus Lines ....426.7838 ....(central Massachusetts, New York City)

Plymouth and Brockton.............423.5810 (the Cape)

Driving

If you have a choice, don't drive. Boston is a pedestrian city, with confusing street patterns in many neighborhoods. Even if you have the derring-do to "compete" with Boston's notoriously brazen drivers, be forewarned that signage is generally poor and there are lots of one-way streets.

On highways, the speed limit is 55 miles per hour. Right turns on a red light are permitted in Massachusetts except where prohibited by posted signs. Tolls are charged for using the **Massachusetts Turnpike** (I-90), tunnels, and various bridges.

Garages

There are numerous parking garages in town, and various open lots, some of which are listed below. Prices vary widely for hourly and day rates, with the most expensive in the **Financial District/ Downtown** area.

In Boston:

Auditorium Garage 50 Dalton St (near the Hynes Convention Center) 247.8006

Boston Harbor Garage 70 East India Row...723.1731

Copley Place Parking 100 Huntington Ave .375.4488

Government Center Garage 50 New Sudbury St........ ....227.0385

Prudential Center Garage 800 Boylston St.267.2965

In Cambridge:

Charles Square Garage 5 Bennett St, Harvard Square 491.6779

Harvard Square Parking Garage 65 JFK St...354.4168

Parking

Street parking is limited and highly regulated, so read signs carefully. Many neighborhoods, particularly Beacon Hill, have almost no parking for nonresidents. It's very common to be ticketed and/or towed away to Boston's hinterlands. If your car is towed, retrieving it will be costly and time-consuming.

Subway

Run by the **MBTA,** Boston's subway system—known locally as the "T"—is the nation's oldest. Four lines—*Red, Blue, Orange, Green*— radiate from downtown. The symbol **T** (pictured above) outside the entrance indicates stops. Inbound trains go to central downtown stations: **Park Street, Downtown Crossing, State,** and **Government Center;** outbound trains head away from these stops. Tokens (available for purchase at stations), exact fare, or passes (see below) must be used.

The **T** has minor eccentricities, best learned from experience. On the *Green Line,* many of the street-level stations do not have ticket booths, so you must have exact change ready (tokens are also accepted, supplemented by change). Drivers do not make change, although helpful passengers often will. Note: Certain inbound lines charge higher fares from outlying stations; always ask. And going outbound on the *Green Line,* no fare is charged if you board at an aboveground station. Smoking is not allowed in stations or on trains.

MBTA operates Monday through Saturday from 5AM to 12:45AM, and Sunday and holidays from 6AM to 12:45AM. Discount passes for senior citizens are available at the **Downtown Crossing Concourse;** student passes are sold at schools (children five to 11 pay half fare, children under five ride free). The Boston Passport, a visitor pass good for three or seven days, is sold at the **Boston Common Visitor Information Center** (open daily from 9AM to 5PM), or at the **Airport** station (open daily between 9AM and 4:30PM).

Telecommunications Device for the Deaf (TDD) can be reached at 722.5146. For daily recorded service conditions, call 722.5050. Those with special traveling needs should call 722.5123, 800/533.6282, or TDD 722.5415. Monthly passes (722.5219) are available at various rates and provide the option to combine subway and bus travel.

Taxis

There are usually plenty around town, except between 3PM and 7PM (especially on Friday) and in the worst weather. They're easiest to find near major hotels, on **Newbury Street,** and at **Downtown Crossing** and **Faneuil Hall Marketplace.** Available cruising taxis have a lighted sign on the roof. Some local companies are:

In Boston:

Checker Taxi	536.7000
Red and White Cab	742.9090
Red Cab	734.5000
Town Taxi	536.5000

In Cambridge:

Ambassador Brattle	492.1100
Cambridge Yellow Cab	547.3000
Checker Cab of Cambridge	497.9000

Tours

By Trolley, Bus, or Car:

Beantown Trolley	287.1900
Boston Trolley Tours (The Blue Trolley)	427.8687
Brush Hill Transportation	986.6100
Commonwealth Limousine Service	787.5575
Gray Line Sightseeing	426.8805
New England Sights	232.1130
Old Town Trolley Tour of Boston	269.7010
Uncommon Boston	731.5854

By Boat:

See the "Waterfront" chapter, which begins on page 58.

By Foot:

Boston by Foot/Boston by Little Feet	367.2345
Historic Neighborhoods Foundation	426.1885
Uncommon Boston	731.5854

Trains

MBTA (722.3200, 800/392.6099) commuter trains leave from **North Station** (150 Causeway St) for destinations north and west of the city. This is where droves of Bostonians catch the *Purple Line* to the **North Shore** and its beaches. The *Rockport Line* commuter rail, nicknamed "the beach train," fills up fast on hot summer days. The **MBTA** *Green* and *Orange Lines* also stop here.

Amtrak (482.3660, 800/872.7245) trains depart from **South Station** (Atlantic Ave, at Summer Street) and stop at **Back Bay Station** (145 Dartmouth St), and at **Route 128 Station** in **Westwood**, 15 minutes west of Boston.

The **MBTA** *Purple Line* also leaves from **South Station** for points south of the city. The *Red Line* stops at **South Station** and the *Orange Line* stops at **Back Bay/South End Station** (which also serves as **Amtrak's Back Bay Station**).

Walking

The entire city could be walked briskly in a day, so a lot of your sight-seeing is best done on foot. Half the fun is wandering along the twisting, nonsensical streets. If you would prefer a more premeditated route, there's always the **Freedom Trail.** For strolling through the grass, you are never more than a few blocks from parkland, thanks to Frederick Law Olmsted's **Emerald Necklace.**

FYI

Accommodations

In addition to the hotels listed in each chapter, there are a variety of guest houses and bed-and-breakfasts in Boston and Cambridge. **Beacon Guest Houses** (248 Newbury St, between Fairfield and Gloucester Sts, M-F 262.1771; evenings, weekends, holidays 266.7142) attracts many tourists and foreign visitors to their inexpensive pension-style accommodations. The office screens guests and provides single and double efficiencies (twin beds only) for brief or long-term stays in converted town houses. The rooms have no telephone, TV, or maid or room service, but all have a private bath and kitchenette with some utensils, linens, and towels.

There are also many B&B referral organizations serving a number of neighborhoods and towns. Some of these include:

A Cambridge House Bed-and-Breakfast Inn	491.6300, 800/232.9989
Bed & Breakfast Associates	449.5302
Bed and Breakfast Cambridge and Greater Boston	576.1492, 800/888.0178
Host Homes of Boston	244.1308
New England Bed & Breakfast Inc.	244.2112

Climate

Boston's weather can be capricious: Summer can be very hot and humid, but is often cooled by the sea; winter is usually cold and damp with snow and ice, or brisk and sunny. The most comfortable times are spring and fall, but each season has its charms.

Months	Average Temperature (°F)
December-February	30
March-May	46
June-August	71
September-November	53

Drinking

You must be 21 years old to purchase liquor. Blue Laws vary slightly in Cambridge and Boston, and also depending on the establishment's license. In general, no liquor is sold in bars after 2AM or before noon on Sunday. In stores, no liquor is sold after 11PM Monday through Saturday, and none on Sunday except near the New Hampshire border.

Money

Boston banks do not commonly exchange monies from other countries, so be sure to handle any such transactions at **Bay Bank Foreign Money Exchange** at **Logan International Airport** (Terminal E, 567.2313). You can buy foreign currency at **Thomas Cook Foreign Exchange** (160 Franklin St, at Congress St, 426.0016), **Shawmut Bank of Boston** (1 Federal St, between Milk and Franklin Sts, 292.2000), and **Bank of Boston** (100 Federal St, between Franklin and Congress Sts, 434.2200). Banks, many stores, and restaurants accept traveler's checks, generally requiring a photo ID. You can purchase them at **American Express** (1 Court St, at Washington St, 723.8400), **Thomas Cook** (160 Franklin St, at Congress St, 426.0016), and at most major banks. Banks are generally open Monday through Friday from 9AM to 4PM.

Personal Safety

Always keep an eye on the traffic, as Boston drivers—and cyclists—are aggressive and often run red lights. Use common sense; be careful if you venture off well-worn paths in the city.

The subways are safe within Boston, Cambridge, and Brookline, but keep your wits about you. After dark, avoid the parks, **Boston Common,** the **Combat Zone** (the red-light district near **Chinatown**), alleys, and side streets.

Publications

Local newspapers and periodicals for news and events information include: the *Boston Globe* (daily), *Boston Herald* (daily), *Christian Science Monitor* (Monday through Friday), *Boston Phoenix* (published on Friday), *Boston Magazine* (monthly), and the *Tab* (weekly, with different editions for specific neighborhoods). Especially helpful for events information are two Friday publications, the *Boston Herald*'s "Scene" section and the *Boston Phoenix,* as well as one Thursday publication, the *Globe*'s "Calendar."

Radio Stations

AM:

WEEI (sports)	590
WRKO (talk)	680
WHDH (adult contemporary)	850
WBZ (pop)	1030

FM:

WBUR (classical/National Public Radio)	90.9
WROR (pop)	93.5
WJIB (pop)	98
WFNX (contemporary/new wave)	101.7
WBCN (rock/pop)	104.1

Restaurants

Reservations are essential at most trendy or expensive restaurants, and it's best to book far in advance at such dining spots as **Biba** and **L'Espalier.** If you want to avoid crowds, ask about late seatings. In general, jackets and ties are not required except at the posh and popular places, and most establishments accept credit cards.

Shopping

Boutiques and galleries bedeck Back Bay's upscale **Newbury Street.** A longer—and not quite so elite—shopping thoroughfare is lower **Boylston Street,** also in Back Bay. For the latest in clothing fashions catering to college students, you can't beat Cambridge (this is also the place for hard-to-find books). Nirvana for bargain hunters is at the original **Filene's Basement** (426 Washington St, at Summer St, 357.2100) in the Financial District. There are also numerous shopping complexes, throughout Boston, including **Faneuil Hall Marketplace, Copley Place,** the **Prudential Center, The Shops at Charles Square,** and more.

Smoking

There's a strong anti-smoking sentiment in Boston and Cambridge, with some restaurants banning it entirely and most offering nonsmoking sections. Many public places forbid smoking.

Street Plan

Logic is useless to figure out the maze of Boston's thoroughfares. It's best to get a good detailed map of the city; even longtime residents have to haul one out when planning to stray from their own well-worn paths.

Taxes

In Massachusetts, a five-percent tax is charged on all purchases except services, food bought in stores (not restaurants), and clothing under $175. There's a 9.7-percent hotel tax.

Telephones

The area code for Boston is 617, 508 for outlying areas, and 413 for the the rest of the state. If you're not sure which area code applies to you, ask the information operator or check the telephone book. At press time, NYNEX and AT&T pay phones cost 10¢ for a local call, with no charge for information (dial 411 for local information). However, a number of other companies have installed pay telephones that cost 25¢.

Tickets

There are a number of ticket sources for Boston-area events. **Ticketron** (720.3434, 800/302.8080) and **Concertcharge** (497.1118, 800/442.1854) offer tickets for sports, theater, dance, and music events. **Hub Ticket Agency** (240 Tremont St, Theater District, 426.8340) also handles sports and theater happenings. **Charge-Tix** (542.8511) specializes in comedy clubs and special shows. **Concertix** (876.7777) sells tickets for the **Regattabar** jazz performances and some other events. **Ticketmaster** (931.2000) is a computerized ticket service for cabarets, concerts, circuses, and sports. If you prefer paper to plastic, ask for cash-only outlet locations or use **Bostix** (Faneuil Hall Marketplace, 723.5181), which has some half-price tickets for same-day events, or **Out of Town Ticket Agency** (Harvard Square Station, Cambridge, 492.1900).

Tipping

Leave a 15- to 20-percent gratuity in restaurants and for personal services. Taxi drivers expect a 15-percent tip.

Visitors' Information Offices

The main visitor's information center is the **Massachusetts Tourism Office** (100 Cambridge St, at Bowdoin St, Government Center, 727.3201, 800/447.6277). Others include the **Boston Common Visitor's Information Center** (147 Tremont St, between Temple Pl and West St, Beacon Hill, 426.3115), the **Cambridge Discovery Information Kiosk** (Harvard St, at Peabody St, Harvard Sq, Cambridge, 497.1630), the **Charlestown Navy Yard Visitor's Center** (Charlestown Navy Yard, Building 5, off Chelsea St, Charlestown, 242.5601), the **Greater Boston Convention and Visitor's Bureau** (Prudential Center, 800 Boylston St, at Gloucester St, Back Bay, 536.4100), and the **National Park Service Visitor's Center** (15 State St, Financial District, 242.5642). All are open daily from 9AM to 5PM, except the **Massachusetts Tourism Office** and the **Greater Boston Convention and Visitor's Bureau,** which are closed on weekends.

Phone Book

Emergencies

Ambulance/Fire/Police	911
AAA Emergency Service	800/222.4357
Dental	956.6828
Massachusetts General Hospital	726.2000
Medical	726.2000, 956.5566
Poison Control	232.2120
Rape Crisis Hotline	492.7273
24-hour Pharmacies:	
In Boston	523.1028/4372
In Cambridge	876.5519

Recorded Information

Marine Weather Forecast	569.3700
MBTA service (daily conditions)	722.5050
Time	637.1234
US Postal Service	451.9922
Weather	936.1234/1212

Sports and Recreation

Appalachian Mountain Club	523.0636
Bicycling	491.7433
Boston Bruins (hockey)	227.3200
Boston Celtics (basketball)	523.3030
Boston Parks and Recreation	635.4505, 725.4006
Boston Red Sox (baseball)	267.8661
Canoeing	965.5110
Ice skating	727.5215
National Park Service	242.5642
New England Patriots (football)	800/543.1776
Sierra Club	227.5339

Skiing conditions	207/773.7669 (Maine), 800/258.3608 (New Hampshire), 802/229.0531 (Vermont)
State Fisheries and Wildlife	727.3151
State Forests and Parks	727.3180

Visitor Information

American Youth Hostels (AYH)	731.5430
Amtrak	482.3660, 800/872.7245
Bay State Cruise Company (ferry service)	723.7800
Handicapped-visitor Information	727.5540
Mass Bay Lines (ferry service)	542.8000
Massachusetts Bay Transportation Authority (MBTA)	722.3200, 800/392.6100
US Passport Office	565.6998

Bests

Michael and Susan Southworth

Urban Designers, Planners, and Authors of the *A.I.A. Guide to Boston*

The ornamental wrought- and cast-iron fences, balconies, and door and window grilles of **Back Bay, Beacon Hill,** and the **South End.**

Friday afternoon at **Symphony Hall,** the Stradivarius of concert halls.

Exploring the underground railroad and the many other significant black history sites in Boston.

Candlelight concerts at the **Isabella Stewart Gardner Museum.**

Chiles rellenos at **Casa Romero,** an intimate Mexican restaurant that transcends tacos and smashed beans.

Bicycling in the **Emerald Necklace,** especially on the **Riverway** under autumn leaves.

The first day the **Swan Boats** paddle the pond in the **Public Garden** each spring.

The *Robert Gould Shaw Memorial,* by Augustus Saint-Gaudens, honoring the first regiment of freed blacks to serve in the Civil War.

The Italian Renaissance Revival interiors of **McKim, Mead & White**'s **Boston Public Library.**

The **Nichols House** and **Gibson House,** museums that transport us to domestic life in 19th-century Boston.

The **Essex Institute** in **Salem,** with its collection of important museum houses, furniture, and artifacts of the China Trade.

Saturday morning shopping at the Italian street markets in the **North End.**

A Sunday afternoon walk through the **Back Bay Fens** with its tall rushes, winding waterway, and stone bridge (by **H.H. Richardson**), followed by visits to the **Museum of Fine Arts** and the **Isabella Stewart Gardner Museum.**

Evacuation Day (17 March), because it's the holiday no other city celebrates.

Trinity Church by **H.H. Richardson,** the best example of Romanesque Revival architecture in the country.

What's All the Ballyhoo in Beantown?

From Boston's Bunker Hill Day to its famous marathon and wildly colorful Italian *feste,* this is a city that knows how to celebrate its life and times. Here are some of the most popular events that take place year after year. For more information on these activities, call the **Greater Boston Convention and Visitors Bureau** (536.4100), or read the *Boston Phoenix* (published on Friday) or the Thursday "Calendar" section of the *Boston Globe.*

January
Chinese New Year (which is sometimes celebrated in February), Children's Museum

February
Black History Month

Chinese New Year (which is sometimes celebrated in January)

Hasty Pudding Awards, Harvard University

Inventor's Weekend, Museum of Science

Kid's Computer Fair, Computer Museum

Massachusetts Camellia Show

New England Boat Show, Bayside Exposition Center

Valentine's Festival, various hotels

March
Evacuation Day (March 17), when the British army fled in 1776

Flower Show, Bayside Exposition Center

Myopia Polo Matches, South Hamilton

St. Patrick's Day Parade, South Boston

April
American Indian Day, Children's Museum

Artists' Ball, the Cyclorama in the South End

The Big Apple Circus, Fan Pier

Boston Kite Festival, Franklin Park

Boston Marathon (the third Monday in April)

Earth Day, Charles River

Myopia Polo Matches, South Hamilton

Opening Day at Fenway Park (baseball)

Patriots Day (the third Monday in April), Reenactment of the Battle of Lexington, Paul Revere's and William Dawes's rides and other events

Swan Boats return to the Public Garden Lagoon

Whale-watching cruises begin

May
All Walks of Life (AIDS march)

Art Newbury Street (open galleries)

Beacon Hill Hidden Garden Tour

Boston Pops season begins, Symphony Hall

Brimfield Outdoor Antiques Show

Lilac Sunday, Arnold Arboretum

Magnolias bloom on Commonwealth Avenue

Myopia Polo Matches, South Hamilton

Walk for Hunger

June
Blessing of the Fleet, Provincetown and Gloucester

Boston Globe Jazz Festival, Hatch Shell and other locations

Bunker Hill Day, Charlestown (June 17)

Dairy Festival, Boston Common

Gay Pride March

Myopia Polo Matches, South Hamilton

Tanglewood Music Festival, Berkshires

July
Bastille Day, Marlborough Street in Back Bay

Boston Harborfest

Boston Pops Esplanade Orchestra Concerts, Charles River Esplanade

Brimfield Outdoor Antiques Show

Chowderfest, City Hall Plaza

Myopia Polo Matches, South Hamilton

North End Italian Feste

US Pro Tennis Championships at Longwood

USS *Constitution* Turnaround (July 4)

August
Myopia Polo Matches, South Hamilton

North End Italian Feste

September
Art Newbury Street (open galleries)

Boston Film Festival

Brimfield Outdoor Antiques Show

King Richard's Fair, South Carver

Myopia Polo Matches, South Hamilton

October
Haunted Happenings, Salem

Head-of-the-Charles Regatta

Myopia Polo Matches, South Hamilton

November
Boston Ballet's Nutcracker, The Wang Center

Boston Globe Book Festival, Hynes Center

December
Boston Ballet's Nutcracker, The Wang Center

Christmas Tree Lighting, Prudential Center

Crafts at the Castle

First Night (December 31 through January 1)

Boston's land area is 48.6 square miles; the Greater Boston land area is 2,100 square miles. Boston has 790 miles of streets, 43 miles of waterfront, 349 bridges, 8 historic or preservation districts, and 8 major medical research centers.

Beacon Hill

Stroll across **Boston Common**, an enormous grassy blanket that Bostonians have used since the city's birth, and then prepare yourself for poking about the nooks and crannies of historic Beacon Hill. This redbrick quarter of handsome houses crowded along crazy-quilt streets is a walker's dream and a driver's nightmare. In one of America's most European cities, this neighborhood looks ever-so-English. Beacon Hill's slopes are easiest to navigate in good weather, but it's well worth a bit of slipping and sliding to enjoy the area's serene winter stillness.

In colonial times, what is now a fashionable enclave was infant Boston's undesirable outskirts—crisscrossed with cow paths and covered with brambles, berries, and scrub. The Puritans called it "Trimountain" because its three-peaked silhouette resembled a person's head and shoulders. Whittled away by early developers to create new lots and landfill, only one hill remains today. The completion in 1798 of the majestic **State House**, designed by **Charles Bulfinch**, spotlighted the area's potential. Affluent Brahmins and a number of cultural luminaries were drawn here as Beacon Hill blossomed in the first half of the 19th century, and the city's intellectual and artistic renaissance unfolded.

Beacon Hill is composed of approximately three districts. The flats, the newer, more orderly section, runs down to the **Charles River** from **Charles Street.** Up from Charles Street is the sunny south slope, extending from **Beacon Street** to **Pinckney Street**, and the shady north slope, descending from Pinckney to **Cambridge Street.** While the south slope's mansions and row houses exude Brahmin privilege, the north slope's smaller houses and former tenement walk-ups relay a history of ethnic diversity and the struggle of many groups—especially African-Americans—to make their way here. Coursing through Beacon Hill, infusing it with vitality, is Charles Street, an eclectic, surprisingly friendly thoroughfare where most of the area's shops, services, and businesses are located.

In older cities, the chicken-or-the-egg question is: Which came first, the streets or the dwellings? It's clear that the houses came first on the hodgepodge "Hill," and that the streets have simply made do. As you wend your way over bumpy brick sidewalks, you'll probably agree that Beacon Hill wouldn't be so appealing without the jigs and jogs of the streets, the surprise of **Louisburg Square**, and the glistening river glimpsed below. In this intimate, people-scaled place, idiosyncrasies reveal the layers of lives that have enriched this large heap of brick and granite. Iron handrails fastened to buildings help you climb up the steeper blocks; gardens and gatherings enliven the rooflines; ornate door knockers, boot scrapers, and wrought-iron embellishments dress up some of the most modest facades; and tunnels lead to concealed courtyards and hidden houses.

Most of the homes are Greek Revival or Federal in style, but refreshing upstarts have sneaked in here and there. Master carpenters, called "housewrights," built most of the structures when the trained American architect was a brand-new breed. Notice the many graceful bowfronts—a local innovation. Officially declared a historic district in 1955, today the Beacon Hill Civic Association watchdogs its precious repository of buildings— even dictating exterior color choices. Come back in 30 years, and the structures will look the same. But, as buildings change hands there's less single ownership, and more condos and luxury apartments belong to young professionals instead of "Proper Bostonians." Today this area is home to Jewish and Italian immigrants, bohemian artists, and college students as well as Boston's famous "First Families"—the Cabots, Lodges, Codmans, and Lowells, to name a few—who have held sway over Beacon Hill for generations.

If the tranquil charm and careful-when-you-touch air begin to grow tiresome, remember that just ahead there's a startling or delightful nuance to discover. Watch the world go by over an espressoo at **Caffè Bella Vita;** find that slip of a street called **Acorn;** then come down from the heights and take an afternoon promenade in the **Public Garden.**

The four subway stops most convenient to Boston Common, Beacon Hill, and the Public Garden are Park Street (*Red* and *Green Lines*), Charles (*Red Line*), and Boylston or Arlington (*Green Line*). The entire neighborhood can be toured by foot easily from any of these stations.

1 Boston Common The oldest public park in the country extends 50 sprawling acres. Now the city's heart, it was once Boston's hinterland. In the early 1600s the grounds were part of the farm belonging to Reverend William Blaxton, the first English squatter on the Shawmut Peninsula. A reclusive bachelor in the style of Thoreau, Blaxton shattered his own blissful solitude by generously inviting the city's Puritan founders to settle on his peninsula and share its fresh water. Then, finding his neighbors too close for comfort, Blaxton sold them the land in 1634 and retreated to Beacon Hill. There the city's first—but not last—eccentric tended to his beloved orchard, reputedly riding about on his Brahma bull for recreation. But when the busybody Puritans tried to convince Blaxton to join their church, he fled south to Rhode Island.

The park has belonged to Bostonians ever since. Cattle grazed its grass until the practice was outlawed in 1830. Justice—of a sort—was meted out here with whipping posts, stocks, and pillories. Indians, pirates, and persecuted Quakers were hanged here, as was Rachell Whall in the late 1700s, for the crime of highway robbery (she stole a 75¢ bonnet). This is where Redcoats camped during the Revolution and Civil War troops once mustered. Until 6 July 1836, African-Americans couldn't pass freely through the land. General Lafayette returned to the US in 1824 and shot off a ceremonial cannon here, and the Prince of Wales, future King Edward VII, reviewed the troops on these very same grassy lawns in 1860.

Long the site of great public outdoor theater—sermons, duels, puppet shows, balloon ascensions, promenades, hopscotch championships, fire-engine and flying-machine demonstrations, horse races, antislavery meetings, fireworks, hoop rolling, and ox roasting—the **Common** still offers some of Boston's best people-watching. Arrive before nine on a sunny morning, and relish your leisure while working folk push on to their jobs, leaving you to saunter among the magicians, musicians, mounted police, artists, babies in strollers, religious proselytizers, in-line skaters, soapbox orators, pigeons, and pushcart vendors along the park's walkways. Return some summer evening to watch a softball game in one corner, while in another corner an unofficial dog-walking group meets after work to chat while their quadrupedal pals romp. One cautionary note: as is true in most urban areas, the park is not a safe place to be after dark. ♦ Bounded by Beacon, Tremont, and Boylston Sts, and Park and Arlington Sts

2 Park Street Station Designed by **Wheelwright and Haven,** the first subway system in the US opened here to incredible fanfare on 1 September 1897. "First Car Off the Earth!" trumpeted the *Boston Globe.* (The subway line originally ran only as far as today's **Boylston Station,** just one stop across the **Boston Common.**) Before you hurry aboveground to escape the dank air, the popcorn and doughnut smells, and the throngs on the platforms, look for the mosaic mural by the turnstiles. It depicts the first subway car—actually a streetcar which became an underground railway here—entering the tunnel, with a woman rider holding aloft that day's *Globe.* Aboveground, the two copper-roofed, granite-faced kiosks are National Historic Landmarks.

Head a short distance down Tremont Street to the blue-trimmed **Visitors' Information Center,** where you can inquire about museum exhibitions, helicopter rides, whale watches, and where Boston's renowned **Freedom Trail**

begins. On the way is **Brewer Fountain** (completed in 1868), a bronze replica of the lauded fountain of the 1855 Paris Exposition and a popular rendezvous. ♦ Park St (between Tremont and Beacon Sts)

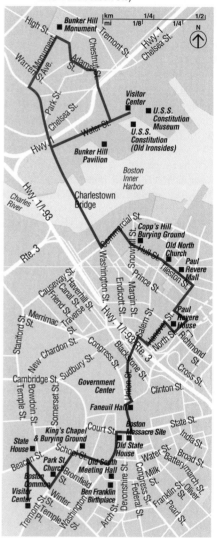

3 The Freedom Trail Begin the famous self-guided, 2.5-mile tourist pilgrimage at the **Visitor's Information Center,** and track an elusive red line connecting 13 historical sites from colonial and Revolutionary times, including **Paul Revere's House** and the **Old North Church** (see the map above). You'll end up in Charlestown, which means a trek or ride back, and you really could invent a more entertaining odyssey of your own. But if you're in the mood to follow in the footsteps of countless others, the tour takes about three hours. If you prefer a guided tour (which lasts about 90 minutes and visits five sites), call the **National Park Service** (242.5642 for daily schedules; 242.5689 for group reservations). ♦ Visitor's Information Center, Tremont St (between Temple Pl and West St)

3 Parkman Plaza Left of the **Visitor's Information Center,** facing the **Boston Common,** the plaza's bronze figures enshrine Puritan values. The path to the left of *Industry* is called Railroad Mall because in 1835 it led to the terminal of one of Boston's first railroads. A brief, lovely stroll down Railroad leads to the Neo-Classical **Parkman Bandstand.** Mount this neglected, but still-handsome structure, where you can watch the skittering squirrels and imagine long-silent strains of music while you try to ignore the graffiti. Surrounded by rustling leaves and frequented by Boston's homeless people in the fall, this is one of the city's most evocative settings. ♦ Boston Common

4 Boston Common Ranger Station Stop on the Tremont Street side of the park for information on the walks led by park rangers, including historic tours of the **Common** and the **Granary Burying Ground,** and a "What's in Bloom?" walk or "Family Stroll" in the **Public Garden.** For kids, there's the "Make Way for Ducklings" tour, which includes reading the famous children's storybook (the walk starts at the garden's bronze ducklings); and the "Horse of Course" program about a day in the life of a park ranger horse. ♦ Free. Daily. Behind the Visitor's Information Center, Tremont St (between Boylston and Park Sts). 635.7389

5 Central Burying Ground Once you're in a thoroughly contemplative mood, follow Railroad Mall to find history etched on 18th-century tombstones. Legend claims that American soldiers who died at the Battle of Bunker Hill and British soldiers who succumbed to illness during the Siege of Boston lie here. At least a dozen Boston Tea Party guests are also in this graveyard, as is portrait artist Gilbert Stuart, who painted Martha and George Washington. Stuart died in poverty, humiliated to be eclipsed by less-talented but more socially skilled painters. The inscriptions that mention "strangers" refer to Irish Catholic immigrants buried here. In early colonial graveyards like this one, headstones often face east—from whence would come the Day of Judgment trumpet call—and are paired with footstones, creating a cozy bed for the occupant's eternal rest. ♦ Boylston St (between Tremont St and Charles St S)

6 Flagstaff Hill Climb the **Common**'s highest point, atop which the *Soldiers and Sailors Monument* commemorates Civil War combatants. Gunpowder was stored here long ago. ♦ Boston Common

6 Frog Pond True, it's a frogless, sometimes-empty concrete hollow instead of the marshy amphibian abode it once was (Edgar Allan Poe derisively called Bostonians "Frogpondians"), but in steamy weather the pond is filled with children cavorting under its fountain. (Even the cynical Poe called the **Common** "no common thing.") ♦ Boston Common

7 William Hickling Prescott House Built in 1808, this graceful pair of brick bowfronts, now joined, is adorned with many of the delicate Greek architectural details favored by architect **Asher Benjamin.** The left-hand house, now a National Historic Landmark and headquarters for the National Society of the Colonial Dames of America, inspired the setting for *The Virginians* by British author William Makepeace Thackery (houseguest of a former owner). On Wednesdays, if you take the tour, you can peruse the colonial and Victorian artifacts collected and preserved by the Dames. ♦ Admission. W. 54-55 Beacon St (at Spruce St). 742.3190

8 Harrison Gray Otis House This is the last (circa 1805) and largest of the three imposing residences designed by **Charles Bulfinch** for the larger-than-life grandee Harrison Gray Otis—one of Boston's first big-time developers, a Boston mayor, and a US senator. Otis, a man who believed in living the good life, added a fourth repast to his regular meals, breakfasted daily on pâté de foie gras, and—surprise, surprise—was a gout victim for 40 years. Otis feted all of fashionable Boston in his magnificent rooms. Each afternoon the politicians and society guests who were gathered in Otis's drawing room consumed 10 gallons of spiked punch from a punch bowl perched on the landing. Amazingly, Harry's house didn't have plumbing. (Bathwater was considered a health menace because it supposedly attracted cockroaches, so tubs weren't allowed until the 1840s.) The American Meteorological Society is the current, fortunate resident of the house. ♦ 45 Beacon St (between Spruce and Walnut Sts)

8 Somerset Club Painter John Singleton Copley lived in a house that once stood on this site, until he went to England in 1744 and never returned. Now an ultraexclusive private club, the Greek Revival granite bowfront that replaced Copley's house aggressively protrudes beyond its neighbors' facades. **Colonel David Sears** erected the right-hand half in 1819, adding the left half in 1831—doubling **Alexander Parris**'s original design and spoiling it in the process. Look for the baronial iron-studded portal with its lion's-head knockers—a very showy touch for Beacon Hill. ♦ 42 Beacon St (between Spruce and Walnut Sts)

Restaurants/Clubs: Red   **Hotels:** Blue
Shops/ 🌳 Outdoors: Green   **Sights/Culture:** Black

9 Appleton-Parker Houses Built in the early 1800s by **Alexander Parris,** these two Greek Revival bowfronts were, respectively, the abodes of Boston's merchant prince Nathan Appleton of the textile-manufacturing family and his former partner, Daniel Parker. Henry Wadsworth Longfellow courted and married Fanny Appleton in her family's front parlor in 1843. And sardonic Edgar Allan Poe, characteristically misbehaving before the ladies at an Appleton soiree, was given the heave-ho. Both houses are National Historic Landmarks. ♦ 39-40 Beacon St (at Walnut St)

9 Purple Windowpanes The famed "purple panes" of Beacon Hill are these lavender-hued windowpanes—the proud possession of a handful of houses on the Hill. Actually, the treasured tint was a fluke—in shipments of glass sent from Hamburg to Boston between 1818 and 1824, manganese oxide reacted with the sun to create the color. Although numerous copies exist, very few authentic panes have survived. ♦ 39-40 Beacon St (at Walnut St), and 63 Beacon St (between Charles St S and Spruce St), and 29A Chestnut St (between Spruce and Walnut Sts)

10 Little, Brown and Company Imagine Louisa May Alcott dropping by to look over the galley proofs for *Little Women.* Established in 1837, this venerable Boston publishing house also has on its backlist John Bartlett (of that household tome *Bartlett's Familiar Quotations*), J.D. Salinger, Evelyn Waugh, Fanny Farmer (of cookbook fame), Margaret Atwood, and Berke Breathed, creator of the retired *Bloom County* cartoon strip. The firm moved its headquarters here in 1909, and although the Adult Trade division decamped to New York several years ago, certain imprints remain. ♦ 34 Beacon St (at Joy St)

10 George Parkman House In one of the most sensational murders of the century, George Francis Parkman's father, Dr. George Parkman, was murdered in 1849, allegedly by Harvard professor John Webster, a fellow Boston socialite who had borrowed money from the doctor. Lemuel Shaw, the judge handling the case, was related to the victim, and sent Webster to his hanging. After the furor, Parkman's son retreated from public scrutiny with his mother and sister, remaining a recluse here until his death in 1908.

Built in 1825 by **Cornelius Coolidge,** the house overlooks the **Common.** Parkman must have found solace in this unchanging landscape because he left $5.5 million in his will for its maintenance. For generations, Boston mayors lived in this house which belongs to the city; it is now used only for civic functions. ♦ 33 Beacon St (between Bowdoin and Joy Sts)

11 Beacon Street Mall In the shadow of the **State House,** this wide, dappled promenade along the **Common's** north side is where Ralph Waldo Emerson and Walt Whitman paced back and forth, arguing about taking the sex out of Whitman's *Leaves of Grass.* Though Emerson was utterly convincing, Whitman concluded: "I could never hear the points better put—and then I felt down in my soul the clear and unmistakable conviction to disobey all, and pursue my own way." Despite their disagreement, the friends went off together to partake of "a bully dinner." ♦ Beacon St (between Park and Joy Sts)

12 The State House The 23-karat gilded dome of the Massachusetts State House (pictured on page 15) glitters above the soft, dull hues of Beacon Hill, luring the eye. In fact, it was the capitol building (always always called "the State House," never the "Capitol") that first drew wealthy Bostonians away from the crowded waterfront to settle in this more salubrious neighborhood, which was still considered "country" at the start of the 18th century.

Charles Bulfinch spun out his remarkable designs at a breathtaking rate, leaps and bounds ahead of city officials in his brilliant urban-planning maneuvers. Completed in 1798, the **State House** is his finest surviving gift to Boston. When construction began, Governor Samuel Adams, the popular Revolutionary War patriot, laid the cornerstone with Paul Revere's help. Looking up from Beacon Street, imagine away the two marble wings, added more than a century later by **Chapman, Sturgis, and Andrews.** Facing the **Common,** the imposing south facade is dominated by a commanding portico with 12 Corinthian columns, surmounting an arcade of brick arches. Topping the lantern above the dome is a gilded pinecone, a symbol of the vast timberlands of northern Massachusetts, which became the state of Maine in 1820.

This striking Neo-Classical edifice cut a much less flashy figure in **Bulfinch's** time: The dome was originally made of whitewashed wood shingles, replaced in 1802 with gray-painted copper sheeting, installed by Paul Revere and Sons; gilding wasn't applied until 1874. The dome was briefly blackened during World War II to hide it from moonlight during blackouts, so it wouldn't offer a target to the Axis bombers (who never came). In 1825 the redbrick walls were painted white (a common practice when granite or marble was too costly); in 1845 repainted yellow; then white again in 1917 to match the new marble wings.

Not until 1928 was the redbrick exposed once more. Around the back is the monstrous yellow-brick heap of an extension, six times the size of the original building.

Statues of the spellbinding orator and US senator *Daniel Webster,* educator *Horace Mann,* and Civil War general *Thomas Hooker* on his charger stand beneath the central colonnade. On the lawns below are more pensive images. There's *Anne Hutchinson* (below the left wing), who was banished from Boston in 1645 by the Puritan community for her freethinking religious views. (Not until 1945 did the Great and General Court of Massachusetts revoke the edict of banishment.) And there's *Quaker Mary Dyer* (below the right wing), who was hanged on the **Common** for protesting Anne's banishment. Note also the statue of a serious, striding *John F. Kennedy.* Climb the steps and enter **Bulfinch**'s **Doric Hall** (named for its 10 colossal columns) on the second floor under the dome. The hall's main doors only open when a US president visits or a Massachusetts governor leaves the building for the very last time.

On the third floor is the resplendent House of Representatives gallery. Here hangs the *Sacred Cod* carved in pine, presented to the legislature in 1784 by Boston merchant Jonathan Rowe as a reminder of the fishing industry's importance to the state economy. This wooden fish effigy garnered such ridiculous reverence that in 1895 it was wrapped in an American flag and carried to the new seat of government by four messengers, escorted by a committee of 15 House members. And on 26 April 1933, when the fish was codnapped by *Harvard Lampoon* as a prank, all business in the House was suspended for several days, the members fuming over their missing fish. The thieves relented, and

phoned to tell the House that their mascot was concealed in a closet beneath their chamber. In the barrel-vaulted **Senate Reception Room,** the original **Senate Chamber,** each of four original Ionic columns by **Bulfinch** was carved from a single pine tree. Directly beneath the gold dome is the sunburst-ceilinged Senate Chamber, where Angelina Grimké became the first woman to address a US legislative body when she gave an antislavery speech in 1838. ♦ Free. M-F. Beacon St (between Hancock and Bowdoin Sts). 727.3676 ዿ

13 Robert Gould Shaw Memorial Across from the main entrance to the **State House,** sculptor Augustus Saint-Gaudens's monument honors the 54th Massachusetts Regiment volunteers of African descent, and the nation's first black regiment, which enlisted in Boston. The troops fought in the Civil War under the command of 26-year-old Shaw, son of a venerable Boston family. For two years, until a shamefaced Congress relented, members of the 54th refused their pay because they received only $10 a month instead of the $13 paid to whites. Shaw and half his men died in a valiant assault on Fort Wagner, South Carolina, in 1863.

Saint-Gaudens took 13 years to complete this beautifully wrought bas-relief, which Shaw's abolitionist family insisted must honor the black infantrymen as well as their son. Erected in 1897, the monument today seems somewhat patronizing for its portrayal of the white Shaw as a heroic figure on horseback, towering above the black troops, but it was, in fact, remarkably liberal in its day. Draw near and study the portraitlike, ennobling treatment of the men's expressive faces. The angel of death hovers above. The story of Shaw and his brave regiment is recounted in the 1989 film, *Glory.* **Charles McKim,** of the architectural firm **McKim, Mead & White,** designed the memorial's classical frame. It sits on a small plaza whose granite balustrade overlooks the **Boston Common.**

The State House

The **Black Heritage Trail,** a guided walking tour that retraces the history of Boston's 19th-century black community, begins at the memorial. Call the **Boston African American National Historic Site** (742.5415) for information. ♦ Beacon St (between Park and Joy Sts)

14 Park Street Called Sentry Lane in the 17th century, this was the pathway the sentry took to the top of Beacon Hill, where a bucket of tar mounted on a post in 1634 was ever-ready for emergency lighting (until it blew down in 1789). An almshouse, a house of correction, an insane asylum, and a "bridewell"—a lovely name for a jail—populated this street when it was part of Boston's outskirts; now Park Street is home to a number of decidedly reputable institutions. In 1804 architect **Charles Bulfinch** straightened out the lane and designed nine residences facing the **Common** that became known as Bulfinch Row. Only the **Amory-Ticknor House** at the corner of Beacon Street survives, although it's disastrously altered. ♦ Between Beacon and Tremont Sts

14 Goodspeed's Book Shop Charles E. Goodspeed began business nearby in 1898, and a branch of his distinguished firm has been in one place or another on the Hill since the 1930s, purveying old maps, prints, manuscripts, and first editions. "We'll always be right on Beacon Hill," George T. Goodspeed, son of the founder, has promised his patrons. One step in the door and you'll sniff the unmistakable and oddly pleasant smell of old books. ♦ M-F. 9 Park St (at Beacon St), Third floor. 523.5970

15 Park Street Church When heading northeast on the **Common,** all eyes irresistibly rise to this majestic 1809 church looming at Park and Tremont Streets opposite the subway station. Henry James heaped praise on the elegant late-Georgian edifice, pronouncing it "perfectly felicitous" and "the most interesting mass of brick and mortar in America." Influenced by his much more illustrious English compatriot **Christopher Wren,** architect **Peter Banner** capped the crowning glory of his career with a stalwart 217-foot-tall telescoping steeple that points to the sky like an orator's emphatic forefinger. Locals have always relied on its easy-to-read clock for time and rendezvous. The illustrious Handel & Haydn Society, formed here in 1815, drew many of its voices from the church choir. And here the anthem "America" was first sung on 4 July 1831; 24-year-old Samuel Francis Smith reputedly dashed off its lyrics a half-hour before schoolchildren sang it on the church steps. The church once stood next to a workhouse, the Puritan answer to homelessness and poverty. ♦ Daily July-Aug; by appointment only Sept-June. 1 Park St (at Tremont St). 523.3383 &

15 The Union Club Formerly separate 19th-century mansions (the right-hand building was demolished in 1896 and replaced) owned by two of Boston's most illustrious families, the flag bearing this club's logo forever waves here. Members use the *Social Register* as their telephone book and chat over lunch about strictly nonbusiness topics. ♦ 8 Park St (off Tremont St)

15 Brimstone Corner Where Park and Tremont Streets meet was supposedly dubbed for the fire-and-brimstone oratory of the Congregational preachers—including abolitionist William Lloyd Garrison, who gave his first antislavery address here in 1829. But a more banal explanation is that brimstone, used to make gunpowder, was stored in the **Park Street Church**'s crypt during the War of 1812. ♦ Park and Tremont Sts

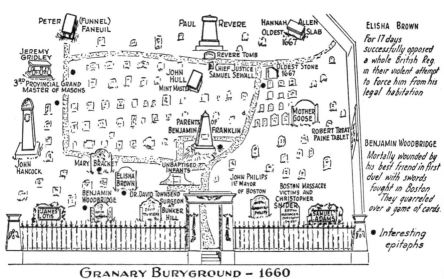

PETER (FUNNEL) FANEUIL

JEREMY GRIDLEY

3RD PROVINCIAL GRAND MASTER OF MASONS

JOHN HANCOCK

PAUL REVERE

REVERE TOMB

JOHN HULL MINT MASTER

CHIEF JUSTICE SAMUEL SEWALL

MARY BRACKET

ELISHA BROWN

BENJAMIN WOODBRIDGE

DR. DAVID TOWNSEND SURGEON BUNKER HILL

JAMES OTIS

PARENTS OF BENJAMIN FRANKLIN

UNBAPTISED INFANTS

JOHN PHILIPS 1ST MAYOR OF BOSTON

HANNAH ALLEN OLDEST SLAB 1667

OLDEST STONE 1667

MOTHER GOOSE

ROBERT TREAT PAINE TABLET

BOSTON MASSACRE VICTIMS AND CHRISTOPHER SNIDER

SAMUEL ADAMS

ELISHA BROWN
For 17 days successfully opposed a whole British Reg. in their violent attempt to force him from his legal habitation

BENJAMIN WOODBRIDGE
Mortally wounded by his best friend in first duel with swords fought in Boston. They quarreled over a game of cards.

● Interesting epitaphs

GRANARY BURYGROUND - 1660

16 Granary Burying Ground Nestled to the right of the Park Street Church, this graveyard (pictured on page 16, with sample epitaphs listed to its right) was named for the 1738 granary that the church replaced. Created in 1660, it is the third-oldest graveyard in the city. In this shady haven lie many Revolutionary heroes–Samuel Adams, John Hancock, James Otis, Robert Treat Paine, and Paul Revere–although the headstones have been moved so often you can't really be sure who's where. The five victims of the Boston Massacre (including black patriot Crispus Attucks), philanthropist Peter Faneuil (for whom Faneuil Hall is named), Benjamin Franklin's parents (he's in Philadelphia), and "Mother" Goose are also here. Judge Samuel Sewell likewise rests easy here, having cleared his conscience as the only judge to ever admit publicly that he was wrong to condemn the Salem Witches.

The best reason to visit this two-acre museum is to examine the tombstones' extraordinary carvings (rubbings are forbidden here) of astonishing skeletons, urns, winged skulls, and contemplative angels. In this haunting place, you will be transported back to the 17th century, from which the earliest tombstones date. The winged hourglasses carved into the Egyptian-style granite gateway (designed in 1830 by **Solomon Willard**) were added in the 19th century. ♦ Free. Daily. Tremont St (between Bosworth St and Hamilton Pl)

17 The Boston Athenaeum Although **Edward Clark Cabot** modeled the 1849 building after **Palladio**'s Palazzo da Porta Festa in Vicenza, Italy, the **Athenaeum** is a Boston institution to its bones. Enlarged and rebuilt in the early 1900s by **Henry Forbes Bigelow,** the

structure is now a National Historic Landmark. Only 1,049 ownership shares exist to this independent research library, founded in 1807, and all can be traced to their original owners. You're invited to tour and look at— but not touch—books on the first and second floors, and to visit the **Athenaeum Gallery,** which offers ongoing exhibitions. Two groups frowned upon in most public places—dogs and smokers—are welcome here. Take a tour and visit Boston's most pleasant place for musing, the high-ceilinged, airy **Reading Room** on the fifth floor, with its sunny alcoves. As poet David McCord wrote, the room "combines the best elements of the Bodleian, Monticello, the frigate *Constitution,* a greenhouse, and an old New England sitting room." Make sure you step out onto the fifth-floor terrace, with its gorgeous plantings and view of the **Granary Burying Ground.**

The superb collections here include George Washington's private library and Confederate imprints, as well as history, biography, and English, American, and Gypsy literature. There's a notable mystery collection too. Members and visitors who've gained special dispensation can actually handle many of the books, but may receive a lesson in the proper way to remove a volume from its shelf (work your fingers "around" its sides, *don't* pull it out from the top!). Take a ride in the charmingly hand-painted elevator, a former employee's handiwork, with its framed bookplate display. Part of the library's appeal is the way Oriental carpets and art treasures are casually strewn about. Keep an eye out for the wonderful statue of *Little Nell* on the first floor next to the stairs. Special exhibits—open to the public—are mounted throughout the year. You'll leave full of envy for the fortunate 1,049 shareholders. ♦ Free. M-Sa; tours Tu, Th (reservations required); closed June-September. 10½ Beacon St (between Park and School Sts). 227.0270 ₠

BLACK GOOSE

18 Black Goose ★★$ Crowds gather regularly for the Coliseum-size Caesar salads and luxuriant pesto served in the midst of majestic Corinthian columns. In good weather, find a sun-warmed table out front for lunch, and watch scholars and book-browsers coming and going beneath the **Boston Athenaeum**'s dignified sandstone facade across the way. ♦ Italian ♦ M-F lunch and dinner; Sa dinner. Reservations recommended. 21 Beacon St (between Bowdoin and Somerset Sts). 720.4500 ₠

18 Lodge's Pushcart A compact showcase of North End Italian treats, this grocery-store-cum-deli-counter serves overstuffed calzone and deep-dish *pizza grande,* along with specialty coffees and *pizzelle* (waffle cookies). ♦ M-F; Sa until 3PM. No credit cards accepted. 23 Beacon St (between Bowdoin and Somerset Sts). 723.5353

The part of Boylston Street that runs along Boston Common was originally called Frogg Lane because of the numerous frogs in the Common and along the Charles (they were reportedly more than a foot long). The name was changed in tribute to Zabdiel Boylston, who inoculated Bostonians against smallpox.

Restaurants/Clubs: Red **Hotels:** Blue
Shops/ 🌳 Outdoors: Green **Sights/Culture:** Black

19 The Golden Dome ★$ The Hill's legislators hold court daily in this clubby little pub, which has been called "the State House Annex," and it's a show worth catching. Whenever roll is called at the government offices, someone phones over and a waitress yells out the names of those missing. Watch how no one winces. They just keep hoisting those delectable turkey clubs (the turkey's roasted on the premises) and toothsome fried-potato wedges. Daily specials keep the pols happy. ♦ American ♦ M-F lunch; pub until 11PM. No credit cards accepted. 150 Bowdoin St (between Ashburton Pl and Beacon St). 227.7100

19 The Fill-A-Buster $ Gracious Vaios Grigas's friendly crew serves hearty fare with Greek highlights—egg-lemon soup, spinach-cheese pie, and kabobs—for a clientele of pols and media types. The breakfast specials are just as bountiful, plus you can smell Grigas's famous homemade muffins a block away. Once you're a regular here, they'll have your coffee poured and waiting before you've crossed the threshold. ♦ Greek/American/Takeout ♦ M-F breakfast and lunch. 142 Bowdoin St (between Ashburton Pl and Beacon St). 523.8164

20 Lyman Paine House This understated house's distinctive character comes from its intriguing asymmetrical windows and refined Greek Revival ornamentation. ♦ 6 Joy St (at Mt. Vernon St)

21 Appalachian Mountain Club Founded in Boston in 1876, the **AMC** can give you plenty of information on outdoor recreation around Boston and New England. ♦ M-F. 5 Joy St (between Mt. Vernon and Beacon Sts). 523.0636

22 32 Mount Vernon Street Julia Ward Howe and Dr. Samuel Gridley Howe took up housekeeping here in the 1870s. Dr. Samuel is best known for founding the Perkins Institute for the Blind, but he also organized the Committee of Vigilance to protect runaway slaves, helping hundreds of fugitives and pulling off an occasional daring rescue when word arrived that slaves were aboard the ships pulling into Boston Harbor. Julia composed "The Battle Hymn of the Republic" as well as many volumes of poetry. A suffragist and social reformer, she wrote and lectured on the rights of women and African-Americans. General Ulysses S. Grant and writer Bret Harte were among the Howes's notable houseguests. ♦ Between Joy and Walnut Sts

23 Nichols House Museum Remarkable Miss Rose Standish Nichols, niece of sculptor Augustus Saint-Gaudens, spent most of her genteel life in this house, built in 1804 by **Charles Bulfinch**. A gardening author, world traveler, peace advocate, and pioneer woman landscape architect who earned her own living, Nichols also founded the International Society of Pen Pals in her front parlor. Stop in to see the furnishings, memorabilia, and ancestors' portraits—collected by her family over centuries—which she bequeathed to the public along with her home. The witty museum curator, William Pear, will take you on an entertaining tour. ♦ Admission. Call for hours. 55 Mt. Vernon St (between Joy St and Louisburg Sq). 227.6993, recorded information 720.0786 &

Within the Nichols House Museum:

The Beacon Hill Garden Club Their annual spring Hidden Gardens Tour is your one chance to roam through greenery that otherwise can only be glimpsed tantalizingly beyond brick walls. ♦ 227.4392

24 John Callender House One of the first houses on the street, Callender's small abode cost $2,155 for the lot and $5,000 to $7,000 for construction when it was built in 1802. Recently, a new roof was affixed to the Federal-style brick house and the entrance moved slightly, but it's still standing. What's more, a lavish garden blooms behind this bargain-basement structure. ♦ 14 Walnut St (at Mt. Vernon St)

25 13, 15, and 17 Chestnut Street Charles Bulfinch kept busy building for patrons' daughters, and, in fact, this most famous trio of row houses was dubbed the "Daughter Houses." In 1805, while her husband, Colonel James Swan, cooled his heels in a French debtors' prison, Boston heiress Hepsibah Swan had these houses built as wedding gifts for her daughters. **No. 13** is a National Historic Landmark. ♦ Between Walnut and Spruce Sts

26 29A Chestnut Street In 1865 tragedian Edwin Booth was enjoying a successful run in *The Iron Chest,* a drama about a murderer haunted by his crime, and was staying here at the home of the theater manager. But on the eve of Edwin's last performance, brother John Wilkes Booth murdered President Abraham Lincoln. Edwin's last performance was canceled, and he left secretly for New York, not appearing before an audience again for nearly a year. ♦ Between Walnut and W Cedar Sts

27 Acorn Street . Stand at the crown of this street, one of Boston's skinniest, and watch cars shimmy and shake as they torturously climb its cobbled length. On one side, look up at the trees waving from the hidden gardens backing Mount Vernon Street; opposite are the diminutive houses that belonged to coachmen serving families in mansions on Chestnut and Mount Vernon Streets. Study the entrances to **Nos. 1, 3,** and **5** and notice the ornamental acorns that correspond in number with each address. The humble original homeowners would be pleased to know their houses now hobnob with the best on the real-estate market. ◆ Between W Cedar and Willow Sts

28 Harrison Gray Otis House (1802) Ever an onward-and-upward kind of fellow, Otis abandoned a spanking-new manse on Cambridge Street, also by **Charles Bulfinch,** to take up residence in this fashionable neighborhood of his own making. One of the only houses in the area with ample elbow room, this towering structure was intended to set a Jones's standard of free-standing mansions on generous landscaped grounds, but Boston's population boom soon made this impossible. The structure is now on the National Register of Historic Places. ◆ 85 Mt. Vernon St (between Walnut St and Louisburg Sq)

29 Louisburg Square Suddenly, the houses open wide and you're swung in a new direction at the edge of one of Boston's most serenely patrician places. Be sure to pronounce that "s"; you'll horrify locals if you say "Louie-burg!" If **Bulfinch** had had his way, the square would be three times larger and three decades older, but the Mount Vernon Proprietors didn't act on his 1826 plan. The redbrick row houses and the oval park they overlook aren't extraordinary in themselves; it's the square's timeless aura that has always appealed to Bostonians. Deteriorating statues of *Aristides the Just* and *Columbus* coolly survey all comers.

Many famous people have crossed the threshholds of houses on this street. After becoming a literary success, Louisa May Alcott brought her perennially penniless

family to **No. 10,** where mercury poisoning—she got it while a Civil War nurse—slowly crippled her. **No. 20** is a happier address: here soprano Jenny Lind ("The Swedish Nightingale"), skyrocketed to fame by P.T. Barnum, was married in 1852 to her accompanist. Samuel Gray Ward, a representative of Lind's London bankers, also lived at **No. 20**; among his banking coups was arranging America's purchase of Alaska from Russia for $7.5 million. ◆ Between Pinckney and Mt. Vernon Sts

30 Pinckney Street Begin at its base, and with luck you'll time your arrival at the summit as the late-afternoon sunlight turns golden, and the trees become sparkling lanterns stretching down toward the Charles River. Called the "Cinderella Street" of Beacon Hill by one author, it was once the dividing line between those who were and those who were not. There are both handsome and humble buildings here, and all are utterly delightful. ◆ Between Joy St and Embankment Rd

31 62 Pinckney Street Built in 1846 and owned by George S. Hilliard, this residence was a stop on the underground railroad that ran through Boston in the 1850s. Whether Hilliard knew fugitives were harbored in his home is debatable, but his staunchly abolitionist wife, Susan Tracy Hilliard, certainly did. Workmen discovered the secret attic chamber in the 1920s. ◆ At Anderson St

32 Boston English High School The first interracial public school in Boston (boys only) opened in this austere cruciform edifice—now condos—in 1844. ◆ 65 Anderson St (at Pinckney St)

COURTESY OF THE BOSTONIAN SOCIETY

Rope making, began in Boston in the 1630s. By the 19th century, ropewalks (long covered buildings where ropes were manufactured) were commonplace fixtures on the town's outskirts. Buildings extended up to 1,000 feet long to house the cumbersome hemp-winding process. Inside, the ropemaker walked backward as the hemp fiber unwound from the skein encircling his waist and was simultaneously twisted into yarn. Ropewalks once crisscrossed the Public Garden and the north slope of Beacon Hill, presenting physical barriers that even influenced how neighborhoods developed. And since a coating of hot pitch was often applied to the rope as a preservative, ropewalks were smelly, hazardous firetraps avoided by townspeople out strolling the streets.

33 Pie-Shaped House The interior reveals what the exterior conceals: squeezed between its neighbors, this house comes to a point like a piece of pie. Look at the roofline for a clue. ♦ 56 Pinckney St (between Joy St and Louisburg Sq)

34 House of Odd Windows When Ralph Waldo Emerson's nephew renovated this former carriage house in 1884, he turned the facade into a montage of windows—each singular and superbly positioned—in an inexplicable burst of artistry. Notice the quirky eyebrow dormer at the top. ♦ 24 Pinckney St (between Joy and Anderson Sts)

34 20 Pinckney Street Bronson Alcott, mystic, educator, "other-worldly philosopher," and notoriously bad provider, brought his wife and four daughters to live here from 1852 to 1855. The close-knit family and their struggle with poverty inspired daughter Louisa's heartstring-tugger *Little Women.* ♦ Between Joy and Anderson Sts

35 91/2 Pinckney Street The Hill's hodgepodge evolution created labyrinthine patterns of streets and housing that led to hidden gardens and even hidden houses. (**No. 74½ Pinckney Street** is the famous "Hidden House," left to your imagination). The iron gate here opens onto a tunnel that passes through the house and into a courtyard skirted by three hidden houses. Crouch down for a glimpse. ♦ Between Joy and Anderson Sts

35 Middleton-Glapion House George Middleton, an African-American jockey, horse-breaker, and Revolutionary War veteran, and hairdresser Louis Glapion, collaborated in the late 1700s on this minute clapboard house, so untouched by time that the pair might have strolled out the front door this morning. ♦ 5 Pinckney St (at Joy St)

36 Myrtle Street When Brahmin elegance begins to stultify, seek out this narrow, down-to-earth street. Tenements and Greek Revival row houses commune along this stretch with the laundries, markets, shoe-repair shops, a playground, a pizza parlor, and other unfashionable establishments that make it the neighborhood's most for-real street. Look at the rooflines and spot the funky gardens that aren't found on any "Hidden Gardens of Beacon Hill" tour. Perched here in the heights, you can see the lazy Charles River and **Massachusetts Institute of Technology.** ♦ Between Primus Ave and Hancock St

---

Boston's nickname, "The Hub," comes from an article published by Oliver Wendell Holmes—doctor, author, and father of the famous jurist—in *The Atlantic Monthly* in 1858. Holmes wrote that the "Boston State House is the hub of the solar system." Bostonians have since stretched his grandiose image to include the entire city.

37 African Meeting House Free African-American artisans built this meeting house (pictured above) in 1806, and **Asher Benjamin**'s architecture influenced its town-house style. A National Historic Landmark, it's the oldest black church still standing in the US. Nicknamed "Black Faneuil Hall" during the abolitionist era, here is where William Lloyd Garrison founded the New England Anti-Slavery Society on 6 January 1832. Late last century, African-Americans began migrating to the South End and Roxbury. By the 1920s, Irish and Jewish immigrants had moved in. The meeting house was sold to an Orthodox Jewish congregation and remained a synagogue until purchased by the **Museum of Afro American History** (see below) in the 1970s. ♦ 8 Smith Ct (off Joy St, between Cambridge and Myrtle Sts)

37 Museum of Afro American History The first grammar and primary school for black children in Boston opened in 1834, replacing the school that had met in the **African Meeting House** basement. It was named for Abiel Smith, the white businessman who bequeathed the funds for its construction. The school closed 20 years later when the state upheld the demand for integrated schools, ending the practice of taxing blacks to support schools that excluded their children. Now you can explore African-American history in New England in the former school building. ♦ Free. M-F. 46 Joy St (at Smith Ct). 742.1854

37 William C. Nell House America's first published African-American historian and a member of William Lloyd Garrison's circle, Nell boarded in this 18th-century wooden farmhouse from 1851 to 1856. He led the crusade for integrated public schools in the city, and his Equal School Association organized the boycott of the neighboring **Abiel Smith School** until the state legislature finally abolished restrictions on black children's access to public schools. African-American clothing-dealer James Scott, who purchased Nell's house and ran it as a rooming house starting in 1865, sheltered fugitive slaves here. The structure is now a National Historic Landmark. ♦ 3 Smith Ct (off Joy St, between Cambridge and Myrtle Sts)

Restaurants/Clubs: Red   Hotels: Blue
Shops/ 🌳 Outdoors: Green   Sights/Culture: Black

38 Venice Ristorante ★$ This is the kind of place you can walk by a hundred times without noticing, but stop in once and try the food and you're sure to become a regular. Crisp-crusted pizzas topped with ultrafresh ingredients even come in a "personal" size for one. Or choose from an enormous selection of salads, pastas, subs, and daily specials. There's free delivery. ♦ Pizza/Takeout ♦ Daily lunch and dinner. No credit cards accepted. 204 Cambridge St (at S Russell St). 227.2094 ♿

39 Rollins Place Countless passersby have glanced down Revere Street and been charmed by this little white house tucked snugly at its end. But the inviting southern-style facade is really a false front. The architectural trompe l'oeil masks an old cliff running between Revere and lower Phillips Streets. Continue down the same side of the street and slip into Goodwin Place (**No. 73**), Sentry Hill Place, and Bellingham Court, all charming cul-de-sacs along Revere Street that also disguise the cliff, but without such fanciful deceit. ♦ 27 Revere St (between Anderson and Garden Sts)

40 Lewis Hayden House A fugitive slave himself, Hayden (pictured above) became one of the most famous abolitionists, and his 1833 home a station on the underground railroad. William and Ellen Craft, a famous couple who escaped by masquerading as master and slave, stayed here. And in 1853 Harriet Beecher Stowe, who had already published *Uncle Tom's Cabin,* visited Hayden and met 13 newly escaped slaves—the first she'd ever met. The Haydens reputedly kept two kegs of gunpowder in the basement, threatening to blow up the house if anyone tried to search it. No one did. ♦ 66 Phillips St (between W Cedar and Grove Sts)

41 The King & I ★$ What started out as a fling with Thai restaurants in the 1980s has turned into a passionate, some say obsessive, affair with that cuisine in Boston. The offspring of this affair are scattered throughout the city, and it's often hard to tell them apart. This bright, courteous restaurant has always stood out, however, for its entrancing, delicate versions of dishes like Paradise beef. For an after-dinner treat of a different sort, cross Charles Street and enter the passage to the left of the Charles Street Animal Clinic. You'll see an arch framing trees, the river, passing cars. Enter here and admire the curved charm of West Hill Place. ♦ Thai ♦ M-Th lunch and dinner; Sa dinner. Reservations recommended for dinner. 145 Charles St (between Storrow Dr Rotary and Revere St). 227.3320. Also at: 259 Newbury St (between Gloucester and Fairfield Sts). 437.9611

42 Danish Country Antique Furniture Brightly colored rugs, tableware, crafts, and folk art can be found in, on, and among the handsome blond furniture dating from the mid-18th century onward. So often antique furniture cringes from returning to active service, but owner James Kilroy's Danish desks, armoires, tables, chests, and chairs sturdily welcome the prospect. His shop is cheery when compared with the dark and dour environments of many other Hill establishments. ♦ Daily. 138 Charles St (between Cambridge and Revere Sts). 227.1804

42 Marika's You'll need to navigate carefully through this crowded collection of glassware, furniture, paintings, tapestries, and treasures from all around the world. Owner Matthew Raisz's grandmother, Marika, emigrated from Budapest and founded this shop in 1944. It's prized particularly for its extraordinary jewelry. ♦ Tu-Sa. 130 Charles St (between Cambridge and Revere Sts). 523.4520

42 George Gravert Antiques The pleasant proprietor of this shop has been in the antiques business for more than 30 years, specializing in European furniture and accessories that are clearly chosen by an expert eye. Something timeless and trustworthy about the place will make you want to linger even after you've ogled everything twice. Although he caters mainly to wholesalers, Gravert won't mind at all if you come in and browse. ♦ M-F. 122 Charles St (between Cambridge and Revere Sts). 227.1593 ♿

43 Period Furniture Hardware Company This almost-80-year-old shop is aglow with gleaming surfaces to stroke. Many antiquers have abandoned their wearisome Holy Grail quest for such-and-such genuine wall sconce from such-and-such period for the somewhat as satisfying pleasures of these reproductions of hardware from the 18th century onward. If only the price tags weren't the real thing. ♦ M-F; Sa until 2PM. 123 Charles St (between Cambridge and Revere Sts). 227.0758

43 Boston Antique Coop I & II These two cooperatives in one building set out a tempting smorgasbord of American, Asian, and European antiques. The place has all the ambience of a garage sale, but it's great fun and local antiques dealers snoop about here, too. Downstairs at **Coop I,** four dealers display sterling, porcelain, paintings, jewelry, bottles, vintage photography, bric-a-brac, and more. Upstairs at **Coop II,** eight dealers specialize in decorative items, vintage clothing, and textiles. The items change constantly, so check back from time to time. ♦ Daily. 119 Charles St (between Cambridge and Revere Sts). Coop I: 227.9810, Coop II: 227.9811

44 Helen's Leather Care to prance about in python or buckle on some buffalo? You can even opt for ostrich in this leather emporium, which boasts an exotic collection of handmade boots. The mammoth wooden boot out front tells you you've arrived at New England's biggest western boot dealer; also for sale are shoes, clothing, briefcases, backpacks, and other leather whatnots in many popular brands. ♦ Daily. 110 Charles St (between Revere and Pinckney Sts). 742.2077

45 Elements Antiques-obsessed Charles Street is not exactly what you'd call trendy, so it's refreshing to see a forward-looking enterprise set up shop. Billing itself—tongue in cheek— as "the ultimate factory store," this producer of avant-garde accessories devotes 80 percent of its space to its own products (from vases to jewelry) and the rest to works by local artisans. The shop is definitely cutting-edge— and fun. ♦ Daily. 103A Charles St (between Revere and Pinckney Sts). 227.3029. Also at: 18-20 Union Park St (between Washington St and Shawmut Ave). 451.9990

46 The Coffee Connection ★$ The coffee is unsurpassable; walk in and let the potent, sultry aroma of the beans engulf you. Sit at one of the tiny window tables and nurse your brew or, better still, carry it over to the **Public Garden.** You can even order beans by mail (800/284.5282). ♦ Cafe/Takeout ♦ Daily. 97 Charles St (at Pinckney St). 227.3812. ♿ Also at: 2 Faneuil Hall Marketplace (in North Market). 227.3821; Copley Place (between Dartmouth and Huntington Sts). 353.1963; 350 Newbury St (between Hereford St and Massachusetts Ave). 859.5751

47 Romano's Bakery & Coffee Shop ★★$ It's short on decor but long on great cheap food, so people keep wending their way back to this cozy downstairs coffee shop. The clutter of newspapers tells you to sit, relax, take your time. The fresh-baked goods, quiches, salads, sandwiches, and soups always hit the spot at lunchtime, and leave you with plenty of money to splurge on dinner. If your energy level is low, grab a lethal pastry or chocolate something to rev you up for the afternoon. ♦ Cafe/Takeout ♦ Daily breakfast, lunch, and dinner. No credit cards accepted. 89 Charles St (between Pinckney and Mt. Vernon Sts). 523.8704

The shortest suspension bridge in the world is the footbridge that crosses the Swan Boat Lagoon in the Public Garden.

47 The Sevens ★★$ No wonder this is the neighborhood's favorite pub. Often crowded, with free-for-all conversations bouncing between the bar and the booths, it's a gregarious place meant for sitting back and sipping a draft when the world seems a little lonely. Try the pub lunch—a generous, satisfying sandwich and bargain-priced mug of draft beer. The chili, soups, and salads are good, too. ♦ American ♦ Daily until midnight. No credit cards accepted. 77 Charles St (between Pinckney and Mt. Vernon Sts). 523.9074

47 The Hungry i ★★$$$$ If you're claustrophobic, think twice before stepping down into this extremely intimate restaurant—one of the city's most romantic choices. For Sunday brunch, you can also dine alfresco in a diminutive courtyard. Fish and game star in the brief, but inventive, menu. ♦ American ♦ M-Sa dinner; Su brunch and dinner. Reservations recommended. 71½ Charles St (between Pinckney and Mt. Vernon Sts). 227.3524

48 Eugene Galleries It's easy to lose all track of time in this enthralling emporium, which specializes in Boston views and maps—old prints, sketches, postcards, and photographs. Stop here after touring the city—it's the ideal place to see how your favorite sights have been commemorated through the centuries. You'll also find oddments of every sort—a Victorian dustpan, sheet music, paperweights, fire-and-brimstone sermons, and *History of the Great Fire of Boston,* to name a few. Some 250 other categories of memorabilia are available: botanical, medical, legal, women, transportation, and on and on. ♦ M-Sa. 76 Charles St (between Pinckney and Mt. Vernon Sts). 227.3062

COURTESY OF JOHN SHARRATT ASSOCIATES

49 Charles Street Meeting House It's a shame they stuck a food shop in the front of this forthright structure completed in 1807 (pictured above)—even if it is a popular outpost of the inimitable **Rebecca's** cafe (see page 25). An octagonal belfry crowns the rectangular central tower, a handsome ensemble by **Asher Benjamin,** the architect who designed **Faneuil Hall** and inherited

Bulfinch's unofficial role of architect laureate of Boston. The meeting house's first congregation was the Baptist Society, who found the nearby Charles River convenient for baptisms. Later, although abolitionists—including William Lloyd Garrison, Frederick Douglass, Harriet Tubman, and Sojourner Truth—often orated from the pulpit, church seating was segregated. Timothy Gilbert, a member of the congregation, challenged the tradition and was expelled for inviting several African-American friends to sit in a white pew. (Gilbert then founded the **Tremont Temple** in 1842, Boston's first integrated place of worship.) The African Methodist Episcopal Church met here from 1867 until the 1930s, with the Unitarian Universalists moving in after the Depression. Later, when the **Afro-American Culture Center** was located here, poet Langston Hughes gave readings. Renovated in 1982 by **John Sharratt Associates** and put on the National Register of Historic Places, shops and private offices have since replaced the community activities that took place here. ♦ 121 Mt. Vernon St (at Charles St)

50 The Church of the Advent The story goes that flamboyant parishioner Isabella Stewart Gardner, who founded her signature museum in the Fenway, scrubbed the church steps during Lent as penance. The tale also goes that proper Bostonians sniffed and wondered why Isabella wasn't required to scour the entire edifice. This Gothic Revival church (completed in 1888 by **Sturgis and Brigham** and pictured above) distributes its great girth on an awkward site through a chain of conical-roofed chapels, accommodating nearby domestic architecture as a good Beacon Hill neighbor should. The interiors are also ingeniously arranged and splendidly embellished. The church boasts one of the finest sets of carillon bells in the US and a restful garden. ♦ 30 Brimmer St (at Mt. Vernon St). 523.2377

51 Sunflower Castle Remodeled in 1878 by **Clarence Luce**, this amusing Queen Anne cottage began life in 1840 as a plain-Jane anonymous little building; now it takes its name from the enormous, gaudy sunflower ornament pressed on its brow. Maybe boredom with Beacon Hill's de rigueur palette and mincing details inspired **Luce** to paint the stuccoed first floor brilliant yellow and sheath the second story in China-red tile. Whimsy now unleashed, he added exuberantly carved brackets and posts, and a griffin. ♦ 130 Mt. Vernon St (at River St)

52 Another Season
★★★$$$ London-born owner Odette Bery proves the English can cook. Her monthly menus are eclectic and international; her food modern, understated, often free of butter and cream, and served in petite portions. The well-heeled clientele includes many Hill regulars, who don't mind if their knees bump in the cramped dining alcoves because they're fond of the Gay Nineties bistro murals, impressed with the inventive turns beef medaillons take here, and enamored of the expressive chocolate or the fruit-based desserts. Insist on the front room. Stroll up to Mount Vernon's summit afterward, and pronounce the evening perfect. ♦ Continental ♦ M-Sa lunch and dinner. Reservations recommended; required for dinner Friday and Saturday. 97 Mt. Vernon St (at W Cedar St). 367.0880

53 Charles Street Supply A really good hardware store is an alluring place. Even if you've never gone to war with weeds or handled a 2 x 4, you'll itch to tackle some project, *any* project, at the sight of all the handy wares spilling onto this overstuffed store's sidewalks. Sure, the prices are high, but the store dispenses a lot more than tools and how-tos. The gregarious owner, Richard Gurnon, and his staff steer disoriented people in the right direction. If you would still prefer that all physical labor be taken off your hands, they'll repair screen doors, broken windows, vacuum cleaners—practically anything you need to smooth the bumpy course of urban life. ♦ Daily. 54-56 Charles St (between Chestnut and Mt. Vernon Sts). 367.9046

53 Blackstone's of Beacon Hill Owner Richard Dowd stocks reproductions for historical societies all across the United States, so this is the place to come for brass and mahogany trivets, candlesnuffers, and doorknockers. They also have porcelain and enamel renditions of the **Public Garden**'s famous **Swan Boats**, designed for the shop by Limoges and Crummles, and handmade stained-glass picture frames. ♦ Daily. 46 Charles St (between Chestnut and Mt. Vernon Sts). 227.4646

53 Paramount Restaurant $ This is a Greek diner squeezed into a Charles Street shoe box. A gathering spot for locals, it offers typical greasy-spoon breakfasts (self-served and very cheap) that one is expected to consume with dispatch during busy hours. You'll know if you're too slow. Yet *so* many are dedicated to the place, there must be some larger appeal a sensitive soul will perceive. Nothing's small here—try the Greek salad, moussaka, or souvlaki. ♦ Greek/American/Takeout ♦ Daily breakfast, lunch, and dinner. 44 Charles St (between Chestnut and Mt. Vernon Sts). 523.8832 ♿

53 Bel Canto ★$ This local chain cooks up tasty *tortas*—thick-crusted (wheat or white) pizzas—perfect for two, so come with an even-numbered party or include a renegade who'll happily tackle a calzone instead. Mix and match toppings to your heart's content, but if you order fresh garlic, advise the waiter that you have no fear of vampires and don't need an entire head thrown on. ♦ Pizza/Takeout ♦ Daily lunch and dinner. 42 Charles St (between Chestnut and Mt. Vernon Sts). 523.5575 ♿

54 Victorian Bouquet One of Boston's most inspired florists, Susan Bates uses locally grown flowers and Holland imports, as well as dried and silk varieties. Her bouquets are simply great. Attentive staff willingly provide street-side service. ♦ M-Sa. 53A Charles St (between Chestnut and Mt. Vernon Sts). 367.6648

54 Ristorante Toscano ★★★$$ Conscientiously patrolled by its ultracivilized owners, this brisk, friendly Florentine trattoria offers a diverting lineup of daily specials, headlining such luscious stars as carpaccio, smoked-salmon pasta, and rack of lamb. And this is one of the only places in Boston you're likely to encounter *bollito misto* (boiled meats). Start out rifling the bread basket for focaccia and its Florentine version, *schiacciata*, and end in dignified rapture over tiramisù and espresso. Sophisticated and self-assured, this restaurant is one of Boston's favorites. ♦ Italian ♦ M-Sa lunch and dinner; Su dinner. Reservations recommended. Valet parking evenings. 41-47 Charles St (between Chestnut and Mt. Vernon Sts). 723.4090

While a prisoner at Charles Street Jail in 1904, legendary Boston Mayor James Michael Curley ran for the city's board of aldermen and won. Curley was doing time for taking a postal exam for a friend.

Restaurants/Clubs: Red   Hotels: Blue
Shops/ 🌳 Outdoors: Green   Sights/Culture: Black

55 James Billings Antiques & Interiors The person handling the antiques here is James Billings, who concentrates on 18th-century English and continental furniture. Lise Davis, his wife and partner, is an interior decorator who specializes in the ever-more-popular English country-house look. Both belong to the British Antique Dealers Association and have been in business in Essex, England, since 1961, and in Boston since 1982. Their talents blend beautifully in this spacious, opulently appointed shop. It's impossible to pass by without peering within, even if the owners' particular interests aren't your cup of tea. As one glance will inform you, everything comes dear here. ♦ M-Sa. 34 Charles St (at Chestnut St). 367.9533

56 Cedar Lane Way When evening has nearly crept over the Hill, enter this skinny lane from Chestnut Street. Say hello to the cats in the windows of the tiny dwellings, and use sonar to sidestep the residents' trash and potted plants while you look up and admire their gardens spilling over brick retaining walls. The lane turns to cobblestones after crossing Pinckney Street and ends beneath a lantern's intimate glow. ♦ Between Chestnut and Pinckney Sts

57 The Book Store Just a few strides away from the commotion of Charles Street, this little shop seems to shrink back into the safe embrace of its residential surroundings. A familiar presence on the Hill, the unassuming store has catered to residents for over 40 years. Soft-spoken owners Susan Timken and Linda Cox stock many books that no one else seems to have, with wonderful choices in art and children's books. They'll special-order anything for you. ♦ M-Sa. 76 Chestnut St (between Charles and Spruce Sts). 742.4531

58 Caffè Bella Vita ★$ We'll tell you up front that the service is inexplicably harried and hare-brained, and the pastries and cappuccino only so-so in this redbrick storefront cafe. But take a look around, and you'll know right away why you came. Long after the last drop of espresso is a memory, people linger here gazing out at the Charles Street parade. Every table is near a plate-glass window, making this a good place to write a long letter on a winter afternoon. Plus, the *biscotti di Prato*—say "almond cookies," or you'll get a blank look—are great dunkers and the gelato *perfetto,* from the amaretto to the zuppa inglese. ♦ Cafe ♦ Daily. No credit cards accepted. 30 Charles St (at Chestnut St). 720.4505 ♿

59 Rebecca's ★★★$$ Yes, it's trendy, and you won't want your heart to suspect how much butter the succulent monkfish is swimming in. But silence those qualms and enjoy owner Rebecca Caras's consistently good formula for seasonal bounty, which made this cheerful bistro such a success that she's launched little take-out satellites all over the city. Watch the chefs in the open kitchen assemble excellent omelettes, salads, and pasta concoctions, or ogle the chorus line of desserts, which always includes pies with sky-high crusts. To avoid the crush, come early for dinner while the loyal clientele are still at their health clubs. While waiting for a table on a late summer's evening, walk down Chestnut Street toward the river and look for **No. 101** on your right. Surrounding a charming interior court, these condos look like English mews. And on your way back, watch for **No. 90,** an architectural oddity on the opposite side of the street. ◆ American/ Takeout ◆ Daily lunch and dinner. Reservations recommended. Valet parking evenings. 21 Charles St (between Chestnut and Beacon Sts). 742.9747 ♿ (takeout only)

60 Beacon Hill Thrift Shop Don't be hoity-toity about stopping in here; Boston's resourceful Brahmins would surely look askance at anyone silly enough to snub a bargain. One of Boston's oldest thrift shops, it's pleasingly cramped and cluttered with knickknacks and doodads, plus some truly fabulous finds. Manager Elizabeth Moore is always ready to make a deal, ably assisted by a loyal corps of women volunteers from the Hill. All proceeds benefit the New England Baptist Hospital League Nursing Scholarships. ◆ M-Th, Sa. 15 Charles St (between Chestnut and Beacon Sts). 742.2323

60 De Luca's Market This market has all sorts of gourmet fixings for a sumptuous picnic on the esplanade or supper by a fire. (If it's Oreos you're looking for, you can find them, too.) Expect lines and tight squeezes because everyone shops here. Of course, such quality commands a high price. There's a little bit of everything here, but if you can't find your favorite treat, they'll order it. In business since 1905, the market wangled a wine-and-liquor license (a major feat on the Hill) some years back and purveys an extensive selection. ◆ M-Sa. 11 Charles St (between Chestnut and Beacon Sts). 523.4343. Also at: 239 Newbury St (at Fairfield St). 262.5990

61 Library Grill ★★★$$$ Built for Brahmins by a Brahmin (**Ogden Codman**), this 1909 town house—known as the **Hampshire House**—borrows from Greek and Georgian Revival and Federal styles. Upstairs in this restaurant, the silver-spoon spirit still thrives, with the polished paneling, leather chairs, and mooseheads creating a men's-club ambience. The Sunday brunch is the meal to try. The decor becomes more and more pleasant, just fine, really, when the splendid eggs Benedict and crisp corned-beef hash arrive. Then it's time for a second impeccable Bloody Mary, while the piano playing gently eases the morning along. Return some evening, with your favorite person, to gaze at the **Public Garden** and gorge yourself on char-grilled beef or grilled shrimp served with any of a number of delectable sauces. ◆ American ◆ M-Sa dinner, Su brunch and dinner. Reservations recommended for dinner; free parking 5-10PM. 84 Beacon St (at Brimmer St). 227.9600

61 Bull & Finch ★$ Downstairs within the **Hampshire House** is the bar that the TV sitcom "Cheers" was modeled after. All the brouhaha has eclipsed a lot of the pub's authentic charm, but if you time it right, you can sidestep the boisterous throngs of tourists and college students by slipping in at a quiet hour for a beer and one of the great burgers or other pub-style fare. One of Boston's nicest bartenders, Eddie Doyle, works here days. Doyle has raised hundreds of thousands of dollars over the years for all kinds of causes. Look for the paper place mats—Doyle's design. ◆ American ◆ Daily lunch and dinner. Dancing F-Sa nights. 84 Beacon St (at Brimmer St). 227.9605 ♿

Known as "The Way to the Poorhouse" in the 17th century because of the almshouse at the corner of Park Street, Beacon Street began as an undeveloped area on the edge of Boston. Here the free-spirited Reverend Blaxton cultivated the first-named variety of American apple—"Blaxton's Yellow Sweeting"—in his beloved orchard near today's Charles Street. Formally laid out in 1708, Beacon Street began to acquire its present sedate and stately character when its brick row houses, most in early Federal style, were built in the first half of the 19th century, following the State House's lead. This bright thoroughfare bordering the Common became known as "the sunny street that holds the sifted few."

62 Public Garden You can't lounge as freely on the grass here (see the map below) as at the **Common,** but this garden is an idyllic, lush retreat that always seems larger than it truly is. Artists love to paint the manicured look, and the advertising and film communities stage photo shoots all over. Several out-of-the-way bowers offer haven from urban tumult. And there's no better place for a springtime romance to bloom.

One of the oldest botanical gardens in America, the property began as desolate, soggy salt-marsh flats located along a great bay of the Charles River estuary. Ropewalks spanned the area (see the description on page 19), and Bostonians clammed and fished when the tides allowed. In April 1775 the British soldiers embarked by boat, near the garden's Charles Street Gate, for Lexington and Concord. There's also a remarkable history of outspoken citizen involvement enshrined in this spot. Throughout the early 1800s, real-estate developers hankered after its 24 acres, only to be thwarted again and again by vigilant citizens dreaming of a magnificent botanical park. Bostonians finally ratified a bill in 1859 that deemed the garden forever public. That same year, **George Meacham,** a novice local architect, won $100 for his English-inspired vision of a public garden dominated by a sinuous pond and ribboned with paths. His grandiloquent scheme was modestly altered in the final form. Today the garden is watched over and beautified by "garden" angels: The Friends of the Public Garden, formed in the 1970s. ♦ Bounded by Beacon and Boylston Sts, and Charles St S and Arlington St

Within the Public Garden:

Footbridge Enter the garden by taking the ceremonial "Haffenreffer Walk" off Charles Street and step onto the spunky, whimsical footbridge, designed in 1867 by **William G. Preston.** It's an appealing exaggeration of the engineering marvel of its day—the suspension bridge. Repaired and reinforced, the bridge's spiderweb cables are only

decorative now. Lean back against the baby bridge and gaze across the garden toward Beacon Street, ignoring the ugly downtown stretch in the distance along Tremont Street. From bridgeside, watch Boston's entire socioeconomic spectrum pass by on the surrounding walkways.

Swan Boats and Lagoon One of Boston's most famous sights, the **Swan Boats** cruise serenely by, while dozens of chatty ducks wait for handouts on the four-foot-deep, four-acre lagoon. A pair of real swans, ceremoniously escorted to the lagoon every spring, also sail snootily about. Rowboats, canoes, and a little side-wheeler named the *Dolly Varden* once plied these waters, but the **Swan Boats** have reigned alone now for more than a century. Their creator, Robert Paget, an English immigrant and shipbuilder, was inspired by Richard Wagner's opera *Lohengrin,* in which the hero crosses a river in a boat drawn by a swan.

Paget's ancestors still own the quaint fleet he launched in 1877. The six existing boats now carry up to 20 passengers per boat instead of the original four, and weigh two tons. The oldest, *Big Bertha,* dates from 1918. Only children are thrilled by this 15-minute figure-eight voyage pedal-powered at two miles per hour—but if you're tired, it's a fine way to rest your feet. In the winter, the lagoon becomes a picturesque skating pond. ♦ Nominal fee. Daily. Swan Boats 522.1966; skate rentals 482.7400

Plants and Trees Amble amid the colorful legacy of William Doogue, the garden's controversial superintendent from 1878 to 1906, who instituted its famous Victorian floral displays that are rotated seasonally. Some Bostonians griped about Doogue's extravagant use of showy hothouse plants, including palms, cacti, and yucca. In 1888, some 90,000 plants were laid out in 150 beds. But most people were thrilled, and Doogue's style has endured, though on a more modest scale. Nearly 600 trees of more than a hundred varieties grow in the garden, most labeled with their Latin and common names, a practice inspired by the 19th-century passion for learning. The garden's weeping willows offer splendid shade for reading. Pick a tree to revisit over the years.

Statues Sure, some of the garden's sculpture is mediocre, but all in all it's an oddly appealing lot. The most striking statue is Charlestown native Thomas Ball's gallant *George Washington* on horseback (erected in 1869), facing

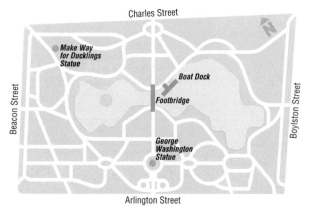

Charles Street

Beacon Street

Make Way for Ducklings Statue

Boat Dock

Footbridge

George Washington Statue

Boylston Street

Arlington Street

Commonwealth Avenue (near the Arlington Street gate). Anecdotes tell how Ball was obsessed with accurately depicting the triumphant patriot's steed; he frequented local stables and employed a famous local charger, Black Prince, as his model. To George's right (facing Commonwealth Avenue) is the granite and red-and-white-marble *Ether Fountain,* the garden's oldest monument, donated in 1867 to honor the first use of anesthesia, 21 years before, at Massachusetts General Hospital.

Some others to seek out: Facing Boylston Street are abolitionist senator *Charles Sumner* (sculpted by Thomas Ball); antislavery spokesman *Wendell Phillips* (Daniel Chester French did the statue in 1914; Henry Bacon designed the base); and Polish independence leader *Tadeusz Kosciuszko* (sculpted in 1927 by Theo Alice Ruggles Kitson). By the Charles Street gate is philanthropist *Edward Everett Hale* (completed in 1912 by Bela Lyon Pratt), patriot Nathan Hale's nephew. Flamboyant Unitarian preacher and transcendentalist *William Ellery Channing* (sculpted in 1903 by Herbert Adams) faces Arlington Street. Channing's writing influenced many young authors of his day, including Ralph Waldo Emerson. Three fountain statues portray images of childhood. Near Arlington Street is sculptor Mary E. Moore's *Small Child* (erected in 1929); and near Charles Street are *Triton Babies* (by Anna Coleman Ladd) and *Bagheera* (erected in 1986) by Lilian Swann Saarinen, wife of architect **Eero Saarinen,** which illustrates the scene from Rudyard Kipling's *Jungle Book* in which the black panther Bagheera tries to trap an owl.

Ducklings The newest and best-beloved garden statues (unveiled in 1987) are Boston artist Nancy Schön's larger-than-life bronzes of Mrs. Mallard and her eight ducklings, the heroes of Robert McCloskey's children's tale *Make Way for Ducklings* (published in 1941). As the story tells, after stopping all traffic on Beacon Street, the canard clan marches off to rendezvous at the lagoon with Mr. Mallard. It's easy to spot the ducks along the path between the lagoon and the gateway at Charles and Beacon Streets; you'll always see children sitting on them, embracing and patting them or waddling nearby quacking. When one of the ducklings was stolen in 1989, a pair of bartenders—Eddie Doyle of the nearby **Bull & Finch,** aka "Cheers" bar, and Tommy Leonard of Kenmore Square's **Eliot Lounge** started the "Bring Back Mack" fund-raising campaign. Now Mack is back with his pack.

The name Boston is an elision of St. Botolph's Town, named for the patron saint of fishing, whose name was derived from *bot* (boat) and *ulph* (help).

Bests

Ann Robert
Co-owner with husband, Lucien Robert, Maison Robert

Visiting the rose garden in **Fenway.**

The Sunday afternoon concerts at **King's Chapel.**

A boat ride on **Boston Harbor.**

The **Arnold Arboretum,** for a walk during any season.

Theater performances at the **Huntington** or by the **American Repertory Theatre (ART).**

Window shopping on **Newbury Street.**

Dining with friends at **Maison Robert**—on the outdoor terrace in warm months, upstairs or in the cafe the rest of the year.

Boston Athenaeum, for tea on Wednesday and for concerts.

Beacon Hill garden tours in the spring.

The **Fine Arts Museum**—special and regular exhibits.

Corby Kummer
Senior Editor/Food and Wine columnist, *The Atlantic Monthly* magazine

Evidently much goes on in the early morning in Boston, but the only time I've ever seen those terrible hours is waiting for the doors to open at **Filene's Basement** during one of the crucial twice-a-year sales. Coffee from one of the several branches of **au bon pain** inside Filene's is essential to endure this. ("FB," as my more-addicted friends call it, is a necessary stop for any visitor.)

Afternoons at the **Fogg Art Museum** at **Harvard,** looking at the Impressionist or early Italian panel paintings, and then walking around the **Cambridge** bookstores, feeling the winds of the four corners of the earth—a far more cosmopolitan feeling than you get anywhere in Boston.

Late afternoon walks along the **Charles River Esplanade,** watching the sun set over the odd Neo-Classic marble dome of **Massachusetts Institute of Technology** across the river and feeling glad you don't have to pass a single engineering course there.

Checking the antiques shops of **Charles Street** in **Beacon Hill,** where you'll find many high-priced shops, and the equally important shops on the hidden parallel River Street.

Tea at the **Bristol Lounge** of the **Four Seasons,** where all is grace without pomp; you can look at the flowering trees of the **Public Garden** across the street, and the scones are flaky and warm from the oven.

Dinner at **Hamersley's Bistro,** in the **South End,** where Gordon Hamersley cooks with Mediterranean invention and French frugality, or at **Ristorante Toscano** in **Beacon Hill,** where Vinicio Paoli, a native Florentine, brings the only authentic whiff of porcini to Boston.

Government Center/ Faneuil Hall

This part of town is not so much a neighborhood as it is a collection of interesting sights sprinkled among impersonal office towers and heavily trafficked, characterless streets. More or less bound by **Cambridge Street** to the west, the tangle of highways at the edge of the **Charles River** to the north, **Court** and **State Streets** to the south, and the **Central Artery** to the east, the main attractions here are **Faneuil Hall Marketplace**, with its blend of history and contemporary consumer delights; **Blackstone Block**, a tiny remnant of "Old Boston"; and the **Boston Garden/Shawmut Center** arena, home of the **Celtics** basketball team and the **Bruins** ice-hockey team.

Established communities that once existed here were swept away during the 1960s, when the city tried to rejuvenate itself through drastic and painful urban renewal, forcing thousands of city residents to move. Architect **I.M. Pei**'s master urban design plan imposed monumental order on 56 acres: 22 streets were replaced with six; slots for big, bold new buildings were carefully plotted; and a vast plaza was created and crowned with an iconoclastic city hall symbolizing "New Boston."

The name **West End**, nearly forgotten now, at one time referred to the 48 acres stretching from the base of **Beacon Hill** to **North Station.** The West End's fashionable days ended in the 19th century, and by the 20th century many considered the area a slum. Yet more than 10,000 people—Russians, Greeks, Albanians, Irish, Italians, Poles, Jews, Lithuanians—inhabited brick-row houses on the lively, intimate streets. Older Bostonians recall when Government Center was the raucous and irrepressible **Scollay Square**, where Boston's racier nightlife crowd caroused in saloons, burlesque shows, shooting galleries, adult theaters, pawnshops, tattoo parlors, and cheap hotels. Many still regret that this historic, freewheeling square was obliterated to make way for businesses and federal, state, and city offices—attracting somewhat more reputable, but much less colorful, residents.

Incredibly altered and dislocated from its past, this area now seems oddly situated. Abutting the history-drenched Waterfront, North End, and Beacon Hill, Government Center is more a passageway to other destinations than a place to linger. Only vestiges of the past remain, like **Old West Church**, the

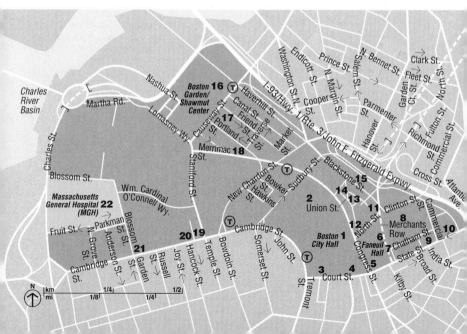

Harrison Gray Otis House, the **Bulfinch Pavilion** and **Ether Dome** at **Massachusetts General Hospital (MGH)**, and the famous **Steaming Kettle** landmark. Most of the contemporary architecture has a 1960s' look, often alienating and aloof. The newest buildings still can't decide what they're doing here. The old, authentic languages, layers, color, and complexity are gone. Some say the West End's demise was necessary to let a new city image live. While it's true that much of what's gone doesn't merit mourning, it's also true that most of the new is nothing to brag about.

The best starting point for touring this neighborhood is the **Government Center T** stop (*Green* and *Blue Lines*) at **City Hall Plaza,** but the **Haymarket** (*Green* and *Orange Lines*) and **Bowdoin** (*Blue Line*) subway stops are also convenient. **North Station** (*Green* and *Orange Lines*) is the stop for **Boston Garden/Shawmut Center;** the **Charles Street** stop (*Red Line*) takes you nearest to **Massachusetts General Hospital** and **Massachusetts Eye and Ear.** (Note: the **Haymarket** bus and subway stop is behind the **Government Center Garage,** about a block's distance down New Congress Street from the outdoor **Haymarket.**)

1 Boston City Hall Dramatically towering over a windswept brick plain, **Kallmann, McKinnell, and Knowles**'s massive structure (pictured below) looks precisely like what it is—a factory where Boston governmental operations crank along. **Gerhard Kallmann** and **Michael McKinnell,** also architects for the Hynes Auditorium in Back Bay and the Boston Five Cents Savings Bank on School Street, won a national competition for this project, the eye-catching centerpiece of New Boston.

Like most old warehouses, the 1968 building's exterior frankly communicates the functions and hierarchies of what's happening inside. Its sprawling, open lower levels house departments that directly serve the public, while more aloof bureaucracy is relegated to the upper floors, and the publicly accountable mayor and city council offices are suspended between. Summertime concerts and year-round political events spill onto City Hall Plaza. Although its interior is somewhat dim and neglected looking, this municipal building remains an edifice of heroic intentions, its massing and shadows always eloquent.
♦ Congress St (at North St). 635.4000

2 John F. Kennedy Federal Office Building Indifferent and impersonal in appearance, this one-million-square-foot building designed in 1967 by **The Architects Collaborative (Walter Gropius**'s firm) and **Samuel Glaser Associates,** is a perfectly appropriate home for the Internal Revenue Service, the Federal Bureau of Investigation, and many of the other federal agencies one doesn't want to tangle with. A Robert Motherwell mural marks the spot where the 26-story tower unites with its long, low-rise mate. ♦ City Hall Plaza (off Sudbury St)

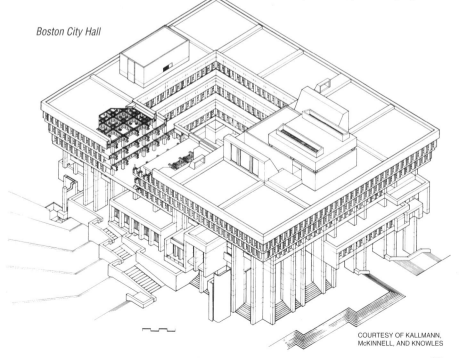

Boston City Hall

COURTESY OF KALLMANN, McKINNELL, AND KNOWLES

3 Sears Crescent Building A holdover from old Scollay Square, this gracefully curving 1816 building—renovated in 1969 by **Don Stull Associates**—moderates **City Hall**'s aggressive stance and softens nine-acre City Hall Plaza's impersonality. The building recalls the days when Boston streets sprouted every which way and the city didn't care that the shortest distance between two points is a line. Built by **David Sears,** whose Beacon Hill mansion is now the **Somerset Club,** this block was once Boston's publishing center, where Emerson, Hawthorne, and other literary types gathered.

Cozying up to this structure is the little **Sears Block** building (completed in 1848), where Boston's homey landmark, the gilded **Steaming Kettle,** puffs round the clock. The city's oldest animated trade sign, the kettle was cast in 1873 by coppersmiths Hicks and Badger, and commissioned by the Oriental Tea Company. Fed steam by a pipe from the company's boiler room, the kettle was an instant curiosity. Its big day came when Oriental Tea held a contest to guess its mascot's capacity. Weeks of fervent speculation ended on 1 January 1875, when more than 10,000 people gathered to watch William F. Reed, City Sealer of Weights and Measures, decree the official measure of 227 gallons, two quarts, one pint, and three gills—now engraved on the kettle's side. Eight winners shared the prize: a chest of premium tea. Reporting on the event, the *Boston Sunday Times* referred to the famous Boston Tea Party and bragged, "The tea-kettle excitement has run nearly as high as the tea excitement of old, and is almost a historical incident in the career of our noble city." Once Scollay Square was razed, the kettle was relocated in 1967 to the Sears Block. Now a landmark, it graces the former **Steaming Kettle Coffee Shop,** which has been transformed into **Coffee Connection** (★$, 227.2284). ♦ 63-65 Court St (at Tremont St)

4 Ames Building Fourteen stories high, this proud and distinctive structure—now on the National Register of Historic Places—was once the tallest office building on the Eastern seaboard. Abounding with arches, modulating from the weighty ones at the base to the delicate chain under the cornice, the vigorous building was designed in 1889 by **Henry Hobson Richardson**'s successor firm, **Shepley, Rutan & Coolidge.** Although the great architect had died a few years earlier, his influence clearly was not forgotten, especially in the Romanesque architectural details and lacy carvings.

One of Boston's first skyscrapers, the sturdy building is supported by nine-foot-thick masonry walls—the second-tallest such structure in the world—not the light-steel frame that became popular soon afterward.

The building only briefly dominated the city's skyline. No matter that it has been dwarfed by 20th-century behemoths—it exerts enduring presence. ♦ 1 Court St (between Cambridge and Congress Sts)

5 Bay Tower Room
★★$$$ It's a private club by day, but come evening, this restaurant offers stunning views, festive atmosphere, and costly but good food selected "to celebrate the seasons." Located on the 33rd floor of the **Sheraton World Headquarters Building** (pictured at right), the dramatic dining room is an assemblage of alcoves and tiers where every table claims a view: miniaturized **Faneuil Hall Marketplace** crowds, the **Custom House Tower,** boats crossing **Boston Harbor,** and planes circling **Logan Airport**.
(Try to arrive before sunset.) The cuisine is sometimes uneven and other times just fine, with successes including lobster ravioli, oysters, chateaubriand, grilled seafood, rack of lamb, roasted venison tenderloin, and an extraordinary fruit shortcake. After dinner, ascend to the postage-stamp-size lounge and dance to music by a small combo. There's free validated parking under the building after 5PM; enter from Merchant's Row. ♦ American ♦ M-Sa dinner. No jeans allowed. Jacket required in dining room. Reservations recommended. 60 State St (at Congress St). 723.1666

5 Houlihan's $$ One in a national chain of more than 50 restaurants, this watering hole has predictable, passable food and is usually packed, especially with the big business-lunch crowd and major after-work singles scene. A DJ entertains nightly, Monday through Friday from 5PM to 2AM and Saturday and Sunday from 4PM to 2AM. ♦ American ♦ Daily lunch and dinner. Dress casual but neat; no tank tops after 7PM. Reservations recommended. 60 State St (at Congress St). 367.6377

5 Dock Square The open area between Congress Street and Faneuil Hall earned its name in colonial times when it was young Boston's landing place. The Town Dock was eventually built out into Town Cove and later filled in to create more land, an important threshold to the New World. Newcomers, visitors, and goods passed constantly across the square to and from the boats docked near its edge. On the way to Faneuil Hall, look for Anne Whitney's 1880 bronze of *Samuel Adams.*

6 Faneuil Hall From the heights of the steps behind **City Hall,** look for the most familiar and beloved of Boston's many curious objects of affection: Spinning in harbor-sent breezes and glinting in the sun atop **Faneuil Hall** (pictured below) is master tinsmith Deacon Shem Drowne's gold-plated grasshopper, a weather vane modeled in 1742 after a similar one topping London's Royal Exchange. Grasshoppers symbolize good luck; and in a city where many a fine old building has been lost to fire or progress, this critter has certainly done right by **Faneuil Hall.** In 1740, when wealthy French Huguenot and English merchant Peter Faneuil offered to erect a market building for the town at his own expense, citizens voted on his proposal. It barely passed, 367 to 360, a lukewarm welcome for a landmark that has been a historic center of Boston life ever since.

Painter John Smibert designed the original structure. Built in 1742, it housed open-market stalls, a meeting hall, and offices. All were gutted by fire in 1761, but an identical building was soon rebuilt. Peddlers and politicians have always peacefully coexisted here, inspiring local poet Francis W. Hatch to write: "Here orators in ages past have mounted their attack/Undaunted by proximity of sausage on the rack." As

the Revolution approached, the impassioned oratory of patriots such as Samuel Adams and James Otis fired up the populace, drawing huge crowds and earning the marketplace the nickname "Cradle of Liberty." At a 1772 town meeting here, Adams proposed that Boston establish the Committee of Correspondence and invite the other colonies to join, thus establishing the clandestine information network that promoted united action against British repression. The hall's nickname was further cemented when Boston's famous antislavery orator Wendell Phillips presented his first address here in 1837. William Lloyd Garrison and Massachusetts senator Charles Sumner joined the battle for the abolitionist cause from the same rostrum.

In 1806, when the crowds just couldn't squeeze in anymore, **Charles Bulfinch** handsomely remodeled and enlarged the cramped hall. He preserved its stalwart simplicity but doubled its width, added a floor, and created a marvelous second-floor galleried assembly room that citizen's groups use to this day. Among the room's dozens of portraits of famous Americans, look for George P.A. Healy's *Liberty and Union, Now and Forever* depicting Massachusetts senator Daniel Webster on the floor of the US Senate defending the Union in 1830 against a southern senator's contention that states could veto federal laws. Gilbert Stuart's well-known portrait of George Washington taking Dorchester Heights from the redcoats is also here. On the third floor are the headquarters and museum of the Ancient and Honorable Artillery Company of Massachusetts, a ceremonial organization with a proud past as the oldest military organization in the Western Hemisphere; it was chartered in 1638 by Massachusetts's first governor, John Winthrop. On display is the company's vast collection of arms, uniforms, documents, and memorabilia.

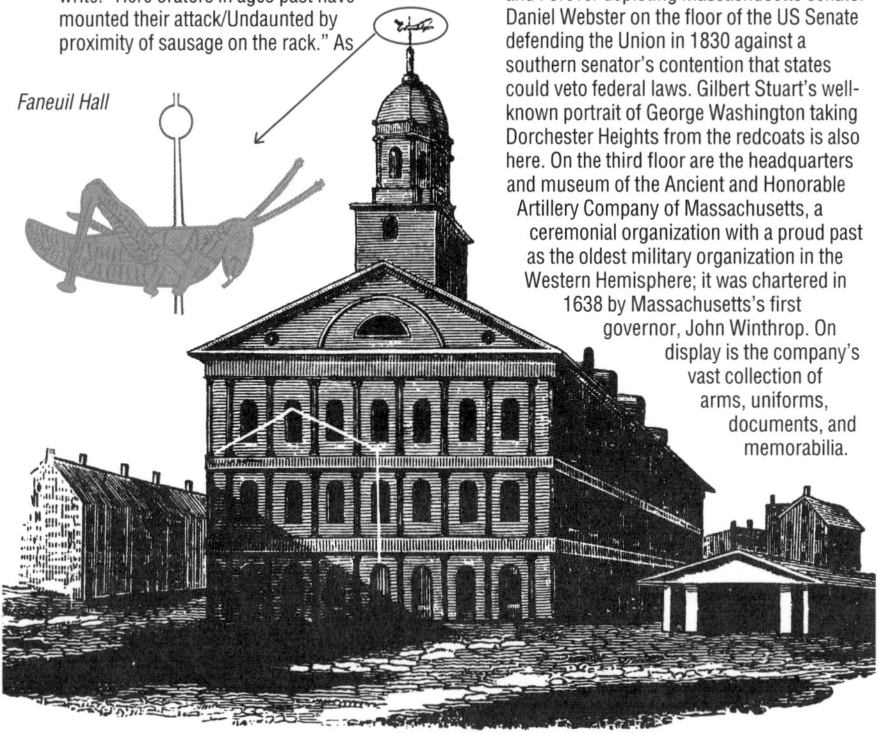

Faneuil Hall

There's only one Faneuil Hall—the brick building with the grasshopper on top—but the entire marketplace is collectively called Faneuil Hall, too, and sometimes it's known as Quincy Market.

Pronunciations of "Faneuil" abound, with little agreement about which is correct. Is it *Fan'l, Fannel, Fan-you-ill, Fan-yul,* or *Fan-ee-yul*? Who knows? But the first two are by far the most common.

Back at ground level, get a foretaste of **Quincy Market** across the way by making a quick tour of the souvenir shops and food counters that have replaced the more down-to-earth provender purveyed in the old hall. Times have changed, but the adaptable hall thrives on. Its political pulse also beats strong; during presidential-election years, contenders in the state's primary debate here. ♦ Daily. Faneuil Hall Sq (between Congress St and Merchants Row). 523.3886

6 Bostix Stop by this outdoor kiosk to purchase half-price tickets on the day of performance, or full-price advance tickets, to many of Boston's arts and entertainment events. This in-person, cash-only service sells tickets for visiting Broadway shows and dozens of local theater, dance, and music companies, plus comedy clubs, sports events, jazz concerts, campgrounds, nightclubs, dinner theaters, tourist attractions, and summer festivals. ♦ Tu-Su. Faneuil Hall Marketplace (on the south side of Faneuil Hall). Recorded information 723.5181

7 The Limited and Express Compagnie Internationale Representative of New Boston's sometimes cavalier attitude toward the city's history, this building by **Graham Gund Associates** strives to relate to the other marketplace structures. But as hard as it tries, it's a new kid on the block with too much style and not enough substance. For a shopping foray that's sure to overwhelm, step inside **The Limited**'s superstore: floor upon floor of moderately priced fashions and accessories primarily for women—but some for men and children, too—including **Express**'s international assortment of pricier "Euro" looks. There's a whole floor of lingerie. Teens and college students go absolutely crazy over this place. ♦ Daily. One Faneuil Hall Sq (in South Market). 742.6837

7 Bertucci's $ Another spacious outpost of the very popular local pizza and pasta chain, this branch hops in tune with nearby **Faneuil Hall Marketplace.** Count on them for tasty fresh pizzas, calzones, and salads. Look for the fun mural, depicting pizza making, above the bar. ♦ Pizza/Takeout ♦ Daily lunch and dinner. 22 Merchants Row (between Broad and Congress Sts). 227.7889

7 Clarke's $$ On one side, there's a big neighborly saloon where crowds flock to watch sports events on TV, eye prospective dates, or wind down after work; on the other, a comfortable, no-frills restaurant and bar where you can order straightforward New England dishes like scrod. Try the big sandwiches and burgers with a side of great fries. A shuttle will take you from here to **Boston Garden/Shawmut Center** arena events. Co-owner Dave DeBusschere, formerly of the **New York Knicks,** sometimes drops by to watch the **Celtics** play.

♦ American ♦ Daily lunch and dinner. Reservations recommended for large parties. 21 Merchants Row (at State St). 227.7800

8 Faneuil Hall Marketplace Beyond **Faneuil Hall** stands a long, low trio of buildings (pictured on page 33) bursting with international and specialty food stalls, restaurants, cafes, boutiques, bars, and an army of pushcarts peddling wares to tempt the impulsive buyer. The extravaganza ranges from junk food to gourmet, kitsch to haute couture. The whole ensemble attracts more than 14 million visitors a year, inviting comparisons to Disney World. But touristy and slick as it is, the marketplace possesses the authentic patina of history. It has lived a long, useful life. Many people are turned off by the throngs and the buy, buy, buy mood of this shop-and-snack mecca, but it definitely deserves a visit—if only to glance over the worthy old buildings and enjoy the outdoor spectacle of pedestrians and street performers. An information desk is located under the South Canopy. It isn't easy to spot among the pushcarts, and the staff is often indifferent, but pick up the extremely helpful printed directory.

The marketplace's 535-foot-long granite centerpiece, a National Historic Landmark, is named for Josiah Quincy, the Boston mayor who revitalized the decrepit waterfront by ordering major landfills, six new streets, and the construction of a market house to supplement overcrowded **Faneuil Hall.** Architect **Alexander Parris** crowned the 1826 Greek Revival central building with a copper dome and planted majestic Doric colonnades at either end. The building projected a noble face seaward, for it was right at the harbor's edge in those days. Two granite-faced brick warehouses, today called **North** and **South Markets,** later rose on either side according to **Parris**'s plans. For a century and a half the ensemble was the dignified venue for meat and produce distribution and storage.

By the 1970s, however, the marketplace was decaying, in danger of demolition. **Ben** and **Jane Thompson** of **Benjamin Thompson & Associates** convinced the city and developers that the complex could become Boston's gathering place again if it were recycled to suit contemporary urban life. The firm restored most of the marketplace in 1978, adding such innovations as glass canopies flanking the central building and festive signage. The cobbled pedestrian way on the **South Market** side isn't quite as narrow as the thoroughfare on the **North Market** side and has plenty of benches. Even in chilly weather, you'll see lots of people enjoying the show while savoring baklava, barbecue, chowder, fudge, gourmet brownies, pizzas, salads, sausage on a stick, raw oysters, Indian pudding, french fries, ice cream—the whole gastronomic gamut. Under

Faneuil Hall Marketplace

the canopy on the north side of **Quincy Market**, a popular piano bar draws a large after-work crowd from the Financial District and nearby offices, inspiring many an impromptu sing-along. When Boston winter finally gives up, sidewalk cafes dot the pedestrian streets. An outdoor flower market near the north side of **Faneuil Hall** blankets the cobblestones with greenery, bringing colors and smells of each season to this corner of the city: autumn pumpkins, Christmas trees and poinsettias, and summer bouquets.

The scheme to gently breathe life back into the old buildings has proven to be a fantastic success, a model for renewal projects across the country. Boston lost its waterside meat-and-potatoes-style market to colorful abundance of another sort. Come early in the morning and enjoy a quiet breakfast in **Quincy Market**'s central rotunda, or brave the Saturday afternoon crowds when the place is full of competing aromas and voices. You'll notice people often gather round the

cobblestoned square between **Faneuil Hall** and **Quincy Market**'s West Portico, the prime spot for musicians, jugglers, and other entertainers. ◆ Daily. 1 Faneuil Hall Marketplace (between Commercial and Congress Sts). 338.2323

Within Quincy Market:

Boston & Maine Fish Company Live lobster, up to a whopping 25 pounds, and other super-fresh seafood are packed for travel or shipped anywhere in the US from this retail market. The prices are high, but sometimes worth it to satisfy a hankering for fruits of the Atlantic. You can get all the fixings for an authentic New England clambake, minus the seaside pit: lobsters, steamer clams, chowder, and utensils. Or, if you just want some steamers to take home for supper, they'll steam them for you here while you wait. ◆ Daily. Colonnade. 723.3474, 800/626.7866

BOSTON & MAINE FISH COMPANY

The Salty Dog Seafood Bar and Grille

★★$$ Get some of the best oysters in town, good chowder and fried clams, and other fresh and undisguised seafood in this noisy little hut of a place. There's no pastry cart here, and they don't take reservations, but you can dine alfresco from April through November. A lot of regulars stay away during the summer to avoid the inevitable throngs. ♦ Seafood/American ♦ M-Sa lunch and dinner; Su brunch and dinner. Lower level. 742.2094

Boston Chipyard The award-winning mouthfuls of the best chocolate chippers in town are always fresh, whether the plain traditional favorite or mixed with ingredients like peanut butter, extra chocolate, nuts, oatmeal, or raisins. A California mom came more than 18 years ago and opened the shop with her own recipe, a favorite of her son and his friends. Come for a late-night fix of milk and cookies. You can mail order, too. ♦ Daily. North Canopy. 742.9537

Within North Market:

Marketplace Cafe ★$$ Dine outdoors in the summer and in a greenhouse setting in the winter on a variety of appetizers, salads, sandwiches, and simple entrées. Light, bright, and casual, the bistro is especially festive and welcoming on warm evenings. ♦ American ♦ M-F lunch and dinner; Sa-Su brunch and dinner. Street level. 227.9660

The Boston Beach Club

Attracting a younger crowd, this place books live bands and plays up its seaside theme with surfboard tables, a fish tank, tropical drinks, Hawaiian leis, and assorted games and toys. T-shirts, hats, records, trips, and other freebies are handed out on promotion nights. Drinks only are served. ♦ Daily 6PM-2AM. Street level. 227.9664

The Marketplace Grill and Oar Bar

★★★$$ A cut above other culinary choices here, this spacious brick-walled room—sparsely decorated with a pair of impossibly long and skinny sculls hung overhead—overlooks the marketplace hubbub and serves exemplary American cuisine at a very reasonable tariff. Chef Jamie Mohn presents artfully composed plates, such as a meal-unto-itself goat-cheese salad, and his improvised pastas of the day—for example, al dente fettuccine topped with grilled salmon, sun-dried tomatoes, and cool slivers of avocado—are nothing less than inspired. It's worth withstanding the allure of the market's clamoring food stands to have a studied, civilized meal in this second-story hideaway—a real find. ♦ American ♦ M-Sa lunch and dinner; Su jazz brunch. Reservations recommended. Second level. 227.1272

Durgin-Park ★★$$ Come here for true Yankee cooking and a taste of Boston's bygone days. Don't listen to detractors who say this place is overrated; give it a try and enjoy a fast-paced, filling meal. Founded in 1827 (the same year their Boston logo—pictured above—was drawn), this cranky, creaky, but well-loved institution dates from the marketplace's old days, when produce held the fort instead of today's gourmet melee. Notice the ancient plank floors and tin ceilings. Waitresses legendary for their brisk gotta-job-to-do manner serve raw clams and oysters, phone-book-size prime rib, starchless fish chowder, Boston scrod (with baked beans, of course), chops, steaks, fresh seafood, chicken potpie, and more solid old favorites. Save room for the scrumptious fresh strawberry shortcake, made on the premises, and rich Indian pudding. Everybody dines family style at tables set for 16 and decked out in red-checkered cloths. Ask about validated parking. ♦ American ♦ Daily lunch and dinner. No credit cards accepted. Street level. 227.2038

Downstairs at Durgin-Park:

The Oyster Bar at Durgin-Park ★★$

Serving appetizers and sandwiches only, this is a great alternative to the noisy place upstairs if you want a light repast and a little calm. Try the soothing clam chowder and briny steamers. There are no tables; just the bar and counters. Dessert is not on the menu, but just ask and someone will bring it down from upstairs. ♦ American ♦ Daily lunch and dinner. 227.2038

Geoclassics Featuring an unusually broad array of fossils, minerals, and gemstones, this shop offers necklaces and rings in simple and tasteful mounts, as well as semiprecious stones set in silver or gold. Though owner Claudio Kraus prices some children's offerings at $1 or $2, other pieces can run $1,000 and up. There are also some unusual paperweights and more run-of-the-mill sundries. ♦ Daily. Street level. 523.6112

The historic Green Dragon Tavern once stood on Union Street, the popular patriots' meeting place that Daniel Webster called the "Headquarters of the Revolution." The Boston Tea Party was planned here.

Restaurants/Clubs: Red   Hotels: Blue

Shops/ 🌴 Outdoors: Green   **Sights/Culture:** Black

Zuma's Tex-Mex Cafe ★$$ Subdued, this basement cafe is not—the very first sight that greets you is a sandpit artfully sporting an O'Keeffe-style cattle skull. The small, packed space is abustle with sizzling fajitas and quesadillas about to be zapped with hot, hot, hot sauce, and abuzz with neon accents and scattered video monitors broadcasting surfer tapes. Owner Steve Immel's mission—to serve "foods of the sun"—extends to Italian pasta and Japanese teriyaki, and is typified in a line of fresh-fruit "neon" margaritas. ♦ Tex-Mex/International ♦ Daily lunch and dinner. Basement. 367.9114

Within South Market:

Serendipity 3 $$ Tourists, families, and the young crowd flock here. This good-humored food boutique makes no bones about its eccentricities, from the whimsical decor to an enormous illustrated menu you'll want to color with crayons. Be basic with a burger or omelette, or venture into blue-corn nachos with goat cheese, scrod Rockefeller (baked with crabmeat and mozzarella), Ftatateeta's Toast (thick slices of bread dipped in egg batter and lathered with cream cheese or other spread, topped with rhubarb ginger jam), an Eiffel Tower sandwich (croissant with ham and brie served with paprika and other spices), or the famous frozen hot chocolate. Complimentary hors d'oeuvres are served weekdays from 4PM to 8PM during "Attitude Adjustment" hours, live jazz plays Friday night and at Sunday brunch, and a magician performs Thursday night. In warmer weather, tables migrate outdoors. By the way, if you see something you like here, be it a T-shirt, statuette, or lighting fixture, it's probably for sale. ♦ American ♦ M-F lunch and dinner; Sa-Su brunch and dinner. Reservations recommended Friday and Saturday nights, and Sunday brunch. Street level. 523.2339

Siam Malee Come here for a feast of fabrics—iridescent, shimmering, gorgeously colored silks, cottons, and linens, all imported from Thailand—metamorphosed into butterflylike day and evening fashions. Almost all are for women, although there's a vivid array of men's ties. The styling is simple but clever, with unusual detailing. Glittery and festive jewelry, beaded bags, jackets, and belts can be found here too. ♦ Daily. Street level. 227.7027

Alan Lawrence The two friendly young owners put their first names as well as their heads together to create this chic and cozy high-end men's boutique with its emphasis on customer service and "Euro-classic" looks in exceptional textures, colors, and fabrics. Men of all ages come in for custom-made suits and shirts, casualwear, and accessories, some designed by the owners, and produced internationally. There's a tailor on the premises. Custom consultations are offered by appointment only. ♦ Daily. Street level. 227.1144

Whippoorwill A standout among the independent stores that have found a home in the market, this subterranean craft shop tends to specialize in the whimsical. Mixed in among the kaleidoscopes, chimes, woven clothes, and other staples are such oddities as Josh and Michael Cohen's heart-bedecked ceramic condom boxes—"the perfect gift for the safety-conscious '90s." This is a good place to look for such one-of-a-kind tokens of affection. ♦ Daily. Basement. 523.5149

9 The Black Rose ★$ Its name is translated from *Roisin Dubh,* a Gaelic allegorical name for Ireland that symbolizes Irish Catholic repression by the British. Famous Irish faces and mementos line the walls, and Irish music accompanies bargain-priced meals that include meat loaf, lamb stew, fish-and-chips, Yankee pot roast, and boiled lobster (don't look for gourmet here). This big, hospitable bar offers numerous Irish beers and stout on tap and live Irish music every day; ask for times. It's a great place to meet after work, sing along with folk music, watch the **Celtics** game on the big-screen TV, and slowly sip Irish coffee. ♦ American/Irish ♦ Daily lunch and dinner. 160 State St (at Commercial St). 742.2286

In 1972 Boston mayor Kevin White bailed the Rolling Stones out of jail so the band could keep a concert date at Boston Garden.

Book Nooks

Boston and Cambridge are internationally renowned meccas for booklovers; after all, both cities have treated the printed word reverentially since their founding days. When the Puritans arrived, books transported from England were among their most prized possessions. Boston's first English settler was William Blaxton, a loner whose idea of perfect companionship was communing with his enviable library of 200 or so volumes. Cambridge remains the true booklover's haven for its critical mass of shops clustered in **Harvard Square**, the bookshop capital of the East Coast, if not the country. Together Boston and Cambridge bookstores can satisfy any literary interest. Here's a sampling of some of the best.

In Cambridge:

Robin Bledsoe and H.L. Mendelsohn (1640 Massachusetts Ave, between Shepard and Langdon Sts, 576.3634) offers out-of-print scholarly works on art history, architecture, archaeology, city planning, graphic design, women artists, landscape architecture, and decorative arts, as well as new, used, and imported books on horses.

The Grolier Poetry Book Shop Inc. (6 Plympton St, between Mt. Auburn St and Massachusetts Ave, 547.4648) has thousands of poetry titles, plus first editions, literary magazines, and small-press publications.

The Harvard University Press Display Room (1354 Massachusetts Ave, between Holyoke St and Dunster Rd, Holyoke Center Arcade, 495.2625) headlines the latest Harvard University Press publications, including the Loeb Classical Library. There's a bargain section, too.

Kate's Mystery Books (2211 Massachusetts Ave, between Chester and Day Sts, north of Porter Sq, 491.2660) spotlights more than 10,000 new and used mysteries amid black cats galore. A tombstone on the front lawn marks the address. This is also the hangout for the Cadaver Club, a cadre of local mystery writers.

Mandrake Book Store (8 Story St, between Brattle and Mt. Auburn Sts, 864.3088) specializes in the social sciences and art, architecture, and design.

The MIT Press Bookstore (292 Main St, at Kendall Sq, 253.5249) carries scholarly books and journals on engineering, computers science, architecture, philosophy, linguistics, economics, and more.

New Words Bookstore (186 Hampshire St, at Prospect St, Inman Square, 876.5310) is a feminist bookstore with books by and about women, plus records, T-shirts, posters, and postcards. Nonsexist and nonracist books for kids are a specialty.

Pangloss Bookshop (65 Mt. Auburn St, between Holyoke and Linden Sts, 354.4003) features used, out-of-print, and rare scholarly books.

Priscilla Juvelis, Inc. (1166 Massachusetts Ave, between Bow and Arrow Sts, 497.7570) purveys *libres d'artiste,* literary first editions, fine bindings, illustrated books, press books, and fine art by appointment only.

Revolution Books (1156 Massachusetts Ave, between Bow and Arrow Sts, 492.5443) sells books and periodicals on revolutionary politics.

Schoenhof's Foreign Books, Inc. (76A Mt. Auburn St, between Dunster Rd and Holyoke St, 547.8855) is America's oldest and largest comprehensive foreign-language bookstore.

Starr Book Shop (29 Plympton St, at Mt. Auburn St, 547.6864) is an academic bookstore in the **Harvard Lampoon Castle.**

WordsWorth (30 Brattle St, between Eliot and Mt. Auburn Sts, 354.5201), the square's busiest bookshop, carries all kinds of titles, and discounts all but textbooks.

In Boston:

Ars Libri (560 Harrison Ave, at Union Park St, South End, 357.5212) possesses the country's largest comprehensive inventory of rare and out-of-print books and periodicals about the fine arts.

Avenue Victor Hugo Bookshop (339 Newbury St, between Hereford St and Massachusetts Ave, Back Bay, 266.7746) stocks new and used paperbacks and hardcovers, magazines, and comic books.

Barnes & Noble (395 Washington St, between Winter and Bromfield Sts, Downtown, 426.5502; also at: 607 Boylston St, between Dartmouth and Clarendon Sts, Back Bay, 236.1308), the giant bookseller of reduced-price books, also carries paperbacks, children's books, and magazines.

Boston Cooks (Quincy Market, Faneuil Hall Marketplace, 523.0242) is blessed with a cornucopia of cookbooks in hardcover and paperback, including many privately printed by organizations from all over America.

Brattle Book Shop (9 West St, between Washington and Tremont Sts, 542.0210, 800/447.9595), the successor to America's oldest operating antiquarian bookshop, occupies three floors stocked with a little bit of everything.

Bromer Booksellers (607 Boylston St, at Dartmouth St, Second floor, Back Bay, 247.2818) handles rare books of all periods, literary first editions, private press and illustrated books, books in fine bindings, and miniature and children's books.

Maury A. Bromsen Associates, Inc. (Prudential Center, 779 Boylston St, at Gloucester St, Suite 23F, Back Bay, 266.7060) showcases rare Americana, Latin Americana, autographs and manuscripts, bibliography and reference works, fine arts (19th-century paintings and prints), and exploration and discovery. This store is open by appointment only.

B.U. Bookstore (660 Beacon St, at Commonwealth Ave, Kenmore Square, 267.8484) is a six-story collegiate department store, as well as New England's largest bookstore.

Buddenbrooks Booksmith (755 Boylston St, between Exeter and Fairfield Sts, Back Bay, 536.4433) gives prominence to its second-floor antiquarian section.

ChoreoGraphica (82 Charles St, between Pinckney and Mt. Vernon Sts, Beacon Hill, 227.4780), a well-established used bookstore, specializes in the performing arts, especially dance. Some reviewers' copies are sold here, too. It shares space with **Sher-Morr Antiques**.

Glad Day Bookshop (673 Boylston St, between Dartmouth and Exeter Sts, Back Bay, 267.3010) is New England's only gay and lesbian full literature bookshop.

The Globe Corner Book Store (1 School St, at Washington St, Downtown, 523.6658; also at: 49 Palmer St, at Church St, Harvard Square, Cambridge, 497.6277—travel and geography only) harbors a wealth of works on New England and books by regional authors; plus a fine selection of guidebooks and world-travel information.

Goodspeed's Book Shop (9 Park St, at Beacon St, Third floor, Beacon Hill, 523.5970), purveyor of rare tomes since 1898, now sells maps, prints, and first editions only.

David L. O'Neal Antiquarian Bookseller, Inc. (234 Clarendon St, between Newbury St and Commonwealth Ave, Second floor, Back Bay, 266.5790) handles fine and rare books from the 15th to the 20th century.

Pepper & Stern—Rare Books, Inc. (355 Bolyston St, at Arlington St, Second floor, Back Bay, 421.1880) specializes in first editions of American and English literature, mystery and detective fiction, rare cinema material, signed and inscribed books, autograph letters, and manuscripts.

Rizzoli (Copley Place, 100 Huntington Ave, at Dartmouth St, Back Bay, 437.0700) highlights art and architecture, design, photography, current fiction and nonfiction, and international and classical music.

Spenser's Mystery Bookshop and Marlowe's Used Books (314 Newbury St, at Hereford St, Back Bay, 262.0880) carries new and used mystery books, first editions, and collectible paperbacks.

Traveldays Bookshop (Copley Place, 100 Huntington Ave, at Dartmouth St, Back Bay, 247.2291) is part of a travel chain owned by Doubleday. You'll find around 5,000 titles, plus maps, videos, globes, atlases, and foreign-language guides here.

Trident Booksellers & Cafe (338 Newbury St, between Hereford St and Massachusetts Ave, Back Bay, 267.8688) has much more than just books. Crystals, incense, scented oils, tarot cards, and bonsai trees are sold here. The little cafe is a popular neighborhood meeting place.

Waldenbooks (2 Center Plaza, between State and Sudbury Sts, Government Center, 523.3044), the popular chain store, sells current paperbacks and hardcovers on general subjects.

Outside Boston:

New England Mobile Book Fair (82 Needham St, between Rte 128 and Winchester St, Newton, 527.5817) is well worth a drive. Not mobile in the least, it's actually a huge warehouse stocking more than 800,000 books. Everything is discounted by 20 percent, and there's a special mark-down section. Many of the titles are arranged by publisher.

10 Marketplace Center This gauche gate-crashing building—erected in 1985 by the **WZMH Group**—tries to look as if it belongs on this important historic site, even mimicking its venerable neighbors somewhat in materials and style. While it could have been worse, the building is awkward, especially its graceless atrium gateway with makeup-mirror–style fixtures. Although the opening preserves the pedestrian walk-to-the-sea leading to Boston Harbor at **Christopher Columbus Park,** the too-tall, too-wide building creates a barrier where none existed before. The marketplace's stockpile of shops includes many chain stores like **Brookstone, Banana Republic, Mrs. Fields' Cookies, Williams-Sonoma, The Sharper Image, The Gap,** and more.
♦ 200 State St (off Atlantic Ave). 478.2040

Within Marketplace Center:

Pavo Real Discover beautifully hued and patterned sweaters here that can't be found elsewhere. The shop imports most of its luxurious alpaca wool and pima cotton. The custom-designed, hand-knit sweaters for men and women from Peru and Bolivia sport hefty markups. The delightful jewelry, hats, gloves, scarves, wallets, and pocketbooks—some quite whimsical in design—make nice gifts.
♦ Daily. Street level. 439.0013

Doubleday Book Shop Spacious and bright, with a friendly staff, this link in the nationwide chain carries books for the general public, with strong sections in fiction, cooking, and local information. It's convenient, too, since bookstores in this neighborhood are scarce. Pick up some reading to accompany a take-out lunch from **Quincy Market.** ♦ Daily. Street level. 439.0196. Also at: 99 Park Plaza (between St. James and Boylston Sts) 482.8453

Peacock Papers Almost always crowded and busy, this gift and novelty shop carries the full Peacock Papers line of giftwrap, gift bags, cards, and mugs; plus other trendy, amusing, and irreverent cards, wrapping paper, office supplies, T-shirts, pencils stamped with mottoes, and just-for-fun gizmos and games. ♦ Daily. Street level. 439.4818

Chocolate Dipper Watch thick streams of fragrant, gooey chocolate blending away here while the staff readies luscious fresh fruit and truffles for dipping. Try strawberries, raspberries in season, banana, pineapple, cherries, grapes, and orange slices and rinds enrobed in dark, milk, or white chocolate. The extra-rich truffles come in more than half a dozen flavors, and a wide variety of other chocolates are also made on the premises. ♦ Daily. Street level. 439.0190

11 The Bostonian Hotel $$$$ Intimate and gracious, this hostelry is one of the most pleasant places to stay in Boston. Much of the charm comes from its residential scale and the way it blends with the historic Blackstone Block. Incorporated into the hotel complex are a structure hailing from 1824 and an 1890 warehouse that was built by **Peabody and Stearns** (architects for the **Custom House Tower**). Many of the 152 rooms have French doors opening onto private balconies that overlook **Faneuil Hall Marketplace;** rooms in the 19th-century **Harkness Wing** have an imprint of history. Ten honeymoon suites have Jacuzzis and working fireplaces, and two of the rooms have canopy beds. The lobby is appealingly low-key, with historic displays on permanent loan from the Bostonian Society. The airy **Atrium** cocktail lounge is a comfortable place to snack on appetizers and listen to live jazz (no jeans or sneakers allowed). Amenities include babysitting and complimentary overnight shoe shines. Request nonsmokers' or wheelchair-accessible accommodations. Rooms equipped for people with hearing impairments are also available. ♦ North and Blackstone Sts (at Faneuil Hall Marketplace). 523.3600, 800/343.0922; fax 523.2454 ᕕ

Within The Bostonian Hotel:

Seasons ★★★★$$$$ The swank, glass-enclosed dining room atop the hotel offers generous cityscapes and marvelous views of **Quincy Market**'s gold dome, the famous **Faneuil Hall** weather vane, and the **Custom House Tower**'s glowing clock; newcomers to Boston are sure to be dazzled. This dining spot is famous as a training ground for Boston's top chefs (Lydia Shire, Jasper White, Gordon Hamersley, et al). An avatar of the new wave of "healthy gourmet" cuisine, Chef Peter McCarthy uses flavor-infused oils and

vinegars in lieu of heavy sauces, and the results scintillate. As befits its name, **Seasons'** menu changes quarterly, featuring such New England and international treats as duckling with ginger and scallions, roasted rack of lamb and pumpkin couscous, baked swordfish with olive compote, and wild mushroom tartlet. Service is gracious. The award-winning, all-American wine list is impressive, and the staff ably recommends. The billowy ceiling balloon shades add a romantic touch, and piano music filters up from the **Atrium** lounge. Politicos and businesspeople come here for power breakfasts, but **Seasons** is a private club at lunchtime. There's valet parking. ♦ American ♦ Daily breakfast, lunch, and dinner. Reservations recommended. No jeans or sneakers at dinner. 523.4119

12 Statues of Mayor Curley Follow North Street to an amiable little park tucked between Union and Congress Streets, which features two statues of Boston's controversial but beloved Mayor James Michael Curley (1874-1958) by Lloyd Lillie. In one, Curley is seated on a bench in a very approachable pose; many a photo has been taken of Curley "chatting" with whomever plops down next to him. The other statue portrays an upright Curley as the man of action and orator. Four times mayor, four times congressman, and former Massachusetts governor, Curley was born in Boston's South End. Truly a self-made man, this flamboyant politician gave Bostonians plenty to admire, gossip about, and remember him by. Curley smoothly ran Boston's infamous and powerful Irish political machine, inspiring poet Francis W. Hatch to quip, "Vote often and early for Curley." Edwin O'Connor had Curley in mind when he wrote *The Last Hurrah*. But Curley was also known as the "Mayor of the Poor," and his civic contributions included establishing **Boston City Hospital.** ♦ North St (between Union and Congress Sts)

12 Marshall House ★★$$ When the **Union Oyster House** is too crowded or too much for your wallet—often the case—come here. You may have a wait, but it won't be as long. This place actually opened in 1982, yet manages to look as if it had been here a century, with plenty of brass and wood. Eat informally at the bar or bar tables, or in the snug rear dining room. Start off with the raw bar—oysters, steamers, cherrystones, littlenecks—and proceed with fresh seafood entrées prepared in the open kitchen in the middle of the restaurant. There are two lobster specials every day, a wide choice of beers, and big burgers and sandwiches. You can't make a reservation, so leave your name and take a stroll around **Faneuil Hall Marketplace;** you won't be bored. ♦ Seafood/American ♦ Daily lunch and dinner. 15 Union St (between Salt La and North St). 523.9396

13 Union Oyster House ★★$$$ Dine in one of the few spots in Boston where time simply refuses to move forward. The city's oldest restaurant (founded circa 1715) and the oldest in continuous operation in the US, this eatery has served its specialty at this spot since 1826. Look in the window and watch oyster-shucking at the bar. This is truly a one-of-a-kind place, best on a cold winter's day when you can follow chilled oysters with steaming chowder or oyster stew and fresh seafood entrées of every kind. The first-floor booths are the original ones, with a plaque adorning the booth where JFK liked to dine.

When the restaurant's original owners, Atwood and Bacon, opened their oyster-and-clam bar, they installed the current half-circle mahogany bar that supposedly became Daniel Webster's favorite haunt. Webster reputedly downed each half-dozen oysters with a tumbler of brandy and water, and rarely consumed fewer than six platefuls. ♦ Seafood/American ♦ Daily lunch and dinner. Reservations recommended. 41 Union St (at Marshall St). 227.2750 ♿ (first floor only)

13 Ebenezer Hancock House This three-story redbrick house was probably completed in 1760 by John Hancock's uncle, Thomas, from whom John later inherited it. Here John's younger brother, Ebenezer, lived and maintained his office as deputy paymaster of the Continental Army. His biggest duty came in 1778, when Admiral D'Estaing's fleet conducted two million silver coins from King Louis XVI of France to pay local troops, salvaging their morale. Restored, the house is now lawyers' offices and not open to the public. ♦ 10 Marshall St (between Union and Blackstone Sts)

13 Blackstone Block A charming snippet of Old Boston, this tiny block is laced with winding lanes and alleys whose names—Salt Lane, Marsh Lane, and Creek Square—echo an era when water still flowed here. The neighborhood's history dates to colonial times; its architecture spans the 18th, 19th, and 20th centuries. People, chickens, geese, hogs, garbage, and carts laden with goods from nearby ships once commingled on the block's dirt streets. This area was on the narrow neck—frequently under water—that led from Shawmut Peninsula to the North End. Meat markets flourished here throughout the city's history, and still do along Blackstone Street, named for Boston's first settler William Blaxton (his name was spelled both ways). ♦ Between North and Hanover Sts

14 Bell in Hand Tavern Operating since 1795, though not always at this site, this is the oldest tavern in the US. On a cold afternoon, duck in here for a giant draft beer and an appetizer, burger, or sandwich. (Kitchen hours vary, so food isn't always available.) Its moniker is illustrated by the curious old sign on its plain

facade, much like pubs in Great Britain. It was named by original proprietor Jim Wilson, Boston's town crier until 1794, who rang a bell as he progressed through town announcing the news. Benjamin Franklin's childhood home once stood on this site. ♦ Daily. 45 Union St (between Marshall and Hanover Sts). 227.2098

15 The Haymarket On Friday and Saturday a fleet of pushcart vendors selling fruits, vegetables, and fish sets up for open-air business along Blackstone Street, in front of old establishments like the Puritan Beef Company and Pilgrim Market, which purvey meats and cheeses supplementing the **Haymarket**'s offerings. There's also a great greasy stand-and-eat pizza place. The narrow sidewalk is clogged with veteran shoppers making their rounds and bewildered novices trying to learn the ropes. Saturdays are busiest. Come for bargains, especially at the end of the day, but be forewarned that the vendors, many of them North Enders, will treat you brusquely if you pick over their merchandise selectively. *They* fill the bags; you just pay, European style. So what if a tomato or two is worse for the wear; it's satisfying to have avoided the supermarkets' boring sterility.

When the market finally winds down for the day, squashed produce and scattered cartons make passage here challenging, but the place is soon restored for the next day's deluge. The debris has been honored in Mags Harries's bronze reliefs of everyday garbage, embedded in asphalt at the intersection of Blackstone and Hanover Streets. ♦ F-Sa dawn-dusk. Blackstone St (between North and Hanover Sts)

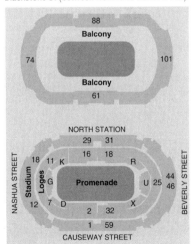

16 Boston Garden/Shawmut Center Visit the venerable old **Boston Garden** center while you can because the new **Shawmut Center** sports arena will be home to the **Boston Celtics** and **Boston Bruins** starting with the 1995-96 season. Many will miss the former's funky Art

Deco facade, interestingly juxtaposed with elevated rails. The spectacular new 755,000-square-foot arena and entertainment complex rests above the new **MBTA** parking garage. Like its beloved predecessor, the arena will host such family events as the circus and the **Ice Capades** as well as concerts year-round. But unlike the **Garden,** the arena will offer air-conditioning and access by both elevator and escalator. The **Garden**'s famous parquet floor—built during World War II when only short wood was available—will be moved to the new arena, along with a rafterful of championship banners (and retired numbers of legendary **Celtics** Bill Russell, Bob Cousy, John Havlicek, and Larry Bird, and **Bruins** Bobby Orr, Johnny Bucyk, and Phil Esposito). The new center, highly visible from both north and south, will feature grand-scaled windows looking out over the city's inner harbor. After the game, head over to the **Commonwealth Brewing Company** (see below); or just follow die-hard fans to the nearby bars. ♦ 150 Causeway St (between Haverhill and Friend Sts). Recorded information 227.3200

Behind Boston Garden:

North Station Trains operating from here transport eager sports fans and daily flocks of commuters from the North Shore. In the summertime, the station rings with voices, as cheerful crowds await the beach train (the route stopping at Beverly, Manchester, Gloucester, Rockport, and other towns with spacious public beaches). Across from the station's main entrance is **MBTA**'s *Green Line,* which carries riders in and out of central Boston. ♦ Causeway St (between Haverhill and Canal Sts). 723.3200

17 Hilton's Tent City The name is no empty boast. What began as a modest army surplus store in 1947 has ballooned into the biggest and best source of tents, with five floors holding the largest tent display in the country and complete accessories for camping and backpacking. It also sells men's and women's clothing for skiing, mountaineering, and backpacking, as well as hiking, work, and sporty boots and shoes (no running shoes or sneakers). Remember the old hardware store in your hometown? This is that kind of funky, dusty place packed with indispensable bargains—it guarantees the lowest prices around on all its stock. ♦ Daily. 272 Friend St (at Causeway St). 227.9242

18 101 Merrimac Street Boston's first faux-historic building, a 10-story office complex that looks like a conglomeration of rehabbed warehouses, was, in fact, designed from scratch by **The Architects Collaborative** in 1991. Duck inside to catch New York muralist Richard Haas's trompe l'oeil palm court, a domed winter garden eked out of two dimensions. The ubiquitous **au bon pain** ($, 248.9441) has a small cafe here, should

you wish to rest and nosh a while. ♦ Between Lancaster and Portland Sts

18 Commonwealth Brewing Company ★$ "Let no man thirst for the lack of real ale" is the motto here. This working brewery and restaurant produces 10 or so kinds of English ale on the premises, including the acclaimed Boston's Best Burton Bitter, all dispensed on tap at the appropriate 52 degrees. The cavernous main level glows with copper fixtures, pipes, and tables (polished nightly), and huge tanks of beer. In the downstairs tap room, redolent with fermenting yeast, you can watch the brewing process through glass walls. Light meals and snacks are available, but the main attraction is definitely the ale. A lot of people come here before and after games at the sports center, and needless to say, it gets pretty noisy. Live bands play Saturday night. Free brewery tours—but no samples—are offered Saturday at 3:30PM and Sunday at noon (the tours are not wheelchair accessible). ♦ American ♦ Daily lunch and dinner. 138 Portland St (at Merrimac St). 523.8383 &

19 Old West Church A 1737 wood-framed church stood on this site until the British razed it in 1775, suspicious that Revolutionary sympathizers were using the steeple to signal the Continental troops in Cambridge. The decorous redbrick Federal replacement, a National Historic Landmark designed by **Asher Benjamin** in 1806, is kin to **Charles Bulfinch**'s **Massachusetts State House** and **St. Stephen's Church,** and **Benjamin**'s **Charles Street Meeting House**—all flat-surfaced and delicately ornamented with classical motifs. Formerly Unitarian and now Methodist, the church exerts quiet composure along Cambridge Street's physical and architectural chaos. Inquire about concerts featuring the fine Charles Fisk pipe organ. ♦ Su service 11AM. 131 Cambridge St (at Staniford St). 227.5088

20 Harrison Gray Otis House This 1796 house—the trial run for Otis and his architect-of-choice—was the first in a series of three increasingly lavish residences that **Charles Bulfinch** designed for his friend (who had a taste for flamboyant living and fine architecture). Otis lived here for just four years before moving his family to grander quarters on Mount Vernon Street, followed by another move to Beacon Street. When he lived at house number one, Harry Otis was a prestigious lawyer and freshman member of Congress. He ultimately became Boston's third mayor and a major land speculator who transformed rustic Beacon Hill into a wealthy enclave, again with **Bulfinch**'s help. Set in what was briefly fashionable Bowdoin Square, this Federalist mansion is austerely handsome, much more opulent inside than out. By the end of the 19th century, Bowdoin Square's elegance had frayed away, and Otis's former home endured a spotty career as a women's Turkish bath, then a patent medicine shop, and finally a boarding house defaced with storefronts.

In 1916 the **Society for the Preservation of New England Antiquities (SPNEA)** acquired the house—now one of 34 New England properties they run—and meticulously restored its former splendor. SPNEA is headquartered here, including its fabulous architectural and photographic archives, and offers tours of the interior. The house's decor dates from 1790 to 1820 and includes some Otis family belongings. With its next-door neighbor, the **Old West Church,** the Otis house steps back into the early years of the Republic—two lonely survivors who refuse to be overwhelmed by their high-rise surroundings. ♦ Admission. Tu-Sa. Guided 40-minute tours on the hour; groups limited to 15, by reservation only. 141 Cambridge St (at Lynde St). 227.3956

21 Holiday Inn-Government Center $$ Adjacent to **Massachusetts General Hospital,** this 15-story hotel has 300 rooms, with the nicest on the Executive level. There's a seasonal outdoor pool, and rooms for nonsmokers and people with disabilities are available. **Foster's Bar and Grill,** located across from the hotel lobby, offers a complete breakfast, lunch, and dinner menu. You can easily walk to **Faneuil Hall Marketplace,** or cross Cambridge Street and meander over to Beacon Hill. Discounted parking is also available. ♦ 5 Blossom St (at Cambridge St). 742.7630, 800/465.4329; fax 742.4192 &

22 Massachusetts General Hospital (MGH) Although a hospital is rarely a voluntary destination, make a trip here to visit this medical center which is consistently distinguished as the nation's best general hospital. To locate the **Bulfinch Pavilion** (a National Historic Landmark) amid the **MGH** maze, enter from North Grove Street off Cambridge Street, or ask directions at the **George R. White Memorial Building** on Fruit Street, the main hospital building. (Built in 1939 by **Coolidge, Shepley, Bulfinch, and Abbott,** this late–Art Deco city landmark building is also worth a look.)

In 1817 Boston's trailblazing architect **Charles Bulfinch** won the commission to create this edifice of Chelmsford granite, quarried by inmates of the state prison. Questions persist about **Bulfinch**'s actual role in the pavilion commission, since it was his last project before he was called to Washington, DC, by the president to design the Capitol rotunda. His assistant, **Alexander Parris**—who later gained fame in his own right, particularly for designing **Quincy Market**—prepared the working drawings and supervised construction, probably influencing the

pavilion's final form much more than its name suggests. Delayed by the War of 1812, the cornerstone was laid in 1818 and the first patient was admitted in 1821. Today the building is still used for patient care, offices, and research.

Progressive for its day and gracefully proportioned, the Greek Revival building's enduring fame derives from the medical achievements that took place in the amphitheater beneath the skylit dome. It was in this theater, the hospital's operating room from 1821 to 1867, now called the **Ether Dome,** that the first public demonstration of the use of ether in a surgical procedure took place. On 16 October 1846, Dr. John C. Warren, cofounder of the hospital and its first surgeon, operated on a patient suffering from a tumor in his jaw. A dentist named Thomas Green Morton administered the ether with his own apparatus, after supposedly almost missing the operation because he was having last-minute adjustments made to the inhaler device. When the operation was finally finished, the patient awoke and said he had felt no pain. Dr. Warren proudly announced to his colleagues, "Gentlemen, this is no humbug." Within a year, ether was in use worldwide to prevent surgical pain.

Not only does the amphitheater house memories of medical success, it's also home to *Padihershef,* a mummy from Thebes, Egypt. Brought here in 1823, it was the US's first mummy. The hospital's original fund-raiser, *Padihershef* is also the only remaining witness to the **Ether Dome**'s finest moments. To visit the **Ether Dome,** call ahead to be sure it's not in use. ♦ 55 Fruit St (bounded by Blossom, Parkman, Fruit and Charles Sts). 726.2000

Bests

Priscilla H. Douglas
Secretary of Consumer Affairs and Business Regulation, Commonwealth of Massachusetts/Radcliffe Instructor

My favorite activities in Boston:

Bicycling with the Charles River Wheelmen, a group known for their 30- to 100-mile "show and go" rides. This diverse group of cycling enthusiasts sees the best of Boston's backroads and cranberry bogs and seashore.

Fourth of July with the **Boston Pops** on the **Esplanade.**

Rollerblading on **Martha's Vineyard** bike path.

Kite Festival in **Franklin Park.**

The cheapest fun: browsing the book stores, watching the sidewalk entertainers, and just watching people in **Harvard Square.** That's why I live in **Cambridge!**

Restaurants/Clubs: Red	Hotels: Blue
Shops/ ♦ Outdoors: Green	Sights/Culture: Black

North End

You'll know you've wandered into the North End when you hear the strains of a plangent tenor solo wafting over the virtually untrafficked streets. North Enders know that if they ever *move* their cars, their precious parking spots will be lost; hence the curbside stasis. The sidewalks, however, are abuzz with impassioned food shoppers and venerated elders who, in summer, haul their lawn chairs down to the sidewalks to create an alfresco living room. Gala window displays brighten up the endless rows of redbrick facades, monotonous except at street level, and alluring aromas from *pasticcerie, trattorie, ristoranti, mercati,* and *caffè* escape into the tangled streets. The happy banter of children, who effortlessly switch between English and Italian depending on whether they're talking to school friends or family, can be heard throughout. And within this insular, fiercely proud Italian enclave winds the red ribbon of the **Freedom Trail**, directing tourists to the **Paul Revere House**, the **Old North Church**, and other vestiges of colonial Boston.

This is the spirited, colorful, bursting-at-the-seams North End. Don't even attempt to come here by car. It's best reached on foot by an ignominious route: from the **Haymarket** subway stop (on the *Green* or *Orange Lines*), a short pedestrian tunnel sneaks under the elevated Fitzgerald Expressway, commonly called the **Central Artery**. Your path may be gritty and noisy, but you'll be cheered on by sculptor Mags Harries's bronze reliefs of typical **Haymarket** garbage embedded in the pavement below, children's mosaics in the tunnel walls, and outdoor murals that greet you at **Cross Street** once you've reached the North End side of the expressway.

The heart of this vivacious, voluble district is Mediterranean, but Italians have held sway here only since 1920 or so. This is Boston's original neighborhood, where the city's early Puritan residents settled during the 17th century, their

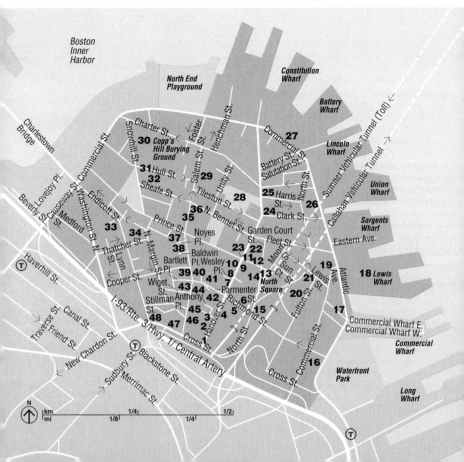

eyes on the sea. As piers, wharves, and markets sprang up along the **Waterfront**, the North End was known as the wealthiest, most populous, and in every way the most important part of town. It has undergone many changes since then. The glory days ended following the Revolution, when the area's aristocratic Tory population fled to England, and elite Bostonians moved to Beacon Hill and Bay Village. The black community gradually migrated to the Hill as well. In the 19th century, waves of immigrants—first Irish, then Eastern European Jews, then Portuguese, then Italians—poured into the North End which had deteriorated into a slum. Over some 70 years, Italian-Americans have industriously restored the neighborhood. Their traditions, rituals, and festivals—focused around the family, the church, and the cafes—have become the North End's bulwark.

Most streets follow a jumbled 17th-century pattern, giving you the flavor of colonial history, but seasoned with Italian culture. When infant Boston still fit onto the Shawmut Peninsula, the North End was a second peninsula—almost an island—divided from the first by **Mill Creek**. Today, following the old creek's track, the Central Artery cleaves the North End from downtown. At press time, work was underway to dismantle and depress the elevated highway; the project is expected to be completed in 2004.

Changes are already afoot, so spend some time here while the fascinating cultural layers remain in place. The people you pass on the streets are still the children and grandchildren of *paesani* from villages in Sicily, Abruzzi, and Calabria. On **Hanover Street**, the main commercial thoroughfare, cafe jukeboxes play Italian pop music. Parallel and to the left is **Salem Street**, where meat and provisions shops do a brisk business. A block to the right brings you to quaint **North Square** and **North Street**, which followed the shoreline until landfill pushed it blocks away. Notice the loaded laundry lines (you won't see *those* on Beacon Hill), minimal building ornamentation (except for a bit of wrought iron here and there), and scarce room for greenery (aside from some well-used parks and rooftop gardens). Glance up; more than one elderly North Ender is leaning out to check on who's coming, who's going, and who's doing what they shouldn't be doing. This is a close-knit place, after all, where people watch out for one another and strangers get the once-over more than once. But don't let that intimidate you. Be sure to visit in July and August when each weekend is dedicated to a different patron saint. Join the throngs for one of these *feste,* when North Enders commandeer the streets for morning-till-night processions, dancing, eating, and praying.

North End Beach and the bridge to Copp's Hill Terrace

Boston's subway service doesn't bring you into the North End, but rather deposits you near its edge. Although making your way into this out-of-the-way neighborhood can be confusing, there are always crowds of tourists headed in that direction. In addition to **Haymarket** (*Green* and *Orange Lines*), the **North Station** (*Green Line*) and **Aquarium** (*Blue Line*) stops are the most convenient.

1 Hanover Street The straightest and widest street in the labyrinthine North End runs through the heart of the district and boasts the greatest concentration of restaurants, bakeries, cafes, banks, services, and shops selling everything from saints' figures to Italian-leather goods. Two famous department stores began here. At No. 168, Eben Jordan started a dry-goods store that eventually became the **Jordan Marsh Company;** and

Rowland H. Macy opened a similar operation nearby that grew into the R.H. Macy Company of New York City. Block after block, four- and five-story buildings crowd in so closely that the Waterfront's nearness stays a secret until you reach the bend by **Charles Bulfinch**'s **St. Stephen's Church.** Tourists stream along the narrow sidewalks as they follow the **Freedom Trail** to the **Old North Church,** or seek out popular dining spots such as **The European Restaurant** or the **Daily Catch.** But most of the street scene belongs to the people who live here. Even on a sleepy Sunday afternoon, this street pulses with the vigor of Italian-American culture. ♦ Between Cross and Commercial Sts

2 Theatre Lobby and Paolo Ristorante
★★$$ This terrific little combination theater/cabaret/restaurant fills a giant gap in Boston's nightlife with aplomb. Nowhere else in the city can you enjoy an evening of entertainment with such leisurely European style. Owners Anthony and Sally Capodilupo have created a graceful, satisfying setting for performers and audiences, offering Tuscan/ New England seasonal fare. The 175-seat wraparound square theater and the mauve-and-cream cabaret/cafe, which also serves as the theater's lobby, are intimate and comfortable; the sound and lighting superb; and the cabaret's handsome antique Steinway beautifully reconditioned. ♦ Italian/New England ♦ Admission. Discounts are usually available on combination tickets. Daily dinner; call for information on the program and show times. 216 Hanover St (between Anthony Pl and Cross St). 227.9872

The Prince Spaghetti Company used to be located at 45-69 Atlantic Avenue. For years, it ran a television ad campaign with the famous line, "In the Italian North End of Boston, Wednesday is Prince Spaghetti Day." Many Americans can still picture the commercial's star, a boy named Anthony, rushing home through the North End's streets as his mother calls him to a steaming plate of spaghetti at the crowded family table.

On 18 January 1950, Tony Pino and 10 partners-in-crime pulled off their famous heist of more than $1.75 million in cash from the Brinks Garage, located at the intersection of Prince and Commercial Streets.

2 The European Restaurant ★$ This restaurant isn't much to look at inside, but its famous clock and neon sign outside have been familiar features since 1917. The finickiest diner will be satisfied with the mammoth menu, and service is usually brisk and friendly. Huge, gloppy portions of Italian-American fare are reasonably priced—no exciting finds, but the extra-large pizza is surely Boston's biggest. Although the lines are long, the elephantine dining rooms mean the wait is generally endurable. The mood here is often boisterous; practically every visit, some table of 20 bursts into strains of "Happy Birthday." Still, once in a while this just seems like the right place to be. Bring the kids—they can bounce off the walls and no one will notice. After your meal, cross Hanover Street to Mechanic Street, which ends in a funky cul de sac. Through the wire fence is a great view of the stalwart **Custom House Tower** downtown and its beautiful clock. To the left is the Sumner Tunnel entranceway, with its wonderful pair of Art Deco reliefs: one angel in flight escorts a vintage truck, the other a car. ♦ Italian ♦ Daily lunch and dinner. Reservations recommended for large parties. 218 Hanover St (between Anthony Pl and Cross St). 523.5694 ⟨

2 Trio's ★$ Using recipes from Abruzzi and Sicily, some of which go back 300 years, the Trio family (Tony, Genevieve, and their son Louis) whips up an awesome array of homemade pastas and companion sauces. To name just a few, you can take home gnocchi, tortellini, tortelloni, agnolotti, cavatelli, ravioli, red-pepper linguine, lemon fettuccine—and top them off any which way with ginger-vermouth, gorgonzola, anchovy-nut, white-clam, piquant marinara, or pesto sauces. Everything's made fresh; look into the kitchen where the pasta machines are churning out that day's supply. The Trios prepare lasagna and other entrées for takeout, but there are a handful of stools if you can't wait to dig in. ♦ Italian/Takeout ♦ Daily. No credit cards accepted. 222 Hanover St (between Anthony Pl and Cross St). 523.9636

Restaurants/Clubs: Red	Hotels: Blue
Shops/ ♣ Outdoors: Green	Sights/Culture: Black

3 A&J Imports Budding vintners and brewers come to this well-stocked store for everything they need to make wine or beer—presses, concentrate, strainers, bottles, hops, and malt. Italian kitchenware, from meat grinders to frivolous cookie presses are also featured. There are plenty of heavy-duty pasta and espresso machines to choose from, plus all those little gizmos for specialized tasks. ♦ Daily. 230 Hanover St (between Cross St and Anthony Pl). 523.8490

4 Caffè Paradiso Espresso Bar ★$ On a bright summer day, you may find other places cheerier, but this place is—for Boston—a night-owl spot, with the only 2AM liquor license on the street. Stop here on the night of a *festa* or other celebration. The whole neighborhood shows up and has a great time. Mirrors are everywhere, magnifying the hectic atmosphere, and the lively crowd keeps the jukebox cranking. There's a full line of Italian bitter aperitifs; homemade gelati, spumoni, and *sorbetti;* plus an enormous array of designer desserts that you won't see in any of the local bakeries. ♦ Cafe ♦ Daily. 255 Hanover St (between Cross and Richmond Sts). 742.1768. Also at: 1 Eliot Pl (at Winthrop St), Harvard Square, Cambridge. 868.3240; 1627 Commonwealth Ave (between Sherborn and Granby Sts). 247.0509; 3 Water St (between Washington and Devonshire Sts). 742.8689

Upstairs at the Caffè Paradiso Espresso Bar:

Il Sole ★$$ A lot of younger locals name this place their favorite North End restaurant. There are interesting offerings, such as a spicy seafood stew, as well as the usual fish, veal, chicken, and pasta selections. ♦ Italian ♦ M-Sa lunch and dinner. Reservations recommended. 742.1768

4 Modern Pastry Giovanni Picariellos Senior and Junior are renowned for their diabolically delicious homemade *torrone,* a nougat-and-almond confection drenched in chocolate. This ever-popular, more-than-60-year-old *pasticceria* offers great *sfogliatelli* (pastry shells filled with vanilla cream and egg), *pizzelle* (a light waffle), and cannoli. ♦ Daily. 257 Hanover St (between Cross and Richmond Sts). 523.3783

5 Villa Francesca ★$$ Not to be outdone by **Felicia's,** its high-profile neighbor across the way, this restaurant claims its share of star diners, too, including a slew of **Red Sox** baseball players. The food is nothing special—large portions spruced up with lots of lemon and white wine—but an Italian singer Monday through Friday draws a big following and provides the finishing touch to the overblown, Old World ambience. When you want a little schmaltz with your romance, try this place. And bring a date who has a sense of humor. ♦ Italian ♦ M-Sa dinner; Su lunch and dinner. 150 Richmond St (between Hanover and North Sts). 367.2948

6 Salumeria Italiana It's definitely worth a stop at this Italian deli to pick up some *prosciutto di Parma,* an import that wasn't available for years. The store also sells a good variety of cheeses, breads, salamis, olive oils, and espresso coffees. Come at lunchtime and proprietor Erminio Martignetti will make what celebrity chef Jasper White calls "probably the greatest cold-cut sandwich in the world." ♦ M-Sa. 151 Richmond St (between Hanover and North Sts). 523.8743

6 Felicia's ★$$ Undeniably a North End institution, owner and chef Felicia Solimine's place banks on past prestige. On your way upstairs to the dining room, look at the gallery of celebrities' photos. See Bob Hope? Tom Selleck? This is a classic overpriced red-sauce-and-Chianti-bottle-lamp kind of spot. Still, most local restaurants overcharge for spiffed-up spaghetti, and this place can be campy and fun if you come with a large group. The chicken *verdicchio* (made with mushrooms, artichokes, and acidic white wine) is worth a try. ♦ Italian ♦ Daily late lunch and dinner. 145A Richmond St (between Hanover and North Sts). 523.9885 ♿

7 Ristorante Saraceno ★$$ Neapolitan recipes are featured at this family-owned and operated restaurant. In addition to the usual antipasti and entrée lineup, specialties include good veal saltimbocca, shrimp and lobster *fra diavolo,* and linguine with seafood. The scrolled menus add a note of pretension to an otherwise straightforward and pleasant place recommended by many North Enders. Dine in the small upstairs room; downstairs is rather confining with gaudy murals of Capri, the Bay of Naples, and Amalfi. ♦ Italian ♦ Daily lunch and dinner. Reservations recommended. 286 Hanover St (at Wesley Pl). 227.5888 ♿

8 Caffè Vittoria ★$ This place is almost too much, with its faux marble tables and ornament, *un cortile* that isn't *really* a courtyard, *un grotto* that isn't *really* a grotto, and more-lurid-than-life murals of Venice and the Bay of Sorrento in the back. But a little braggadocio isn't all bad, and this more-than-60-year-old cafe—Boston's first—exerts a full-bodied charm all its own. The antique coffee grinders are absolutely real, as are the black-and-white photos of North Enders on the walls and the operatic espresso makers by the windows. Venture beyond cappuccino; try an anisette, grappa, Italian soda, or maybe a gelato. Come during the day when your companions will be older men lingering over newspapers, chatting in Italian, and you'll get a sense of how deeply rooted Italian culture is in this neighborhood. At night it's a totally different place—festive and boisterous. ♦ Cafe ♦ Daily 8AM-midnight. No credit cards accepted. 296 Hanover St (at Wesley Pl). 227.7606 ♿

8 Mike's Pastry Every type of caloric Italian treat one could possibly crave—cream cakes, candy, cookies, breads, cannoli, even that most un-Italian of baked goods, the oat-bran muffin—is sold at this perpetually busy bakery. Since this place is trying to cover all the bases, quality varies, and you should scout out the smaller *pasticcerie* for your favorite sweets. The *biscotti di Prato* are very good and cinnamony here, or go whole hog and try a "lobster tail," a particularly diet-devastating concoction of pastry with cheese, custard, *and* whipped cream. There are some tables, and **Freedom Trail** pilgrims find this to be a useful place to rest their weary feet and fuel up with a cup of coffee before continuing their trek. ♦ M-Sa. 300 Hanover St (between Wesley Pl and Prince St). 742.3050

9 Caffè Graffiti ★$ Depending on the time of day, stop in for a glass of wine, a generous calzone, or one of Boston's best cappuccinos and a tasty, award-winning homemade pastry. ♦ Cafe ♦ Daily. 307 Hanover St (between Richmond and Prince Sts). 367.3016

10 Caffè dello Sport ★$ No question about which sport this sunny cafe's name refers to: fluttering everywhere are pennants for Italian soccer teams. Take a windowside seat, and sip an intense espresso or foamy cappuccino while you join in the North End's favorite pastime: people watching. It gets ever more lively as the day progresses. ♦ Cafe ♦ Daily. 308 Hanover St (at Prince St). 523.5063 ᛐ

11 Pomodoro ★★★$$$ Seating a maximum of 24 diners, this cozy restaurant is a joy. Dazzling daily specials expertly prepared by Chef Rich Hanson span game to seafood. Try the rack of venison or pan-roasted whole fish with risotto and spicy clams. Whimsical modern art and a full list of Italian wines complete the sensory experience. ♦ Italian ♦ Daily lunch and dinner. 319 Hanover St (between Prince and Fleet Sts). 367.4348

11 Daily Catch ★★$$ That's the tiny restaurant's official moniker, but the name **Calamari Cafe** and the portrait of a squid lovingly hand-painted on the front window tell the real story. Owners Paul and Maria Freddura have dedicated their culinary careers to promoting this cephalopod, which can be devoured here in many delicious ways. The menu's supporting cast includes Sicilian-style seafood options. The linguine with white or red clam sauce is another hit. Half-a-dozen-or-so tables flank the open kitchen, so enjoy the show as the young chefs deftly, flamboyantly toss your meal (intense garlic is in practically every dish) together. The drawback: there's no bathroom. But it doesn't take much resourcefulness to find neighboring facilities (and there's always a line, so come in good weather when you feel gregarious, or eat early). ♦ Italian ♦ Daily lunch and dinner. No credit cards accepted. 323 Hanover St

(between Prince and Fleet Sts). 523.8567. ᛐ Also at: 261 Northern Ave (at Fish Pier), Waterfront. 338.3093; 441 Harvard St, Brookline. 734.5696

12 Ristorante Carlo Marino ★★$$ The gay green awning announces Anna Marino's place, named for her late father. When you've had your fill of silk flowers, travel posters of *Italia,* and red-and-gold-splashed dining rooms, Anna's crisp, forest-green-and-white-enamel decor is downright refreshing. And her flowers are real. Seating's snug but doesn't detract from the pleasant spirit. The affable owner is committed to tasty classical renditions of enduring Northern Italian peasant dishes. ♦ Italian ♦ Tu-Su dinner. 8 Prince St (between Hanover St and North Sq). 523.9109 ᛐ

12 Artu ★★★$$ Don't let the small entry fool you. Owner/chef Donato Frattarolli serves dishes that rival the best food anywhere, whether it's *quazzetto alla Donato* (shrimp, squid, mussels, clams, and sole in a stew) or *agnello arrosto* (roast leg of lamb with marinated eggplant and roasted peppers). Take-out orders are available. ♦ Italian ♦ Daily lunch and dinner. No credit cards accepted. 6 Prince St (between Hanover St and North Sq). 742.4336 ᛐ

13 North Square Idiosyncratic interpretations of the civic "square" abound in Boston. This plaza is, in fact, a cobbled triangle. Nearly overwhelmed by the massive chain along its perimeter—a heavy-handed, almost ludicrous nod to a nautical past—the square is still winsome, made more so by its circular garden. The first part of the North End to be settled, a stone's throw from the Waterfront, the square soon boasted a diverse community of artisans, merchants, seafarers, and traders. The **Second Church of Boston,** nicknamed "Old North," the seat of the powerful, preaching Mathers family, was located where Moon Street enters the square until the church was torn down by the British in 1776. By late colonial times this had become a very prestigious neighborhood. Boston's two most lavish mansions overlooked the square, then called Clark Square. Today, 17th- to 20th-century structures commune here. Just off the square is Boston's most charmingly named intersection: the celestial meeting of Sun Court and Moon Street. Just around the corner is 4 Garden Court Street, home for eight years to John F. "Honey Fitz" Fitzgerald, ward boss, congressman, Boston mayor, and one of the city's most famous citizens. His daughter Rose, President John F. Kennedy's mother, was born here in 1890, in what she described as "a modest flat in an eight-family dwelling." While in residence at No. 4, Honey Fitz began his political ascent with his election to Congress in 1894, soon acquiring the nickname the "Napoléon of the North End." After leaving Garden Court, Honey Fitz took his family to No. 8 Unity Street, also in this section. Throughout his career, Honey Fitz spoke so often of the "dear old North End" that North Enders were dubbed the "Dearos," a name that was adopted by the Irish political and social organization he led.

Honey Fitz was born nearby on Ferry Street in 1863. (Both the Fitzgeralds and the Kennedys emigrated to Boston in the mid-1800s to escape the Irish potato famine. Honey Fitz's father became a grocer on North Street and on Hanover Street.) US senator Ted Kennedy has reminisced about how he and brothers John and Robert used to play a game to see who could cross Hanover Street first "in a hop, a skip, and a jump." ♦ Prince St (between Garden Court and Moon Sts)

13 Sacred Heart Church Walt Whitman described this former bethel (a place of worship for seamen) as "a quaint ship-cabin-looking church." It opened in 1833, and for 38 years seamen flocked to hear the legendary Methodist preacher Father Edward Taylor, once a sailor himself. "I set my bethel in North Square," said Taylor, "because I learned to set my net where the fish ran." Whitman came to the services, calling Father Taylor the only "essentially perfect orator." Ralph Waldo Emerson anointed Taylor "the Shakespeare of the sailor and the poor" and often spoke from his close friend's pulpit. On one of his Boston visits, Charles Dickens made a special trip to hear the preacher, accompanied by Longfellow and Charles Sumner, abolitionist and US senator. In 1871 the bethel was sold and enlarged as a Catholic church. ♦ 12 North Sq (at Moon St). 523.1225

14 Mariners' House Dedicated to the service of seamen, this respectable Federalist edifice was erected in 1838 and converted into a seamen's boardinghouse in the 1870s. A remnant of Boston's great seafaring days, now long gone, it fueled the city's rapid growth and the residents' fabulous fortunes. From the cupola atop its roof, mariner residents reputedly kept watch on the sea, much nearer then than it is today (due to landfill). Peer in the windows at the exceedingly nautical decor. Bonafide seamen still board here. ♦ 11 North Sq (at Garden Court St).

Boston is full of public squares that are named after someone, but the North End has an especially large supply. Most of them honor Italian public figures, war heroes, and the like, such as Joseph S. Giambarresi Square, Arthur A. Sirignano Square, and Gus P. Napoli Square.

14 Paul Revere House Here is where America's most famous messenger hung his hat. A descendant of Huguenots named Revoire, Paul Revere was an exceptionally versatile gold- and silversmith, as well as a copper engraver and a maker of cannons, church bells, and false teeth—reputedly including a pair for George Washington.

Busloads of tourists stream in nonstop, but it doesn't take long to see the humble rooms in Revere's tiny, two-story wooden clapboard abode (pictured above). It's worth inching along because this house and the **Pierce-Hichborn** residence next door are remarkable rare survivors of colonial Boston. Constructed in 1680 (nearly 100 years before the "Son of Liberty's" midnight ride), rebuilt in the mid-18th century, and restored by **Joseph Chandler** in 1908, this National Historic Landmark has reverted to what it looked like originally, before Paul added an extra story to accommodate his big family. Revere and his second wife, Rachel (who gave birth to eight of his 16 children), owned the house from 1770 to 1800 and lived here for a decade until the war-ruined economy forced them to move in with relatives. From here Revere hurried off to his patriotic exploits, including participating in the Boston Tea Party. By the mid-19th century, the house slipped into decrepitude and became a sordid tenement with shabby storefronts. The wrecking ball loomed at the start of this century, but a great-grandson of Revere's formed a preservation group that rescued the house.

From across North Square, look toward the medieval overhanging upper floor and leaded casements. These throwbacks to late 16th-century Elizabethan urban architecture are reminders that architectural styles were exported to the colonies from England and adapted with Yankee ingenuity long after they were out of fashion in Europe. Built after the devastating Boston fire of 1676, the fashionable town house violated the building code because it was made of wood, not brick.

Today 90 percent of its frame and one door are genuine; its clapboard shell and interior are reproductions. See how artfully the house tucks into its tiny site in the colonial North End, where rabbit warren clusters of small houses are linked by a maze of alleyways. The dark, low-ceilinged, heavy-beamed rooms with their oversize fireplaces bear few traces of the Revere family, but recall colonial domestic arrangements. The pretty period gardens in back are equally interesting when you study them with the help of the posted key and a pamphlet sold at the ticket kiosk. The multipurpose plantings—with old-time names like Johnny-jump-up, Bee-balm, Dutchman's-pipe, and Lady's-mantle—remind visitors that gardens were once commonplace sources of ornament, pharmaceuticals, food, and domestic aids. ♦ Admission. Daily; closed Monday January-March, and major holidays. 19 North Sq (at Bakers Alley). 523.1676

Across the street:

Rachel Revere Park This tiny park is used chiefly as a playground for schoolchildren. It was dedicated to Paul's wife by the Massachusetts Charitable Mechanics Association, a philanthropic group that was founded in 1795 with Revere as its first president.

14 Pierce-Hichborn House This stalwart structure to the left of Paul Revere's house was home to Paul's cousin, a boat-builder by the name of Nathaniel Hichborn. A prized colonial urban relic, the house was built around 1710 by a glazier named Moses Pierce. Overstimulated modern eyes might not notice, but this English Renaissance brick structure stylistically leaps far ahead of the Revere's Tudor in a very brief time span. Even the central stair is innovative—simple and straight instead of windy and cramped like that of the Revere House. The pleasing three-story residence reflects a pioneering effort to apply formal English architectural principles to early Boston's unruly fabric. When the house left Hichborn's family in 1864, it, too, fell on hard times, becoming a tenement until it was restored in 1950. Four rooms are open to the public for guided tours given twice daily, the only times to see the interior. Enter at the **Revere House** gate. ♦ Admission. Tours daily; closed Monday January-March, and major holidays. 19 North Sq (at Bakers Alley). 523.1676

Around the corner:

Bakers Alley Walk down this alley to a pretty residential plaza ingeniously tucked in among the backsides of apartment buildings. The lucky residents have a number of handsome specimens of that scarce North End commodity: trees.

15 V. Cirace & Son Jeff and Lisa Cirace are the third generation and the second brother-sister act to run this almost 90-year-old Italian wine establishment. About half of the store's 1,500-plus wines are Italian, and there's an extensive collection of cognacs, cordials, and venerable vintages. Also on sale are cheeses, pâtés, and other gourmet items. This is not a self-service place; the friendly staff will assemble gorgeous gift baskets if you desire. The "V" in the name, by the way, is for Vincenza, the owners' grandmother. ♦ M-Sa. 173 North St (at Richmond St). 227.3193

16 Bibelots Housed in the **Mercantile Wharf Building,** an enormous 1857 granite warehouse renovated by **John Sharratt Associates** in 1976, Renée Koller and David Bastian's gift store is great fun. Practically  every item is one-of-a-kind and at least slightly eccentric. Most are handmade, imported from Mexico, Guatemala, Africa, England, and other far-off places. There are amusing interpretations of teapots, napkin rings, and salt-and-pepper shakers; jewelry shaped like flora, fauna, and creatures that can't be categorized; plus more practical items such as dinnerware that resembles a stylish version of Fiestaware. A small gallery downstairs exhibits local artists' work. ♦ M, W-Su. 75 Commercial St (between Cross and Richmond Sts). 523.7336

17 Michael's Waterfront and Wine Library ★★$$$ Its windows crowded with wine bottles and books, this restaurant announces up front the two features that keep it from being just another fern bar. The books, some of which are quite old, are donated by libraries and individuals, and patrons may borrow them. The sports-oriented bar, which offers a large selection of international wines by the glass, is frequented by a nonbookish crowd that occasionally includes rock musicians, entertainers, and TV people. As for the food, it's basic New England cuisine and seafood, featuring a great rack of lamb. Shuttle service is available to **Boston Garden/Shawmut Center** events, the theater district, and local hotels. ♦ American ♦ Daily dinner. Reservations recommended. Valet parking. 85 Atlantic Ave (at Commercial Wharf E). 367.6425

18 Lewis Wharf In the mid-19th century Boston's legendary clipper-ship trade centered on this wharf, originally named for Thomas Lewis, native of Lynn, Massachusetts, a canny merchant who acquired much of Boston's waterfront property after the American Revolution. Ships carried tea to Europe, and foodstuffs that were sold at exorbitant rates to California Gold Rush prospectors (eggs went for $10/dozen; flour for $44/pound). The warehouse was built of Quincy granite between 1836 and 1840, attributed to **Richard Bond,** and renovated in the late 1960s by **Carl Koch and Associates,** at which time the graceful gabled roof was replaced with an unwieldy mansard one. The building now houses residential and commercial units. To the right stretches an attractive harborside park. The **Boston Croquet Club** rents a portion and sets up their wickets—a genteel sight that brings home how long gone the city's seafaring era really is. One story claims that Edgar Allan Poe's tale, *The Fall of the House of Usher,* was inspired by tragic events that took place on the wharf's site in the 18th century. Two lovers, a sailor and another man's wife, were trapped by the angry husband in their rendezvous, a hidden tunnel underneath the Usher house. When the structure was torn down in 1800, two skeletons locked in embrace were discovered behind a gate at the foot of the tunnel steps.

Set back at the Boston Harbor end of the wharf—where old, fallen-in wharf structures look ready for a harbor burial—is the popularly acclaimed **Boston Sailing Center,** which offers a variety of sailing and racing lesson packages, as well as captained harbor cruises aboard 23- to 30-foot-long sailboats. Boats also embark on day sails among the Boston Harbor Islands and on overnight trips to Provincetown, Martha's Vineyard, Newport, and Block Island. The sailing center acts as broker to arrange more extensive charters. ◆ Fee. Daily May-Oct. Off Atlantic Ave (between Eastern Ave and Commercial Wharf E). 227.4198

19 Jasper's ★★★★$$$$ Offer to take a Bostonian out for an extravagant, sumptuous dinner—no matter the price—and this will be one of his or her first choices. Owner and chef Jasper White is lauded nationally for his culinary wizardry, which, Pygmalion-like, transforms even the heartiest fare into an elegant, refined dish (not *too* refined, however). White clearly thinks food is just wonderful and that it should always taste that way. Some of White's inventions are his famous grilled lobster sausage; pork and clams *Alentejo* style (with garlic and tomatoes); Maine rock crab cakes; and grilled duck salad with papaya and spiced pecans. Soups and desserts are incredible here. The dining rooms are spacious, muted, yet unremarkable—a perfect unobtrusive setting for any evening drama you'd like to enact. Service is highly professional, although some critics have experienced off nights, especially when White's not around. But throw caution to the winds—innumerable Bostonians have gone before you and been delighted. There's piano music on weekends. ◆ American ◆ Tu-Sa dinner. Reservations recommended. Valet parking. 240 Commercial St (at Atlantic Ave). 523.1126 ⅖

20 McLauthlin Building The soft brownish-mauve facade of New England's first cast-iron building is adorned with lacy rows of arched windows crowned by fanlights. Built circa 1850, the structure was renovated in 1979 by **Moritz Bergmeyer.** The McLauthlin Elevator Company once resided here; now condos do. ◆ 120 Fulton St (between Richmond and Lewis Sts)

21 Piccolo Nido ★★★$$$ Chef Mark Donohue has developed an imaginative and tempting table of entrées at this trattoria, ranging from the *code di gamberi alla Ruth* (shrimps, cucumber, basil in white-wine and plum-tomato sauce) to *pollo scarpariello* (sautéed boneless chicken with artichoke hearts, white wine, garlic, and lemon). ◆ Italian ◆ Tu-Su dinner. Reservations required. 257 North St (at Lewis St). 742.4272 ⅖

Enrico Caruso loved the North End. When the Italian tenor came to Boston, he often ate at a restaurant called the Grotta Azzura on Hanover Street (the establishment no longer exists). A famous anecdote about Caruso tells how he wasn't able to cash a check at a neighborhood bank because he had no acceptable identification. Caruso launched into "Celeste Aida," immediately delighting and convincing the skeptical bank manager.

Restaurants/Clubs: Red   Hotels: Blue
Shops/ 🎣 Outdoors: Green   **Sights/Culture:** Black

22 Giacomo's ★★$$ The open kitchen is close, but not too close, which means you're enveloped in tantalizing, spicy-sauce aromas, but you won't leave this cozy bistro drenched in the smell of garlic and smoke. The grill's the thing here—meaty swordfish and tuna steaks arrive succulent and smoky from the charcoal flame, and grilled chicken and sausage are a fine duo. Try linguine with *frutte di mare* (seafood), a house specialty, with "Giacomo" sauce—a feisty combination of white and red sauces. The unfinished brick walls and refinished wood floors—signs of unwanted gentrification throughout the North End—suit owner Jack Taglieri's unpretentious place. A handsome tin-stamped ceiling, oils on wood of Rome and Venice, and black-and-white cafe curtains add warmth and character. ◆ Italian ◆ M-Sa dinner. 355 Hanover St (between Prince and Fleet Sts). 523.9026

22 Alloro ★★★$$ This relative newcomer to the North End has quickly taken its place among the area's best eateries. Owner Armando Galvao has put his trust in the able hands (and palates) of chefs Stuart Cameron (formerly with **Cornucopia**) and Suzanne Salter. Their Portuguese, Spanish, and French-influenced Italian menu features such stunning multicultural dishes as *coniglio* (rabbit) wine-braised, and served over *pappardelle* (thick noodles); *cozze* (mussels) steamed in a spicy-tomato broth with garlic, cilantro, and cumin; and *fedelini* (thin spaghetti with calamari, shrimp, mussels, and clams in a saffron-tomato broth). ◆ Mediterranean ◆ Daily dinner. 351 Hanover St (between Prince and Fleet Sts). 523.9268

The most popular *feste* are the "Big St. Anthony" and the colorful Feast of the Madonna del Soccorso (nicknamed the "Fisherman's Feast"). This feast's most famous feature is the "light of the angel," in which a young girl "flies" from a window over North Street to offer a bouquet to the Madonna. The *feste* have become commercial over time, and many North Enders avoid them now because they draw hordes of outsiders and turn the neighborhood into a circus. Still, these exuberant celebrations are the fullest expression of North End culture you'll ever encounter.

23 St. Leonard's Church Peace Garden With flowers and statuary that are spotlit at night, this place is more like a garden center than a garden. It's a cheery spot, especially when decked out with lights at Christmastime. Planted at the close of the Vietnam War and maintained by the Franciscans, the garden and the church (designed in 1891 by **William Holmes,** and pictured above) possess the mark of distinction. This is the first Italian church erected in New England, and the garden contains two shrubs that were brought over from the altar on the **Boston Common** where Pope John Paul II celebrated mass. ◆ Daily until 1PM. Hanover St (at Prince St). 523.2110

24 St. Stephen's Church Located at Hanover Street's bend, on its sunny side, is **Charles Bulfinch**'s sole surviving church in Boston. In 1804 he transformed a commonplace meeting house called the New North into an elaborate, harmonious architectural composition, for which the congregational society in residence paid $26,570. Paul Revere cast the bell that was hung in the church's belfry in 1805. Although **Bulfinch** was usually drawn to English architecture, Italian Renaissance campaniles also inspired him in this work—an architectural foreshadowing of the North End's future ethnic profile. The dramatic tower crowds to the front of the wide-hipped facade, a bold counterpoint to the subtle Federal architectural gestures inside. Notice how the windows and column styles metamorphose as they move toward the gracefully curving ceiling. Most of the woodwork is original, including the pine columns. The 1830 organ was restored by Charles Fisk of Gloucester, Massachusetts, a famous American organ conservator. In 1862 the Catholic Diocese of Boston bought the church to serve the North End's enormous influx of Irish immigrants and gave it its present name. In 1869 they moved the entire building back approximately 12 feet to accommodate the widening of Hanover Street, and in 1870 they raised it six feet to install a basement church underneath. Rose Kennedy, JFK's mother, was christened here. In 1964 Cardinal Richard Cushing launched a successful campaign to renovate and restore the church to **Bulfinch**'s design (**Chester F. Wright** carried out the restoration), respectfully returning the edifice—now on the National Register of Historic Places—to its original prominence. ♦ 401 Hanover St (at Clark St). 523.1230

25 Ristorante Lucia ★$$ The food here is pretty good, featuring dishes from Abruzzi. One pasta concoction reproduces the Italian flag with a white-cream, red-tomato, and green-pesto sauce. The walls are covered with takeoffs on Italian masterpieces. Upstairs is the opulent pink-marble barroom, whose ceiling is painted with replicas of scenes from the Sistine Chapel. Note the tasteful touch the indiscreet Michelangelo omitted: under-garments resembling diapers and swaddling clothes. ♦ Italian ♦ M-Th dinner; F-Su lunch and dinner. Valet parking evenings. 415 Hanover St (at Harris St). 367.2353 ♿

26 Davide ★$$$ The interior of this restaurant is bordelloesque, right down to the overstuffed red-velvet banquettes and the overheated color scheme—be sure to come with a group that can live up to its melodramatic setting. The menu changes seasonally (uncommon in the North End). Try the duck served in a port sauce flavored with figs, risotto with seafood, or pan-fried bass with lemon-caper butter. ♦ Italian ♦ M-F lunch and dinner; Sa-Su dinner. Reservations required. Jacket requested. Valet parking. 326 Commercial St (opposite Union Wharf). 227.5745

27 Bay State Lobster Company The East Coast's largest retail and wholesale seafood operation, this more-than-70-year-old business's biggest draw is the live lobsters you can buy on the spot for tonight's dinner or have shipped UPS to anywhere in the continental US. Fish of all kinds—shellfish with all the trimmings, as well as the company's own clam and fish chowders, and lobster pies—are sold here and can be packed for traveling. As you might guess, it's often a madhouse. ♦ Daily. 379 Commercial St (at Battery Wharf). 523.7960

28 Paul Revere Mall (The Prado) Laid out in 1933 by Arthur Shurcliff, this tree-shaded park could have been plucked from Italy. It offers residents a comfortable cushion of space in their jam-packed quarter, and sight-seeing pilgrims a pleasant passage from **St. Stephen's** to the **Old North Church** looming up ahead on Salem Street. This modest, slightly scruffy park has more personality than any of Boston's grander spaces. Though it isn't very old, it has a very lived-in look. The mall's brick walls and paving carve out a reposeful realm where all generations of North Enders cheerfully converge. A serious game of checkers or cards often goes on among the elders while perambulators are wheeled past, kids play, and dogs race about. The bronze equestrian statue of *Paul Revere* (designed by Cyrus E. Dallin in 1885 and erected in 1940) towers near the Hanover Street edge, giving the young park a historical stamp. Hardworking, pragmatic artisan that he was (not to mention unremarkable in physique), Paul Revere wouldn't recognize himself in this dashing figure. On some of the side walls, plaques commemorate North Enders' contributions to their city.

The mall ends at Unity Street; cross and enter the gate leading into the courtyard behind the **Old North Church.** On the way, look for the **Clough House** (built in 1715) at 21 Unity Street. Ebenezer Clough lived here, one of the Sons of Liberty, a Boston Tea Party Indian, and a master mason who laid the bricks for the church. The courtyard itself occupies the former site of 19 Unity Street, which Benjamin Franklin bought for his two widowed sisters. ♦ Bounded by Hanover and Unity Sts, and Charter and Tileston Sts

28 Maurizio's ★★★$$ Bright, quiet, and understated, this restaurant serves some of the best Mediterranean cuisine in Boston. From the grill, the *filetto di salmone* (salmon fillet) with fresh plum tomatoes and tuna steak with lemon and capers are superb. The roasted rack of lamb with rosemary and garlic in a Chianti sauce, served with assorted grilled vegetables and roasted potatoes, is impeccable. All of the artwork on display is by local artists and is available for purchase. Owners Linda and Maurizio Loddo provide a thoroughly satisfying and tasteful dining experience. ♦ Italian ♦ Tu dinner; W-Su lunch and dinner. 364 Hanover St (at the Prado). 367-1123

Reverend Samuel Mather's home (since demolished) on Moon Street formerly belonged to a sea captain who is remembered in history as the man put in the stocks on Boston Common in 1673 for "lewd and unseemly conduct." The captain's crime: kissing his wife on their doorstep after returning from a two-year voyage—unspeakable behavior, indeed, in Puritan times.

29 Old North Church (Christ Church)

Called the "Old North Church" by nearly everyone, this is the oldest church building in Boston (pictured below) and the second Anglican parish founded in the city. Architect **William Price,** a local draftsman and print dealer, emulated **Christopher Wren** quite nicely in this 1723 brick edifice, now a National Historic Landmark. Coping with a tiny site in cramped quarters, **Price** gave the church needed stature and eminence by boldly attaching a 197-foot-high, three-tiered steeple—one of New England's earliest.

What points to the sky today, however, is the 1955 replica of the original steeple, which was toppled by a gust of wind in 1804 and once again in 1954. The weather vane on top was made by colonial craftsman Deacon Shem Drowne. The eight bells that ring from the belfry were cast in 1744 by Abel Rudhall of Gloucester, England, and range in weight from 620 to 1,545 pounds. Their inscription recalls long-extinguished aspirations: "We are the first ring of bells cast for the British Empire in North America, Anno 1744." The oldest and sweetest-sounding church bells in America, they have tolled the death of every US President since George Washington died in 1799. When he was 15, Paul Revere and six friends formed a guild to ring the bells.

Years later, Revere starred in the celebrated drama that has enveloped this landmark building with enduring legend, though a lot of the facts are cloudy. On the night of 18 April 1775 Revere rode on horseback to warn the Minutemen at Lexington and Concord of the approaching British troops. And as Revere arranged before departing, or so the story goes, the church's sexton—Robert Newman—hung signal lanterns in the belfry to alert the populace that the British were on the march. Although a number of other messengers, including William Dawes, rode out into the towns, Paul Revere has eclipsed them all in fame. Henry Wadsworth Longfellow can take the real credit for Revere's glory. Spellbound by the nearly forgotten tale, he wrote the inaccurate but entertaining poem "Paul Revere's Ride," published in *The Atlantic Monthly* in 1861. Every April, on the eve of Patriots' Day, descendants of Revere or Newman hang lanterns in the church belfry to commemorate that spring night. An unresolved controversy, however, concerns whether this is the real **Old North Church,** or whether the **Second Church of Boston** on North Square—nicknamed "Old North," which was burned by the British–truly held the leading role in the events on the eve of the American Revolution. If this theory is ever proven, it will cause a major re-routing of the **Freedom Trail,** so no one is rushing to verify it. No matter what the truth is, a sad and genuine chapter in this church's past was the divided loyalties of its Episcopalian congregation. Once the Revolution ignited, the church was closed until 1778 because of the tensions unleashed between Patriot and Tory parishioners.

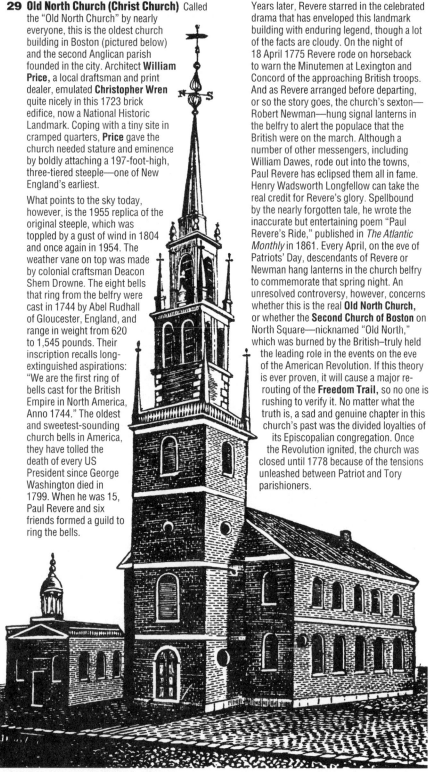

Old North Church (Christ Church)

The structure's white interior shimmers with light entering through pristine glass windowpanes. It's too bad there's rarely a chance to enjoy the unusual serenity and architectural clarity in solitude. Originally owned by parishioners, with brass plaques indicating which was whose, the tall box pews were designed to hold the warmth of hot bricks and coals during the winter. Look for the Revere family pew—No. 54. Inscriptions abound in the church and on the walls of the **Washington Memorial Garden** in back. Many offer interesting slants on colonial Boston. The clock ticking reassuringly at the rear of the gallery was made by a parishioner in 1726, and it's the oldest still running in an American public building. The brass chandeliers, also gifts, were first lighted on Christmas Day 1724. To the right of the apse, a 1790 bust of *George Washington* rests in a niche. When General Lafayette returned to Boston in 1824, he noticed this bust and said, "Yes, that is the man I knew, and more like him than any other portrait." Before leaving the church, look for the tablet on the left side of the vestibule, which identifies 12 bricks set into the wall. These were taken from a cell in Guildhall in Boston, England, where William Brewster and other Pilgrims were held after attempting to flee that country in 1607. In 1923, on the church's 200th anniversary, the mayor of Boston, England, sent the bricks as a gesture of friendship.

To the left as you exit is a curious museum and gift shop amalgam, housed in a former chapel built in 1917 to serve the North End's tiny community of Italian-speaking Protestants, now vanished. In front of the street entrance, notice the amusing, stout little columns resting on the pair of lions' backs. Inside, look for the "Vinegar Bible," a gift of King George II in 1733 and so nicknamed for its famous typo: on one page heading, the "Parable of the Vinegar" appears instead of the "Parable of the Vineyard." Tea retrieved from the boots of a Boston Tea Party participant is also on display. There are lots of fun things to buy here, from spice gumdrops and maple sugar candy to copies of Longfellow's poem and Wedgwood china decorated with the church's image.

Behind the church on both sides are charming small gardens nestled among clusters of nearby residences. In early summer the courtyard of the **Washington Memorial Garden** is awash in the fragrance of roses. Among its many commemorative tablets, one intriguingly states, "Here on 13 Sept. 1757, John Childs, who had given public notice of his intention to fly from the steeple of Dr. Cutler's church, performed it to the satisfaction of a great number of spectators." Said Childs did indeed leap from on high, strapped to an umbrella-like contraption that carried him safely for several hundred feet.

Cross Salem Street and look back at the church. Ever since its completion, the steeple has towered over the swath of redbrick that makes up the North End's fabric. The church's colonial neighbors are gone now, but unlike the **State House,** it has not been overwhelmed by 20th-century urbanism. None of the newer buildings in the area exceed five stories, so you still get a vivid picture of the early 18th-century landscape. Historical talks are offered by staff ad hoc. ◆ 193 Salem St (between Hull and Charter Sts). 523.6676

30 Copp's Hill Burying Ground Another of Boston's wonderful outdoor pantheons, this cemetery not only offers the finest gravestones in Boston, but also some of the best views of the city's most elusive feature—the Waterfront. From this promontory you can see down to the boat-clogged Boston Harbor and over to Charlestown and its **Naval Yard,** where the venerable warship "Old Ironsides," the *USS Constitution,* is in dry dock. This cemetery was established in 1659 when **King's Chapel Burying Ground** got too crowded. Once an Indian burial ground and lookout point, "Corpse Hill" (as it is also known) has accommodated more than 10,000 burials. In colonial days black Bostonians settled in the North End in what was called the New Guinea community, at the base of the hill. A granite pillar marks where lies Prince Hall, black antislavery activist, Revolutionary War soldier, and founder of the Negro Freemasonry Order.

Sexton Robert Newman, who flashed the signals from **Old North Church**—and was imprisoned by the British for doing so—is also buried here. And the formidable dynasty of the Puritan Mathers, churchmen and educators—Increase, his son Cotton, and Cotton's son Samuel—reside in a brick vault near the Charter Street gate. (Increase was awarded the first doctor of divinity degree conferred in America.) During the Revolution, British generals directed the shelling of Bunker Hill from here and their soldiers used the gravestones for target practice—as you can still discern. Look for Captain Malcolm's bullet-riddled marker. His patriotic epitaph particularly incensed the soldiers: "a true son of Liberty/a friend to the Publick/an enemy to oppression/and one of the foremost/in opposing the Revenue Acts on America." Legend tells of two tombs that were stolen here: interlopers ejected the remains of the graves' rightful owners, whose names were carved over with those of the thieves for future burial. ◆ Snowhill St (between Charter and Hull Sts)

Restaurants/Clubs: Red   Hotels: Blue
Shops/ 🌳 Outdoors: Green   Sights/Culture: Black

30 Copp's Hill Terrace After scrutinizing the Puritan view of death, head downhill to this graceful plaza set into the sloping hill, beleaguered by neglect and vandals. It's still a wonderful architectural progression, most frequented by the youngest and oldest neighborhood residents. Near this site on Commercial Street below, the Great Molasses Flood occurred on 15 January 1919. A four-story tank containing 2.5 million gallons of molasses burst, releasing a lavalike torrent that destroyed several buildings, killed 24 people, and injured 60. It took a week to clear the streets after the explosion, and a sticky-sweet aroma clung to the neighborhood for decades. Some North Enders claim they can still smell molasses from time to time in the heat of summer. ♦ At Copp's Hill

31 Hull Street Leading up the hill from the **Old North** and abutting the **Copp's Hill Burying Ground,** is this tree-lined, winding street—one of the North End's most pleasant streets. It was named after Boston's first mintmaster, John Hull, who coined the city's famous "pine-tree shillings" and had an estate that encompassed this neighborhood. ♦ Between Salem and Snowhill Sts

32 44 Hull Street Located across from the Hull Street entrance to **Copp's Hill Burying Ground** is a circa-1800 house that is indisputably the narrowest in Boston, one window per floor at the street end, squeezing up for air between its stout companions. An amusing tale claims that this house was an act of revenge, built solely out of spite to block the light and view of another house behind. In truth, this is a lonely survivor of the breed of modest dwellings called "10 footers," depicted in old prints of colonial Boston-town. This picturesque dwelling is nine feet, six inches wide, to be precise. A floral wrought-iron fence leads to its charming entry. ♦ Between Salem and Snowhill Sts

33 Oasis Cafe ★$ If you aren't in the mood for marinara, hop off the Italian express at this casual, comfy little cafe, where the order of every day is American home-style cookery: meat loaf, barbecue pork, cajun catfish, burgers, and corn bread. The signature offering is the roast of the day, which can be accompanied by real mashed potatoes, if you like. There's a special daily fritter, too, either fruit or vegetable. Everything's homemade right down to the salad dressings. Be ready for whopping portions. Come hungry and have a dessert like key lime pie. You'll dine to the tune of 1930s and 1940s jazz in a pink-and-black Art Deco setting. When you leave, find where Endicott Street intersects North Margin Street at odd, appealing Alfred Wisniski Square. Looking down Endicott Street toward downtown from here, you get one of the North End's few unimpeded views. ♦ American/Takeout ♦ Tu-Sa lunch and dinner, Su brunch. 176 Endicott St (at Alfred Wisniski Sq). 523.9274

34 Pizzeria Regina ★$$ In Boston everybody but everybody knows the city's most famous (not best) pizza joint. This is brick-oven pizza of the thin-crust, oily variety. Customers from New York and Florida fly home with as many as eight pizzas. It's a little tricky finding the curved corner building, but any North Ender can point you in the right direction. ♦ Pizza/Takeout ♦ Daily lunch and dinner. No credit cards accepted. 11½ Thatcher St (at N Margin St). 227.0765. Also at: Quincy Market (Faneuil Hall Marketplace). 227.8180

35 Salem Street This intimate, bustling street was dominated in the 19th century by the millinery and garment businesses owned by Jews who settled in this area. Now butcher shops, restaurants, markets, and great produce markets, many with no signs and run by proprietors who serve *all* customers—North Enders or not—with the same brusqueness, are tucked into tiny shopfronts. Most of the people you see lugging parcels are returning from this street; here one gets a glimpse of daily North End goings-on. From the south end of the street you get a great view of the trucks and cars creeping along on the elevated Central Artery. Enjoy your pedestrian freedom. ♦ Between Cross and Charter Sts

36 North Bennet Street School Founded in 1881 by Pauline Agassiz Shaw, this school originally helped North End immigrants develop job skills. No longer a social service agency, it now offers classes in furniture making, carpentry, piano tuning, violin making and restoration, bookbinding, jewelry making, watch repair, and other fields. Its graduates are trained in the traditional way and respected throughout New England. ♦ 39 N Bennet St (at Salem St). 227.0155

37 Bova Italian Bakery If ever you suffer from insomnia, why not discover what the North End is like at four in the morning, when nary a tourist blocks your way, and get some fresh bread and pastries in the bargain at the Bova family's corner shop that's open round-the-clock. For more than 70 years, this clan's been baking all its goods right on the premises—there's nothing fresher. ♦ Daily 24 hours. 134 Salem St (at Prince St). 523.5601

37 A. Parziale & Sons Bakery This is a businesslike shop, and its business is to make lots of great bread. The place is bursting with it. The Parziale family sells a thousand loaves a day of French bread alone. But why not stick to the Italian varieties and try a handsome loaf of *scali, bostone,* or fragrant, rich raisin bread? The *pizzelle* (waffle cookies) and anisette toasts are great, too. ♦ Daily. 80 Prince St (at Salem St). 523.6368

The first Boston Marathon, run in 1897, listed only 16 contestants.

Pick of the Pasta

Oodles of noodles, some of the best in the world, are served in Boston's North End, where the thriving Italian community tends to center around restaurants and cafes. Knowing you want "spaghetti" just isn't good enough anymore. This primer should help you identify which pasta you desire.

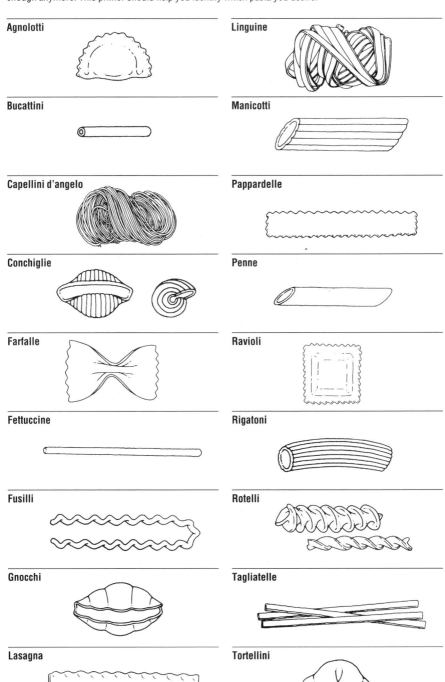

Agnolotti

Linguine

Bucattini

Manicotti

Capellini d'angelo

Pappardelle

Conchiglie

Penne

Farfalle

Ravioli

Fettuccine

Rigatoni

Fusilli

Rotelli

Gnocchi

Tagliatelle

Lasagna

Tortellini

38 Lo Conti's ★$ If you like your Italian fare fresh and light, and are not keen on the heavy trappings of typical bordello-style decor, try this small, bright restaurant with teal-laminate wooden tables and modernist leanings. Some specialties include *gnocchi mascarponi* (potato dumplings tossed in a rich cheese sauce) and *calamari bianco* (fresh squid simmered with white wine). The service here is brisk and no-nonsense; the pricing and portioning quite generous. ◆ Italian ◆ Daily lunch and dinner. 116 Salem St (at Baldwin Pl). 720.3550 ♿

39 L'Osteria Ristorante ★★$$ This Northern Italian eatery recently moved to a larger space across the street where there is a downstairs dining room ideal for business meetings or festive gatherings. The delectable entrées are still made from the very freshest ingredients. House specialties include chicken *finiziare* (served with veal, shrimp, and assorted vegetables) and veal *bocconcini* (rolled and stuffed with tomato cream sauce). ◆ Italian ◆ Daily lunch and dinner. Reservations recommended. 104 Salem St (at Cooper St). 723.7847 ♿

40 Polcari's Coffee A fragrant North End fixture since 1932, congenial Ralph Polcari sells more than a hundred spices from all over the world as well as his fine selection of coffees. Innumerable specialty items fill every inch of shelf and floor space: chamomile flowers, *ceci* (dried chickpeas), Arborio rice, flax seed, carob and vanilla beans, pine nuts, braided garlic, and bunches of fresh oregano. Polcari's wares are the stuff of alchemy in everyday cooking. ◆ M-Sa. 105 Salem St (at Parmenter St). 227.0786

41 Boston Public Library, North End Branch Come by when the library is open to inspect the remarkable 14-foot-long plaster model-diorama of the Doge's Palace in Venice. This clever creation was the consuming passion of Henrietta Macy, who taught kindergarten in this neighborhood before moving to Europe. After she died in Venice, her handiwork was presented to the library. Painted settings and dolls enacting 16th-century scenes were added by Louise Stimson of Concord, Massachusetts. Architect **Carl Koch**'s attention to Italian-American cultural heritage in this 1965 building has tempered and transformed the coldness of 1960s modernism into an extraordinary neighborhood addition. The library's atrium is cobbled like an Italian piazza, with plants and a small pool. Umbrellalike concrete vaults supported by nine columns form a roof, raised to create a clerestory that illuminates the library interior. The brick exterior is punctuated by colored glass ceramics, adding festive notes to what is an otherwise drab streetscape. ◆ M-F. 25 Parmenter St (between Salem and Hanover Sts). 227.8135

42 Fratelli Pagliuca's ★$$ There's decidedly nothing fancy about the Pagliuca brothers' very popular place. Joe, Freddy, and Felix changed the name from **Sabatino's,** but everything else is the same. A goodly number of locals eat here, Monday and Tuesday especially, as do businesspeople who know their way around. This is satisfying, stick-to-the-ribs Northern Italian red-sauce cuisine served in a family atmosphere. Favorites include the chicken-escarole soup, chicken marsala, and sweet roast peppers with provolone and sausage, which come in large portions for reasonable prices. Don't look for the four basic food groups here: pasta and meat, not veggies, get priority. ◆ Italian ◆ Daily lunch and dinner. Reservations recommended Friday-Sunday. 14 Parmenter St (between Salem and Hanover Sts). 367.1504

43 Terramia ★★★★$$$ Nestled along narrow Salem Street is one of Boston's smallest but very best restaurants. Owner and chef Mario Nocera has won the hearts and palates of sophisticated critics and diners alike. Don't look for veal parmesan here. Nocera, assisted by David Tannaccio, prepares authentic Italian cuisine. (Italians visiting the US have been known to fly in to Boston just to eat here.) Featured are dried salted cod, reconstituted with potato and onions in white truffle oil; roast quail risotto with porcini and shiitake mushrooms; and swordfish stuffed with pine nuts and raisins. It's all served in an elegant but spare setting, with views of the copper-laced Old World kitchen. ◆ Italian ◆ M-W, Su dinner; Th-Sa lunch and dinner. 98 Salem St (at Parmenter St). 523.3112

44 Mottola Pastry Shop Armando Mottola has been baking since he was nine years old. In addition to cookies, cannoli, and other traditional pastries, the Mottolas (Armando's brother bakes here, too) turn out a wonderfully rich rum cake—the weight-watcher's nemesis. Another specialty is Armando's black-and-white cake made to look like a volcano—there's surely someone or some occasion it will suit perfectly. ◆ Daily. 95 Salem St (between Cross and Parmenter Sts). 227.8365

44 Ristorante Positano ★★★$$ You'll feel as though you've stepped into a field in Northern Italy when you enter this place—the walls are green, there's loads of fresh flowers on each table, and plants galore. Strands of garlic hanging from the ceiling, wine bottles, olive oil, and fresh-baked breads accent the sumptuous surroundings, and for their part, chefs Robert O'Brien and Jack Goucem offer a formidable menu. Two popular pasta dishes are the penne *boscaiola* (ham and mushrooms in a pink cream sauce with mascarpone cheese), and gnocchi Positano (served with a red sauce with melted romano and mozzarella cheeses). Choosing among the blueberry, strawberry, or peach pancakes for breakfast can also be a difficult dilemma. ♦ Northern Italian ♦ Tu-F lunch and dinner; Sa breakfast, lunch, and dinner; Su breakfast and dinner. 93 Salem St (between Cross and Parmenter Sts). 367.4878

RABIA'S

45 Rabia's ★★$$ Talented chef Julie Fiore offers traditional Italian dishes with some interesting twists. Her tomato *torta basilico* (smoked tomato topped with fresh basil, garlic, lamb strips, and mozzarella cheese) is a favorite appetizer here. Among the pasta dishes, the ziti *amatriciana* (with sautéed bacon, plum tomatoes, onion, and spices), and shrimp and scallops Orvieto (in a creamy garlic sauce with artichoke hearts served over fresh linguine) are superb. Try the chicken *braciolettini* (stuffed with smoked ham and cheese and sautéed with mushrooms in a marsala sauce). ♦ Italian ♦ M-Sa lunch and dinner; Su dinner (from noon-10PM). 73 Salem St (between Cross and Parmenter Sts). 227.6637

45 Giorgio's $ "Every pizza weighs a minimum of two pounds," says a sign in the window, a promise that will lure those who like a hefty pie. Judging by the enormous slices, not to mention blimplike calzone (one-pound minimum), the promise is kept. But what's really special about this popular pizzeria is the simple sauce, sweet with crushed ripe tomatoes and oil only; the wide selection of fresh toppings; and the owners, Albert and Steven Giorgio and their mother, Lillian, who like to get acquainted with their customers. Try to sit by the window overlooking the street. ♦ Pizza/Takeout ♦ Daily lunch and dinner. No credit cards accepted. 69 Salem St (between Cross and Parmenter Sts). 523.1373

46 La Piccola Venezia ★★$ Forget decor, forget romance, forget trendy angel-hair pasta concoctions—there's a whole slew of other reasons to frequent this no-frills spot. First, there's the hearty Italian home cooking that runs the gamut from familiar favorites—lasagna, spaghetti with meat sauce, sausage cacciatore—to such hard-to-find, traditional Italian fare as gnocchi, polenta, tripe, *baccala* (salt cod), and *scungilli* (conch). Second, everything's inexpensive and arrives in hefty portions, so when your wallet's light but your appetite's immense, this place is perfect. Third, it's noisy, it's hectic, it's tacky, it's bursting with people, but it's perpetually cheerful. And finally, look who's dining with you. Among the tourists are a lot of locals, many who've been coming to John and

Jimmy's place for more than a decade. ♦ Italian ♦ Daily lunch and dinner. No credit cards. 63 Salem St (between Cross and Parmenter Sts). 523.9802

46 Dairy Fresh Candies If you like sweets, it's impossible to pass by without stopping; once you're inside, it's all over. Those who suffer from chocoholism will tremble at the sight of loose chocolates of every sort, including massive chunks of the plain-and-simple sinful stuff and gorgeous packaged European assortments. The entire confection spectrum is here, including hard candies, old-fashioned nougats, and teeth-breaking brittles. But the amiable Matara family, in the retail and wholesale business for more than 30 years, goes way beyond candy: they have Italian cakes and cookies, dried fruits, nuts, exotic oils and extracts, vinegars, antipasti, pastas, cooking and baking supplies, and more—an extravaganza of delicacies. You can assemble a wonderful gift box here. "Thank you, stay sweet," says the hand-lettered sign by the door. ♦ Daily. 57 Salem St (at Morton St). 742.2639, 800/336.5536 &

47 Maria's Pastry Shop What's a *pasticceria* without a display of marzipan in fruit and animal shapes, lurid with food coloring? Here you'll find that popular almond-sugar confection, and plenty more. Butter, anise, and almond scent the air, and through the kitchen door you can see bakers taking cookies out of the oven. Try the *savoiardi napolitani* (citrus-layered cookies), or, at Halloween time, the intriguing *moscardini ossa di morta* (cinnamon cookies that really do resemble bones). The *sfogliatelli* (clam-shaped pastries) are creamy, citrony, and not too sweet. ♦ Daily. 46 Cross St (between Endicott and Salem Sts). 523.1196

48 Purity Cheese Company Four people make all the marvelous ricotta and mozzarella sold fresh in this unobtrusive shopfront. It's easy to miss unless you glance in and spot the giant, pungent wheels of parmesan and tubs of olives. Grating cheeses, pastas, oils, and big serving bowls are available, too. The business began in 1938, and the operation is as unfussy as ever. People come from all over for the high-caliber cheese choices. And it smells delicious inside. ♦ Tu-Sa. 55 Endicott St (at Cross St). 227.5060 &

48 Pat's Pushcart ★$$ The decor here is nothing to speak of (the place looks like a dive from the outside), but it's packed with North Enders and everyone else wily enough to it track down. Entrées are basic, tasty, and inexpensive. ♦ Italian ♦ Tu-Sa dinner. 61 Endicott St (between Cross and Stillman Sts). 523.9616

Restaurants/Clubs: Red	**Hotels:** Blue
Shops/ ☂ Outdoors: Green	**Sights/Culture:** Black

Waterfront/ Fort Point Channel

Newcomers to Boston who have heard of its great maritime past are often surprised to discover how elusive its waterfront is. Hills that once overlooked **Boston Harbor** were leveled long ago, and the shoreline, for centuries Boston's lifeline, has been sheared from the city's core by **Atlantic Avenue**, the **Central Artery**, and a shield of modern buildings. With a little perseverance, however, you can cross this divide to see where Boston began. An urban treasure, the Waterfront is vibrant with light and hue and the constant motion of water and air. The history of the neighborhood's heyday is recorded in the street and wharf names, and captured in grand old buildings getting a new lease on life. The harbor itself, among the nation's most polluted, has undergone a massive cleanup: sludge dumping has ceased, and at press time, there were plans to build a new primary sewage treatment plant. Eventually, the sprinkling of the more than 30 islands here should have the sparkling setting they deserve. From little **Gallops, Grape**, and **Bumpkin** to big **Peddocks** and **Thompson**, the **Boston Harbor Islands** will entice you with picturesque paths, beaches, and views of the city.

In colonial times young Boston looked to the Atlantic Ocean for commerce and prosperity. Throughout the 17th, 18th, and 19th centuries profit-minded Bostonians industriously tinkered with the shoreline, which originally reached to where **Faneuil Hall** and **Government Center** are today, once the **Town Dock** area. Citizens built piers, shipyards, warehouses, and wharves extending ever farther into the sea, until the shoreline resembled a tentacled creature reaching hungrily for its nourishment: trade. The ocean brought profitable European and Chinese trade and established the city's legendary merchant princes.

One of Boston's most glorious moments was the clipper-ship era of the 1850s, when the harbor horizon was alive with masts and sails. Toward the turn of the century, as rails and roads replaced sea routes and manufacturing

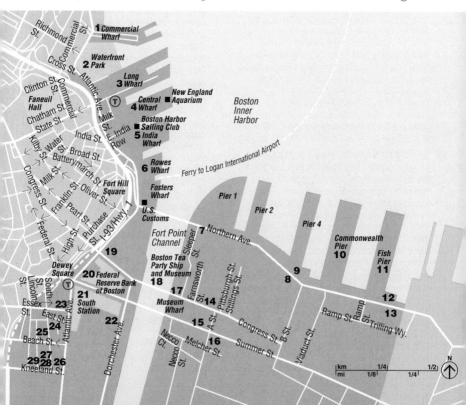

supplanted maritime trade, fishing, and shipbuilding, Boston's liaison with the sea began to suffer, languishing for decades until the late 1960s, when the city began to reclaim it. Now the Waterfront is being resurrected gradually, its connections to the heart of Boston reforged. The harbor activities that remain have shifted elsewhere, primarily to Charlestown and **Fish Pier** in South Boston.

Boston is also reinterpreting the Waterfront's role as a place for leisure, luxurious residences and offices, pleasure boats, and waterside restaurants and hotels. Excursion and commuter boats depart from the numerous wharves for the Boston Harbor Islands, **Provincetown** on **Cape Cod, Cape Ann,** and **South Shore** communities. **Harborwalk,** the pedestrian route along the Waterfront, is lengthening; it ultimately will stretch from the Charlestown Navy Yard, where *Old Ironsides* is temporarily dry-docked, to **Fort Point Channel,** linking with walks along the **Charles River**—a total of more than 20 miles. For now, however, you can take one great stroll that begins at **Waterfront Park** and **Commercial Wharf,** proceeds past the **New England Aquarium** and around sumptuous **Rowes Wharf,** crosses over the channel via the **Northern Avenue Bridge** into the area where Fish Pier, the **Children's Museum,** and the **Computer Museum** are located, then doubles back past **South Station,** concluding with a brief meander in the little **Leather District.**

Fort Point Channel and the Leather District aren't part of the historic Waterfront per se, but are natural companions because they, too, reveal facets of Boston's workaday life. Developed during the late 19th century, the Fort Point Channel neighborhood was the center for Boston's fishing, shipping, warehousing, and manufacturing industries; during the same era, the garment and raw leather goods industries thrived in the Leather District. In both atmosphere and architecture, these two neighborhoods, like the Waterfront, are acquiring new vitality as galleries, restaurants, and shops move in, following the trail of artists and other urban pioneers. Walking the entire length of this far-flung neighborhood at one time is an ambitious undertaking, but definitely can be achieved if you're not with children. It's a great Boston experience.

The best way to get to the Waterfront/Fort Point Channel area is to take the subway to the **Government Center** stop (*Green* and *Blue Lines*) and cross City Hall Plaza to the right of **City Hall,** descending the steps behind to Congress Street, crossing to **Faneuil Hall Marketplace,** and continuing straight to **Christopher Columbus Park**—the walk-to-the-sea route. Or, the **Aquarium T** stop on the *Blue Line* brings you directly to the Waterfront, to the right of the park. And the **South Station** stop (*Red Line*) brings you to the edge of the Leather District and Fort Point Channel.

Waterfront

1 Commercial Wharf When Atlantic Avenue sliced through the Waterfront in 1868, it sadly split a rugged 1834 building of Quincy granite and Charlestown brick in two. Now the western half of the building, renovated by **Anderson, Notter, Feingold** in 1971, is home to **Michael's Waterfront and Wine Library,** and the larger eastern half, renovated by **Halasz and Halasz** in 1969, houses offices and upscale apartments with enviable views. Original architect **Isaiah Rogers** also designed Boston's famed Tremont Hotel, long

gone, the nation's first luxury overnight digs. If you walk to the wharf's end, you'll see ramshackle buildings, relics of days gone by. Now pleasure boats in the adjacent yacht marina crowd the pier and clamor for attention. ♦ Off Atlantic Ave (next to Waterfront Park)

1 Boston Sail Loft $ Strange as it seems in a seaside city, there aren't many restaurants in Boston where you can sit and look out at the water. This is one of the few. Longtime residents fondly recall its predecessor, a run-down, quiet hole-in-the-wall called **The Wharf.** But things change; even if this is now a hopping touristy spot on the Happy-Hour trail, you get a nice view of Boston Harbor along with your oversize portions of decent seafood. ♦ American/Seafood ♦ Daily lunch and dinner. No tank tops allowed. 80 Atlantic Ave (next to Commercial Wharf). 227.7280. Also at: One Memorial Dr (at the base of Longfellow Bridge), Cambridge. 225.2222

Bostonians never call Boston "Beantown," a nickname that lingers nonetheless.

1 Cornucopia ★★★$$ In years past, Chef Bill Kousky's eclectic seasonal bounty, superb seafood, and peerless pan-roasted duck made a trip to this restaurant at its former location near the Combat Zone (Boston's red-light district) worth the venture. Since owner Kristine Fayerman-Piatt moved her operation here, the view of Boston Harbor and **Christopher Columbus Park** is even more reason to come and indulge in culinary excellence. Choose from broiled scrod with roasted garlic mashed potato and braised leeks, almonds, and green beans; tea-smoked chicken with crispy sesame noodles and orange–star anise sauce; or spring vegetable phyllo tart topped with feta cheese and scallion oil for dinner; then choose from the neighboring wharves, the North End, or **Faneuil Hall Marketplace** for a postprandial stroll. ♦ American ♦ M-F lunch and dinner. Reservations recommended. Validated parking nearby. 100 Atlantic Ave (at Commercial Wharf). 367.0300

2 Waterfront Park This friendly park, designed by **Sasaki Associates** in 1976, opened a window to the sea and drew Bostonians back to where their city began. In fact, the park was built to complete the "walk to the sea" that starts at City Hall Plaza in Government Center, proceeds through **Faneuil Hall Marketplace,** then passes under the Central Artery to end by the water. A handsome trellis promenade—short on greenery—crowns the park's center, with huge bollards and an anchor chain marking the seawall. The park offers views of the harbor and wharves, and a sociable scene: From morning until late at night, this versatile oasis hosts sea-gazing, ledge-sitting, suntanning, frisbee-throwing, dog-walking, and romantic rendezvous. Watch planes take off across the harbor at **Logan International Airport** and the steady boat traffic. On a summer afternoon sit and read amid the grove of honey locust trees or in the **Rose Fitzgerald Kennedy Garden,** fragrant with her namesake blooms. **Quincy Market** is just a five-minute walk away; pick up some treats and picnic with the cool ocean breezes rustling by. ♦ Bounded by Long Wharf, Commercial Wharf, and Atlantic Ave

3 Long Wharf Boston was already America's busiest port when farsighted Captain Oliver Noyes constructed this wharf, the city's oldest—and now a National Historic Landmark—in 1710. It originally extended from what is now State Street far out into what was then Town Cove, creating a dramatic half-mile avenue to the farthest corners of the world. It was the **Logan Airport** of its day, where even the deepest-drawing ships could conveniently unload cargo on the pier lined with warehouses. The painter John Singleton Copley played here as a child, where his mother ran a tobacco shop. Landfill and road construction demolished most of the wharf by the 1950s, but the restoration of its remaining buildings and the arrival of the **Boston Marriott Long Wharf** hotel have made it a destination once more. Walk to the spacious granite plaza at the wharf's end for fresh air and lovely views. Off Atlantic Ave (at State St)

On Long Wharf:

Boston Marriott Long Wharf $$$$ It's certainly pleasant to stay here at the city's edge in rooms surveying the lively Waterfront, with **Christopher Columbus Park** next door, the **New England Aquarium** one wharf over, and the North End *ristoranti* and **Faneuil Hall Marketplace** mere minutes away. Many of the 400 rooms have good views, and two luxury suites have outside decks. The **Concierge Level** offers premium services; general amenities include a business center, an indoor swimming pool, other exercise facilities, and a game room. This 1982 hotel, designed by **Cossutta and Associates,** has a couple of counts against it as a Waterfront neighbor, however. It rudely crowds what should have remained a generous link in the Harborwalk, and the architects' attempt to mimic Waterfront warehouses and the lines of a ship has resulted in an awkward, aggressively bulky building. The hotel's red-garbed porters are a striking sight. Be sure to see the 19th-century fresco depicting Boston Harbor that is mounted in the lobby upstairs. Relax by a window in **Rachael's Lounge;** there is also the formal **Harbor Terrace** restaurant and a more casual cafe. ♦ 296 State St (at Atlantic Ave). 227.0800, 800/228.9290; fax 227.2867 &

The Chart House ★★$$$ The **Gardner Building,** a simple and solid circa 1763 brick warehouse—the Waterfront's oldest, renovated in 1973 by **Anderson, Notter, Feingold**—was recycled for this chain restaurant. Inside, rustic bricks and beams recall the building's former life. Steak, prime rib, and seafood are the ticket, with children's plates available. Lots of stories circulate about the building's history—some possibly true—claiming it was called "Hancock's Counting House" because John Hancock had an office here, and that tea was stored here prior to the Boston Tea Party. When closed for the night, the sealed shutters outside convey a snug, sleepytime look. The free valet parking is a great boon in a neighborhood born long before the days of autos. ♦ Seafood/American

♦ Daily dinner. 60 Long Wharf (off Atlantic Ave). 227.1576

Custom House Block Before his writing career finally freed him from ordinary pursuits, Nathaniel Hawthorne spent two years (1838-40) recording cargoes in the cramped predecessor to this building, demolished in 1847. The "new" structure, designed by **Isaiah Rogers** and restored as a National Historic Landmark by **Anderson, Notter, Feingold** in 1973, was never used for customs collection. Nonetheless, this building bears the signature eagle and a misleading sign on its imposing granite facade. Always held privately, it now accommodates offices and apartments. ♦ Long Wharf (off Atlantic Ave)

4 Central Wharf In the early 19th century Boston was rebounding economically from the American Revolution and becoming a booming seaport once more. The brilliantly daring developer Uriah Cotting formed the Broad Street Association of businessmen to modernize the dilapidated, disorderly Waterfront. With architect **Charles Bulfinch** designing, the association created broad streets flanked by majestic four-story, brick-and-granite warehouses, and completed this pier, as well as **India Wharf,** in 1816. Only a fragment of the original wharf remains, with a handful of its structures stranded forlornly on the opposite side of the expressway. A seamen's chapel was also located here. ♦ Off Atlantic Ave (between Central and Milk Sts)

On Central Wharf:

New England Aquarium School kids and plenty of adults hurry eagerly across the expansive plaza, pausing to spot the harbor seals in their year-round outdoor pool (watch for Rigel the seal, who barks like a parrot). Inside is the aquarium's most spectacular attraction, a three-story, 40-foot-diameter tank swirling with fish, sea turtles, and sharks. Dim lighting is provided by the aquarium's illuminated displays and exhibit tanks, creating a murky underwater ambience. Visitors walk up the ramp winding around the central tank, transfixed by the constantly circling parade of flashing fins, spiky teeth, waving tails, and opaque eyes. Watch for the divers who feed the fish five times a day, only after the sharks have otherwise dined. And check out the walls opposite the tank, inset with aquariums. At the tank's base, endearing penguins stand at attention or zip about a shallow pool, braying noisily. Next door floats the **Discovery Theater,** where you can see the ever-popular marine mammal shows. On the outdoor plaza, summertime snack stands draw steady business.

Don't miss the kinetic sculpture *Echo of the Waves,* which can move for hours without repeating the same pattern. The work of Susumu Shingu, the sculpture has dampers to control its movement during high winds.

The boxy, concrete aquarium (designed by **Cambridge Seven** in 1969) is now like a sea creature grown too big for its shell. A model in its day, the aquarium (see the map below) is poised for a fabulous renaissance. (At press time, a major expansion was slated for the year 2000.) ♦ Admission. Daily. Central Wharf (between Central and Milk Sts). Recorded information 973.5200 &

 New England Aquarium Whale Watching Since the aquarium considers whales to be another important exhibit, it organizes trips to visit the extraordinary mammals at **Stellwagen Bank,** a rich feeding ground 25 miles due east of Boston. During the five- to six-hour voyage (round-trip), aquarium naturalists tell whale tales and describe other marine life. Sometimes whales come up to the boat and let out a blow right into your face and camera. Whales frequenting New England coastal waters include humpbacks, finbacks, and, occasionally, right whales. In 1987 two blue whales, the largest creatures ever to live on earth, were sighted off Cape Cod.

Be sure to dress warmly in layers—even in summer—and bring waterproof gear, rubber-soled shoes, and sunscreen. The boat offers a full-service galley. Children under 36 inches in height aren't permitted on board. ♦ Apr-Oct.

New England Aquarium

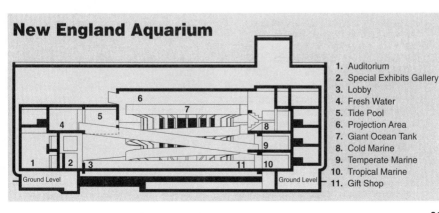

1. Auditorium
2. Special Exhibits Gallery
3. Lobby
4. Fresh Water
5. Tide Pool
6. Projection Area
7. Giant Ocean Tank
8. Cold Marine
9. Temperate Marine
10. Tropical Marine
11. Gift Shop

Reservations by credit card; payment in cash only. Boat leaves from Central Wharf (off Milk St). Recorded information 973.5277 &

5 India Wharf The other major result of the Broad Street Association's 19th-century scheme to revamp the Waterfront, this wharf (begun in 1805) was once a half-mile stretch of piers, stores, and warehouses designed by **Charles Bulfinch.** The last vestiges of the handsome structures were leveled to make room for the upstart **Harbor Towers.** ◆ Off Atlantic Ave (between Central Wharf and Rowes Wharf)

On India Wharf:

Harbor Towers Whereas Boston's historic Waterfront buildings stretched like fingers into the harbor, waves lapping among them, these modern towers aren't so involved in the maritime scene. The standoffish pair (designed by **I.M. Pei** in 1971) is more intrigued by the sky. At their nascent stage, the 40-story interlopers brought dramatic new style and scale to this part of town. Originally somewhat alienating, the towers have acquired a kind of folk appeal, partly because newer buildings more brazen and far less clever have pushed their way in—such as **International Place** across the street. The towers are more exciting to live in than to look at; the residents enjoy stunning views. David von Schlegell's *India Wharf Project,* a stark 1972 sculpture composed of four folded planes, stands at the edge of the harborside terrace. The flat surfaces clad in stainless steel also ignore the harbor and reflect what's happening above instead. The human hustle-bustle and colorful disorder this wharf once knew have been replaced by lonely, silent forms. But you won't find it gloomy here, just introspective—like the sea's occasional gray, foggy face.

Boston Harbor Sailing Club Sail in the harbor and among the islands that once witnessed stirring arrivals and departures of Boston's majestic clipper ships. In a city famous for its exclusive clubs, this is not a club per se, but rather a private enterprise founded in 1974 to offer sailing classes that are taught by experts. The one-week courses are very popular, attracting novices from all over. Properly certified visitors can rent boats from a fleet of 65, ranging in length from 26 to 39 feet. ◆ Daily May-Oct. 72 E India Row (at India Wharf). 523.2619

6 Rowes Wharf Many Bostonians consider **Skidmore, Owings, and Merrill**'s grand, redbrick complex—luxury condos, offices, shops, a 38-slip marina, and a hotel—the best addition to Boston in years. A resplendent six-story arch lures pedestrians from Atlantic Avenue to the water's edge. The 15-story development was built in 1987 on the 1760s' **Rowes** and **Fosters Wharves.** Many don't

even realize it's new, because unlike **Harbor Towers,** the complex looks backward in time. The ornamental overkill borders on kitsch, but the building is generous, capable of grand gestures. **Rowes Wharf** has further privatized the Waterfront, yet gives back to Bostonians the heroic arch, an observatory, open space, a splendid **Harborwalk** extension leading past enormous yachts, and best of all, an entry to the city via the water shuttle that zips between **Logan International Airport,** and the wharf. This speedy journey is worth taking for its own sake, sans baggage, to enjoy the most picturesque approach to Boston and see the flipside view through the monumental portal. It's not a cheap thrill, but do it once (see the "Orientation" for more information). ◆ Off Atlantic Ave (between India Wharf and Fosters Wharf)

On Rowes Wharf:

Boston Harbor Hotel $$$$ This 230-room hotel's public spaces are tranquil and attractively dressed in warm woods, pearly grays, and subdued burgundies, with companionable textures and tapestry patterns. Cove lighting adds a subtle glow and paintings by Massachusetts artists decorate the first two floors. Pay more for a room where you can gaze out at Boston Harbor instead of peering across the elevated expressway at the Financial District. Amenities include a posh health club and spa with a pristine three-lane lap pool, 24-hour room service, rooms for nonsmokers and people with disabilities, and pet services from counseling to catnip. The airport water shuttle, indoor parking, and marina slips are also available.

In the hotel's **Magellan Gallery** is a largely undiscovered treasure: a private collection of early maps and charts depicting New England and Boston. Owned by The Beacon Companies, developers of the **Rowes Wharf** complex, the display includes Virginian Captain John Smith's 1614 map of the New England coast, the first ever produced, which later guided the Pilgrims to Plymouth. Another fascinating map (created in 1625 by Sir William Alexander) records The Council of New England's scheme to turn the region into an elite association of English estates, which was ultimately overturned by competition from the Massachusetts Bay Colony and support for the Puritan cause.

Pretty **Harborview Lounge** with its comfortable furnishings is a wonderful place to have a drink and watch the light fade to harp or piano music. A Sunday breakfast buffet is accompanied by a live trio, high tea is served Monday through Saturday, a dessert buffet is offered every evening, and a bar dinner menu is available on weekdays. Inquire about live music and dancing on weekends. Away from the water overlooking empty sidewalks, **Rowes Wharf Bar** is unfortunately placed but blissfully quiet. ♦ 70 Rowes Wharf (off Atlantic Ave). 439.7000, 800/752.7077; fax 330.9450 ♿

Within Boston Harbor Hotel:

Rowes Wharf Restaurant ★★★★$$$$
The views from here are so splendid it would be easy not to care much about what's on your plate. But in fact, the hotel lavishes attention on the roomy restaurant's cuisine. Chef Daniel Bruce hails from New York's 21 and Le Cirque, not to mention Venice and Paris ports-of-call. A blend of such regional American and seafood specialties as a trio of fish with triplet sauces, bouillabaisse, and crab cakes are served with finesse amid a sophisticated rendition of the obligatory nautical theme, with fabric-covered walls and lush carpeting to soak up wayward sound. Look for Dr. Robert Levine's mahogany, teak, and lemonwood replica of the renowned 1851 clipper ship *The Flying Cloud*. ♦ American ♦ M-F breakfast, lunch, and dinner; Sa breakfast and dinner; Su breakfast and lunch. 439.3995 ♿

Rowes Walk Cafe ★★★$$ During spring and summer, weather permitting, enjoy lunch, cocktails, or dinner on the patio outside of the **Harborview Lounge.** The kitchen is outdoors too, so the menu is simple, but the setting is gorgeous, and you don't have to dress up. ♦ Cafe ♦ Daily lunch and dinner; closed September-June. 439.7000 ♿

Fort Point Channel

Most Bostonians have yet to stumble upon this fascinating place, and those who love it hope that won't change too soon. This no-nonsense neighborhood exposes some of the city's practical inner workings. The slender channel is now all that divides the original **Shawmut Peninsula** from **South Boston**, once a far-off neck of land. In the 1870s the Boston Wharf Company cut the channel and erected warehouses on the South Boston side to store lumber, sugar, coal, imported fruit, wool, raw pelts, and ice. **Fish Pier** and **Commonwealth Pier** were both built on landfill, the second becoming the center of the Boston fishing industry. By the 1890s the area was the major transfer point for raw materials fueling most New England industries, and was bursting with wharves, machine shops, iron foundries, glassworks, wagon factories, soap producers, brickyards, and printing trades. Business boomed through the early 20th century, then slackened as the fishing and wool industries, shipping, and manufacturing declined. The construction of the **Central Artery** isolated the area further and speeded its decline.

Artists rediscovered the neighborhood in the 1970s, creating a SoHolike atmosphere that early on earned the district the affectionate nickname "NoSo," short for North of South Boston. Now more than 300 artists belong to the **Fort Point Arts Community (FPAC),** the largest community of visual artists in New England. Headquartered at 249 A Street, an artists' cooperative, FPAC sponsors several open-studio weekends annually. A few pioneering galleries and museums moved in as well, followed by creative and service industries.

The **World Trade Center** and the massive **Boston Design Center,** the latter New England's major showroom facility for the interior-design trade, have comfortably settled in now, too. What port activity remains in Boston is located along **Northern Avenue** and at Fish Pier, home of the New England Fish Exchange. Megadevelopment of the vacant **Fan Pier** nearby—an on-again, off-again proposal for a city-in-a-city—would transform the neighborhood. But for now it's great fun to poke around the revival and rubble, still full of the old Waterfront district's industrial flavor and vitality. Look for the Boston Wharf Company's architecturally inventive warehouses on **Summer** and **Congress Streets.** Trucks and tractor-trailers rule the roads in this part of town. Back across the channel, skyscrapers spread like weeds; here, low-rise buildings and empty lots let light flood in. Unfamiliar vantage points show off the city's skyline.

For such a tiny waterway, the Fort Point Channel bridges offer a remarkable survey of mechanical engineering. Each operates differently: the creaky **Northern Avenue Bridge** is a trussed rolling bridge that swivels 90 degrees on a single axis to clear the channel for ships (at press time there were plans to replace it with a fixed bridge); the **Congress Street Bridge** has a giant counterweight to drive a large gear system that lifts up the bridge; and the **Summer Street Bridge** is engineered to slide sideways out of the way on rails built on piers.

Boston sailor-historian Samuel Eliot Morison wrote: "A summer day with a sea-turn in the wind. The Grand Banks' fog, rolling in wave after wave, is dissolved by the perfumed breath of New England hayfields into a gentle haze, that turns the State House dome to old gold, films brick walls with a soft patina, and sifts blue shadows among the foliage of the Common elms. Out of the mist in Massachusetts Bay comes riding a clipper ship, with the effortless speed of an albatross."

Restaurants/Clubs: Red	**Hotels:** Blue
Shops/ ♣ **Outdoors:** Green	**Sights/Culture:** Black

Sojourns to the Sea: Short Trips to the Boston Harbor Islands

Whether you'd prefer to quietly bask in the summer heat or the silvery winter light, the 30 islands dotting the inner and outer harbors offer wonderful respite from city crowds and new perspectives on Boston's connection to the sea.

Georges Island, the hub of the chain, is dominated by **Fort Warren,** massive 19th-century granite fortifications where Confederate soldiers were imprisoned during the Civil War. Guided tours and programs are offered by state park staff (Metropolitan District Commission; MDC; 725.9547) six months of the year. The 30-acre island is the perfect place for a picnic overlooking the distant cityscape, and has rest rooms, an information booth, and a first-aid station.

Sixteen-acre **Gallops Island** also has picnic grounds, a pier with a large gazebo, shady paths, meadows, and remnants of a World War II maritime radio school. **Lovell Island,** 62 acres large, offers a supervised swimming beach—though you'd probably prefer to do no more than wade a bit until the harbor is cleaned up—a picnic area with hibachis and tables, campsites, and walking trails that take you through meadows, salt marsh, dunes, and woods.

One of the harbor's biggest islands, 188-acre **Peddocks** also has picnic and camping areas and the remains of **Fort Andrews** occupying its **East Head.** Because the **West Head** is a protected salt marsh and wildlife sanctuary, access beyond recreational areas is restricted to organized tours or by permission of park staff. Tranquil **Bumpkin Island** offers trails to an old children's hospital ruins and stone farmhouse, and its rocky beach is popular for fishing. Wild rabbits and raspberry bushes proliferate. Some campsites are available. **Grape Island,** named for the vines that grew here in colonial times, feeds many birds with its wild bayberries, blackberries, and rose hips. Come here for birding, picnicking, camping, and meandering. Rugged **Great Brewster Island**'s 23 acres afford splendid views of **Boston Light,** the country's oldest lighthouse, on **Little Brewster,** but can only be reached by private boat. The lighthouse on Little Brewster began blinking in 1716. Destroyed by a 1751 fire, rebuilt, destroyed by the evacuating British in 1776 and rebuilt again, **Boston Light** is visible 27 miles out to sea. One of only six lighthouses in the country that is still manually operated, the 89-foot-tall lighthouse has been threatened with automation— forestalled for now with the help of

Senator Edward Kennedy. The first lightkeeper, George Worthylake, drowned with his family when his boat capsized on the way back to Little Brewster in 1718. Benjamin Franklin wrote a poem about the tragedy. The names of the present and former keepers are etched on island rocks. Owned by the Thompson Island Outward Bound Center (328.3900), 157-acre **Thompson Island** is open on a limited basis for guided tours, hiking, picnicking, educational programs, and conferences—you must call ahead. The center provides boat transportation to the island.

No fresh water is available on Gallops, Lovells, Bumpkin, Grape, or Great Brewster Islands. Day-use permits are required for large groups; permits are also necessary for camping and for alcohol consumption on some islands. A number of the islands belong to the **Boston Harbor Islands State Park** and are reached by ferries departing from **Long Wharf** or **Rowes Wharf** on the Waterfront. Privately operated, the ferries charge fees and most go to Georges Island, where free water-taxis take you to five other islands. For more information or to obtain permits for Georges, Lovell, and Peddocks Islands, call the MDC (727.5290). For Gallops, Bumpkin, Grape, and Great Brewster Islands, call the Department of Environmental Management (DEM; 740.1605). Georges, Bumpkin, and Thompson Islands are wheelchair-accessible.

Friends of the Boston Harbor Islands (523.8386), a nonprofit organization dedicated to preserving the island's resources, sponsors year-round public education programs, history tours, and boat trips.

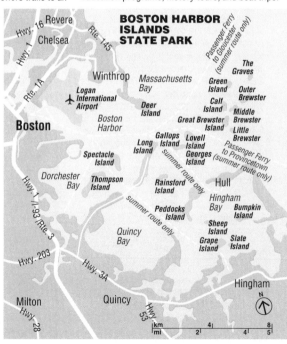

BOSTON HARBOR ISLANDS STATE PARK

7 The Barking Crab ★★$$ Take a hard right rudder after the Northern Avenue Bridge and you'll find this restaurant, formerly **Venus Seafood in the Rough**. John Geoffrion and Bill Lombardi have extended the traditional clambake fare with all kinds of fried, boiled, steamed, and grilled seafood. Sit at tables under the giant heated tent, with a wonderful view juxtaposing lobster boats and the city skyline. ♦ Seafood ♦ Daily lunch and dinner. 88 Sleeper St (at Northern Ave). 426.2722 &

8 Our Lady of the Good Voyage Chapel In addition to regular weekend Masses, an annual "Blessing of the Animals" service is held at this humble little chapel. ♦ 65 Northern Ave (opposite Pier 4). 542.3883

9 Anthony's Pier 4 ★$$ There are better places to go in Boston for an expensive seafood dinner, but this place is worth a visit at least once to experience a big-time restaurant formula that keeps 'em coming, and coming, and coming. Owner Anthony Athanas, an Albanian immigrant, started out as a shoe-shine boy, built a restaurant, and wound up ruling a fiefdom of five gigantic seafood houses. After the inevitable wait, enjoy towering popovers, raw oysters or clams, steamed lobster, or simply cooked seafood, and end with Indian pudding or a dessert soufflé. The wine list may be New England's biggest and best.

The colonial-nautical motif is milked for all it's worth, but Anthony needn't have gone to the trouble: big views of Boston Harbor steal the show. There are no quiet corners here, where as many as 3,000 meals a day are served. Take a good look at the "Wall of Respect"—make that "Walls"—crammed with photographs of Anthony and the Pope, Anthony and John F. Kennedy, Anthony and Frank Sinatra, Anthony and Liz Taylor, Anthony and Gregory Peck. . . . ♦ Seafood/American ♦ Daily lunch and dinner. Jacket required and tie preferred for main dining room at dinner; no jeans or sneakers. Valet parking. 140 Northern Ave (at Pier 4). 423.6363

10 Commonwealth Pier/World Trade Center Excursion boats depart from this pier for Provincetown, the Harbor Islands, and other points. The beflagged business center accommodates all kinds of enormous functions. Across the street from its lower main entrance, a pedestrian walkway winds to the elevated Viaduct Street, a little-known route that offers unusual cityscapes. Behind lies hectic Fish Pier; in another direction looms the Postmodern **Boston Design Center** and giant **Boston Edison** with its towering stacks; and on the right is Boston's southern flank. Continue straight on Viaduct's sidewalk until you reach Summer Street, then turn right. Look back for the best view of the trade center's monumental pomp and circumstance. ♦ Off Northern Ave (between Pier 4 and Fish Pier)

11 Fish Pier Two long, arcaded rows housing fish-related businesses stretch more than 700 feet out onto the water, with the heroic New England Fish Exchange dominating the far end. The century-old building's arch is crowned with a wonderful carved relief of Neptune's head, with more fabulous fishy ornamentation above.

No longer the center of New England's—let alone America's—fish industry, Boston's catch keeps shrinking, with more and more fish brought in by trucks, not boats. But the venerable fish auction still starts up every morning around 6:30, presided over by exchange president Marie Frattollilo. It's well worth arriving by 6AM to watch the buyers haggle over that day's cod, hake, and pollack, sold right off the boats and rushed to refrigerated trucks. Off Northern Ave (between Commonwealth Pier and Trilling Way)

11 No-Name ★★$$ Once upon a time this eatery had a name, but it sure doesn't need one now. The hungry hordes all know where to find this big-business restaurant that has been cooking up meals for fishers and pier workers since 1917: in the righthand building of Fish Pier, just past the arcade's first curve. The dinnertime line out the door helps point the way; don't fret at the sight—you may meet some amusing fellow diners. Enlarged to accommodate the tourists, businesspeople, and locals who have joined the old crowd, its original hole-in-the-wall look has been preserved right down to the concrete floor. Hope for a table in the back overlooking the pier (and the boats that brought your dinner). Sitting elbow-to-elbow at boisterous communal tables, fill up on "chowdah" and big portions of impeccably fresh fried seafood, boiled lobster, broiled fish, fish o' the day, and delicious homemade pie. Expect to wait in line; they don't take reservations. ♦ Seafood ♦ Daily lunch and dinner. No credit cards accepted. 15¹/₂ Fish Pier (off Northern Ave). 338.7539 &

12 Jimmy's Harborside Restaurant ★$$ This Waterfront fixture has been around since 1924, starting out as a nine-stool joint serving Fish Pier workers and fishers. The cavernous seafood house's dated decor shows a refreshing lack of interest in fads. Notice the funky fish mosaics and neon on the facade. Showcased in walls of glass, the views are among the Waterfront's most colorful, with big boats docked close by. The reliably fresh seafood is at its best in simpler preparations, especially the chowder. The title "Home of the Chowder King" was earned in the 1960s when the late owner, Jimmy Doulos, was invited to bring his great fish chowder to Washington, DC. It pleased the palates of John F. Kennedy and members of Congress, and will undoubtedly please you. Jimmy's son is in charge now, but politicians and other celebs still crowd in with the tourists and regulars.

While waiting for a table, have a drink at **Jimmy Jr**, the boat-shaped bar. ◆ Seafood/American ◆ M-Sa lunch and dinner; Su dinner. Reservations recommended. Jackets requested; no jeans, sneakers, or T-shirts allowed at dinner. Valet parking. 242 Northern Ave (at Fish Pier). 423.1000 ♿

JIMBO'S

13 Jimbo's Fish Shanty ★$ Geared toward the family trade, this casual joint is run by the Doulos family, which also owns **Jimmy's Harborside Restaurant** across the way. Children are delighted with the trains-and-hobos decor and the three train sets zipping by them on overhead tracks. You won't find harbor views, but the low prices for chowder, basic seafood, pizzas, salads, burgers, and other no-frills American food make up for it. Children's plates are available. The restaurant's tiny newsletter-menu advises you to check out the **New England Aquarium** "for a close look at the seafood on the hoof." ◆ Seafood/American ◆ Daily lunch and dinner. Valet parking at Jimmy's Harborside. 245 Northern Ave (at Fish Pier). 542.5600 ♿

13 Daily Catch ★$$ An offspring of the popular North End hole-in-the-wall, this larger place is just as redolent with garlic and serves the same great seafood, although the original has much more personality. Try one of the many variations on the calamari theme; the owners love to turn people on to their favorite seafood. ◆ Seafood ◆ Daily lunch and dinner. No credit cards accepted. 261 Northern Ave (at Fish Pier). 338.3093. Also at: 323 Hanover St (between Lothrop Pl and Prince St), North End. 523.8567

Boston aristocracy does not, as many believe, hark back to the early Puritan settlers or the Mayflower set; instead, Boston's elite descended from 19th-century merchant princes, some of whom had made money in rather unsavory ways. Many of these early, privileged Bostonians justified their worldly gains by founding and funding cultural and charitable organizations. Brahmins came to epitomize high standards of thrifty, moral, and simple living. Oliver Wendell Holmes—doctor, author, and father of the famous jurist—coined the term "Brahmin," after the ascetic Hindu caste that performed sacred rituals and set moral standards, in a series of articles written for the *Atlantic Monthly* in 1860 entitled, "Autocrat of the Breakfast Table." Cabot, Coolidge, Forbes, Lawrence, Lodge, Lowell, Saltonstall—their names have been recycled and intermingled through the years, but still convey the best and worst of their all-powerful ancestors who once ruled the city.

14 Mobius The name refers to both the **Mobius Performing Group** of 17 artists and to the multimedia gallery and performance space on the fifth floor of a former leather-sole manufacturing building where other artists can also present their work. The founding group works in performance, installation, sound art, new music, film, video, dance, and intermedia. Works-in-progress are presented frequently. Performances change just about every weekend; call ahead for times and to alert the staff you're coming. ◆ Admission. 354 Congress St (between Farnsworth and Pittsburgh Sts). 542.7416 ♿

14 Boston Fire Museum This chunky little 1891 granite-and-brick firehouse is now owned by the Boston Sparks Association, which welcomes visitors. ◆ Free. Sa or by appointment; closed December-April. 344 Congress St (at Farnsworth St). 482.1344 ♿

15 Marco Polo Cafe ★$ Frequented by employees of local architecture offices, this stylishly sparse cafeteria-style lunch spot serves great coffee and Mediterranean fare, ranging from minestrone to moussaka. Most everything's made on the premises, including from-scratch morning muffins. ◆ International/Takeout ◆ M-F breakfast and lunch. 274 Summer St (between A St and Fort Point Channel). 695.9039 ♿

16 A Street Deli Express $ While the rest of the city's asleep, get a hearty breakfast with lots of good grease to jumpstart your day. For lunch, the food is cheap, basic, and good: pizza, soup, and salads. Walk up Melcher Street to see its gracefully curving warehouses. ◆ American ◆ M-Sa breakfast and lunch. 324 A St (at Melcher St). 338.7571 ♿

17 The Milk Bottle $ A landmark in its own right, this vintage 1930s highway lunchstand (pictured above) was installed in front of **The Children's Museum** in 1977, having first been sawed in half and floated down the Charles River. Donated to the museum by the H.P. Hood Company, the 40-foot-tall wooden bottle would hold 50,000 gallons of milk and 860 gallons of cream if filled. Served from within are a variety of soups and salads, and, of course, ice cream. ♦ American ♦ Daily. 300 Congress St (at Museum Wharf). 426.7074 &

17 The Children's Museum Kids adore this lively participatory museum located in a former wool warehouse (see the plan below). Whatever your age, a visit here will

revive that urge to touch and get into things, even if you restrain yourself and just watch. In ongoing exhibitions for toddlers to teens, kids may blow bubbles and spin tops in the **Science Playground;** scramble on the two-story **Climbing Sculpture;** learn personal health and well-being in "Mind Your Own Business"; visit "The Kid's Bridge," an exhibition that addresses Boston's multicultural heritage; and investigate what daily life is like in a Japanese silk-merchant's reconstructed home from Kyoto, Boston's sister city. One of the museum's newer exhibits is "Teen Tokyo," which is about the international culture of youth in Japan today; it includes a Japanese subway car, a karaoke booth, and an animation computer. The **Resource Center** offers educational materials and services to parents and teachers, such as RECYCLE, which sells in bulk dirt-cheap industrial raw materials discarded by local

factories. **The Children's Museum Shop** is an unbeatable source for unusual gifts, toys, and books. The museum has an active outreach program, working with local neighborhoods on a variety of cultural events, so this is the place to find out about all sorts of family activities going on around Boston.
♦ Admission; reduced admission Friday evenings. Tu-Su. Open Monday during Boston school vacations and holidays. 300 Congress St (at Museum Wharf). Recorded information 426.8855 &

17 The Computer Museum A remarkable repository of technologies past and present, this is the only museum in the world devoted entirely to computers. Forget those graceless terms—nerd, hack, dweeb—computer "companions" are made here, the museum says. Whether you're computer-literate or -leery, more than a hundred interactive exhibitions chronicle computers and their role in society. Walk through a spectacular 50-times-larger-than-life, two-story computer model that demonstrates how a personal computer functions, complete with a 25-foot-long keyboard, a 108-square-foot color monitor, and six-foot-tall floppy disks. David Macauley, writer and illustrator of *The Way Things Work* and other delightfully reassuring show-and-tell-style books,

The Children's Museum

1 Studio 10/15
2 Science Playground
3 Backstage at the Big Top
4 Fort Point Garage
5 El Mercado del Barrio
6 Mind Your Own Business
7 Teen Tokyo
8 Families
9 Favorites

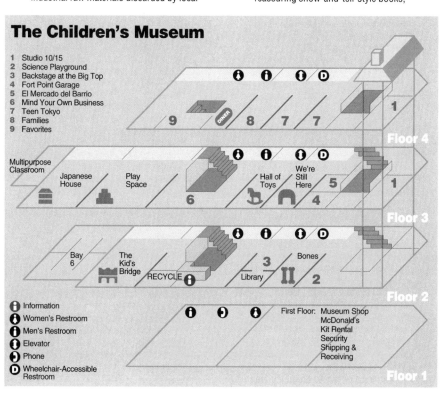

Walk-Through Computer Exhibit

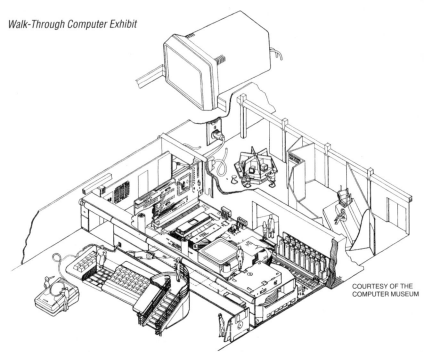

COURTESY OF THE
COMPUTER MUSEUM

illustrated the "Walk-Through Computer" exhibit (pictured above). Hands-on exhibitions let you "paint" pictures, compose melodies, create programs, simulate aircraft flight, design a house or car, even remodel your face.

Visit the amusing **Animation Theater,** and **Smart Machines Gallery** starring more than 25 robots. "People and Computers: Milestones of a Revolution" tracks the development of computers from the punch-card machines of the 1930s to today's microprocessors. "Tools and Toys: The Amazing Personal Computer" explores all the fascinating functions a PC can perform, including animation, video, and virtual reality. Ride the massive glass-enclosed elevator overlooking the Fort Point Channel. The techy gift shop even sells chocolate "chips." ◆ Admission; reduced admission Saturday 10AM-noon. Summer: daily; winter: Tu-Su. 300 Congress St (at Museum Wharf). 426.2800, computerized information 423.6758 ♿

17 Lightships $ A lengthy, if not especially inventive menu and fabulous views of the downtown skyline distinguish this congenial restaurant—that and the fact that it's afloat. A rehabbed barge, it serves a family-pleasing assortment of sandwiches and seafood, with a nod to traditional Mexican standbys. ◆ International ◆ Daily lunch and dinner. 310 Congress St (at Museum Wharf). 350.6001 ♿

18 Boston Tea Party Ship and Museum
The Boston Tea Party took place near here on Griffin's Wharf, long gone (its site is now landfill on Atlantic Avenue between Congress Street and Northern Avenue). On a cold December night in 1773, angry Colonists dressed as Mohawk Indians boarded ships and heave-hoed 340 chests of costly British tea into the harbor to protest the tax imposed on their prized beverage. A cuppa was a costly commodity in those days. Moored alongside the Congress Street Bridge is the *Beaver II,* a Danish brig resembling one of the three Tea Party ships and sailed here in 1973. For kids, it's an adventure to climb about the 110-foot-long working vessel, listen to costumed guides, and finally toss a bale of tea defiantly over the side (the fact that it's roped to the ship and hauled back up again doesn't lessen the thrill). On the adjacent pier, a small museum contains exhibitions, films, ship models, and memorabilia, with printed information available in seven languages. Tax-free tea is served at all times. ◆ Admission. Daily. On the Congress St Bridge (near Dorchester Ave). 338.1773

In the summer, tourists fill the gap left by vacationing college students. The National Park Service reports that in 1993 the Paul Revere House had 3,376 visitors in January, ballooning to almost 27,000 in August, while monthly tallies of people touring the USS *Constitution* grew from 4,681 to 95,866.

Restaurants/Clubs: Red   **Hotels:** Blue
Shops/ 🌳 Outdoors: Green   **Sights/Culture:** Black

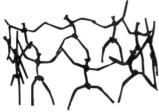

19 Artsmart This roomy, smart-looking shop features personal adornments and quirky home furnishings fashioned by some 120 local artisans. "It's comfortable, rather than pretentious—we make sure people can touch everything," says co-owner Dror Ashuah. Among the "unique objects" you may indeed want to fondle are their velvet hats, hand-painted picture frames, and faux-finished armoires. Be sure to duck next door to visit a sibling enterprise, the **Ashuah-Irving Gallery** (286 Congress St, 482.3343), a small, raw space whose selections are singularly astute. ♦ Call for hours. 272 Congress St (between Dorchester and Atlantic Aves). 695.0151

20 Federal Reserve Bank of Boston
Whether you think this building (designed by **Hugh Stubbins & Associates** in 1977) resembles an old-fashioned washboard, goal posts, or a radiator, its shimmering aluminum-sheathed form is remarkably visible from many vantage points. The bank's art gallery on the ground floor is an alternative space where nonprofit New England–based artists and arts organizations mount six professional-level exhibitions annually.

A performance series is held in the adjacent auditorium September through December and March through June; call for program information. Free group tours of the bank's operational departments are offered with a month's notice. Public tours are held every Friday; and individual bank tours are offered by appointment only, generally on Friday. Visitors leave with souvenir packets of shredded money. ♦ Call for hours. 600 Atlantic Ave (between Congress and Summer Sts). Recorded gallery information 973.3453. Tours 973.3451 &

21 South Station When construction on this station (designed by **Shepley, Rutan, and Coolidge**) at Dewey Square was completed in 1900, it was the world's largest railroad station, holding that title for many years. And by 1913, handling 38 million passengers a year, it was the busiest station in the country—even topping New York City's Grand Central Station. In peak year 1907, some 876 trains plied the rails on weekdays. The majestic five-story edifice, its shapely curved facade adorned with a nine-foot-wide clock surmounted by a proud eagle, proclaimed Boston's important place in the world. In its heyday, the station's comforts included a theater that screened newsreels and **Our Lady of the Railways Chapel.** But when airplanes, trucks, and autos eclipsed trains, the station slid into decrepitude. Eventually, most of it was demolished, except for the handsome headhouse, which nearly gave up the ghost in the 1960s.

Modern construction, respectful restoration, and intelligent planning have made the terminal (on the National Register of Historic Places) an exciting destination once more, with pushcart vendors, a food hall, coffee bar, newsstand, bank, and other services to lure pedestrians from nearby streets. Look for the old tin ceilings and beautiful carved details. More than 200 commuter trains and dozens of **Amtrak** runs come and go on the busiest travel days. At press time a new bus station was under construction on the top level. With the *Red Line* subway conveniently on site, travelers are linked to the rest of Boston and suburbs. ♦ Bounded by Dorchester and Atlantic Aves, and Summer St.

22 US Postal Service-South Postal Annex
Boston's general mail facility looks like a 1920s ocean liner berthed alongside the channel. Always open, this is the mail processing hub for the Boston Division, with more than 1.2 million square feet of space and 12 miles of conveyors. Groups of 10 or more, minimum age 13 or eighth grade, can take a guided tour of the automated and mechanized facility and see how employees sort a daily average of nine million pieces of mail with the help of optical character readers, letter-sorting machines, bar-code sorters, and other sophisticated equipment. Call to arrange a tour at least one week in advance. ♦ Free. Tours Tu-F Jan.-Nov. 25 Dorchester Ave (behind South Station). 654.5081 &

Leather District
Like the Fort Point Channel area, this tiny appendage to the Financial District has a businesslike personality and lots of integrity. You can cover the entire seven-block neighborhood in one half-hour stroll. When Boston's Great Fire of 1872 swept clean more than 60 acres, it wiped out the city's commercial and wholesale centers, including the dense leather and garment district concentrated here. But slowly, businesses rose from the ashes and built sturdy new warehouses and factories, most along **Lincoln** and **South Streets,** some Romanesque in style and quite distinguished. Except for a few firms, the leather warehousing industry long ago departed for other countries. In the 1970s artists and urban pioneers began to move in, followed by art galleries, shops and services, and restaurants. The neighborhood's new identity is still in the making. But arty attempts to update and upscale the neighborhood are like dressing up a business suit with a Day-Glo tie.

23 The Essex Grill ★$$ On the first floor of the former **Hotel Essex,** now spiffed up as the **Plymouth Rock Building,** this big dining room looks across at trains idling in the **South Station** yards and fronts a major street, so diners can survey the urban scene. Nicely prepared seafood—including fresh-water varieties—dominates the menu. On the same floor is the high-ceiling, airy **Essex Bar,** a throwback to another era with wonderfully fussy columns and drapes. The old hotel, built about the same time as **South Station,** was a popular haunt, and it's easy to imagine the days when both rail-weary and raring-to-go travelers came and went from here, baggage in tow. As you come or go, look for the handsome old clocks in the lobby. ◆ Seafood ◆ M-F lunch and dinner. Reservations recommended for lunch. 695 Atlantic Ave (at Essex St). 439.3599 &

24 Populuxe Four collectibles dealers contribute to this "20th Century Collective," and the pickings are ultra-kitsch: everything from vintage clothing and accessories to movie star portraits and religious icons. If you'd like to re-create the ambience of decades gone by, this is the place to prowl. ◆ M-Sa. 92 South St (between East and Beach Sts). 482.5207

24 Ware on Earth The showroom for Pot Specialists, Inc., local importers, this shop sells containers and planters from Thailand, Malaysia, Greece, Italy, China, and other countries. Many of the striking vessels are one-of-a-kind or antique, and some are enormous—such as the antique Greek oil drums. Prices start very low and keep climbing. ◆ M-F. 104 South St (between East and Beach Sts). 451.5995

As for the raucous Boston Tea Party of 16 December 1773, the 342 chests of tea, weighing several tons, were lowered into the harbor so quietly that not one crew member of a British frigate, anchored no more than a quarter-mile away, reported seeing or hearing anything unusual that chilly night.

24 Gallery Per Tutti Bulgarian-born painter Gedy Moody opened this semi-subterranean gallery to showcase affordable art in a variety of media (paintings, prints, photographs, and furniture, from $50 to $5,000) and to foment discussion of art's function. The gallery's 40 or so artists are also featured in monthly receptions, and on alternate Sunday afternoons, Moody hosts a salon, free and open to all. ◆ Tu-Sa; call for additional hours. 112 South St (between East and Beach Sts). 482.2710

25 Whit's End Most Bostonians have yet to discover this captivating shop purveying inexpensive trinkets and toys. Yet many are familiar with its biggest seller: clever rubber stamps of animals, buildings, cartoons, patterns, names, and hundreds of other designs—practical and outrageous—all manufactured right on the premises. Custom orders are taken, too.

And if rubber stamps aren't your thing, for peanuts you can get a plastic Hula girl, chocolate cow, lobster-claw-shaped harmonica, blinking Christmas-bulb earrings with matching necklace, itsy-bitsy plastic ants and creepy bigger bugs, plus all sorts of stationery, cards, handmade jewelry, mugs, and wind-up toys—the whole kit and kaboodle of eccentric doodads. ◆ M-Sa. 105A South St (between East and Beach Sts). 426.3458

25 Bromfield Gallery Boston's oldest artist-owned cooperative gallery exhibits work ranging from realist to abstract and conceptual art, displaying prints, paintings, photographs, and other media by a stable of a dozen-or-so artists. Shows change frequently and are individual, group, invitational, and juried. ◆ Tu-Sa. 107 South St (between East and Beach Sts). 451.3605

25 John Gilbert Jr. Co. Established in 1830, this is Boston's oldest spirits shop. It began as a purveyor of fancy groceries and delicacies. (The ancient store ledgers are fascinating for their flowery handwriting alone.) In addition to fine wine and beers, all kinds of liquid treasures are sold. ◆ M-Sa. 107 South St (between East and Beach Sts). 542.8900

CECIL'S

25 Cecil's on South Street ★$ Located in the 1888 **Beebe Building,** this friendly place has warmed up its exposed bricks-and-beams interior with vivid Caribbean posters, fish statues, mobiles, ceiling fans, wooden booths, and background jazz. The Colombian chef orchestrates an interesting rapprochement among Mexican, Latin, Caribbean, Italian, and

American dishes at lunch, with a dinnertime focus on excellent Cuban-Latin cuisine. Try *ropa vieja* (Cuban-style beef stew), *pollo borracho* ("drunk chicken" marinated in beer and wine), *pargo a ajillo* (red snapper with salsa), or turkey potpie. ◆ International/Takeout ◆ Cover charge for music Saturday night. M-F breakfast, lunch, and dinner; Sa lunch and dinner; closed mid-June–Labor Day. Reservations recommended for dinner. 129 South St (between East and Beach Sts). 542.5108

26 Howard Yezerski Gallery A bright, inviting gallery that strives to be a little offbeat and untraditional, it shows contemporary painting, sculpture, and photography by established and emerging artists from the US and Europe. The core group of 20-plus artists and guest exhibitors includes Natalie Alper, Domingo Barreres, and Paul Shakespear. ◆ Tu-Sa. 186 South St (between Beach and Kneeland Sts). 426.8085

27 Genovese Gallery Annex An outpost of the South End gallery, this pristine space favors big, bold, minimalist art. ◆ Tu-Sa. 195 South St (between Beach and Kneeland Sts). 426.2062

27 Robert Klein Gallery An important destination for photography collectors, this fifth-floor gallery exhibits, appraises, purchases, and sells stunning international 19th- and 20th-century photographs, many rare. More than 150 photographers are represented, including William Henry Fox Talbot, Diane Arbus, Ansel Adams, Robert Mapplethorpe, Eugene Atget, Edward Weston, Richard Avedon, and Man Ray. Special offerings have included Lucien Aigner's limited-edition *Einstein Portfolio*. ◆ Tu-Sa. 207 South St (between Beach and Kneeland Sts). 482.8188 &

28 The Blue Diner ★$ There's no place like it in Boston. Straddling this corner since 1947, the bluer-than-a-bluebird diner was carefully refurbished to keep its old character but acquire a new sheen. A wonderful hangout—unfortunately, a *lot* of people think so—the diner has its original working Seeburg sound system, with Wall-o-Matic selectors at every booth. Two plays per quarter let you listen to a parade of vintage 45s from the likes of Elvis, Aretha Franklin, Jerry Lee Lewis, and Louis Armstrong.

To the requisite rib-sticking diner fare—the daily Blueplate Specials include meat loaf,

roast turkey and homemade gravy, and franks and beans—owner Don Levy has added imaginative grilled seafood items, Mississippi barbecue, and vegetable fritters. Unlike the average diner, all the food is "real" here—no mixes—right down to the maple syrup and magnificent mashed potatoes. The french fries are from scratch, too. The day starts early here, as any respectable diner's should, with hearty breakfasts. Order a cup of coffee to go; it comes in a great, kitschy paper cup. ◆ Diner/American ◆ M, Su 7AM-midnight; Tu-Sa 24 hours. 178 Kneeland St (at South St). 338.4639

28 Akin Gallery Owner Ali Righter was among the first to set up shop in this formerly charmless area, and her pick of mid-level artists, along with the occasional discovery, is still worth searching out. ◆ Tu-F. 164 Kneeland St (between Lincoln and South Sts). 426.2726 &

28 The Art Zone ★$$ Located in a former warehouse, this barbecue pit has art gallery aspirations. The food is pretty good, with best bets including the pulled pork (entrée or sandwich), smoked-beef brisket, babyback ribs, Killer Chili, sweet-potato chips, and onion rings. Or come for a down-home breakfast complete with grits. But the real draw here is the artful tables: each glass-topped shadow box holds the creation of a local artist, and they range from funny to whimsical to outrageous and arresting. Every few years, the tables are auctioned and a new round commissioned. ◆ Barbecue ◆ M-F, Su lunch and dinner; Sa dinner. Reservations recommended Thursday-Saturday nights. 150 Kneeland St (between Lincoln and South Sts). 695.0087 &

29 F.C. Meichsner Company Founded in 1916, this family-owned and -operated business is the only East Coast establishment that can actually fix and repair all makes and models of binoculars and telescopes. Considered *the* source for binoculars, telescopes and accessories, barometers and ships' clocks, and replicas of old telescopes, it'll give you the best optics for your money. ◆ M-Sa. 182 Lincoln St (between Beach and Kneeland Sts). 426.7092

Boston's greatest admirer, as legend has it, was Charles Dickens. Said Dickens: "Boston is what I would like the whole United States to be." The city's greatest detractor, Edgar Allen Poe, who was "heartily ashamed to have been born in Boston," referred to his native city as "Frogpondium."

Restaurants/Clubs: Red	**Hotels:** Blue
Shops/ 🌳 Outdoors: Green	**Sights/Culture:** Black

Financial District/ Downtown

Boston's most on-the-go neighborhood is bounded by the **Boston Common** to the west, the **Central Artery** and **Waterfront** to the east, **Government Center** and **Faneuil Hall Marketplace** to the north, and **Chinatown** and the **Theater District** to the south. Celebrating the city's economic good health, the bumper crop of skyscrapers found here transforms the Boston skyline. The revitalized **Downtown Crossing** shopping area is cheerfully chaotic with pedestrians, pushcarts, and outdoor performers luring shoppers to the internationally famous **Filene's Basement** and dozens of other stores and boutiques.

History's imprint is here as well: important **Freedom Trail** stops such as the **Old State House, Old South Meeting House,** and **Globe Corner Bookstore** impart a vision of a Revolution-era "Main Street." The **Custom House Tower, State Street Block,** and surviving wharf buildings designed by **Charles Bulfinch** speak of early wealth from the sea. Come during weekday work hours, when everything is open and in full swing. Walk along the profusion of twisty, tiny colonial lanes that have turned into busy arteries shadowed by architectural giants, creating windy, dark New York City–style canyons. Businesslike street names—State, **Court, Broad, Federal, School**—reflect the neighborhood's no-nonsense character. Numerous commercial palaces bear carved or fading traces of their original names, paying tribute to past lives.

From the city's earliest days, State Street was Boston's business artery—the most prestigious and spacious in town. Called **King Street** until the Revolution, State Street stretched 800 feet from the **Old State House** to **Long**

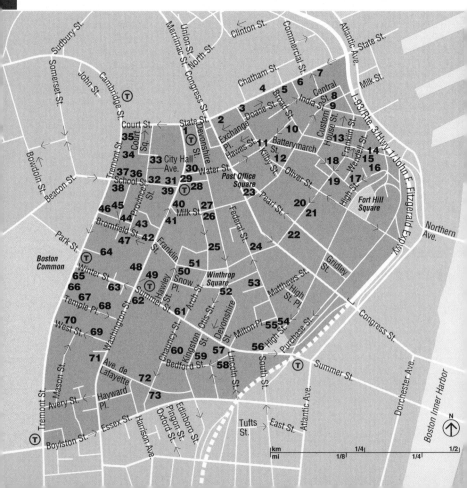

Wharf, the noble pier that once served as the city's highway to the sea. Where State Street intersects **Washington Street** was the epicenter of Boston's commercial and financial life.

An old Indian trail, Washington Street is now the major downtown commercial way, with great streetscapes down the **Ladder Block** side streets toward the **Common**. Always an important thoroughfare, it was the only road in the 17th and 18th centuries that ran the full length of Boston, linking the **Old State House** with the town gate at the neck of the Shawmut Peninsula. The street was renamed to honor George Washington's visit to the city in 1789. Today, it becomes seedy beyond **Temple Place** as it heads south toward the shrinking red-light district, the infamous **Combat Zone** (not a good place to be at night). Much of the existing Washington Street area was built after the Great Fire of 1872, which leveled 65 acres bounded by Washington, Broad, **Milk**, and **Summer Streets**; destroyed the heart of major New England industries; and left thousands without jobs. Many buildings still show scars and burns from the conflagration, which stopped just short of a number of Boston's historical treasures. Although the neighborhood was rapidly rebuilt, its residents had fled and commercialism took over. Boston's publishing and newspaper concerns flourished along **Newspaper Row** where Washington Street meets State and Court Streets, and insurance, banking, retail, garment, manufacturing, and other industries stuck by their roots. The famous **Omni Parker House** hotel and **Locke-Ober** restaurant also persevered in the face of change, and to this day remain pleasant, if somewhat stodgy, oases of gentility.

Economically, Boston was a Sleeping Beauty from 1895 until around 1965, when its building-boom prince finally arrived. Early skyscrapers are in short supply, but Boston does have its pleasing, peculiar **Custom House Tower**, Art Deco **Batterymarch Building** and post office, and lithe and lovely **Winthrop Building**. "If it ain't broke, don't fix it" is the Yankee credo, and Bostonians have always had a talent for recycling old structures. The city's fiscally conservative streak even influences new architecture. Unlike Chicago, where buildings shoot up to the sky unimpeded, Boston prefers a modest scale for its towers, so they politely accommodate older neighbors. Developers are subjected to stringent regulations and reviews. Some new buildings are dressed to the nines in decoration, but many are quite plain, even dowdy. It's as if the city is just getting used to its growing cosmopolitan stature and doesn't quite know how to dress the part.

The Financial District/Downtown neighborhood is large, but easily walked from any subway station in the area, including **Park Street** (*Red* and *Green Lines*), **State** (*Orange Line*), **Washington/Downtown Crossing** (*Red* and *Orange Lines*), **South Station** (*Red Line*), and **Government Center** (*Green* and *Blue Lines*). The **Park Street** and **Washington/Downtown Crossing** stops are most convenient to the downtown shopping area; one block apart, either station can be reached from the other via an underground passage. The **Government Center** and **State** stops are near the historical and financial districts, and the **South Station** stop is just beyond the neighborhood's south-eastern edge.

1 Old State House This lovable 1713 brick building (pictured on page 74) has stubbornly survived centuries of tumult and transformation, witnessing more than its share of dramatic moments in local and American history. The National Historic Landmark has been remodeled and restored so often (**Goody, Clancy & Associates** performed the latest shoring-up in 1992) that its parts date from many eras. Situated at the head of State Street, the so-called "Temple of Liberty" originally commanded a clear view to the sea, and in the mid-18th century became the political and commercial center of the Massachusetts Bay Colony. Its first floor was a merchants' exchange, with the wheels of government turning on the floors above. Even the site occupied an important place in the town's history, for the earliest Boston market square was located here, as were the stocks, pillory, and whipping post used to mete out 17th-century Puritan justice. The building started life as a meeting place used by the British crown's provincial governor, as well as the seat of the government after the Revolution sent the British packing once and for all. The ceremonial balcony at the Congress Street end overlooks the site—within a circle of cobblestones—where on 5 March 1770, frightened British soldiers fired on a large, angry mob of Bostonians, killing former slave Crispus Attucks and four others in the Boston Massacre. From this same balcony, the Declaration of Independence was first read to Bostonians on 18 July 1776. The fantastical cavorting lion and unicorn on the elder edifice's gable, emblems of the hated crown, were frowned upon and removed (they have now been restored to their original home). Every year since, the Declaration has been read from the same spot on the Fourth of July. John Hancock was inaugurated here as the first governor under the new state constitution. And when George Washington visited Boston in 1789, he surveyed the great parade in his honor from here. But after the new **State House** was built on Beacon Hill, this monument became a jack-of-all-trades building, used and abused as a commercial center, newspaper office, and, for a decade, Boston's City Hall.

The outcast's cause was championed just in time in 1881, when a private nonprofit organization called the Bostonian Society organized to restore the building and preserve the rich history it had witnessed. Ever since, the society has called it home and maintained a marvelous museum featuring changing and permanent exhibitions on the Revolutionary era, maritime history, and other important chapters in the city's life. The history of the building is chronicled, too. Paintings, portraits, figureheads, military and domestic artifacts, and other treasures tell the tale of this city quite well. A vial of the original tea from the Boston Tea Party is on view, for

instance, as is the coroner's report on Crispus Attucks. Look for John Hancock's family Bible and some of his clothing, and for Fitz Hugh Lane's painting *View of Boston Harbor*. A lovely spiral staircase leads to where inaugurations, daily government, and momentous meetings took place. For those who want to dig deeper, the society's splendid library across the street on the third floor of 15 State Street comprises more than 6,000 volumes and a thousand maps and architectural plans, plus rare manuscripts and broadsides.

The library also owns more than 10,000 Boston views in photographs, prints, watercolors, and drawings. Another great resource is librarian Philip Bergen, who holds much of Boston's history right in his head. Happily, the **Old State House** has flourished under the society's care. Unicorn and lion now prance with pride, copies elevated to the original animals' lofty perches. Another testament to the building's resilience: the presence of the **State Street** subway station that's tucked underneath. ♦ Admission. Daily. 206 Washington St (at State St). 720.3290

1 Visitor Center Located across the way from the **Old State House,** the center is operated by the Boston National Historic Park Service, which also runs the **Old South Meeting House, Faneuil Hall, Paul Revere House, Old North Church, Bunker Hill Monument, Charlestown Navy Yard,** and **Dorchester Heights.** In addition to offering information about these places, including a brief slide-show presentation, the center's staff of park rangers and volunteers answers questions about Boston and the entire National Park system. Find out about tours, many of which start from here. Pick up free **Freedom Trail** maps and pamphlets about all kinds of places, activities, and events. The center also sells books and souvenirs. And equally important, well-kept rest rooms, water fountains, and

Old State House

telephones are available here, public conveniences hard to come by in Boston. There are also places to sit and rest weary bones. ◆ Daily. 15 State St (between Washington and Devonshire Sts). 242.5642 ⟨&⟩

2 Exchange Place Opinions vary wildly about this blending of old and new. Actually, all that remains of the original 1891 Stock Exchange Building designed by **Peabody and Stearns** is a 60-foot segment of its worthy granite facade on the State Street side, now engulfed by a glassy tower added in 1984 by the **WZMH Group.** From some vantage points, its dark reflective surfaces shimmer interestingly, but overall the new building is, well, tacky. A handsome restored marble staircase is the atrium's incongruous centerpiece. This was the site of the historic **Bunch of Grapes Tavern,** located at the head of Long Wharf during the 19th century. A favorite watering hole for patriot leaders before the Revolution, the tavern reputedly served the best bowl of punch in Boston. ◆ 53 State St (between Congress and Kilby Sts)

3 75 State Street Also known as "Fleet Center," this unabashedly gilded and gaudy showpiece, erected in 1988 by **Graham Gund Associates,** is loved by some and hated by others. The lobby looks like an example of tender loving care gone too far, with its plethora of patterns, types of marble, and fancy fixtures—but the vast atrium lets in plenty of pure, unadulterated light. ◆ At Kilby St

4 Cunard Building The boldly inscribed name on this Classical Revival building built in 1901 by **Peabody and Stearns** recalls another bright moment in Boston's past. The building was once the headquarters for the famous **Cunard Steamship Line,** which pioneered transatlantic steamship routes. Boston was proud to beat out New York City as the first American city to enjoy the innovative service. Nautical motifs aplenty—crowned Poseidon heads, anchor-and-dolphin lighting stanchions, a wavelike ornamental band—add an adventurous air to an otherwise sober structure. ◆ 126 State St (between Broad and Kilby Sts)

5 Board of Trade Building This elaborate, urbane building designed in 1901 by **Winslow and Bradlee** has aged well. Its allegorical figures and vigorous stone carvings harken to seafaring days gone by, especially the galleons rushing forward into the viewer's space. ◆ 131 State St (between Broad and India Sts)

6 Custom House Tower A preposterous marriage of convenience between a Greek Revival temple dating from one century (**Ammi Young** was the architect in 1847) and a 30-story tower plunked on top during the next (**Peabody and Stearns** added it in 1915)

originally appalled many Bostonians. After all, the proud **Custom House** was once the focal point of the thriving waterfront.

Situated at the base of State Street, the important colonial route that once led from the **Old State House** and neighboring financial establishments out onto the wharves, the original structure was mammoth to begin with, each of its 32 Doric columns a single 42-ton shaft of Quincy granite. As the 20th century progressed and skyscrapers sprouted in other cities, Boston was mired in an economic slump. The federal government forked over the funds for the tower addition, which at 495 feet became the city's first—and, for a long time, only—skyscraper. It took a while, but Bostonians have become very attached to their peculiar landmark, now a familiar friend. No matter how many new structures crowd the skyline, the steadfast tower is the most memorable silhouette, its refurbished clock aglow at night. The little 25th-floor observation balcony is still a great place to scan the harbor and Financial District, and the lobby beneath the original building's rotunda—skylit until the tower leapt on top— deserves a look. Unfortunately, the interior remains off-limits until the building's fate is decided. The city bought the entire edifice from the federal government in 1987, and the plan all along has been to open offices and possibly a museum of the City of Boston, but the building remains shut during the funding scramble. ◆ State St (at India St)

7 State Street Block Gridley J.F. Bryant, one of the architects for the **Old City Hall** on School Street, not to mention **Boston City Hospital** in the South End and the **Charles Street Jail** on Cambridge Street, also built a number of large granite warehouses that once extended to the harbor. He designed this massive granite block in 1858. Look for the big granite globe squeezed under the arched cornice facing the **Custom House Tower.** The mansard roofs were added later. ◆ 1 McKinley Sq (at State St)

7 Dockside $ At one of Boston's most popular sports bars, fans look at seven TVs and two big screens to watch the games. Drinks, rah-rah decor, camaraderie, and celebrity customers are the draw—not cuisine. Expect bar-food basics like pizzas, barbecue, and burgers. Many fans bring autograph books because sports stars have been known to drop by, including Larry Bird, Marvin Hagler, several **Bruins,** and assorted visiting players. One memorable night, Jack Nicholson tended bar. ◆ American ◆ Daily lunch and dinner. 183 State St (between Surface Rd and McKinley Sq). 723.7050

Restaurants/Clubs: Red	**Hotels:** Blue
Shops/ 🌿 Outdoors: Green	**Sights/Culture:** Black

75

7 Tatsukichi ★★$$ Its unremarkable looks are deceiving, since this is one of Boston's most authentic Japanese restaurants. Explore the enormous sushi selection, and try teriyaki, sukiyaki, *kushiage* (skewers threaded with meats and vegetables, then batter-fried), or *shabu shabu* (pot-cooked dinners for two). Twenty percent of the menu is raw fish, and many uncommon entrées will pique an adventurous eater's curiosity. If you'd like privacy for your party, request a tatami room. ♦ Japanese ♦ M-F lunch and dinner; Sa-Su dinner. Reservations recommended. 189 State St (between Surface Rd and McKinley Sq). 720.2468

8 Central Wharf Buildings On the opposite side of the Central Artery, Central Wharf concludes at the harbor's edge. The humble but handsome row of eight brick buildings between India Street and the elevated expressway are all that remain of the 54 designed by **Charles Bulfinch,** which together extended nearly 1,300 feet to where the **New England Aquarium** now stands. All of these buildings, built in 1817, originally opened onto the water to receive goods from the ships docked out front. ♦ 146-176 Milk St (between India St and the John F. Fitzgerald Expwy)

9 Flour and Grain Exchange Building This commercial castle brings a surprising fillip of fantasy to the hard-nosed Financial District. The conical roof of the exchange's curvaceous corner is bedecked with pointy dormers that look like a crown. Architect **Henry Hobson Richardson**'s influence is palpable in this 1893 design by his successors, **Shepley, Rutan, and Coolidge,** who also built the impressive **Ames Building** on Court Street. Look for the extraordinary cartouche adorned with an eagle straddling a globe and cornucopias spilling fruit and coins. The exchange was built for the Chamber of Commerce and once housed a large trading hall on the third floor. Now architects hold court within. Don't bother to visit the lobby, as the original was renovated into oblivion. With its lanterns and scattering of trees, the building's triangular plaza is an oasis in this unexpectedly quiet corner of the city. ♦ 177 Milk St (at India St)

10 Broad Street Indefatigable developer Uriah Cotting led his Broad Street Association in many ambitious 19th-century urban redevelopment schemes, of which this street was but one by-product. Laid out around 1805 according to **Charles Bulfinch**'s plans, it quickly became a handsome commercial avenue to the sea, bordered by many Federal-style **Bulfinch** buildings. A scattering of these still stand among more recent but distinguished structures such as **No. 50**

(which was completed in 1863). With its many low-rise buildings, this street is one of the neighborhood's most open, sunny spots. A historical note: In a store located on this very thoroughfare, Francis Cabot Lowell, one of Cotting's partners, developed a power loom that ultimately revolutionized American textile manufacture. ♦ From State St to Surface Rd

10 Sakura-bana ★★★$$ Sushi is the house specialty—as you might guess if you notice the poem by the entrance extolling "sushi rapture"—and you can even order "sushi heaven," a sampler of more than two dozen varieties of sushi and sashimi. If you order à la carte, you can be as daring or timid as you wish, staying with salmon, tuna, and mackerel, or exploring exotica like flying fish roe and sea urchin. The daily *bento* (lunch box) specials served with soup, salad, rice, and fruit are also very good choices. For dinner, try seafood *teppan yaki* (broiled with teriyaki sauce and served on a sizzling iron plate). Not only is this trim and tidy restaurant's cuisine outstanding, its prices are reasonable and portions generous. Lots of Financial District workers regularly queue up for lunch. The name, by the way, means "Cherry Blossom." ♦ Japanese ♦ M-Sa lunch and dinner; Su dinner (closed first Sunday of the month). Reservations recommended for dinner. 57 Broad St (between Water and Milk Sts). 542.4311 &

10 Bakey's ★★$ This upscale delicatessen with a full bar serves all sorts of sandwiches for lunch and supper, plus an extensive continental breakfast. An amusing logo of a man asleep on an ironing board (see the illustration above) indicates imagination at work. The story is, owner George Bakey once found his father in this pose, ensconced on the family ironing board. There are two very pleasant dining rooms—one called **The Snug,** named for the room women retired to when it wasn't considered proper for the sexes to mingle in bars. George has gone all out in his establishment's decor: wooden bars and booths imported from England (be sure to notice **The Snug**'s cozy little square bar), antique lighting, Oriental rugs, fresh linen and flowers. Be forewarned—smoking isn't allowed anywhere. ♦ American/Deli ♦ M-F lunch and dinner. 45 Broad St (at Water St). 426.1710 &

11 Liberty Square At this triangular intersection is another of Boston's quaintly misnamed "squares" squeezed into a busy block. This one commemorates angry

Bostonians' destruction on 14 August 1765 of the British Stamp Tax office that was located here. (A year later, England repealed the Stamp Act.) The square was formally named in 1793 in a gala ceremony honoring the French Revolution, complete with extravagant feasting and 21-gun salute, and is dominated by Gyuri Hollosy's memorial to the Hungarian Revolution of 1956, dedicated in 1986. For those who love old urban pockets lingering in modern cities, this site is a treat. It's surrounded by businesslike 19th-century buildings that reveal curious and delightful details, if you take time to notice. The old street pattern's turns and angles provide interesting vistas. ♦ Bounded by Water, Kilby, and Batterymarch Sts

12 Appleton Building Coolidge and Shattuck designed this powerful, austere Classical Revival edifice in 1924; **Irving Salsberg** renovated it in 1981. Named for Samuel Appleton, a Boston insurance magnate, the building's most expressive gesture is its generous curve to accommodate converging streets on Liberty Square, its best side. (The Milk Street facade is far less interesting.) All else is measured, pragmatic, restrained—just right for the industry it housed. But the more you study the structure, the more inventive it appears, especially its syncopated window patterns and entrance facade friezes depicting a violinmaker, carpenter, glassblower, sculptor, draftsman, and other artisans. Peek into the elliptical lobby with its elegant gilded ceiling. ♦ 110 Milk St (between Oliver and Batterymarch Sts)

13 Sultan's Kitchen ★$ Located in a remnant of **Charles Bulfinch**'s 19th-century Broad Street development, this self-service restaurant cooks up fresh and delicious renditions of Middle Eastern and Greek favorites for the lunch crowd: kabobs, grape leaves, Greek salad, *baba ganooj,* egg-lemon-chicken soup, falafel, and tabbouleh. Try the cool, crisp Sultan's Salad or rich *tarama* salad made with fish roe. If too many dishes tempt you, order one of the sampler plates. ♦ Turkish/Takeout ♦ M-Sa lunch. 72 Broad St (between Franklin and Custom House Sts). 338.7819, recorded menu 338.8509

14 Ayers Rock ★$ Weary of your walkabout? Try Kristian Strom's Australian roadhouse, named for the world's largest rock, found in the center of Australia where four deserts meet. Naturally, Foster's is on tap. You'll delight in the Bushman's black bean soup, sandwiches named for places down under, and entrées from the barbie. ♦ Australian ♦ M-Sa lunch and dinner. 112 Broad St (at Surface Rd). 542.2021

15 Nara ★$$ Lawyers, brokers, bankers, et al., favor this cozy, private little place located along an alley. One might easily miss it altogether, so watch for the Japanese lanterns and red awnings. Sushi lovers find happiness in the extensive selection, and others can sample tempura, teriyaki or *katsu* (deep-fried) entrées. This friendly, family-run restaurant is crowded by day, quieter by night, but always enjoyable. ♦ Japanese/Korean/Takeout ♦ M-F lunch and dinner; Sa dinner. Reservations recommended. 85 Wendell St (at Broad St). 338.5935 &

16 Country Life ★$ Boston's most complete vegetarian dining experience allows you to sample plentiful all-you-can-eat lunch, brunch, and dinner buffets. Absolutely no dairy, meat, refined grains or sugar sneak into any of the dishes. Substitutes include "milk" and "cheeses" made from nuts and soy. The inventive menu changes daily—with a new one printed each month—featuring soups like garbanzo dumpling, lentil, and Russian potato; entrées such as lasagna, enchiladas, and vegetable potpie; and an interesting choice of vegetables. Afterward, treat yourself to one of their desserts. Everything is self-serve, and the decor is neat but plain; the emphasis of this restaurant is entirely on hearty, healthy food. ♦ Vegetarian/Takeout ♦ M-Th lunch and dinner; F lunch; Su brunch and dinner. Reservations requested. No credit cards accepted. 200 High St (between Surface Rd and Broad St). 951.2534, recorded menu 951.2462

17 Chadwick Leadworks Though one-upped by the bulky Neo-Classical **International Place,** a near-by high-rise, this forceful rustic structure still holds its own on the Financial District fringe. Built in 1887 by Joseph Houghton Chadwick, once described as "Lead King of Boston," it was designed by **William Preston,** who also created the former **New England Museum of Natural History** in Back Bay, now the upscale **Louis, Boston** clothing store. Handsome three-story arches with a graceful ripple of spandrels are topped by a row of little windows and a bold parapet. A gargoyle glares from one corner, and other grotesques and dragonlike lizards cling to the facade. At the back is the square shot tower, inside which molten lead was poured from the top, cooling into shot before reaching the bottom floor. ♦ 184 High St (between Batterymarch St and Leman Pl)

18 Batterymarch Building Named for the street it adorns—once part of a marching route for military companies from **Boston Common** to now-leveled Fort Hill—this heroically optimistic Art Deco assemblage designed by **Henry Kellogg** in 1928 is wonderful to behold in the midst of a district becoming ever more crowded and shadowed by impersonal modern giants. The three slender towers linked by third-story arcades undergo a truly marvelous transformation as they push through the crowded block to the sky. Their dark-brown brick at ground level gradually lightens in color until it becomes a glowing buff at the top, as if bleached by sunlight (the one commodity always in short supply in congested downtowns). Under the handsome entrance arches, look for the charming reliefs of boats, trains, planes, stagecoaches, and clipper ships. Unlike the heavy-handed gilding of nearby 75 State Street, this building's discreet touches of gold enhance rather than bedizen its fine form. ◆ 60 Batterymarch St (at Franklin St)

19 Brandy Pete's ★★$$ During Prohibition thirsty Bostonians flocked here in droves after a flip of the venetian blinds signaled that a new shipment of booze had come in. When that period ended, owner Peter Sabia was persuaded by his customers to transform his speakeasy into a restaurant. Today Bostonians on the hunt for traditional "Beantown" fare come to the large brass- and mahogany-appointed pub where current owner Owen Burke provides good, simple fare, including scrod, chicken potpie, and an award-winning meat loaf. There's also alfresco dining for eight on the patio. Whether eating indoors or out, you'll find the best of the basics here. ◆ American ◆ M-F lunch and dinner. 267 Franklin St (at Batterymarch St). 439.4165

20 Le Meridien $$$ The **Old Federal Reserve Bank,** a Renaissance Revival palazzo designed by **R. Clipston Sturgis** in 1922, has been happily preserved—to the tune of $33 million—as part of this prestigious European hotel.

The 326 guest rooms are contemporary in decor, while the lobby and public spaces feature restored original architectural details. Because a glass mansard roof was plunked on top of the old structure to add additional floors, many rooms feature sloping glass walls with electric drapes, offering great views. Suite 915 is especially popular, as are the loft suites. There are 15 rooms specially equipped for people with disabilities, and three floors are reserved for nonsmokers. There's a posh health club called **Le Club Meridien** on the third floor, featuring a pool, whirlpool, sauna, and exercise equipment; and a full-service business center complete with foreign currency exchange. French chocolates and a daily weather report appear bedside nightly in each of the rooms—a nice touch. Other amenities include a multilingual staff, valet parking, 24-hour concierge and room services, and express laundry and dry cleaning. Paid parking is offered in the 400-car garage.

Because the hotel is owned by **Air France,** it is often associated with major French cultural events in Boston, such as those hosted by the **French Library** and **Alliance Française.** Another plus is the location in the heart of the Financial District; it's an easy walk from here to many popular attractions and the Theater District. Adjoining the hotel is **One Post Office Square,** a 41-story tower that was added in 1981 by **Jung/Brannen Associates** and **Pietro Belluschi,** and houses conference rooms, business offices, and the **Julien** and **Cafe Fleuri** restaurants. ◆ 250 Franklin St (between Oliver and Pearl Sts). 451.1900, 800/543.4300; fax 423.2844 &

Within Le Meridien:

Julien ★★★$$$$ Named for Boston's first French restaurant, which opened on this same site in 1794, this restaurant draws a predominantly business clientele. Yet the restaurant's lofty refined splendor and classic French cuisine make it a good choice for a serious evening out. Consulting chef Marc Haeberlin of France's three–Michelin-star Auberge de l'Ill works with resident chef Charlie Prentis, combining fresh native ingredients with French creativity in dishes like roasted rack of lamb with *herbes de Provence* (assorted herbs), ragout of New England scallops with puree of white beans and truffles, and salmon soufflé (a classic Haeberlin masterpiece). Desserts are inspired, and the wine list exceptional.

The vast dining room is located in the high-ceilinged hall that once served as the bank's boardroom; tables are all generously spaced and diners settle into Queen Anne wingback chairs, promoting privacy and conversation. The **Julien Bar,** resplendent with gilded coffered ceilings and wonderful carved details, provides background piano music. Look for the pair of N.C. Wyeth murals portraying Abraham Lincoln and George Washington. ◆ French ◆ M-F lunch and dinner; Sa dinner. Jacket and tie required at restaurant; no blue jeans allowed at bar. Reservations recommended. Complimentary valet parking for dinner. 451.1900 &

Cafe Fleuri ★★$$$ Situated beneath the six-story atrium in **One Post Office Square,** connected to the hotel, this airy and open cafe features brasserie-style cuisine. It is popular for business breakfasts and lunches, and the spectacular, belly-bludgeoning Sunday jazz brunch.

Attention all chocoholics: on Saturday afternoons (except in the summer) the cafe puts on a sumptuous all-you-can-eat Chocolate Bar buffet, a truly hedonistic, decadent display of cakes, pies, tortes, fondues, mousses, cookies, brownies, and the like. ♦ Cafe ♦ Daily breakfast, lunch, and dinner. Reservations recommended. Valet parking. 451.1900

21 State Street Bank & Trust Company
Erected in 1966 by an architectural consortium (**Hugh Stubbins & Associates, F.A. Stahl & Associates,** and **LeMessurier Associates**), this bank is noteworthy for its **Concourse Art Gallery** on the lower level. At least four shows are mounted here each year on art and architecture, often in collaboration with such local nonprofit groups as the Boston Architectural Center and the Massachusetts Horticultural Society. The bank owns a fine maritime folk art collection and 19th-century maps and charts. Works by city youth are shown every summer. ♦ Free. M-F. 225 Franklin St (between Pearl and Oliver Sts). 786.3000 ♿

22 NYNEX Headquarters Building A 1947 design by **Cram & Ferguson,** this step-top Art Deco throwback occupies its place with pride. **Goody, Clancy & Associates** renovated the facade in 1992 in a spiffy homage; check out the spiky beacons, echoed in the phone booths on either side. (Everything has been touched with a Deco wand, from the garden guardrails and trash receptacles, right down to the sidewalk pattern.) Off the main lobby, you can see a re-creation of inventor Alexander Graham Bell's garret. Dean Cornwell's frenzied and colorful mural, which circles the lobby, is really something—Norman Rockwellesque eyefuls. Called *Telephone Men and Women at Work,* the 160-foot-long, action-packed painting depicts 197 lifesize figures in dramatic groupings. Painted in 1951, it lionizes not only Bell and other telephone pioneers, but also employees on the job and those risking life and limb in the face of disaster to keep those calls coming. Cornwell was an old hand at this sort of thing, creating murals honoring steelworkers, pioneers in medicine, various states' histories, etc.

Bell's laboratory is a painstaking replica of his original studio at 109 Court Street in old Scollay Square, where he electrically transmitted the first speech sounds over a wire on 3 June 1875. (The following March, in a different lab, Bell succeeded in sending not just sounds but intelligible words, when he issued his famous line: "Mr. Watson, come here, I want you.") The studio was saved from demolition, dismantled, and eventually brought here in pieces and rebuilt. On display are models, telephone replicas, drawings,

references, and historic artifacts, plus a wonderful diorama of the view of Scollay Square from Bell's window. Pamphlets about Cornwell's creation and Bell's garret are usually available. ♦ Free. M-F. 185 Franklin St (between Congress and Pearl Sts). 743.4747 ♿ (enter from Franklin St)

23 Post Office Square Another of Boston's many triangular "squares," this popular public space tops a 1,400-car garage. One of the busiest and most visually exciting pockets in the city, it's surrounded by the Art Deco post office and telephone company headquarters, and overlooks wonderful views of the city's densest blocks, where new and old exist cheek by jowl. The square was landscaped by Craig Halvorson, and harbors 125 species of plants, including seven vines climbing an elegant 143-foot-long trellised colonnade. **Harry Ellenzweig** designed the sparkling glass quarters of the **Milk Street Cafe** (see page 80); sculptor Howard Ben Tre the handsome green-glass fountains. ♦ Bounded by Milk, Congress, and Pearl Sts

23 Angell Memorial Plaza At the triangle's tip opposite the post office is a pocket park dedicated to George Thorndike Angell, founder of the Massachusetts Society for the Prevention of Cruelty to Animals and the American Humane Education Society. A sculpture of a small pond and its inhabitants is located in the middle of a brick circle inset with reliefs of birds, beasts, and bugs. Look for Angell's wise words: "Our humane societies are now sowing the seeds of a harvest which will one of these days protect not only the birds of the air and beasts of the field but also human beings as well." Looming near the pond is the fountain designed by Peabody and Stearns as a watering place for horses in 1912. ♦ Pearl and Congress Sts

23 John W. McCormack Post Office and Court House A commanding Art Deco building with plenty of crisp ornament and vertical window ribbons, this post office (designed in 1931 by **Cram & Ferguson** with **James A. Wetmore**) has a nicely weathered gray facade. ♦ Congress St (at Post Office Sq). 654.5684

24 Bank of Boston Gallery Campbell, Aldrich & Nulty designed this ungainly brown tower with a big belly in 1971. It quickly earned a famous nickname, "The Pregnant Building." The First National Bank of Boston operates the marvelous gallery on the 36th floor, which displays the bank's own collection and exhibitions, ranging from fine arts to architecture, design, and furniture. The curator, employed by the bank, often organizes collaborative art shows with Boston-area institutions, museums, and schools. ♦ Free. M-F. 100 Federal St (at Franklin St) 434.2200 ♿ (on the Congress St side)

25 Hole in the Wall One of the district's tiniest tidbits of real estate, this diminutive deli manages to turn out a huge assortment of breakfast and lunch items to go. You'd be hard-pressed to think of a hot or cold sandwich that isn't served here (okay, so there's no peanut butter), not to mention the salads, soups and stews, egg combos, burgers, and snacks. Owner Benny Yanoff and his family run the place at top speed. Join the line at the outside counter, or step inside to watch how skillfully counter staff dart past each other in close quarters. It was a passerby's chance remark—"Look at that hole in the wall"—that gave the 12-by-4-foot deli its apt appellation. With brown bag in hand, take a moment to examine Richard Haas's trompe l'oeil mural across the street, painted on the back of 31 Milk Street, which portrays a cutaway of the actual facade. Haas also painted the well-known mural on the **Boston Architectural Center** in Back Bay. ♦ M-F 4AM-4PM. 24 Arch St (between Milk and Franklin Sts). 423.4625 ♿ Also at: 125 Summer St (at Devonshire St). 345.0515

26 International Trust Company Building Max Bachman's allegorical figures *Commerce* and *Industry* adorn the Arch Street side, while *Security* and *Fidelity* are ensconced on Devonshire Street, adding a fanciful representation of business rectitude modern buildings sorely lack. This edifice, built in 1893 by **William G. Preston,** enlarged in 1906, and now listed on the National Register of Historic Places, incorporated the remains of a building partly destroyed by Boston's terrible 1872 fire. ♦ 39-47 Milk St (between Arch and Devonshire Sts)

27 Milk Street Cafe ★$ Downtown shoppers and Financial District denizens love this crowded cafeteria, and many a politician stops in for kosher dairy, vegetarian home-style cooking that includes muffins and bagels, soups, pizzas, pastas, quiches, salads, and sweet treats. ♦ Cafe/Takeout ♦ M-F breakfast and lunch. 50 Milk St (at Devonshire St). 542.3663 ♿

28 Bob Smith Sporting Goods Specializing in running, tennis, skiing, fishing, and, of late, in-line skating, this small shop is staffed by "professionals who play and understand the sport they sell." The service is indeed more than perfunctory—it's educational—and the selections are top-of-the-line. In 1643 this corner was the site of Governor Winthrop's home, conveniently located by Great Spring, for which it's named (that source ran dry in the mid-19th century). ♦ M-Sa. 9 Spring La (off Washington St). 426.4440 ♿

29 Winthrop Building Boston's first building with a steel skeleton instead of load-bearing masonry walls, this sliver slips gracefully into a tapering lot. Conceived in 1893 by one of Boston's more adventurous architects,

Clarence H. Blackall, the gently curving building flows between Spring and Water Streets. Now on the National Register of Historic Places, its golden airiness and dressy decoration, especially on the lower levels, delight the eye. **Blackall**'s Chicago training was a fantastic boon to Boston. He designed a number of majestic theaters and other public buildings. Among Boston's other early steel-frame office buildings are a charming pair nearby: **Cass Gilbert's Brazer Building** of 1896 and **Carl Fehmer's Worthington Building** of 1894, standing side by side at 27 and 33 State Street. ♦ 276-278 Washington St (between Spring La and Water St)

Within the Winthrop Building (around the corner, facing Water Street):

Caffè Paradiso $ Another spin-off of the favorite North End meeting place, this cafe sells quick Italian treats to take away (there are counters, but no tables). In addition to steaming cappuccino, espresso, and Italian beverages, they carry savory calzones, pizzas, quiches, cannoli, and delicious desserts, including a popular hazelnut truffle torte. ♦ Italian/Takeout ♦ M-Sa breakfast and lunch. No credit cards accepted. 3 Water St (at Washington St). 742.8689 ♿ Also at: 255 Hanover St (between Cross and Richmond Sts). 742.1768; 1 Elliot St (at Winthrop St), Harvard Square, Cambridge. 868.3240

29 Mrs. Fields Cookies Ultrarich, chewy, and chocolaty cookies bring a steady stream of sweet-toothed customers to this cookie cove, one of hundreds in the national chain. Choose from the rich repertoire of chocolate-chip varieties, or try oatmeal raisin or cinnamon sugar. The brownies and muffins are equally tempting. ♦ Daily. 264 Washington St (at Water St). 523.0390 ♿ Also at: 426 Washington St (at Summer St, in Filene's). 357.9727; Copley Place Shopping Center, 100 Huntington Ave (at Dartmouth St). 536.6833; Faneuil Hall Marketplace, 200 State St (at Commercial St). 951.0855

30 Merchants Wine & Spirits This former bank now secures a liquid treasure. One of the city's finest wine and spirits shops, offered here are unusual vintages as well as inexpensive drinkable monthly specials. Rare cognacs and superior Burgundies are a specialty; there's also a large California section. Tastings are held regularly in the old bank vault at the back, its walls still lined with safety-deposit boxes. A voluptuous cheese department sells superb cheeses from small New England farmsteads, plus imports. Pick up the very informative, chatty house newsletter. ◆ M-Sa. 6 Water St (between Washington and Devonshire Sts). 523.7425

31 The Globe Corner Bookstore This prized relic of colonial Boston is quite comfortably ensconced on its corner site. The redbrick, gambrel-roofed house (pictured above), now on the National Register of Historic Places, was built circa 1711 for Thomas Crease, who opened Boston's first apothecary shop within. In 1828 Timothy Carter, a bookseller, took over, installed printing presses, and opened the **Old Corner Bookstore** on the first floor. Thus was inaugurated the building's long career as the locus of Boston's publishing industry and literary life.

Here Ticknor & Fields published works by Harriet Beecher Stowe, Charles Dickens, Alfred Lord Tennyson, Elizabeth Barrett Browning, Henry David Thoreau, Nathaniel Hawthorne, William Makepeace Thackery, Julia Ward Howe, and Ralph Waldo Emerson, helping to establish a native literature. Gregarious Jamie Fields in particular gained respect as counsel, friend, and guardian to writers, and was especially loved as an innovator who believed writers ought to be paid for their pains. Here, too, the *Atlantic Monthly* was founded and rose to cultural eminence. The *Boston Globe*'s downtown offices once occupied the building, whose preservation the newspaper ensured by opening its namesake bookstore in 1982.

The current shop sells a wealth of works on New England and books by regional authors, plus a fine selection of guidebooks, maps, globes, atlases, and world travel information. You can always find unusual cards, calendars, cookbooks, and marvelous children's books. ◆ Daily. 1 School St (at Washington St). 523.6658. ᕦ Also at: 49 Palmer St (at Church St), Harvard Square, Cambridge. 497.6277 (travel and geography only)

32 Brookstone The brainchild of engineer Pierre de Beaumont, a frustrated hobbyist who sought unusual tools that weren't available, this specialty store stocks more than a thousand well-made, practical, and sometimes pricey tools and gifts. The inventory focuses on unusual, hard-to-find items, and includes shop and gardening tools, small electronics, housewares, personal care items, exercise and sports equipment, indoor and outdoor games, office supplies, and travel and automotive accessories. De Beaumont started simply with a mail-order catalog business, then launched the innovative retail system that resulted in more than 100 outlets nationwide. It works this way: each store is like a giant 3D catalog, with information cards accompanying all displayed goods. Customers pick up and examine whatever interests them, fill out order forms and present them at the desk, then wait for purchases to be delivered by conveyor belt. Mail-order catalogs are available, too. ◆ Daily. 29 School St (between Tremont and Washington Sts). 742.0055 ᕦ Also at: Copley Place, 100 Huntington Ave (at Dartmouth St). 267.4308; Faneuil Hall Marketplace (Marketplace Center). 439.4460

33 Boston Public Library, Kirstein Business Branch This branch of the Boston Public Library, designed by **Putnam and Cox** in 1930, specializes in noncirculating business and financial references. It's located off the beaten trail on a pedestrian lane connecting School and Court Streets. An interesting feature of the building is its Georgian Revival facade, which replicates the central pavilion of daring **Charles Bulfinch**'s architecturally innovative (for America) and financially disastrous Tontine Crescent residential development, built on Franklin Street in 1794 and demolished in 1858. It was this speculative real-estate scheme's failure that cost **Bulfinch** his inheritance and turned him from an architect by choice into one by necessity. Several blocks away, part of Franklin Street still follows the footprints of the vanished Tontine's curve. ◆ M-F. 20 City Hall Ave (between School St and Pi Alley). 523.0860

33 Pi Alley The printer's term "pi," meaning spilled or jumbled type, is what this alley is probably named after. As the story goes, type would spill from printers' pockets as they went to and from a popular colonial tavern located at the alley's end. A less common account claims the alley is actually Pie Alley, paying tribute to the tavern's popular pies. ◆ Off City Hall Ave (between Court and School Sts)

A bookshop once stood near the Old State House, where the first Bibles printed in America were sold and where Edgar Allan Poe's first volume of verse was published. No copies of Poe's work were sold here, a first blow among the many that darkened his view of life.

Restaurants/Clubs: Red **Hotels:** Blue
Shops/ 🌳 Outdoors: Green **Sights/Culture:** Black

34 Hungry Traveler $ Across from the **Kirstein Business Branch**, tucked into a quiet street behind **Old City Hall**, is an ideal cafeteria-style restaurant for early-bird eggs and bacon or a quick, cheap sandwich. Five or six hot entrées are prepared daily, plus salads and soups. Hang back until you know what you want, because once the no-nonsense counter-help spots you, they'll demand your order. A lot of people come here—tourists and on-the-job Bostonians—and the staff likes to keep things moving. ♦ Cafeteria/Takeout ♦ M-F breakfast (from 5:45AM) and lunch. No credit cards accepted. 29 Court Sq (at Pi Alley). 742.5989 ♿

35 Rebecca's Cafe ★$ They're popping up all over Boston, offering made-from-scratch hot entrées, pastas, soups, salads, sandwiches, pastries, and dreamy desserts; and are winning more and more fans. ♦ Cafe/Takeout ♦ M-F breakfast, lunch, and dinner; Sa breakfast and lunch. No credit cards accepted. 18 Tremont St (between Court and School Sts). 227.0020 ♿ Also at: 112 Newbury St (between Clarendon and Dartmouth Sts). 267.1122; 800 Boylston St (at Gloucester St), Prudential Center. 266-3355; 560 Harrison Ave (at Waltham St). 482-1414

36 Old City Hall Replaced by modern **City Hall** at **Government Center,** this empress dowager is an exuberantly ornamental artifact of a more flamboyant era. The days when colorful Boston politicos like James Michael Curley held sway are long gone. Retired in 1969, the 1865 hall designed by **Gridley J.F. Bryant** and **Arthur Gilman** is no longer in the thick of things. For many visitors, it's a surprise to discover this French Second Empire edifice tucked away from the street. Still graced with ample arched windows and an imposing pavilion, the National Historic Landmark building now accommodates offices and a restaurant; the foyer contains a nice trompe l'oeil reminder of its former finery by muralist Josh Winer, and further embellishments are planned. The exterior was painstakingly renovated by **Anderson, Notter Associates** in 1970.

On either side of the entrance stand Richard S. Greenough's 1855 statue of *Benjamin Franklin* and Thomas Ball's 1879 statue of *Josiah Quincy,* Boston's second mayor, who built **Quincy Market** and served as president of **Harvard College.** Franklin's likeness was the first portrait statue in Boston. Embedded in the sidewalk in front of the hall's cast-iron fence is Lilli Ann Killen Rosenberg's appealing 1983 mosaic, *City Carpet,* which commemorates the oldest public school in the US. Erected near this site in 1635, the **Boston Public Latin School** gave School Street its name and contributed influential alumni to American history books, including Franklin, John Hancock, **Charles Bulfinch,** Charles Francis Adams, and Ralph Waldo Emerson. The school is now located near the Fenway. Rosenberg also created the mosaic located on the wall side of the *Green Line's* outbound platform in **Park Street Station,** offering a delightful pictorial account of Boston's first subway. ♦ 45 School St (between Tremont St and City Hall Ave)

Within Old City Hall:

Maison Robert ★★★$$$$ The colorful political wheelings and dealings of **Old City Hall** belong to the past. But deals are still made here, love affairs launched, marriages proposed, and other momentous occasions celebrated. For more than 20 years, this superb French restaurant has made a happy home in the old hall. Look for the vaulted brick ceilings and distinguished old doors—vestiges of the original interiors. Ann and Lucien Robert offer such fine classic dishes as lobster bisque, rabbit sausage, country pâté, Dover sole, rack of lamb, and wondrous *tarte tatin* (apple tart) and crème brûlée. (Lucien has been honored by the French government with the *Chevalier du Mérite* award for his contributions to French culture.) Wine- and champagne-tasting dinners (put your name on the mailing list) are held here. And on the first Friday of each month, there's "The French Table" prix-fixe dinner, beginning with an aperitif social hour. As many as 80 attend, native speakers and novices alike (reservations are required).

Upstairs is **Bonhomme Richard** ("Poor Richard," in honor of Benjamin Franklin and his famous almanac). These beautiful formal dining rooms with butternut woodwork overlooking the **King's Chapel Burying Ground** are used for formal affairs and catered functions. Downstairs is the less fancy, very inviting **Ben's Cafe** (★★★$$$). It, too, was named for Franklin, and serves somewhat lighter and less expensive dishes. When spring comes, cafe tables and umbrellas appear on the lovely outdoor terrace, and the garden blooms again, signaling the return of a delightful spot.

The Roberts's daughter Andrée skillfully undertakes the duties of chef for all three restaurants. The third Friday of every month, a guest chef helps Andrée prepare a Scandinavian dinner with special dishes from countries like Finland and Norway. For private parties of 10 to 12 people, ask about dining in **the Vault,** the original City Hall vault. ♦ French ♦ M-F lunch (cafe); M-Sa dinner (cafe and upstairs); Su open for private parties. Jacket and tie required upstairs. Reservations recommended. Valet parking W-Sa. 45 School St (between Tremont St and City Hall Ave). 227.3370 ♿

Restaurants/Clubs: Red   Hotels: Blue

Shops/ 🌳 Outdoors: Green   Sights/Culture: Black

37 King's Chapel The original 1688 chapel stirred Bostonians' ire, since it was the city's first place of worship for Anglicanism, the official Church of England that had driven Puritans from their homeland. The plain wooden structure was built at the behest of Sir Edmund Andros, the royal governor who took the reins when the Massachusetts Bay Colony charter was revoked—just one early link in the long chain of events leading to the Revolution. To avoid interrupting services, the substantial 1754 Georgian chapel of Quincy granite standing today (a National Historic Landmark) was actually erected *around* the original building, which was then dismantled and heaved out the windows of its replacement. If the chapel seems squat, it's because the elaborate stone steeple architect **Peter Harrison** envisioned atop its square tower was never built; funds ran out. But in one splendid finishing touch, the facade was embellished with a portico supported by Ionic columns.

The Georgian interior has weathered the centuries well. Its raised pulpit is the oldest still in use in America on the same site. The pew dedicated to early royal governors' use later accommodated George Washington on his Boston visits, and other American worthies. Slaves sat in the rear gallery on the cemetery side, and condemned prisoners sat to the right of the entrance for a last sermon before being hanged on the **Common.** After the Revolution, once the British and Loyalists had evacuated Boston, the chapel was converted around 1789 into the first American Unitarian church. Some of the rich presents given to the earlier chapel by William and Mary of Britain are still in use, but most are now displayed at the **Boston Athenaeum.**

One of the church's other treasures is Paul Revere's largest bell, which he called "the sweetest bell we ever made." Come hear the resonant Charles Fisk organ, a replica of the church's 1756 original; every Tuesday there are free musical recitals, every Wednesday an organ prelude before the worship service. On Thursday there are free poetry readings in "the King's English." No tours are offered, but guides are on hand to answer questions during the summer months. ♦ Tu-Sa May-Oct until 4PM, Nov-Apr until 2PM. 58 Tremont St (at School St). 523.1749 ♿

Adjacent to King's Chapel:

King's Chapel Burying Ground Boston's earliest town cemetery's first resident was Isaac Johnson, who owned the land and was buried here in his garden in 1630. So many Boston settlers so quickly followed suit that some wag noted, "Brother Johnson's garden is getting to be a poor place for vegetables." A pleasant neighbor today, the church next door was erected on land seized from the burying ground. Burials continued until 1796,

although a gravedigger complained in 1739 that this and two other local graveyards "were so fulled with dead bodies that they were obliged oft times to bury them four deep."

As in other Boston cemeteries, grave markers were moved about to accommodate newcomers, an unsettling practice that caused Oliver Wendell Holmes to complain: "The upright stones have been shuffled about like chessmen and nothing short of the Day of Judgment will tell whose dust lies beneath. . . . Shame! Shame! Shame!" The burying ground's inhabitants include governors John Winthrop and John Endicott. On the chapel side, look for the 1704 gravestone of Elizabeth Pain, who supposedly bore a minister's child and probably was Nathaniel Hawthorne's model for Hester Prynne in *The Scarlet Letter.* Also buried here is Sons of Liberty courier William Dawes, who rode through the night just as bravely as Paul Revere, but didn't have the posthumous good fortune to be lionized in a Longfellow poem. And for a sample of the Puritans' pessimistic stance on the snuffing of life's candle, look for Joseph Tapping's marker. Stone rubbings are not allowed. ♦ M-Sa ♿

38 Omni Parker House $$$ Boston's genteel dowager hotel proclaims itself "the choice of legends since 1854," and it's true: US presidents and celebrities of every stripe, from Joan Crawford to Hopalong Cassidy, have made themselves at home here. The oldest continuously operating hotel in America (it has been lovingly restored and is once again luxurious, with the centerpiece lobby clad in original oak woodwork and carved gilt moldings), it represents the success story of Maine native Harvey D. Parker, who came to Boston with less than a dollar and became its leading hotelier. Rebuilt numerous times, the current structure dates to 1927 and attracts mainly business-oriented clientele. There are 541 rooms on 14 floors including rooms for people with disabilities and floors for nonsmokers. The concierge in attendance in the lobby is supplemented by a computerized concierge system. Paid valet parking is available.

Starting around 1855, the famous erudite Saturday Club met here on the last Saturday of every month, its circle including American literary and intellectual luminaries such as Nathaniel Hawthorne, John Whittier, Ralph

Waldo Emerson, and Henry Wadsworth Longfellow; a spin-off group founded the *Atlantic Monthly* in 1859. During one long Boston visit, the high-spirited, sociable Charles Dickens stayed at the hotel and joined the club's congenial gatherings, often fixing gin punch for his pals. The sitting-room mirror before which Dickens practiced his famous Boston readings now hangs on the mezzanine. On a more somber note, just 10 days before assassinating Abraham Lincoln, actor John Wilkes Booth stayed here while visiting his brother Edwin, also an actor, who was performing nearby. John spent some time practicing at a nearby shooting gallery. It was from the hotel's Press Room that JFK announced his candidacy for US president.

Parker's Bar is known for its classic martini; try one with hors d'oeuvres, which are complimentary from 5PM to 7PM. By the way, the famous secret recipe for the soft "Parker House roll" was first created here (they bake more than a thousand of the fragrant rolls each day), as was the tasty, but very unpielike, Boston cream pie. Both are available in the restaurants and to take out. ♦ 60 School St (at Tremont St). 227.8600, 800/843.6664; fax 227.2120

Within Omni Parker House:

Parker's Restaurant ★★$$$ With vaulted ceilings and high, wing-backed chairs, the restaurant is tranquil, roomy, and timeless. The good, reliable American cuisine—accompanied by those famous rolls—is undeservedly overlooked in Boston's frenetic dining scene. A guitarist strums during the award-winning Sunday brunch, and piano music drifts in from the bar the rest of the week. ♦ American ♦ M-F breakfast and lunch; Th-Sa dinner. Reservations recommended. Jacket required at dinner, requested at lunch. Valet parking. 227.8600 ৬

The Last Hurrah! Bar and Grill ★$$ The place looks dated, but that's the point—the walls are plastered with political memorabilia nostalgically harking back to when **Old City Hall** down the street was in full swing. And speaking of swing, there's a swing brunch on Sunday. You can dine as well as drink here, but the food is nothing special. The bar is popular with the **State House** and **City Hall** sets. ♦ American ♦ M-Sa lunch and dinner; Su brunch and dinner. Reservations recommended. 227.8600

39 Boston Five Cents Savings Bank Adding on to a sedate Renaissance-style bank designed in 1926 by **Parker, Thomas & Rice**, architects **Kallmann and McKinnell** (who also designed the new **Boston City Hall**) created a dynamic building. The remarkable 1972 addition has no secrets: its five-story colonnade and enormous beams conduct their structural functions in plain view, and a glass wall exposes all that goes on inside the bank. Big as it is, the building gracefully adapts to a tricky site and has earned its place in one of Boston's most historic quarters. The little park out front offers breathing space from Washington Street crowds, as well as good views of the nearby **Globe Corner Bookstore** and the **Old South Meeting House**. ♦ 10 School St (at Washington St)

40 Old South Meeting House After the **Old North Church** in the North End, this is Boston's oldest church. Built in 1729 by **Joshua Blanchard**, the National Historic Landmark (pictured on page 85) is a traditional New England brick meeting house fronted by a solid square wooden tower that blossoms into a delicate spire. When nearby **Faneuil Hall**'s public meeting space grew too cramped, Bostonians congregated here for town meetings peppered with fiery debate to prepare for the coming Revolution and plan such events as the Boston Tea Party of 1773. That cold December night, which Boston loves to remember, more than 5,000 gathered within to rally against the hated tea tax. Three ships filled with tea to be taxed were anchored at Griffin's Wharf, and the royal governor refused Bostonians' demands that the tea be sent back to England. Samuel Adams gave the signal igniting the protest that turned Boston Harbor into a teapot. During the British occupation, Redcoats struck back at the patriots by using their revered meeting place for the riding school of General "Gentleman Johnny" Burgoyne's light cavalry, complete with an officers' bar. By the time the British had evacuated, the church was in a sorry state. The congregation finally moved back in, then decamped in 1875 to the **New Old South Church** in Copley Square. Among the early congregation members were Phillis Wheatley, a freed slave and one of the first published African-American poets; Elizabeth Vergoose, aka "Mother Goose"; and patriots James Otis, Samuel Adams, and William Dawes.

After escaping destruction by the Great Fire of 1872, the edifice was then nearly demolished in a plan to make room for commercial businesses. But Bostonians, including Julia Ward Howe and Ralph Waldo Emerson, contributed funds to purchase and restore the historic property, which has been maintained as a national monument and museum by the Old South Association ever since. Step inside and experience restful simplicity. Because the British stripped the interior in 1776, only the sounding board and corner stairway are original. The award-winning, permanent multimedia exhibition *In Prayer and Protest: Old South Meeting House Remembers,* includes walls that talk, tapes of Boston Tea Party debates, a scale model of colonial Boston, profiles of famous churchgoers, and artifacts. The museum shop sells cards and such souvenirs as penny whistles, quill pens, and soldiers' dice made from musket balls. "Middays at the Meeting House," an excellent series of monthly concerts and weekly lectures on American history and culture, runs October through April. Events are free with museum admission. In addition to hosting educational programs and performances, the church hosts public debates, forums, and announcements of candidacies for office. During July and August, re-creations of 18th-century Boston town meetings are staged every Saturday in Boston Five Cents Savings Plaza across the street, and bystanders are encouraged to participate. Outside on the corner is one of Boston's largest and prettiest flower stands. ♦ Admission. Daily. Tours for groups larger than 10 arranged with two weeks' notice. 310 Washington St (at Milk St). 482.6439 ♿

Old South Meeting House

41 Blazing Salads $ This cheap quick-eats place serves all sorts of salads—chicken, tuna, Greek, salad niçoise, crabmeat, and tabbouleh, to name a few—with lots of pita bread. Or try a tuna melt, chicken Oriental, or steak teriyaki. It's usually crowded here, but in the afternoons a piano player will rescue you from boredom and the efficient staff keeps traffic humming along. ♦ International/Takeout ♦ M-F breakfast, lunch, and early dinner; Sa breakfast and lunch. No credit cards accepted. 330 Washington St (between Milk and Franklin Sts). 338.9614 ♿

42 Bromfield Street This brief little street was once the location of Revolutionary hero Thomas Cushing's residence, where the Massachusetts delegates to the first Continental Congress assembled, among them Samuel and John Adams and Robert Treat Paine. Today it's one of Boston's more interesting, lively commercial streets, packed with small establishments specializing in cameras, antiques, collector's coins and stamps, jewelry, watches, and pens, not to mention pawnshops. Some great old buildings reside here, too, such as **Nos. 22** and **30** of 1848 and the **Wesleyan Association Building** at No. 36 of 1870, all made of granite. ♦ From Tremont to Washington Sts

43 Skylight Jewelers Edward Spencer, an old-fashioned artisan with a gift for modern design, has been a Bromfield Street fixture for more than two decades. His studio display cases suggest his range and feature fluid settings for organic shapes (freshwater pearls are a specialty, as are moonstones—carved into mysterious moon faces). He's happy to accommodate your own design suggestions. ♦ M-Sa. 52 Province St (at Bromfield St). 426.0521 ♿ (will assist)

43 Sherman's It's an unlikely spot for a department store, but once people find it, they come back often for last-minute gifts, travel items, and housewares. In addition to major appliances and office equipment, cameras, calculators, electronics, luggage, TVs, telephones, small appliances, cookware, and jewelry, miscellany for the manse are sold here. They also carry a number of items in overseas electrical currents, and arrange all shipping—including customs—to foreign destinations. ♦ M-Sa. 11 Bromfield St (between Tremont and Washington Sts). 482.9610

44 Province House Steps From Province Street, mount the weathered steps that once led to the gardens of this 17th-century house, the luxurious official residence of the royal governors of Massachusetts Bay. Renamed **Government House** after the Revolution, the mansion was inhabited until 1796. Here General Gage ordered the Redcoats to Lexington and Concord. Here, too, General

Howe ordered his men to flee after George Washington and his troops managed to fortify Dorchester Heights, aiming big guns at the British. Years later, Nathaniel Hawthorne wrote about the by then decaying tavern and inn in *Twice-Told Tales*. Nary stick nor stone remains of the mansion except these steps. ◆ Province St (at Bosworth St)

44 Cafe Marliave ★$$ Dressed up with bits of wrought iron and balconies, this restaurant has stood on its corner for so long—more than a century—that many Bostonians forget it exists. Then again, a cadre of loyalists keeps coming back. The Italian-American cooking is nothing to swoon over, but it's good and reasonably priced, with plenty of dishes to choose from. The same family has run the place since 1935. The cafe sits high above the street, at the top of the Province House steps; dine on the second floor by the windows and become part of the streetscape. ◆ Italian-American ◆ M lunch; Tu, Th-Sa lunch and dinner. 10 Bosworth St (in the alley off Province St). 423.6340

45 Bromfield Pen Shop Accustomed to cheapo, use-and-abuse disposable pens? Wander into this little shop, gaze upon gleaming rows of new and antique pens, and reconsider your choice of writing instrument. Imagine what that handsome handful of a lovingly restored Bakelite pen might do for your prose! In addition to such standard brands as Parker and Sheaffer, Mont Blanc, Lamy, Pelikan, Yard-O-Led of England, S.T. Dupont, Waterman, Omas of Italy, delicate glass pens, and plenty of ink varieties are in stock. Engraving is free. The best store of its kind in New England, a plethora of local politicians, and medical, literary, legal, and media types (including author Jimmy Breslin) choose their pens here. Longtime manager George Salustro is not only expert at reconditioning or repairing customers' trusty old pens, he's a charmer, too. And he won't shame you if you decide what you *really* need for now is the same never-fail inexpensive pen used by Boston traffic cops. The shop also stocks art supplies. If you have a nice old pen to sell, George might be interested. ◆ M-Sa. 39 Bromfield St (between Tremont and Washington Sts). 482.9053 &

45 J.J. Teaparty Quality Baseball Cards A city that's passionate about sports in general and baseball in particular is the perfect place for this business. The tiny storefront, often crowded with wheeling-and-dealing kids, is owned by Peter Leventhal, whose father runs the coin shop with the same name one door away.

Leventhal buys and sells mostly baseball cards, but also some for football, basketball, and hockey. He's got cards from the 1950s and 1960s, including past and future Hall of Famers. Unusual items crop up, like turn-of-the-century tobacco cards. Collectors can pick up the latest series by Score, Topps, Fleer, and others. ◆ M-Sa. 43 Bromfield St (between Tremont and Washington Sts). 482.5705 &

45 J.J. Teaparty Coin Numismatists take note: Owner Ed Leventhal has been buying and selling coins at Bromfield Street's premier coin shop since 1963. Both casual collectors and serious investors come by to drop some coins of their own for proof sets, mint sets, and bullion coins like the American Eagle and Canadian Maple Leaf. ◆ M-F, Sa until 2PM; closed July-August. No credit cards accepted. 51 Bromfield St (between Tremont and Washington Sts). 482.2398

46 Tremont Temple The fanciful Venetian stone facade of this structure, made of 15 delicate shades of terra-cotta, incongruously hides an office and church complex inside. It gets more and more curious with the added adornment of several elaborate balconies. The 1895 building, designed by **Clarence H. Blackall,** stands on the site of the famous **Tremont Theater,** where illustrious 19th-century thespians, performers, lecturers, and politicians—including Abe Lincoln—enthralled the public. ◆ 88 Tremont St (between School and Bromfield Sts). 523.7320

47 Bruegger's Bagel Bakery $ Ten varieties of excellent bagels—Boston's best—are baked throughout the day at this family business, and are never more than a few hours old. Bruegger's own factory also produces nine different cream cheeses to spread on top. If you want a more filling meal, try a sandwich-on-a-bagel accompanied by freshly made soup. Its decor is fast-food basic, but the restaurant is neat and clean, with plenty of seating. ◆ Bagels/Takeout ◆ Daily breakfast and lunch. No credit cards accepted. 32 Bromfield St (between Tremont and Washington Sts). 357.5577 & Also at: 636 Beacon St (between Brookline and Massachusetts Aves). 262.7939; 64 Broad St (between State and Franklin Sts). 261.7115; 83 Mt. Auburn St (between John F. Kennedy and Dunster Sts), Cambridge. 661.4664

48 Jewelers Building Though stripped of its frilly original copper trim, this Beaux Arts–inspired early "skyscraper" designed by

Winslow and Wetherell in 1898 still serves the function it was designed for: housing nearly 100 jewelry dealers, most of whom sell retail as well as wholesale. In the lobby, you can't miss a crude but informative bronze bas-relief depicting the history of diamond mining and cutting. ◆ M-Sa. 379 Washington St (between Winter and Bromfield Sts) &

48 Barnes & Noble Discount Bookstore
This big general bookstore specializes in reduced-price best-sellers and discounted paperbacks and hardbacks, plus publishers' overstocks. It also sells children's books, magazines, board games, cards, and local maps, and classical and jazz records, tapes, and CDs. ◆ Daily. 395 Washington St (between Winter and Bromfield Sts). 426.5502 & Also at: 603 Boylston St (between Clarendon and Dartmouth Sts), Back Bay. 236.1308

Boston by the Book

To learn more about the history, residents, architecture, and life in general in this popular East Coast city, here are a few pages worth flipping through before you tour the town.

About Boston: Sight, Sound, Flavor and Inflection by David McCord (1973; Little Brown)

The Bell Jar by Sylvia Plath (1991; Bantam)

Blue Laws, Brahmins and Breakdown Lanes: An Alphabetic Guide to Boston and Bostonians by Karen Cord Taylor (1989; Globe Pequot)

Boston: A Topographical History by Walter Muir Whitehill (1968; Belknap Press)

The Bostonians by Henry James (1992; Knopf)

The City Observed: Boston by Donlyn Lyndon (1982; Random House)

Cityscapes of Boston: An American City Through Time by Robert Campbell and Peter Vanderwarker (1992; Houghton Mifflin)

Frederick Law Olmsted and the Boston Park System by Cynthia Zaitzevsky (1982; Harvard University Press)

Imagining Boston by Shaun O'Connell (1992; Beacon Press)

Lost Boston by Jane Holtz Kay (1982; Houghton Mifflin)

Make Way for Ducklings by Robert McCloskey (1993; Puffin Books)

The Proper Bostonians by Cleveland Amory (1984; Parnassus Imprints)

Saturnalia by Paul Fleischman (1992; HarperCollins)

Uncommon Boston by Susan Berk with Jill Bloom (1990; Addisson-Wesley)

What They Never Told You About Boston by Walt Kelley (1993; Down East Books)

Restaurants/Clubs: Red   **Hotels:** Blue
Shops/ 🌳 Outdoors: Green   **Sights/Culture:** Black

48 The Food Emporium $ Inside the otherwise undistinguished **Corner Mall** is a food court teaming with international cuisine. Among the 13 fast-food stands are giants such as **McDonald's** and **Sbarro** and tiny local favorites like **Vouros Pastry,** featuring fresh Greek specialties: moussaka, gyros, and spinach pie. Other offerings range from Mexican to Japanese. This bustling arena is a standby for local office workers, and a great place to pick up a multicultural picnic to enjoy on the **Boston Common.** ◆ International/Takeout ◆ M-Sa breakfast, lunch, and dinner until 6:30PM; Su lunch and dinner until 6PM. 425 Washington St (between Winter and Bromfield Sts). &

49 Filene's One of 33 stores in New England and New York, this full-service department store sells formal, casual, and career fashions (designer and major brand labels) and accessories for men, women, children, and the home. The **Gift Gallery** stocks fine crystal, sterling, porcelain, and other specialty merchandise. Founder William Filene opened his first retail business in 1851. The present building was designed by **Daniel Burnham & Company** in 1912. It was the first—and probably only—department store to have a "zoo" on its roof, with a baby elephant flown in from Bangkok, plus lions, monkeys, and other wild animals; sixty thousand children visited the zoo before it was demolished by the same hurricane that toppled **Old North Church**'s steeple in 1954. The distinguished Chicago-style building boasts a grand corner clock. ◆ Daily. 426 Washington St (at Summer St). 357.2100

Downstairs in Filene's:

FILENE'S BASEMENT

Filene's Basement Far surpassing the fame of its parent store (the companies are now separately owned), America's first off-price store opened in 1908. There are now 40 replicas in nine states. You can enter the unbeatable original's two shopping levels from **Filene**'s proper, or underground from the **Downtown Crossing** subway station (on the *Red* and *Orange Lines*). Determined do-or-die shoppers regularly make it their mission to snag the best buys here. Many a quickie course has been offered locally on how to come away flushed with success and laden with uncostly treasures from the legendary bargain emporium. The simple formula: perseverance, skill, and luck. Every day, trailers replenish the vast supply of overstocks, clearances, samples, and irregulars sold at 20 to 60 percent less than in fine department stores. The inventory includes designer-label and bargain clothing and accessories for men, women, and children, and housewares of all kinds. Retail stock is regularly featured from such prestigious stores as **Saks, Brooks Brothers, Bergdorf Goodman,** and **Neiman Marcus.** Strike it lucky and you might come away with a steal of a wedding dress, a winter coat, business suit, evening attire, luggage, lingerie, diamond ring, goose-down comforter, or fine linen. On the lower level, there's also a designer boutique for women.

The famous automatic markdown system works this way: After 14 selling days on the floor, merchandise is reduced 25 percent; after 21 days, 50 percent; after 28 days, 75 percent. After 35 days, whatever is unsold goes to charity. If you find something after the 35 days, go to the "charity desk" and write a check directly to one of the organizations listed on the charity list. Crowds gather on the legendary "Big Sale" days, when doors open early. Try to flip through a local Sunday paper, since many sales begin Monday. If you watch, you'll see how veterans work the room; you'll also see neat piles and racks of clothing and goods reduced to colorful, chaotic heaps, and glassy-eyed, overstimulated novices escaping to the upper levels in defeat. A women's dressing room was added in 1991 after complaints of sexism (the men's department has long been thus equipped). However, true shopping mavens won't stand for the lines that form and instead take advantage of the liberal return policy (14 days, with receipt) for home tryouts. Many also still use the time-honored method of slipping stuff on in an out-of-the-way aisle. ♦ Daily. 542.2011 & (enter from Filene's, use the elevator)

50 Lauriat's Books Part of a chain throughout New England and New York, this store caters to the general public, selling mass-market hardcover and paperback books. ♦ Daily. 45 Franklin St (at Hawley St). 482.2850 & (rear entrance). Also at: Copley Place, 100 Huntington Ave (at Dartmouth St). 262.8858

51 The London Harness Company Rest assured you'll find only the finest in very proper gifts for travel, home, office, and personal use, tastefully arrayed amid the shop's gleaming old wooden fixtures. The oldest operating retailer in the country, the shop has done business in this general location since the 1700s. Benjamin Franklin was among the early shoppers, and traveled with trunks purchased here. Honor momentous occasions—weddings, graduations, christenings—or get yourself something indispensable that will last forever. Perhaps you'd like a wooden box with **Fenway Park** hand-painted on it, or an illuminated globe, or a chess set, or an umbrella that will stand up to Boston's gusty winds. Clocks, candlesticks, luggage, wallets and accessories, scarves, photo albums, jewelry boxes, briefcases, bookends, desk sets, old prints and maps, and more—all the

appurtenances for a civilized existence. ♦ M-Sa. 60 Franklin St (between Hawley and Arch Sts). 542.9234 & (through rear entrance)

52 One Winthrop Square Ralph Waldo Emerson's nephew, **William Ralph Emerson,** is responsible for several vigorously unconventional Boston structures, including the **House of Odd Windows** (see page 20) on Beacon Hill and the **Boston Art Club** in Back Bay. In this collaborative effort carried out with **Carl Fehmer** in 1873, **William Emerson**'s influence dominates in the eccentric mixing of architectural motifs. Originally a dry-goods emporium and later headquarters for the *Boston Record-American* newspaper, the building has since been adapted to offices. Out front, where trucks once loaded up with newspapers, is an attractive park with Henry Hudson Kitson's bronze of *Robert Burns* briskly striding along, walking stick in hand and collie at his side. ♦ Between Devonshire and Otis Sts

Off Winthrop Square:

Winthrop Lane Opening onto the right-hand side of the square (if you're facing **One Winthrop**), this short-and-sweet brick lane would be unremarkable except for the florist and **Boston Coffee Exchange** shops at one end, and an imaginative work of public art called *Boston Bricks: A Celebration of Boston's Past and Present,* created by Kate Burke and Gregg Lefevre in 1985. The artists have inset dozens of bronze brick reliefs amid the lane's bricks from start to finish. Each relief tells a significant, interesting, or entertaining piece of Boston's story. Have fun trying to figure out what's what. Some images and references are quite familiar: the **Custom House Tower, Boston Common**'s cows, the **Boston Pops,** the city's ethnic groups, the Underground Railroad, the **Boston Marathon,** the **Red Sox,** whale watching, rowers on the Charles River, swans in the **Public Garden,** and an amusing representation of the notorious Boston driver. Others may keep you puzzling a while. Collectively, the clever bricks present a good likeness of the city. ♦ Enter from Devonshire St

53 Champlain Chocolates Hard to find outside their native Vermont, these treats are surpassingly tasty. Offerings range from truffles and Turkish delight to edible gift packs such as a chocolate heart stuffed with nonpareils. There's also a small ice-cream bar on the premises. Be sure to stroll the building lobby, too. The building is a new **Kohn Pederson Fox** structure appended to the Deco-era **75 Federal** (get a look at the elevators); the result is a handsome hybrid. ♦ M-F. 101 Federal St (between Franklin and Matthews Sts). 951.4666 &

54 United Shoe Machinery Corporation Building Now renovated, placed on the National Register of Historic Places, and renamed "The Landmark," Boston's first Art Deco skyscraper—built in 1929 by **Peter, Thomas, and Rice**—forms a handsome ziggurat crowned by a pyramid of tiles. At street level, look for the fine cast-metal storefronts set into limestone. Rude new buildings shove against this proud bulwark, which recalls the era when shoes were big business in Boston. ♦ 140-156 Federal St (at High St)

55 Boston Airline Center This is a handy walk-in center—with no phone number— where you can make on-the-spot reservations or pick up tickets for various airlines, including **American, Continental, Delta, Northwest, United, TWA,** and **USAir.** ♦ M-F. 155 Federal St (at High St) &

Schroeder's

56 Schroeder's ★$$$ Despite its relative youth (it opened in 1977), this restaurant has the look of old money—with a client list and menu to match. All the standbys are here— from vichyssoise and escargots to lobster thermidor and chateaubriand—plus a quartet of signature schnitzels *à la maison*. Although the decor leans more toward a ladies' club than a gentlemen's, this dining spot clearly aspires to **Locke-Ober**'s (see page 90) prestige, and judging from the pleased looks on the well-fed, prosperous faces, it's succeeding quite well. ♦ Continental ♦ M-F lunch; Tu-Sa dinner. 8 High St (between Summer and Federal Sts). 426.1234 &

57 Church Green Building This fine addition to the city's stock of 19th-century granite mercantile buildings is named for Church Green, the triangular intersection of Summer, Lincoln, High, and Bedford Streets, which in turn was named for the lovely church designed by **Charles Bulfinch** that once stood here (just another example of how history haunts many Boston place names). It was built circa 1873 by an unknown architect, although it is widely attributed to **Jonathan Preston.** Behind this structure rises red-roofed **99 Summer Street,** a 1987 interloper by **Goody, Clancy & Associates** that tries mightily to fit in. Across the way is **125 Summer Street,** a 1990 building by **Kohn Pederson Fox,** lurking behind an eclectic row of commercial facades now belonging to **No. 125.** A swath of old streetscape has been nicely preserved, but the huge modern tower bursting from its midst is a little disconcerting in contrast. ♦ 105-113 Summer St (at Bedford St)

The first regularly issued American newspaper, The *Boston News-Letter,* was published in 1704.

58 Bedford Building Red granite, white Vermont marble, and terra-cotta blend well on the Ruskinian Gothic–style facade of this 1876 **Cummings & Sears** creation, renovated in 1983 by the **Bay Bedford Company,** and placed on the National Register of Historic Places. The proud building lost its original clock, but its new stained-glass timepiece (created by Cambridge artisan Lynn Hovey) is particularly striking at night. ♦ 89-103 Bedford St (at Lincoln St)

59 Proctor Building On sunny days, it's bathed in light, the perch for many pigeons. On any day, the small Spanish Renaissance-style building, built in 1897 by **Winslow, Wetherell, and Bigelow,** is an orchestra of ornament crowned by a tiaralike cornice. Shells, birds, flowers, garlands, cherubs, urns, and more parade across the curving cream-colored facade. ♦ 100-106 Bedford St (at Kingston St)

60 Slesinger's Fabric Store When the do-it-yourself urge strikes, dust off the sewing machine and come to Jack Laven's fabric emporium for bridal, drapery, upholstery, sewing, and craft projects. Search among discontinued decorator fabrics and leftover lots of woolens, cotton, challis, silk, and more. Notions are a steal here. Laven also sells muslin and canvas to artists. Lycra spandex is popular these days, he says, and the shop is especially busy around Halloween. His father-in-law, a woolen jobber, began the business; Jack himself started out in Boston's garment district more than four decades ago, at age 23. He's usually on the job about 7AM, and often lets early-bird shoppers in. ♦ M-Sa. 30 Chauncy St (between Summer and Bedford Sts). 542.1805 &

Dakota's

61 Dakota's ★★$$$ Hailing from Dallas, this clubby-looking dining spot does big business in Boston, attracting the briefcase crowd at lunchtime and the *Playbill* crowd in the evening. The menu's focus is on American grill with a southern accent. Many dishes are good and colorfully presented: try the calamari, venison-sausage quesadillas, onion rings, gulf seafood chowder, tortilla soup, roast chicken, or lamb chops. Desserts are intensely rich, and the freshly made breads pleasantly fragrant. Sit in the elevated bar area and look over the fast-paced dining room, spiffed up with marble, ceiling fans, Roman shades, and club chairs.

The restaurant inhabits the second level of a 21-story office tower called **101 Arch,** which preserved under glass a section of the facade of **34 Summer Street** (an 1873 commercial palace) as a decorative piece in the lobby. And, if you're arriving by **T**, look for a vintage wooden escalator—more than 80 years old!—on the outbound Chauncy Street side of the *Red Line*'s **Downtown Crossing** stop. The grooved slats are so slanted, it's a challenge to ascend. ◆ American ◆ M-F lunch and dinner; Sa dinner. Reservations recommended. Complimentary valet parking after 5:30PM on Summer St side. 101 Arch St (entrance on Summer St). 737.1777 &

61 Society of Arts and Crafts at 101 Arch
A satellite of the nonprofit crafts organization headquartered at 175 Newbury Street in Back Bay (266.1810), this educational outreach gallery on the second level of **101 Arch** is the first step toward establishing **The Craft Museum of Boston.** (The hope is that the museum's opening will coincide with the prestigious society's centennial in 1997.) The 1,200-square-foot gallery showcases contemporary works-for-sale in a variety of media by society member artists, plus works on loan from museums and private collections, and rotating exhibitions of crafts by distinguished and emerging artists. In addition to bringing crafts to a part of town that can always use a little color and creativity, the gallery is a great place to find exceptional, interesting objects like jewelry, glass, ceramics, and small furniture. ◆ M-F. 101 Arch St (at Summer St). 345.0033 &

62 Jordan Marsh A stiff competitor to **Filene's** across the way (via a pedestrian mall that's the site of many a summertime concert or impromptu dance performance), this department store is upscale and comprehensive, part of a long-established northeast chain. You'll find the whole kit and kaboodle here: clothing for men, women, and children, jewelry, shoes, cosmetics, housewares, home furnishings, etc. Don't leave without trying the bakery's blueberry muffins. The slogan, "A tradition since 1851," refers to the store's beginning as a small, high-quality dry-goods establishment. Founded in Boston by Eben Dyer Jordan and partner Benjamin L. Marsh, it, too, has a discount basement store, but it's not in the same big-bargain league as the famous **Filene's Basement.** ◆ Daily. 450 Washington St (at Summer St). 357.3000 &

Restaurants/Clubs: Red	**Hotels:** Blue
Shops/ 🌳 Outdoors: Green	**Sights/Culture:** Black

63 Locke-Ober ★★★$$$ The winds of change may howl through Boston, but this bastion of Brahmin traditions mutes them to a whisper. After trying his hand at numerous occupations, including taxidermy and barbering, Louis Ober, an Alsatian, opened **Ober's Restaurant Parisien** in 1870 in this tiny residential alley. In 1892 Frank Locke opened a wine bar next door. Ober's successors combined the two restaurants and their founders' names, an ingenious partnership that has flourished to this day. For nearly a hundred years, the **Men's Cafe** downstairs was reserved for men; escorted women were admitted only on New Year's Eve and on the night of the **Harvard-Yale** game. (Incidentally, if **Harvard** lost, the nude painting of *Yvonne* in the first-floor barroom was draped in black.) But one fateful day in 1974, modern times came knocking, and this hallowed enclave reluctantly began admitting women. Both sexes now enjoy its Victorian splendor, tried-and-true rich Yankee-European cuisine, and perfectly discreet—if not exactly friendly—black-tie, old-world service. Who knows—you may share the dining room with political heavies like the Kennedy family, and those ubiquitous **Harvard** students who come from across the Charles River to toast their graduations.

The famous downstairs is all dark-wood splendor, the hand-carved bar agleam with German silver, but the revamped and gilded upstairs is nice also. Private dining chambers are available for a fee. You'll see plenty of loyalists, mostly male, sitting in their customary places and dining on such delicious old favorites as oysters, lobster Savannah, steak tartare, filet mignon, Dover sole, roast-beef hash, rack of lamb, calf's liver, Indian pudding, and baked Alaska. Follow their example and keep to the time-tested selections. After solicitously notifying the regular clientele well in advance that more—gasp!—change was in the works, healthful new dishes were introduced to the ancient menu. The cafe's lock-shaped sign, by the way, was inspired by one that adorned Locke's original establishment. Women are discouraged from wearing slacks here—another barrier to breach? ◆ Continental ◆ M-F lunch and dinner; Sa-Su dinner (hours vary in July and August). Jacket and tie required. Reservations recommended. Valet parking after 6PM. 3-4 Winter Pl (at Winter St). 542.1340

64 Orpheum Theatre Originally called the **Music Hall,** this worldly theater, built in 1852 by **Snell and Gregorson,** has seen a thing or two. It housed the fledgling **New England Conservatory** and witnessed the **Boston Symphony Orchestra**'s debut concert in 1881. The **Handel and Haydn Society** performed here for years. Tchaikovsky's first piano concerto had its world premiere, Ralph Waldo Emerson and Booker T. Washington lectured, and Oscar Wilde promoted a Gilbert and Sullivan operetta here. Vaudeville shows took a turn, too. In the early 20th century the theater was extensively altered, becoming Boston's first cinema, then later reverted back to a performance space. Today the theater mostly books rock concerts. ♦ No credit cards accepted at box office. Hamilton Pl (enter from Tremont St, between Bromfield and Winter Sts). Recorded information 482.0650; Ticketmaster 931.2000 &

65 Fanny Farmer A Boston classic, this shop has been selling chocolates, fudge, and other candy, ice cream, and nuts on this site for more than 50 years. It is part of the huge national chain named for Fanny Merritt Farmer, Boston's legendary cookbook author. Among other innovations, Fanny introduced the level measurement system that revolutionized food preparation. The company also owns all rights to Fanny's immensely popular *The Boston Cooking School Cookbook,* which can be purchased here. ♦ Daily. 130 Tremont St (at Winter St). 542.8677 & Also at: 288 Washington St (between Water and Milk Sts). 542.7045; 3 Center Plaza (between Congress and Cambridge Sts). 723.6201

66 Cathedral Church of St. Paul Most of Boston's old buildings mingle comfortably enough with their modern neighbors, but this dignified edifice looks uncomfortable sandwiched between two towering commercial structures—as if wondering what happened to the spacious rural town of its day (the 1820s). Once surrounded by handsome homes, the Episcopalian cathedral, on the National Register of Historic Places, is now situated in Boston's workaday district. The church is a simple temple of gray granite, Boston's first example of Greek Revival architecture. The massive sandstone Ionic columns supporting its porch add conviction to a stretch of street that can use it. Architect **Alexander Parris,** the avid practitioner of the Greek Revival style, also designed **Quincy Market.** If the temple's tympanum looks strangely blank, that's because the bas-relief figures intended for it were never carved— another example of a Boston building where

ambitious aspirations exceeded funds. Visit the starkly impressive interior, which was revised somewhat by architect **Ralph Adams Cram** in the 1920s. ♦ M-F noon service. 138 Tremont St (between Temple Pl and Winter St). 482.5800 & (enter through the side entrance)

67 Santacross Distinctive Shoe Service In business since 1917, this shop will heal your footwear woes. Walk-in repairs, shoe shines, reheeling, and handbag repairs done on the premises. And orthopedic shoes are a specialty here. ♦ M-Sa. 16 Temple Pl (between Tremont and Washington Sts). 426.6978 &

68 Stoddard's Open since 1800, the country's oldest cutlery shop sells plenty of other invaluable items, too: row upon row of nail nippers—who'd ever think so many kinds existed?—pocket knives, corkscrews, clocks, manicure sets, mirrors, magnifiers, binoculars, brushes, shaving brushes, scissors, lobster shears, fishing rods and lures, and almost anything else that could possibly come in handy. A great source for practical presents, this place is also one of only a handful remaining where cutlery is sharpened by hand—the only way to give blades their proper edge. An expert grinder works upstairs, giving scissors and such a new lease on life. ♦ M-Sa. 50 Temple Pl (between Tremont and Washington Sts). 426.4187 & Also at: Copley Place Shopping Center, 100 Huntington Ave (at Dartmouth St). 536.8688

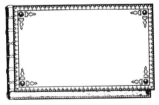

69 Brattle Book Shop Both foreign and domestic bibliophiles find their way to this humble-looking establishment. Not only is it one of America's few surviving urban-based bookshops of its kind, it's also the successor to the country's oldest operating antiquarian bookshop (founded in 1825). For a good part of this century, this literary establishment was run by the late George Gloss, a former fruit peddler. Gloss once exchanged a bunch of grapes for a paperback Dickens novel, and truly earned the nickname "the Pied Piper of book lovers." At one time, he drove a covered wagon through the city, tossing free books to passersby. His son Ken now runs the place, having worked here since age five.

The three-level shop holds every sort of used and rare book imaginable, with fine selections on Boston and New England, and a wealth of autographs and photo albums. The resilient store has risen from the ashes of two big fires and relocated numerous times. Many a treasure has passed through these portals, including a well-read copy of *The Great Gatsby,* given by F. Scott Fitzgerald to T.S. Eliot, which contained Fitzgerald's misspelled inscription and Eliot's annotations. Be sure to peruse the outdoor racks—under the watchful eyes of 18 influential authors (from Leo Tolstoy to Gish Jen) painted by South End artists Jeffrey Hull and Sarah Hutt. Valuable volumes are appraised here, often for free, and the helpful staff are expert book sleuths. ♦ M-Sa. 9 West St (between Tremont and Washington Sts) 542.0210, 800/447.9595 ♿

69 15 West Street This three-story town house, described as "Mrs. Peabody's caravansary" by Nathaniel Hawthorne, was home to the Peabody family from 1840 to 1854. In the rear parlor, Hawthorne married his beloved Sophia, the Peabody's youngest daughter, and Mary Peabody wed Horace Mann, the founder of American public education. In the front parlor, headstrong and brilliant Elizabeth Peabody opened Boston's first bookstore selling foreign works. The eldest daughter, Elizabeth was a fervent abolitionist, a pioneer for kindergartens in America, and the model for the formidable Miss Birdseye in Henry James's novel *The Bostonians.* Here, with Ralph Waldo Emerson, Elizabeth published *The Dial,* the quarterly journal of the Transcendentalists. And each Wednesday local ladies came to hear journalist Margaret Fuller's "Conversations"—landmark lectures on the history of American feminism. These days, the town house is given over to the **West Street Grill.** ♦ Between Tremont and Washington Sts

Within 15 West Street:

West Street Grill ★★$$ Especially popular with the late-night crowd, this spot offers three levels of dining and drinking. The downstairs bar seats about 15, but there are always plenty of standees here and at the smaller upstairs bar. For lunch, the grilled chicken salad sandwich served over wild greens with warm goat cheese and rasberry vinaigrette is wonderful. If you arrive at dinnertime, don't pass up the berber-spiced swordfish sautéed in a lemon-basil sauce and served over couscous. The grill's customers are always satisfied and eager to return. ♦ American ♦ Daily lunch and dinner. 423.0300

70 Fajitas & 'Ritas ★$ Unabashedly fun, this ultraloose joint attracts a surprising number of buttoned-up types. Not content to scribble on the paper tablecloths (crayons are provided), the clientele have spread their doodles and graffiti across every surface; the whole place is a communal work of art in progress. When you fill out your own order forms for assorted fajitas and other Tex-Mex dishes, you can also check off a 'rita (that's margarita) or beer or wine, including sangria by the liter. ♦ Tex-Mex/Takeout ♦ Daily lunch and dinner. 25 West St (between Tremont and Washington Sts). 426.1222 ♿

71 Opera House Sadly dilapidated, the stage of this theater has been dark since 1991. Though this building and the **Paramount Theatre** next door have been marked for preservation by the National Registry of Historic Places, so far the funds to restore the 1928 theater—designed by Thomas Lamb—and the 1932 Art Deco **Paramount** (take note of Arthur Bowditch's marvelous sign) to their former splendor have not come through. The house was first named the **B.F. Keith Memorial Theatre** to honor the show-biz wizard who coined the term "vaudeville." Keith introduced the concept of continuous performances of high-quality variety acts suitable for family viewing, to contrast with the lowlife entertainment offered at Scollay Square's notorious Old Howard theater. He owned a chain of 400 such theaters, after which early movie "picture palaces" were modeled. More recently, this one was called the **Savoy Theatre.** Later it became the home to Sarah Caldwell's **Boston Opera Company.** The Spanish Baroque terra-cotta facade is best seen from Avenue de Lafayette across the way. The lobby and auditorium are the worse for wear, but their decadence is impressively dramatic, perfect for opera. It's easy to imagine what a thrill it was to come here during the theater's heyday. ♦ 539 Washington St (at Ave de Lafayette)

71 Metropolis Adjacent to the old **Opera House** is this three-story dance club. Its severe black facade and urbane lighting contrast starkly with the faded opulence of its ancient neighbor. The action is upstairs at **The Domain:** a dark, DJ'd disco that spins Top 40, R&B, and high-energy "techno" tunes. Although not quite the tony attraction it was when it opened in 1989, if you're game, it's as good a place as any to get down. ◆ Admission. Disco Th-Sa 10PM-2AM. Validated parking at Lafayette Pl. 533 Washington St (at Ave de Lafayette). 338.6999 ♿

swissôtel ✚

72 Swissôtel Boston $$$ Having recently undergone an $11 million makeover, the 500 rooms and suites on this hotel's 16 floors are far more sumptuous and contemporary in decor than the severely impersonal exterior implies. In fact, this hotel is one of the best-kept secrets in Boston, as many don't anticipate finding such stellar accommodations in this part of town. Guest services include a concierge, parking, a multilingual staff, same-day laundry and valet services, an indoor swimming pool and exercise equipment, and a sun terrace. There are rooms for people with disabilities plus two floors for nonsmokers. Swiss chocolates appear not only in guest rooms, but in a monstrous bowl at the registration desk.

Divided into four atriums, each with its own lounge, the **Executive Level** (encompassing 135 rooms) offers 24-hour Swiss Butler service. Other **Executive** perks include a complimentary continental breakfast, afternoon hors d'oeuvres, a fax machine, a private Board Room, and two-line phones in every room. The hotel was the anchor to the adjoining **Lafayette Place** shopping complex, which was built in the early 1980s and has since gone bust. At press time the space was attempting a revival. ◆ 1 Ave de Lafayette (between Washington and Chauncy Sts). 451.2600, 800/621.9200; fax 451.0054

Within the Swissôtel Boston:

Caffe Suisse ★$$ The setting's a bit bland, except for some contemporary artwork by Swiss emigré artists. The bill of fare is a mix of American and continental, with a few Swiss specialties (*rösti* potatoes and spaetzle dumplings) thrown in for color. The ambience livens up a bit on Sunday for the jazz brunch buffet. ◆ International ◆ M-Sa breakfast and lunch; Su brunch. 451.2600 ♿

73 Baker's Plays The oldest American play publishing company was established under the name of the Herbert Sweet Company on Washington Street in 1845. Relocated after the great Boston fire of 1872, it was handed down through several generations, and survives today under the genial custodianship of manager Jack Welch and two resident cats "who let us think we run the place." Boston's small but impassioned theater community counts on finding the latest scripts, trade papers, and casting news here. ◆ M-F. 100 Chauncy St (at Ave de Lafayette). 482.1280

Bests

Chris Pullman

Design Manager, WGBH Boston (Public Broadcasting)

The third Sunday of October is the Head-of-the-Charles regatta, an amazing spectacle of rowing (one boat leaves the starting line every 10 seconds from 9AM to 4:30PM) and schmoozing. It's *the* social event for the East Coast college crowd. Best places to watch are **Magazine Beach** (the launch site), **Weeks Bridge** near **Harvard,** and the sharp curve near the **Cambridge Boat Club.**

The most interesting food in **Cambridge** is at the **Harvest Restaurant.** Conceived by **Ben Thompson** (architect of **Faneuil Hall** and founder of **Design Research**), the place feels comfy and unpretentious, like it's been there forever, and serves imaginative seasonal concoctions. Great bread. Not cheap.

The **Isabella Stewart Gardner Museum** is a funky treasure trove of stuff (from Rembrandts to personal letters) collected by Gardner early in this century. The centerpiece is a magnificent three-story courtyard with seasonal plantings. In the middle of January, leaning out of the balcony into this space is a great refreshment. The little restaurant serves a nice lunch. It's minutes from the **Museum of Fine Arts.**

Try weiner schnitzel, pan-fried potatoes, and spinach at **Locke-Ober;** insist on a table downstairs.

Walk from the **Hatch Shell,** down the esplanade along the **Charles River** to Cambridge, and back the other side (or take the *Red Line* back from **Harvard Square**).

At **Harvard** visit the **Fogg Art Museum,** the **Houghton Library** (for rare books), and the **Carpenter Center for the Visual Arts** (by Corbusier). Then have lunch at **Bartley's Burger Cottage** on Mass Ave.

In Cambridge, start at the **Harvard Square T** stop and walk down **Brattle Street** through the shops and into the residential area (wonderful colonial and Richardsonian houses) as far as you have time for. Take a different route back.

Chinatown/ Theater District

This checkered neighborhood's story has had many acts, characters, triumphs, and tribulations over the years. Here, in a geographically awkward and angular fringe of the city, three principal dramatis personae converge— and sometimes collide: the **Theater District**, the **Combat Zone** (Boston's red-light district), and **Chinatown.**

Beginning in the 1920s, Boston was a favorite tryout city for Broadway-bound plays—a glittering, glamorous mecca when all the big stage names were in town. After cinema outstripped theater in popularity and the suburbs eclipsed the city, great playhouses such as the **Wilbur** and the **Majestic** deteriorated. As roofs leaked, walls crumbled, and paint and plaster peeled, the shadow of the wrecking ball loomed. But Boston's 1980s boom, also known as the "Massachusetts Miracle," rescued a number of theaters. The **Wilbur** is now repaired, the **Shubert** refurbished, the **Majestic** resuscitated, and the **Colonial** forges on. Other houses cling to life or remain dark, awaiting a savior. Today, Boston's rialto is clustered around **Tremont** and **Stuart Streets.**

The Combat Zone, a sleazy "adult-entertainment" district concentrated on lower **Washington Street,** took root in the 1960s and flourished during the 1970s as home to many X-rated movie houses and dozens of seamy strip joints, peep shows, and porn shops. Developers and neighborhood associations have almost succeeded in strangling the Zone—nearly 30 establishments have been closed down since 1986, reducing the size of the area from seven blocks to one. Shady sorts still hang out here, so it's unsafe at night, but the Zone's days are numbered—or so residents hope.

Chinatown's official entry point is a massive ceremonial gateway on **Beach Street,** but pedestrians approach this quarter from every which way. Bounded by **Kneeland,** Washington, and **Essex Streets** and the **Central Artery,** this four-block-long neighborhood is known for its exotic restaurants, close-knit family life, and colorful storefronts. Cramped it may be, but Chinatown is always full of activity, and exudes a festive ambience with its subtitled signs and banners and pagoda-topped phone booths. Popular events are Chinese

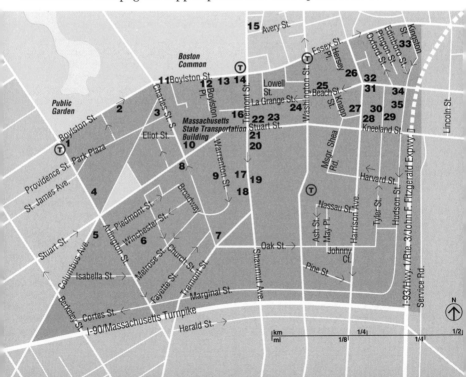

New Year and the August Moon Festival, when local martial-arts groups don dragon costumes and dance through the streets amid exploding firecrackers and crowds of celebrants. Jammed into these dense blocks are about 200 restaurants (many open as late as 4AM), bakeries, gift and curio shops, and markets selling live poultry, fresh fish, and vegetables. The remains of the textile and garment industry (Chinatown's economic mainstay before restaurants and grocery wholesalers took the lead) are located where **Harrison Avenue** intersects Kneeland Street. **Tyler Street** is the showiest thoroughfare, with some of the most flamboyant storefronts, while Beach Street harbors the workaday scene.

A community at a crossroads, Chinatown is struggling to preserve its ethnic character. The first Chinese came to Boston soon after the Revolution. Subsequent China trade brought workers to the seaport, but a permanent community wasn't established until 1875. With the liberalization of immigration laws in the mid-1960s, Chinatown ballooned, but then lost half its land to highway expansion, downtown encroachment, and the **New England Medical Center (NEMC).** Today, the population has swelled to more than 8,000, with Vietnamese, Laotians, and Cambodians enriching the ethnic composition. Bursting at the seams, troubled by refuse-strewn streets, and demoralized by the decaying of the Combat Zone and lack of affordable housing, Chinatown seemed destined to face a grim future. Recently there have been signs of change. The Neighborhood Council now acts as liaison to the mayor's office and reviews all plans for development; in fact, nothing happens in Chinatown anymore without the council's involvement.

A denouement to the neighborhood drama could be the proposed urban megadevelopment called the **Midtown Cultural District.** Not yet approved at press time, it would be a two-square-mile mixed-use community of office towers, department stores, hotels, restaurants, clubs, and cultural space that would encompass **Park Square**, the Theater District, the Combat Zone, and **Downtown Crossing** (the intersection of Washington Street and **Winter/Summer Streets**). This program would serve as the catalyst for restoring historic theaters, ensuring Chinatown's prosperity and **NEMC's** growth, and boosting downtown nightlife. And one unsavory character would be eliminated in the process—the troublemaking Zone.

But, whatever the story's outcome, this neighborhood will remain the source for great performances in the gorgeous old theaters, vibrant comedy club acts, authentic Chinese culture and cuisine, and sophisticated new restaurants perfect for a night on the town.

The subway stations most convenient to this neighborhood are the **New England Medical Center** and **Chinatown** stops (both on the Orange Line), and the **Arlington** and **Boylston** stops (Green Line). The **Park Street** stop (Red and Green Lines) is also within easy walking distance.

1 The Heritage on the Garden One of Boston's more accommodating architectural presences is this mixed-use complex of retail and commercial space and luxurious residential condos designed by **The Architects Collaborative** in 1988. A number of high-powered shops and restaurants are located on the premises—albeit with confusingly varied street addresses—including **Sonia Rykiel Boutique** (280 Boylston St, 426.2033); **Waterford**

Wedgwood (288 Boylston St, 482.8886); **Escada** (308 Boylston St, 437.1200); **Hermès** (22 Arlington St, 482.8707); and **Doubleday Book Shop** (99 Park Plaza, 482.8453). ♦ 300 Boylston St (at Arlington St) &

Within the Heritage on the Garden:

Biba ★★★★$$$ Boston's wild about the adventurous inspiration of Boston-born and-trained chef Lydia Shire, who rose to eminence through stints at several renowned local restaurants. After a hiatus in California, she returned and opened this dining spot filled with joie de vivre. A daring chef, Shire experiments with international cooking styles, and appetizers and entrées are

intermixed, so diners may choose any combination suiting their fancy. Marvelous flatbread arrives hot from the Indian tandoori oven in the corner. The menu changes daily, but surprises have included fried, boned quail with parsnip chips, calf's brains with crisp-fried capers, green-tea duck with ginger-and-scallion pancakes, maple- and rum-smoked salmon, wood-roasted chicken, and sour-cherry ice cream with chocolate cake and "something crunchy." Service is spotty, but always good-natured, and the restaurant gets pretty noisy, so don't plan on sotto voce confidences. New York architect **Adam Tihany** designed the restaurant, a quirky ensemble of styles. The second-floor dining room features an expansive view of the **Public Garden** lagoon. But if upstairs is booked, you can mix and match a delightful eccentric repast from the bar menu downstairs. The sultry ground-floor bar, decorated with a Robert Jessup mural depicting well-fed people, is where many stylish singles find each other.
♦ Continental ♦ Daily lunch and dinner. Reservations recommended for dining room. Valet parking, except Sunday daytime. 272 Boylston St (between Arlington St and Charles St S). 426.7878 &

The Spa

The Spa at the Heritage Six kinds of massage; facials; body wraps; manicures; any kind of pampering for your body, skin, or hair; or an aerobics class is available to the public—for a fee—at this ultrachic and expensive European-style spa/health club/salon. The workout facilities and the three-lane lap pool are limited to members or guests of member hotels. Plenty of special packages with the works are available, some including hotel accommodations and food. **Schwartz/Silver Architects** designed the pristine interior, collaborating with artist Stephen Knapp. The same owners operate the equally elite **Le Pli** in Cambridge. ♦ 28 Arlington St (between Boylston St and Park Plaza). Spa 426.6999, salon 482.2424

Arkansas Congressman Wilbur Mills, former chairman of the powerful House Ways and Means Committee, met his political downfall in the shape of stripper Fannie Fox, with whom he cavorted on stage at the racy Pilgrim Theatre in the Combat Zone in December 1974.

Restaurants/Clubs: Red   **Hotels:** Blue
Shops/ 🌳 Outdoors: Green   **Sights/Culture:** Black

2 Four Seasons Hotel $$$$ Half of the 288 rooms and the restaurants at this luxurious hostelry feature views of the lovely **Public Garden** across the way. You can also watch the world go by in the lobby. Among the celebrities who have stayed in the posh Presidential Suite are Bruce Springsteen, Glenda Jackson, Christopher Plummer, Luciano Pavarotti, and Mick Jagger. Maybe they like the friendly and solicitous staff or the hotel's concern for niceties. For those traveling with children, every crib comes with a teddy bear, kids get bedtime milk and cookies and kits with cameras or magic tricks. The concierge distributes duck and squirrel food for those voracious park denizens across the way, and the hotel will pack picnic baskets for guests on request. For joggers, running shoes are provided, along with maps outlining trails that start right outside the front door. The accommodations are on eight floors, with rooms for people with disabilities and for nonsmokers available. Amenities feature concierge services, around-the-clock room service, same-day laundry and 24-hour valet and pressing services, valet parking, and business services. The health spa has a lap pool, Jacuzzi, sauna, and on-call trainers.
♦ 200 Boylston St (between Arlington St and Charles St S). 338.4400, 800/332.3442 in the US, 800/268.6282 in Canada; fax 426.9207 &

Within the Four Seasons Hotel:

Aujourd'hui ★★★$$$$ An ultra-refined setting for an elegant meal, this restaurant is the most pleasant when light lingers in the **Public Garden** beyond (be sure to reserve a windowside table). Chef Jamey Mammano's acclaimed menu is complemented by a lengthy international wine list. Recent offerings included grilled North Atlantic salmon with couscous, watercress salad, and preserved lemon vinaigrette; poached Maine lobster with black-pepper linguine, served in a broth of shiitake mushrooms, corn, and broccoli; and roast tenderloin of veal, black-truffle polenta, pancetta, and sage. There are always special dishes on the menu—such as pepper-crusted loin of venison, served with gingered rhubarb and celery-root puree—that have reduced calories, sodium, and choles-terol. For a cozier party, reserve one of two private dining rooms. Local designers and shops are featured at lunchtime fashion shows every Wednesday (September through June). Theatergoers pressed for time may opt for the prix-fixe pre-theater menu. ♦ Conti-nental ♦ M-F breakfast, lunch, and dinner; Sa breakfast and dinner; Su brunch and dinner. Reservations recommended. Jacket and tie requested at dinner. Valet parking. 451.1392 &

The Bristol ★★$$ Pick one of the discretely positioned clusters of chairs and sofas for lunch, afternoon tea, cocktails, before- and after-theater supper, and dessert (there's a lush Viennese dessert table from 9PM to midnight on Friday and Saturday evenings). A children's menu is offered here, a rarity in Boston. Pianists provide classical music and soft jazz in the afternoon and evening. A fireplace warms the place during the cold winter months, and tea is served daily from 3PM to 4:30PM. ♦ Continental ♦ Daily. Reservations recommended for lunch. 338.4400 ＆

Adesso Co-owners Rick Grossman and Françoise Theise are retail pioneers, dedicated to discovering and introducing Americans to up-to-the-moment furniture and lighting from France, Italy, West Germany, Holland, and Austria (and some from the US, too). Called "new classics" by the owners, these smashing, versatile pieces are often architect-designed and may be available only to the trade in other cities. They'll ship anywhere in the world, and publish newsletters and catalogs. ♦ M-Sa; Th until 8PM. 451.2212 ＆

3 The Great Emancipator Across the street from the **Park Plaza** (see below), in a motley little green space, stands one statue Boston could do without. This 1879 hero-worshiping homage to Abraham Lincoln, copied from the Washington original and sponsored by legislator Moses Kimball, portrays the president anointing a kneeling former slave, with the inscription "A race set free/A country at peace/Lincoln rests from his labors." From today's vantage point, the work appears paternalistic and demeaning. ♦ Charles St S (between Columbus Ave and Park Plaza)

4 Boston Park Plaza Hotel & Towers $$$
Steps away from the theaters and one block from the **Public Garden,** this 1927 hotel has nearly 1,000 rooms, more than 80 of which are in the **Plaza Towers** atop the main hotel. Decor and room sizes vary considerably: At higher rates, the **Towers** offer more luxurious quarters, a concierge, continental breakfast, and other personalized services. Ask for a room overlooking the **Public Garden.** There's individual voice-mail for every room; a weight room; privileges at the nearby elegant **Spa at the Heritage,** including pool and sauna; 24-hour room service; floors for nonsmokers; and a pharmacy. You can check out and order breakfast via video. On the premises are major airline-ticket offices, a travel agency, and a ticket agency for sports, theater, and concert

events. Within or adjacent to the hotel are restaurants and lounges. **Swans Lobby Lounge,** where Liberace began his career, serves tea and pastries and offers a full bar, with piano music after 4PM. *Forever Plaid,* a popular "doo-wop" musical comedy, is performed Tuesday through Sunday in the **Terrace Room.** ♦ 64 Arlington St (between Stuart St and Park Plaza). 426.2000, 800/225.2008; fax 426.5545

Within Boston Park Plaza Hotel & Towers:

Legal Sea Foods ★★$$$ "If it's not fresh, it's not Legal." The Berkowitz family lives up to their slogan in their fleet of seafood restaurants. This one's the flagship. Observe the long and patient lines—it's hard to believe the empire began as a lowly fish-and-chips joint. Now an endless menu offers all the fruits of the sea, always superior and flapping-fresh. First, choose your fish, then decide on broiled, grilled, fried, stuffed, sautéed, steamed, pan-blackened, Cajun-style, even spicy Chinese recipes devised by visiting chefs from China's Shandong province. The fish chowder could double for wallpaper paste in consistency but wins hordes of fans—including US presidents—as do the smoked salmon and bluefish pâtés. And this is one place where it's always safe to eat raw clams and oysters—every batch is tested at an in-house laboratory. The extraordinary, extensive wine list lives up to the menu.

But be forewarned: This is not the spot for lingering conversation. There are no reservations, so you can easily cool your heels interminably while the loudspeaker incessantly barks out names. The dining rooms are both noisy and jammed, and the policy is to bring food when ready, not necessarily when your companions receive theirs. Still, superb seafood is worth some concession. When you require brain food yet can't endure a mob scene, the smaller cafe/take-out operation next door is the answer. The seating here is more snug, but the cafe offers almost the same menu plus full bar, and operates a little faster. And if the cafe is too full, get your dinner to go. ♦ Seafood ♦ Daily lunch and dinner. 35 Columbus Ave (near Park Plaza). Restaurant 426.4444, Cafe/Takeout 426.5566. ＆ Also at: Prudential Center, 800 Boylston St (at Gloucester St). 266.6800; Copley Place Shopping Center (between Huntington and Dartmouth Sts). 266.7775; 5 Cambridge Center (at Main and Sixth Sts), Cambridge. 864.3400

Legal Sea Foods Cash Market The gargantuan Berkowitz enterprise has yet another giant offshoot: this one-stop gourmet shop featuring a counter stocking at least a dozen kinds of fresh fish from the same supplier used by the restaurant. Pick up live lobster packed to travel, whatever fish you wish, the clan's own famous chowders, pâtés, cheeses, crackers, salads, soups, sauces, condiments, marinades, coffees and teas, chocolates, even the house cookbook. The liquor department carries 600 wines, cold beer, and a full liquor selection. All bases are covered. But don't expect any bargains. ♦ Daily. 15 Columbus Ave (at Park Plaza). 426.7777 &

Ben & Jerry's Ice Cream This franchise sells exclusively the populist entrepreneurs' delicious ice cream, shipped fresh from their Vermont factory. Chocolate Chip Cookie Dough, Coconut Milk Chocolate Almond, and Cappuccino Chocolate Chunk are the current favorites, with all flavors available in sundaes, shakes, cones, and ice-cream cakes, as well as between brownies and cookies. Coffee and muffins baked on the premises are sold in the morning until they run out. ♦ Daily. No credit cards accepted. 20 Park Plaza (between Charles St S and Arlington St). 426.0890 &

5 Park Plaza Castle The imposing granite "Castle," as the eye-catching landmark is universally known around Boston, was built in 1897 by **William G. Preston** as an armory for the First Corps of Cadets, a private Massachusetts military organization founded in 1741 and commanded at one time by John Hancock. The Victorian fortress, now on the National Register of Historic Places, was a social center for prominent Bostonians in the late 1800s, and its luxurious, clubby interior was the site for billiards, imbibing fine wine, and the popular **Cadet Theatricals.** The corps now operates a private military museum in Back Bay. The lofty hexagonal tower, turrets, crenellated walls, lancet windows, and drawbridge, create the illusion of a strong structure that's ready for medieval-style combat. But much calmer events transpire at this exhibition and convention center owned by the **Boston Park Plaza Hotel & Towers.** Bostonians flock to the annual "Crafts at the Castle" sale held in early December and sponsored by Family Services of Greater Boston. Next door is the **Back Bay Racquet Club**—built in 1886 as **Carter's Ink Factory**— which boasts an impressive terra-cotta and brick facade. ♦ 130 Columbus Ave (at Arlington St). For events information, call Boston Park Plaza Hotel & Towers' sales office 426.2000 & (use the Columbus Ave entrance)

6 Bay Village For the flavor of 19th-century Boston, take a 15-minute stroll along this insular nook on Piedmont, Church, Melrose, and Fayette Streets. Difficult to find by car and easy to miss on foot, the tight cluster of short streets bordered by diminutive brick houses was mostly laid out during the 1820s and 1830s. Many of the artisans, housewrights, and carpenters who worked on fashionable Beacon Hill's prestigious residences concurrently built their own small homes here. The neighborhood's residents once encompassed other colorful professions: sailmakers, paperhangers, blacksmiths, harness- and ropemakers, painters, salt merchants, musical instrument makers, and cabinetmakers. Edgar Allan Poe was born in a lodging house in the vicinity in 1809; his parents were actors in a stock company playing nearby. Because it's so close to the Theater District, Bay Village gradually acquired a bohemian flavor and spillover nightlife. Just off Fayette Street, look for brief Bay Street with its single house, a concluding punctuation mark. ♦ Bounded by Arlington and Church Sts, and Stuart and Fayette Sts

7 Beacon Hill Skate This is where you can rent or purchase roller blades, skates, skateboards, and safety equipment to whiz along the esplanade that borders the Charles River, or, in winter, ice skates to skim over the **Public Garden** lagoon while it's vacated by ducks and **Swan Boats** for the season. (Skates are available lagoonside, too, through this shop.) ♦ Daily. 135 Charles St S (between Warrenton and Tremont Sts). 482.7400

8 57 Park Plaza Hotel/Howard Johnson $$ Smack dab in the middle of this neighborhood is a hotel with 350 rooms on 24 floors, two restaurants and a bar, an indoor heated pool, a sauna, a sun deck, room service, and free on-premises parking with direct access to the hotel. Rooms designed for people with disabilities are also available. ♦ 200 Stuart St (at Charles St S). 482.1800, 800/468.3557; fax 451.2750 &

9 Nick's Entertainment Center A fixture on Boston's entertainment scene that has survived by changing with the times, this happening spot once had a cabaret/dinner theater, a comedy club, and a sports bar. Now, it is home to the popular **Nick's Comedy Stop,** a club featuring local and national comics, as well as the new addition—a 1970s-style disco, **Eight Tracks.** ♦ Admission. Box office: daily. Nick's Comedy Stop: nightly. Eight Tracks: Th-Su. No sneakers, ripped jeans, or caps at Eight Tracks. 100 Warrenton St (between Tremont and Stuart Sts). Nick's Comedy 482.0930, Eight Tracks 426.0300

9 Charles Playhouse The Theater District's oldest playhouse—built by **Asher Benjamin** in 1843, renovated by **Cambridge Seven** in 1966, and listed on the National Register of Historic Places—began life as a church and today is a rental facility for private productions, all managed separately. The show playing on **Stage I** changes sporadically, but on **Stage II,** *Shear Madness* has played for over 14 years, and is likely to go on as long as new visitors come to town. It has already made the *Guinness Book of World Records* for longest-running nonmusical play. The comedy-whodunit, set in a Boston beauty salon, often stars good local professional actors. An eccentric concert pianist who lives upstairs is bumped off, and everybody has a motive. Boston police officers enlist the audience to find the culprit, with the solution changing nightly and new improvisations, local color, and topical humor added continually. ♦ Box office daily; shows Tu-Su. Cash only at box office. 74-78 Warrenton St (between Tremont and Stuart Sts). Stage I 426.6912, Stage II 426.5225, Charge-Tix 542.8511

Within the Charles Playhouse:

The Comedy Connection Attracting the under-30 crowd, especially college students, this well-established stand-up comedy cabaret books headliner plays Wednesday through Sunday, with new or established talent launching new material on Monday and Tuesday. Full bar and bar food are served throughout shows. If you charge your tickets in advance, seats will be reserved for you; if you pay cash, you can reserve seats the day of the performance. ♦ Admission. Daily. Credit cards accepted in advance; cash only at door. 391.0022, Charge-Tix 542.8511 ♿

10 Massachusetts State Transportation Building The architectural firm of **Goody, Clancy & Associates** designed this enormous (it occupies an entire city block) state transportation office complex (pictured below), with the participation of local business, cultural, and neighborhood groups, to relate to the surrounding low-rise brick structures. The redbrick exterior, with asymmetrical cantilevers, is fairly self-effacing. The real excitement awaits within, where an atrium—with trendily exposed endoskeletal support beams—vaults above a pedestrian mall with shops and restaurants to draw that vitality inward. Noontime music concerts entertain the milling lunchtime throngs, and a small art gallery operated by the Artists Foundation adds an avant-garde frisson. ♦ Gallery Tu-Sa

afternoons. 10 Park Plaza (bounded by Stuart St, Charles St S, and Tremont St)

Within the Massachusetts State Transportation Building:

rocco's ★★★$$$
Dining at this theatrical restaurant is like joining in a perpetually improvised performance, always festive and fun. Painted murals, enormous arches, flamboyant draperies, and artful props give the place a fantastic stagestruck look perfect for this part of town. Kevin Schopfer created the decor, and Julia Roe Clay painted the rococo-inspired ceiling frescoes.

Owners Patrick and Jayne Bowe deserve an ovation for letting collective imaginations run wild—and the extensive use of fabric (which muffles intimate conversations) means you can talk as well as gawk. Dine cafe-style and less expensively on appetizers and wine, or indulge more extravagantly, like the lush, fleshy figures overhead. The Tuscan menu is supervised by chef Barbara Lynch, whose most popular dishes are roasted glazed chicken served with potatoes and carrots, and basil gnocchi accompanied by yellow tomatoes, garlic, and herbs. ♦ Northern Italian ♦ Daily lunch and dinner. Reservations recommended. 5 Charles St S (between Boylston and Stuart Sts). 723.6800 ♿

Joyce Chen ★$$ Run by the son of famous local chef Joyce Chen, this restaurant is both fancier and pricier than most other Chinese restaurants in the neighborhood. It isn't the place to seek exotic new tastes—the tiny, nondescript eateries are much better for that—but to enjoy reliable Mandarin and Szechuan dishes in comfort. Popular choices include General Gau's chicken, lobster with ginger and scallions, and Peking duck. On weekdays, there's a fixed-price luncheon buffet. ♦ Chinese/Takeout ♦ Daily lunch and dinner. Reservations recommended for five or more. Valet parking. 115 Stuart St (at Tremont St). 720.1331 ♿, 825.3688 (for deliveries). Also at: 390 Rindge Ave (at Alewife Pkwy), Cambridge. 492.7373

Massachusetts State Transportation Building
COURTESY OF GOODY, CLANCY & ASSOCIATES

STUART STREET   PARKING   WATER TANKS   BOYLSTON PLACE   BOYLSTON STREET   BOSTON COMMON

11 Boylston Street The slice of this thoroughfare facing the **Boston Common** was once known as "Piano Row" for its concentration of pianomaking and music-publishing establishments—enterprises in which music-loving Boston led the nation during the 19th and early 20th centuries. The businesses occupied—some still do—several handsome buildings that are physical expressions of the city's traditional high esteem for music: The Wurlitzer Company (now at 96-98 Boylston), resided at **No. 100** with its elegant, elaborate storefront designed by **Clarence H. Blackall;** the building was also home to the distinguished **Colonial Theatre.** The Steinway Piano Company is located at Beaux Arts–style **No. 162,** designed by **Winslow and Wetherell** in 1896. And the **E.A. Starck Piano Company Building** at **Nos. 154-156** houses **Carl Fischer Music.** While you're on this stretch, look for the **Little Building, No. 80,** a 1916 commercial edifice designed by **Blackall**'s firm with a Gothic-influenced terra-cotta facade. Step inside and take a look at its arcaded lobby decorated with naïf murals of Boston history. Then cross Tremont Street to see **No. 48,** the eye-catching Ruskinian Gothic Young Men's Christian Union of 1875, by **Nathaniel J. Bradlee,** listed on the National Register of Historic Places. A few steps farther is the **Boylston Building,** an 1887 edifice, also on the National Register of Historic Places, and the work of **Carl Fehmer,** architect of numerous important Boston office buildings and homes, including the grandiose **Oliver Ames Mansion** in Back Bay. It's now home to the **China Trade Center,** an office/arcade complex organized by the Bay Group and the Chinese Economic Development Group. **The Boston Architectural Team** carved out an appealing atrium, decorated with a mosaic walkway and wall plaque by Lilli Ann and Marvin Rosenberg, elucidating the Chinese lunar zodiac. Several food shops are on the premises, and at noon a group of actors called the **Winter Company** performs on a small stage in the atrium's well. ♦ Between Park Dr and Tremont St

12 Boylston Place Located off Boylston Street along Piano Row, this pedestrian cul-de-sac reputedly was where football was born in 1860, when a student of **Mr. Dixwell's Private School** organized the first game. The rubber sphere used for a ball is in the Society for the Preservation of New England Antiquities' collections. Enter via a fanciful arch replete with theatrical and local allusions, and pass through a phalanx of night spots popular among the young and impecunious, such as **Alley Cat** (1 Boylston Pl, at Tremont Ave, 351.2510) and **Avenue C** (25 Boylston Pl, between Charles St and Tremont Ave, 423.3832). At the end, a pedestrian passage leads through the **Transportation Building** to Stuart Street, a handy shortcut. ♦ Cul-de-sac off Boylston St (between Charles St S and Tremont St)

On Boylston Place:

Zanzibar One of the city's most popular dance and party spots is this two-story, tropical paradise-theme playhouse, with soaring palm trees, Caribbean-motif architecture, ceiling fans, and a spacious dance floor. A DJ spins a mix of Top 40 and rock 'n' roll floor-burners for an upscale crowd, generally ranging in age from mid-20s to mid-40s. ♦ Cover. W-Su. Jacket and tie requested. No one under 21 is admitted. Valet parking on weekend. 1 Boylston Pl (between Charles St S and Tremont St). 351.7000 &

Sweetwater Cafe $ When you want to be casual and anonymous, try this laid-back, cheap-eats place for big portions of Tex-Mex and bar food like nachos, tostadas, burritos, barbecue beef, and super-hot Buffalo wings. There's a bar on the second level, but the downstairs is quieter, with booths. Two jukeboxes crank out tunes, one stocked with old 45s. You can eat outdoors in nice weather. ♦ Tex/Mex ♦ M-Sa lunch and dinner. 3 Boylston Pl (between Charles St S and Tremont St). 351.2515

The Tavern Club Only open to women only since the late 1980s, this exclusive club has resided since 1887 in three quaint brick row houses built in the early- to mid-19th century. For generations the club has been famed for its private performances of outrageous plays starring club members. ♦ Daily. 4-6 Boylston Pl (between Charles St S and Tremont St). 338.9682

13 Walker's Riding outfitters since 1932, this stuffed-to-the-ceiling store doesn't play favorites, carrying both English (black velvet helmets and modern Lycra jodhpurs) and Western (cowboy shirts and pointy boots) gear. It's got to be the only place in town to stock scorpion belt buckles. ♦ M-Sa. 122 Boylston St (between Boylston Pl and Tremont St). 423.9050 &

13 Marais ★★★$$$ This more-than-a-century-old, stylishly retro restaurant still has the facade, hardwood floors, and mahogany paneling of one of its former tenants—the **Boston Music Company** (see below). A marble-and-mahogany bar was added, however, and the place has been SRO since day one. Founders Gillian Troy, Kevin Troy, and Steven Foster have a knack for gauging the recreational cravings of their late-30s/early-40s contemporaries: their first venture, **Jillian's Billiards** (in the Fenway), spawned a national franchise. Their surefire formula for success includes a romantic setting (low lights, period posters) divided between the endless bar and two cozy back rooms with fireplaces. Chef Jackson Kenworth trained with Wolfgang Puck of Los Angeles's Spago, and his menu features a delectable list of "premiers" (inventive mix-and-match appetizers, with complementary wines available by the glass and even the shot) and a handful of rather more substantial entrées, such as grilled lobster with creamy bourbon corn sauce. Your best bet is to pile on the internationally influenced premiers: cuisine this skilled and exotic is rare in Boston, so take advantage and sample the fire-roasted dates stuffed with spicy sausage, or charred sweetbreads with maple and bitter greens. Swapping and sharing are encouraged; the energy and camaraderie here are irresistible. ♦ International ♦ Daily dinner. Bar until 2AM. 116 Boylston St (between Boylston Pl and Tremont St). 482.7799 &

Within Marais:

Esmé To the back of the restaurant, accessible either via the bar or from adjoining Boylston Place, is an intimate, opulent nightclub where talking 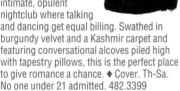 and dancing get equal billing. Swathed in burgundy velvet and a Kashmir carpet and featuring conversational alcoves piled high with tapestry pillows, this is the perfect place to give romance a chance. ♦ Cover. Th-Sa. No one under 21 admitted. 482.3399

14 Colonial Theatre The most gloriously grand theater in Boston, built in 1900, is also one of the most handsome in the country. The play may disappoint, but the arena, never. Actually, this is a very uncolonial-style structure, a 10-story office building with a theater tucked in. It does, however, brim with classical ornament, ebulliently gilded and mirrored. H.B. Pennell's interiors feature glittering chandeliers, lofty arched ceilings, sumptuous frescoes and friezes, allegorical figures—all the ruffles and flourishes imaginable. Yet the 1,658-seat theater is also intimate and comfortable, with excellent sight lines and acoustics. **Clarence H. Blackall**'s other local credits include the nearby **Wilbur and Metropolitan** (now the **Wang**) theaters, as well as the **Winthrop Building** downtown. Thankfully, **Blackall** and Pennell's masterpiece has been spared the ups, downs, and indignities of many ravaged Boston theaters, and has been lovingly preserved.

The theater continues to book major productions, often musicals, many on the way to Broadway. In its 90-odd years in business, Flo Ziegfeld, Irving Berlin, Rodgers and Hammerstein, Bob Fosse, and Tommy Tune have launched shows here. Ethel Barrymore, Frederic March, Helen Hayes, Katharine Hepburn, Henry Fonda, Fred Astaire, Eddie Cantor, W.C. Fields, the Marx Brothers, Will Rogers, Danny Kaye, and Barbra Streisand have all trod the boards. Those lucky enough to find their way deep into the backstage recesses discover a wealth of history and memorabilia from past productions. ♦ Half-price tickets are offered for persons with disabilities and one companion. Box office daily. 106 Boylston St (at Tremont St). 426.9366 &

14 Jack's Joke Shop "Yes, We Have Warts!" a shop notice reads. Pick out your latest disguise at Harold Bengin's wholesale/retail emporium for tricksters. Or make an unforgettable impression with a unique gift from an inventory topping 3,000 different items, including backward-running clocks, instant worms, garlic gum, sneeze powder, or the gross but ever-popular severed heads, fake wounds, and worse. Open since 1922 (it's the oldest shop of its type in the US), this is definitely one of the city's more colorful institutions. Halloween is the shop's biggest selling season, naturally, but kids and adults stream in throughout the year for jokes, tricks, magic, novelties, complete costumes, masks, wigs, beards, flags of all countries, and oddities galore. Bengin and his staff clearly get a kick out of this business. ♦ M-Sa. No credit cards accepted. 197 Tremont St (at Boylston St). 426.9640 &

15 The Boston Music Company Open for over 100 years, this august music emporium purveys New England's largest selection of sheet music and books about music. One glance inside tells you this shop's an oldie but goodie. Its clientele encompasses music lovers and musicians, professional and amateur, who seek anything from choral pieces to the latest rock 'n' roll hit. This place is proud of its enormous collection of music-related gifts, like its cases of music boxes for $5,000 or so. A musical instrument department sells traditional and electronic instruments. Owned by Hammerstein Music and Theatre Corp., which, in turn, is owned by the estate of the legendary Oscar Hammerstein, this subsidiary is the educational music publisher, whose titles are distributed throughout the world. ♦ M-Sa. 172 Tremont St (at Avery St). 426.5100.

16 Emerson Majestic Theatre Originally famous for its musicals and opera performances, this extravagantly ornate, Beaux Arts–style theater, designed by **John Galen Howard** in 1903, was bought by a movie-theater chain in the 1950s that slapped tacky fake materials on top of marble and Neo-Classical friezes. **Emerson College** rescued the theater in 1983, spent several million dollars on renovations, and has made it "majestic" once more. Today, the 859-seat multipurpose performance center serves as a stage for nonprofit groups, including **Dance Umbrella, Boston Lyric Opera,** the **New England Conservatory,** and **Emerson Stage.** Patrons favor the theater for its sense of excitement and inclusion with performers; entertainers like the space for its rococo high style and fine acoustics. This was the first theater in Boston to incorporate electricity into the building's design. ♦ Box office daily, except when theater is dark. 219 Tremont St (between Boylston and Stuart Sts). 578.8727 ♿

17 Shubert Theatre Hill, James & Whitaker designed this refined 1,680-seat theater, with its graceful marquee, in 1910. Now listed on the National Register of Historic Places, it's part of the famous chain, but has a fine reputation in its own right among actors and audiences. Kathleen Turner heated up the town in recent times in Tennessee Williams's *Cat on a Hot Tin Roof;* the illustrious Sir Laurence Olivier, John Barrymore, and Sir John Gielgud performed on this stage, as did Sarah Bernhardt, Mae West, Humphrey Bogart, Ingrid Bergman, Cary Grant, and Helen Hayes. ♦ Discounted tickets are offered to persons with disabilities and one companion. Box office daily, except when theater is dark. 265 Tremont St (south of Stuart St). 426.4520 ♿

TREMONT H·O·U·S·E

18 The Tremont House $$ Named after Boston's first grand hotel, long gone, and filling the shoes of the former **Bradford Hotel,** where 1950s big bands played, this 15-floor renovated hostelry bills itself as "Boston's Affordable Alternative." There are 281 rooms, including accommodations for people with disabilities and for nonsmokers. It caters to the theater crowd (both performers and spectators): Casts often stay here, and special packages, including tickets, are available. Amenities include room service and valet parking. The hotel's brass **Elks Club** doorknobs recall when the hotel was built in 1926 as the national headquarters for the Benevolent and Protective Order of Elks, which explains why the public spaces are so grand. ♦ 275 Tremont St (south of Stuart St). 426.1400, 800/331.9998; fax 482.6730 ♿

Within The Tremont House:

Broadway Deli ★$ Glitzy and frenetic (actors and fans alike flock here), this New York–style delicatessen is doing its best to satisfy the cravings of deli-starved Boston with provisions trucked in fresh from the Big Apple. Formerly the **Stage Deli of New York,** this place is known for its corned beef and pastrami, huge hot entrées, and sky-high Dagwood sandwiches, including more than two dozen named for local and national celebrities. Tackle the Larry Bird Triple Decker, the Raymond Flynn Reuben, or the Chet and Natalie Triple Decker, named for Boston's husband-and-wife TV anchor team. Dive into knockwurst and sauerkraut, stuffed cabbage, potato pancakes, blintzes, apple strudel, and New York–style cheesecake. Somewhat more modest sandwiches are offered for less courageous appetites. Celebrities from whatever shows are in town drop in all the time; their particular deli addictions sometimes make it into a local gossip column. ♦ Deli/Takeout ♦ Daily breakfast, lunch, and dinner. 426.1344 ♿

NYC Jukebox and VHF This is one club with two rooms and two DJs playing two different kinds of music. In one room, Bostonians can shake, rattle, and roll to 1950s through 1970s dance music; in the other, a younger crowd flocks to watch Top 40 videos on dozens of TV screens. There's a full bar, but no food. ♦ Cover. NYC Jukebox: Th-Sa. VHF: F-Sa. No one under 21 admitted. No T-shirts, tank tops, or sweats allowed. 542.1123 ♿

18 The Roxy If you want to kick loose, this may be just the place. A gorgeous setting for any kind of dancing, the younger crowd is attracted here on Friday nights for inter-national industrial rock, and "techno" (you must have high energy for this!) dancing. On Saturday nights, the flavor changes to Top 40 and disco. Bystanders can watch from any of seven bars and the stunning balcony. ♦ Cover. F-Sa. No T-shirts or sneakers allowed. 279 Tremont St (south of Stuart St). 338.7699 ♿

Restaurants/Clubs: Red	Hotels: Blue
Shops/ 🌳 Outdoors: Green	Sights/Culture: Black

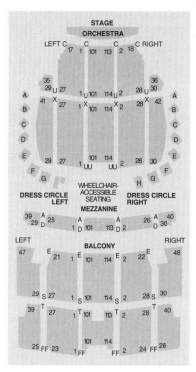

The center's Young at Arts educational outreach program involves Boston children in the visual and performing arts through workshops, performances held in the theater's lobbies, and an annual art contest. Subsidized tickets are available and many events are free; call to inquire. The theater also brings back a hint of its past history with a classic film series shown on one of the world's largest screens.

The **Boston Ballet** makes its home here, and famous visiting companies such as the **Alvin Ailey American Dance Theater** and the **Bolshoi Ballet Academy** perform frequently. Recent restoration work has brought back more of the auditorium's former splendor, and updated its facilities and theater technology. ◆ 268 Tremont St (south of Stuart St). General information 482.9393, Ticketmaster 931.2000 &

20 Wilbur Theatre This distinguished Colonial Revival theater has witnessed its share of dramatic debuts, including the pre-Broadway production of Tennessee Williams's *A Streetcar Named Desire* starring Marlon Brando and Jessica Tandy. Another of Boston's **Clarence H. Blackall** treasures, built in 1914 and now on the National Register of Historic Places, this stage endured dark days and decay, its nadir a brief stint as a cabaret that flopped. But the lights are on again: the proud theater has rebounded.

The 1,200-seat fan-shaped house was renovated to accommodate Off Broadway–style productions. Some recent smash runs were *Five Guys Named Moe* and A.R. Gurney's *Love Letters.* Look up at the facade and note the three theatrical masks—grinning, grimacing, and agape—above the upper windows. ◆ Half-price tickets are offered for people with disabilities and a companion. Box office M-Sa; during shows daily. 246 Tremont St (south of Stuart St). 423.4008 &

21 Hub Ticket Agency Located in a trailer parked on a corner, this agency sells sports and theater tickets, including those for New York events and sometimes for Providence, Rhode Island, and Worcester, Massachusetts. The friendly staff is often willing to drop tickets off at box offices for pickup before shows. Many local performances are sold out well in advance, so call first. The day of the game or performance is a good time to check on last-minute availability. For those who plan ahead, order by mail; the zip code is 02116. ◆ M-F; Sa until noon. 240 Tremont St (at Stuart St). 426.8340

22 Charlie Flynn's ★$ Whether you're up for a game of darts or looking for some wide-screen televised games, Charlie Hoyt and Bob Flynn's pub-style sports bar provides all the traditional food you'd expect: burgers, fries, and generous club sandwiches. ◆ American ◆ Daily. 228 Tremont St (at Stuart St). 451.5997 &

19 The Wang Center for the Performing Arts It's worth the ticket price to whatever performance you can catch here just to see the inside of this former motion-picture cathedral. Predating New York City's Radio City Music Hall, this mammoth entertainment palace, designed by **Blackall, Clapp and Whittemore,** was considered the "wonder theater of the world" when it opened in the Roaring Twenties, built to pack in huge crowds four times daily for variety revues and first-run movies. An architectural extravaganza, the seven-story, 3,800-seat theater (see plan above) boasts a succession of dramatic lobbies—concluding with the five-story Grand Lobby—bedecked with Italian marble columns, stained glass, bronze detailing, gold leaf, crystal chandeliers, and florid ceiling murals. In the theater's early days, billiards, ping-pong, card parties, and other games in four ornate lobbies occupied the crowds until the next show got started.

First called the **Metropolitan Theater** and later the **Music Hall,** it was expanded by **Jung, Brannen Associates** in 1982, renamed for benefactor An Wang in 1983, and renovated by **Notter, Finegold & Alexander** in 1990 to accommodate a variety of performing arts, including opera, ballet, and Broadway musicals. On the National Register of Historic Places, it now has one of the largest stages of any theater in the world. For plays, try to get down-front center seats in the orchestra, where the sight and sound are best.

23 Montien ★★$$ A solid favorite with theatergoers, businesspeople, and staff from the nearby medical complex, all the classic Thai favorites are served here, plus such unusual specials as *kat-thong-tong* (a crisp pastry shell filled with ground chicken, onions, corn, and coriander with a sweet dipping sauce). The tamarind duck and fried squid are superb. The hot-and-spicy set will find their pleasure, as will palates preferring subtler sensations. Service is respectful and prompt, so you'll make that curtain. ♦ Thai/ Takeout ♦ M-Sa lunch and dinner; Su dinner. Reservations recommended for large parties. 63 Stuart St (between Tremont and Washington Sts). 338.5600 &

23 Jacob Wirth ★$$ Amid the whirl of Boston's dining fads and fashions, this venerable establishment—built in 1845 by **Greenleaf C. Sanborn** and now on the National Register of Historic Places (see the illustration above)—plods along unwaveringly on its own steady course. It has been offering up the same hearty traditional German fare— bratwurst, knockwurst, sauerbraten, and sauerkraut, accompanied by heady, specially brewed dark beer—in the same bowfront row house since its doors opened in 1868. All the furniture and fixtures—globe lighting, brass rails, dark paneling—are original. Even the waiters' attire looks vintage. It's easy to step into the past here; in fact, that's the reason to come. The cavernous beer hall is a great place to bring a crowd and sample the long list of lagers. Those in your party with big appetites might attempt the German boiled dinner: pig's feet, pork roast, ribs, and cabbage. Sing along with piano music on Friday. ♦ German ♦ Daily lunch and dinner. Two free hours of parking at the adjacent lot. 37 Stuart St (between Tremont and Washington Sts). 338.8586 &

The first paper money in America was issued in 1690 by the Massachusetts Bay Colony, and was used to pay the soldiers who served on the ill-fated expedition attempting to capture Quebec from the French.

24 Hayden Building Modest-sized and overlooked, this 1875 office building isn't one of **Henry Hobson Richardson**'s finer works but does display his characteristically vigorous Romanesque Revival approach. Unfortunately, the building, which is on the National Register of Historic Places, has been put to demoralizing uses and poorly maintained. It patiently awaits better days at the head of La Grange Street, once a thriving mercantile stretch with hatters, tailors, shoemakers, and such. From the 1960s onward, La Grange was caught in the midst of the Combat Zone and its once-reputable appearance has been shamefully besmirched. ♦ 681 Washington St (at La Grange St)

25 East Ocean City ★$ This sparkling restaurant looks like a yuppie haven (marble entrance, snowy tablecloths), but promises— and delivers—Hong Kong–style exotica. Take a good look at the teeming tanks by the door; if you order seafood, one of these creatures will soon turn up tableside for your pre-dining inspection. Steamed and topped with ginger, coriander, and soy sauce, fish doesn't come any fresher. Nonmarine specialties include scallion pancakes, stir-fried watercress, and assorted "porridges"—rice cooked in flavorful stock. ♦ Chinese ♦ Daily lunch and dinner; Sa-Su dim sum. 25-29 Beach St (between Washington St and Harrison Ave). 542.2504

26 North End Fabrics Not only are the largest selection of fake "fun-furs" around offered here— great for a come-as-you-were-half-a-million-years-ago party—but there's just about everything else in the way of fabrics you could possibly want: wool challis, velvets and velveteen, Thai silk, drapery and upholstery materials, bridal and theatrical fabrics, handkerchief linen, imported lace, odd bolts and remnants, notions—you name it. Professional dressmakers, designers, and home sewers all frequent this shop, around now for more than 30 years. ♦ M-Sa. 31 Harrison Ave (between Beach and Essex Sts). 542.2763

27 Dong Khanh ★$ Come to this clean and bright establishment for Vietnamese-style fast food, including more than a dozen great noodle-soup dishes. The *bi cuon* (meat rolls) are very tasty, as are the fish in spicy soup and assorted barbecue meats with vermicelli. Be daring and try a *durian* juice drink, made from the southeast Asian fruit that looks like a hedgehog and smells like rotting garbage, but has plenty of fans for its flavor. ♦ Vietnamese ♦ Daily breakfast, lunch, and dinner. No credit cards accepted. 83 Harrison Ave (between Beach and Kneeland Sts). 426.9410

28 Siam Square ★$ This Thai interloper at Chinatown's edge offers its own distinctive palette of tastes. Lemon grass infuses a dish of steamed mussels; a pepper-garlic sauce spices frog's legs; the squid *pik pow* is at once spicy and sweet; and Thai seasonings lend a signature kick to Chinese *chow foon* (fat noodles). ◆ Thai ◆ Daily lunch and dinner. 86 Harrison Ave (between Beach and Kneeland Sts). 338.7704

29 China Grove ★★$ Run by a young brother and sister, John and Rita Lin, this bustling little restaurant features highlights from four provinces— Szechuan, Taiwan, Shanghai, and Yangzhou—and the city of Beijing. Such old standbys as Beijing ravioli are state-of-the-art; among the more adventurous offerings are sour cabbage and *hog mow* (intestine) soup, jellyfish with sesame oil and a garlicky seaweed salad, shredded eel with yellow leeks, and squid *satay*. Bring an open mind and a ravenous appetite. ◆ Chinese/Takeout ◆ Daily lunch and dinner. 10 Tyler St (between Beach and Kneeland Sts). 542.5857

29 Golden Palace ★★$ Many Chinatown restaurants are so innocuous looking that they're easy to miss, but not this one—it has the fanciest facade around. The main attraction is excellent dim sum—perhaps Boston's best—served daily until 3PM. There's no menu; when the carts roll up, simply select whatever tidbits strike your fancy in the sea of little plates loaded with dumplings, fried and steamed pastries, and noodle dishes. Try *har gao* (shrimp dumplings), spareribs in black-bean sauce, steamed *bao* (meat-filled buns), *shu mai* (pork dumplings), or more adventurous items like tripe and curried squid. This sprawling place—aglitz with reds, golds, pinks, and painted and carved dragons—is a noisy neighborhood favorite. People come to eat, not unwind, so the service is hurried and the atmosphere minimal. But the dim sum are piping hot, and the regular menu offers loads of superior dishes, including abalone and squab treatments. ◆ Chinese/Takeout ◆ Daily breakfast, lunch, and dinner. Reservations recommended for 10 or more. 14-20 Tyler St (between Beach and Kneeland Sts). 423.4565

Restaurants/Clubs: Red   **Hotels:** Blue
Shops/ 🌂 Outdoors: Green   **Sights/Culture:** Black

Mug Shots: Where to Find the Best Home Brews

Beer was the favored colonial beverage. During the 17th century Boston ship crews were issued beer rations of more than a quart per day; Puritan minister Richard Mather recommended beer consumption along with fresh air and churchgoing; and **Harvard College** operated its own brewery in its backyard.

The right to brew was jealously guarded by Puritan leaders, who had the power to giveth and taketh away licenses, and readily did so when a brewer's beer was deemed inferior. The American Revolution interfered with beer production, and in 1789 the state of Massachusetts exempted brewers from taxes for five years to "encourage the manufacture and consumption of strong beer." National and statewide prohibitions during the 19th and early 20th centuries and the growth of beer conglomerates increasingly disrupted Bay State brewing. In fact, there wasn't a single working brewery in the state by the early 1980s. But several have opened in the last several years, and these are the best of them:

Boston Beer Company (30 Germania St, at Bismarck and Boylston Sts, Jamaica Plain, 522.9080) brews the famous award-winning Samuel Adams Boston Lager here, plus Boston Lightship Beer, Samuel Adams Double Bock Beer, Samuel Adams Summer Wheat Beer, Samuel Adams Dark Wheat Beer, and others. One-and-a-half hour tours and tastes on James Kock's impressive facility are given on Thursday at 2PM and Saturday at noon and 2PM.

Boston Beer Works (61 Brookline Ave, at Kenmore Sq, 536.2337) has developed 25 brews to date, but serves only 13, including some imaginative fruit selections such as watermelon beer. Of the eight or so varieties on tap at any given time, Boston Red (an amber) and Buckeye Oatmeal Stout are particularly popular.

Cambridge Brewing Company (1 Kendall Sq, at Hampshire Ave and Broadway, 494.1994) features its own Regatta Golden, Cambridge Amber, Charles River Porter, Summertime Wheat Ale, and pub fare.

Commonwealth Brewing Company (138 Portland St, between Causeway and New Chardon Sts, 522.8383) serves a variety of its own creations, including Golden Ale, Boston's Best Burton Bitter, Classic Stout, Golden Export, and Famous Perter, plus pub cuisine. Ask about free tours.

John Harvard's Brew House (33 Dunster St, at Mt. Auburn St, Harvard Square, 868.3585) has the former head brewer for San Francisco's very popular Anchor Steam Brewing Company, Tim Morse, cooking up English-style ales and Germanic lagers in this handsome cellar restaurant.

Mass. Bay Brewing Company (306 Northern Ave, beyond Jimmy's Harborside, Waterfront, 574.9551) provides 45-minute tours Friday and Saturday at 1PM where you can sample Harpoon Ale and any other brews on hand.

30 Carl's Pagoda ★★$$ Yes, there is a Carl, and many diners rely on his judgment when it comes to ordering. Carl is like a potentate ruling his personal fiefdom. But even if he's not there, a great meal can be had with tomato soup, Cantonese-style lobster, clams in black-bean sauce, and superb steamed fish. A shrimpy little place it is, but this is one of the few Chinatown restaurants with tablecloths. ♦ Chinese/Takeout ♦ Daily dinner. Reservations recommended on weekends. No credit cards accepted. 23 Tyler St (between Beach and Kneeland Sts). 357.9837

31 Chau Chow Seafood ★★$ Definitely a Chinatown gem, this very busy, very basic place does great things with all sorts of seafood. There's crab with ginger and scallions, steamed sea bass and flounder, fried noodles with seafood and vegetables, salted jumbo shrimp in the shell, baby clams in black-bean sauce, and seafood *chow foon* (a mix of shrimp, scallop, and crabmeat), to name a few. Pork, beef, chicken, and duck dishes abound, and all are excellent. Sample stir-fried watercress, Swatowese dumplings (stuffed with pork and shrimp), or soup with sliced fish and Chinese parsley. Beer is served. Understandably, there's always a long line for dinner. ♦ Chinese/Takeout ♦ Daily breakfast, lunch, and dinner. No credit cards accepted. 52 Beach St (at Harrison Ave). 426.6266

32 Grand Chau Chow ★★$ For the price, you can't do better. The seafood is out of this world, but the bill isn't. Try the delicate steamed striped bass with ginger, the spicy, fried salted squid, or a plate of sizzling noodles with seafood. Presentation and service here are outstanding. ♦ Chinese ♦ Daily lunch and dinner. Reservations recommended. 45 Beach St (at Harrison Ave). 292.5166

33 Dynasty ★$$ This big-league kind of restaurant has lots of mirrors and golden columns and offers good Cantonese dishes: pan-fried spiced shrimp, chicken with cashews, clams in black-bean sauce, and steamed sea bass and gray sole, to name a few. Even better, it stays open nearly round the clock. ♦ Cantonese ♦ Daily breakfast, lunch, and dinner until 4AM. 33 Edinboro St (off Essex St). 350.7777

Chinatown—originally composed of tents— was born when Chinese workers were imported from the West to break a shoe-industry strike in the 1870s.

33 Moon Villa $ By no means the romantic place its name implies, this hangout for hungry night owls serves family-style Cantonese dishes while the rest of the city snoozes. For dim sum, however, you have to come Saturday or Sunday during the day. The waiters tend to be brusque. ♦ Chinese/Takeout ♦ Daily lunch and dinner until 4AM. 15-19 Edinboro St (off Essex St). 423.2061

34 Imperial Tea House ★$ Right at the gateway to Chinatown, this noisy, cavernous restaurant is a good choice for its second-floor dim-sum parlor, where a fleet of carts laden with arrays of little treats—pork dumplings, shrimp balls, bean curd, stuffed meat buns, braised chicken's feet, and so forth—whiz past the packed tables. Just point to your selection and it's whisked onto your table. Always mobbed, the tearoom attracts a fascinatingly mixed clientele. There's usually a short wait. Downstairs, order traditional Cantonese dishes from the regular menu. ♦ Chinese/Takeout ♦ M-Th, Su breakfast, lunch, and dinner until 2AM; F-Sa breakfast, lunch, and dinner until 4AM. Reservations recommended for large parties at dinner. No credit cards accepted. 70-72 Beach St (at Hudson St). 426.8439

35 Ho Yuen Ting ★$ People flock to this no-frills restaurant not for ambience or decor, but for such delectable seafood specials as lobster with ginger, salted and spiced squid, shrimp with spicy sauce, or stir-fried sole and vegetables served in a crunchy edible bowl made of batter-fried shredded potatoes. Also recommended are the pork-and-watercress soup and fish-stomach soup with mushrooms or sweet corn. This is a good place to explore the unknown. The restaurant's located below street level, so be on the lookout or you'll pass right by. ♦ Chinese/Takeout ♦ Daily lunch and dinner. No credit cards accepted. 13A Hudson St (between Beach and Kneeland Sts). 426.2316

35 New Shanghai ★★★$$ You won't be hungry one hour after finishing a meal here, nor will you crave more elegant decor. Chef C.K. Sau prepares an extraordinary Peking duck; another favorite is scallops with black pepper. Top off the meal with a dessert of fried banana fritters. It's all served in the sleekest of settings. ♦ Chinese ♦ Daily breakfast, lunch, and dinner. 21 Hudson St (between Beach and Kneeland Sts). 338.6688

Bests

Julia Goldrosen
DJ/Host "Africa Kabisa"

Welcome to Boston, where our reputation for rigidity is not entirely warranted. For some things, like using indicator lights and posting street signs, we're incredibly nonchalant. In a city where people, cars, and the weather all flaunt laws of man and nature with equal aplomb, you know that the unexpected must lie around the corner (or wherever that 17th century cow decided to wander).

African music clubs are here, but they keep changing location. The local hotels (especially the **Howard Johnson's** in Cambridge) are rented out by *soukous/makossa/zouk* lovers for disco and live entertainment. Check the record stores for flyers or tune into the radio stations to keep abreast. **The Roxy** caters elegance and American music on weekends and occasionally world music acts during the week. **Middle East** in Central Square offers belly dancing and loud music several times a week.

Free entertainment: **Harvard Square** during warm weather. Hear street musicians perform flamenco, reggae, blues, and more all within inches of one another. Less humanistic types can browse newspapers and magazines from around the world at **Out of Town News** while counting cars that jump the red light.

For a quieter Cambridge moment, walk down JFK to the Charles River or stroll down Brattle Street past mansions to the **Longfellow House** and garden. For the ultimate in peace and quiet, continue your walk across the Watertown line to the **Mount Auburn Cemetery.**

Record stores: **Looney Tunes** and **Cheapo Records** for jazz and blues. **Tower** for world music.

Foreign language books: **Schoenhof's** (the only place I've located a Lingala dictionary). Used books: **Harvard Bookstore** (downstairs), **Starr Bookstore, Victor Hugo.**

Cheap clothes: **The Garment District** where office workers from Kendall Square biotech companies and disenfranchised youth equally discover the stylish and cheap. If these prices are too steep, stop downstairs on weekend mornings for the "Dollar a Pound" experience where the eclectic crowd sifts through mounds of polyester to discover clothing gems. What they weigh is what you pay.

Spinnaker—Top of the **Hyatt Regency.** Top of the world, Ma! Sip cognac, pretend you're rich, and watch Boston's ultimate architectural achievement, the flashing Citgo sign, go around.

Dali restaurant—Fantastic decor, ambience, sherry list, tapas, and cute bartenders.

Other advice: Don't drive. If you drive, ignore all information signs, they're probably wrong. Take the **T** but remember that "Inbound" and "Outbound" refer to **Park Street** station. And be sure to scan the lower left part of your FM dial for some of the most numerous and eclectic college/community radio stations in the nation.

Patrick B. Moscaritolo
President & CEO, Greater Boston Convention & Visitors Bureau, Inc.

Sports Museum of New England—An opportunity to relive some of the most dramatic moments in the history of professional and collegiate athletics. Boston is a sports town and a college town, and the museum, founded by Dave Corveas (former **NBA** All Star and world-champion center), captures the essence of Boston's sports tradition. You can also tour the **Boston Garden,** which will be torn down, with the new **Boston Garden** (aka **Shawmut Center**) opening for the 1995-96 season. **Fenway Park** also provides tours of its famed facility—home of the Boston **Red Sox.**

Freedom Trail and **Black Heritage Trail**—Boston is America's walking city and what better way to relive America's history than to walk the **Freedom Trail** and the **Black Heritage Trail.**

Water Shuttle—operates to and from **Logan Airport** to **Rowes Wharf** in downtown Boston; it's the most elegant way to enter or leave Boston. A short 8-minute trip from the airport takes you across Boston Harbor with its beautiful waterfront skyscrapers, condos, sailboats, fishing boats, and cruise ships as your backdrop. Best of all: on the harbor crossing you encounter no stoplights, tolls, or traffic!

David R. Godine
Publisher

First, everyone should read Walter Muir Whitehill's *Boston: A Topographical History.*

For entertainment, always check out **Jordan Hall** at the **New England Conservatory of Music,** for faculty and student concerts are frequently scheduled here (no admission).

Spend at least a day walking around Cambridge and visiting its many museums (**Fogg, Busch-Reisinger, Semitic, Houghton Library, Sackler, Carpenter,** etc).

Walk through the **North End;** it's intact, safe, and as close to Little Italy as you'll find in New England.

Ride the subway; it's cheap and will get you everywhere quickly. If you value your sanity, do not (repeat DO NOT) even think about driving in the city.

Eat at least one dinner or lunch at **Locke-Ober;** it's pricier than **Durgin-Park,** but far more civilized. Also consider tea at the **Ritz-Carlton Hotel,** a great bargain and very relaxing.

Remember: Boston is a small city. Everything is accessible by foot and the city is best seen that way.

Finally, attend a Sunday morning service at **King's Chapel** or **Trinity Church** in Copley Square.

Try to understand that for the New World, this is an *old* city. Its charms are often hidden within its history, but its history is beguiling.

Restaurants/Clubs: Red	**Hotels:** Blue
Shops/ 🌳 Outdoors: Green	**Sights/Culture:** Black

Back Bay

Boston's sumptuous centerpiece of illustrious institutions and architecture is also the best place in the city for extravagant shopping sprees and leisurely promenades. Back Bay attracts a stylish international crowd that's as fun to look at as any of **Newbury Street**'s artful windows. It is also a comfortable, compact neighborhood of broad, gracious streets bordered by harmonious four- and five-story Victorian town houses. Its residents are well-to-do families, established professionals, footloose young people, and transient students for whom the **Public Garden** is an outdoor living room and the **Charles River Esplanade** a grassy waterside backyard.

In the 19th century Boston's wealthy old guard and brash new moneymakers together planted this garden of beautiful homes and public buildings, creating a cosmopolitan, Parisianlike quarter wrapped in an aura of privilege and prosperity. The lingering mystique has even tricked some Bostonians into believing Back Bay is one of the city's oldest neighborhoods, when it's really one of the youngest. What began as Boston's wasteland was transformed in the late 1800s into its most desirable neighborhood by a spectacular feat of urban design.

In the 1850s Boston boasted a booming population and exuberant commercial growth. Railroads and manufacturing supplanted the sea as the city's primary source of capital. The nouveaux riches were hungry for spectacular domiciles, but the almost waterbound city was already overcrowded on its little peninsula. The problem: where to get land? In 1814 a mile-and-a-half-long dam had been built from the base of **Beacon Hill** to

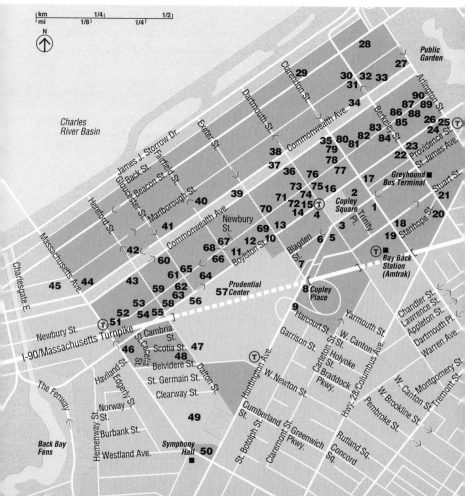

what is now **Kenmore Square** to harness the **Charles River**'s tidal flow and power a chain of mills. The scheme failed, and the acres of water trapped by the dam became a stagnant, stinking, unhealthy tidal flat called Back Bay that Bostonians longed to eradicate. This became the unlikely canvas that developers clamored to fill with daring urban design schemes. To do so, land had to be reclaimed from the sea by a fantastically ambitious landfill program. Inspired by the Parisian boulevard system Baron Haussmann had built for Emperor Louis Napoleon, architect **Arthur Gilman** proposed Back Bay's orderly layout. Starting at the Charles River, the principal east-west streets are **Beacon Street**, **Marlborough Street**, **Commonwealth Avenue**, Newbury Street, and **Boylston Street**, all bisected by eight streets (named alphabetically after English peers) from **Arlington Street** to **Hereford Street**. Sixteen-foot-long public alleys interlace these blocks and provide access to the rear of buildings, originally designed for service and deliveries. **Gilman**'s rational grid remains a startling departure from Old Boston's labyrinthine tangles.

In 1857 the gigantic landfill wave began its sweep across the marshland block by block, from Arlington Street at the **Public Garden**'s western edge toward **Fenway**. As soon as a lot was ready, another architectural beauty debuted. By the time the wave subsided in 1890, 450 acres and more than 1,500 new buildings had been added to the 783-acre peninsula. Gone was the loathsome eyesore; in its place was a charming neighborhood of the same name. Completed in just 60 years, Back Bay is an extraordinary repository of Victorian architectural styles, perhaps the most outstanding in America. As an urban design scheme, it was surpassed in its era only by **Pierre-Charles L'Enfant**'s plan for Washington, DC.

The newborn Back Bay instantly became Boston's darling, a magnificent symbol of civic pride and the city's coming of age. No Puritan simplicity or provincialism here. Affluent Boston had learned how to stage a good show, from **Copley Square**'s lofty cultural aspirations to Commonwealth Avenue's architectural revue of fancy brickwork, stained glass, cut granite, ornate ironwork, gargoyles, and other European conceits. In Back Bay's golden hours, the city's leading financiers, authors, industrialists, artists, architects, and legendary Brahmins lived here. But as the city's economy soured late in the 19th century, the ostentatious single-family dwellings were gradually converted to more modest uses. Though Back Bay's shining moments as a residential district faded after the Great Depression, the neighborhood has resiliently adapted to 20th-century incursions of shops, offices, apartments, and condominiums.

The **T** stops most convenient to Back Bay are **Arlington, Copley, Prudential,** and **Hynes Convention Center/ICA** (*Green Line*). The **Back Bay/South End** (on the *Orange Line* and also a railway station) and **Symphony** stops are handy, too. Access to and from the Massachusetts Turnpike is easy; there's an eastbound exit and a westbound entrance at **Copley Place.**

1 John Hancock Tower When towering new edifices invade historic neighborhoods, they often try to gain public acceptance with lame gestures—by aping local architectural modes or bribing with street-level shops, skimpy parks, or outdoor art. Making no such insincere overtures, in 1976 **I.M. Pei & Partners** designed a cool, aloof, and inscrutable tower (pictured at right) with its own singular style. And that's why more and more Bostonians have grown fond of this skyscraper—New England's tallest—as the years pass. A 62-story glass rhomboid, its shimmering surface acts as a full-length mirror for **Trinity Church** while reflecting the constant shifts of New England weather. The tower's crisp form is mesmerizing from all angles, whether you glimpse the broad faces or razor-blade edges.

It's amazing the tower has become so popular, considering its rocky start. When it was first erected, inadequate glass was used in the tower's sheathing and the windowpanes randomly popped out due to wind torquing, raining onto the square below. Sidewalks were cordoned off to protect pedestrians. All 13 acres of the 10,344 glass panels were replaced; today the panes are continuously monitored for visible signs of potential breakage. Making matters worse, a later engineering inspection revealed that the building was in danger of toppling, which required reinforcing its steel frame and installing a moving weight on the 58th floor to counter wind stress. Once Bostonians could walk by the tower without flinching, they began to notice what a dazzling addition it is to the Boston skyline.

For stunning views that will put all of Back Bay and Boston into perspective, visit the **John Hancock Observatory** on the 60th floor. Binoculars are already zeroed-in on some of the city's most famous sights. The taped narrative by the late architectural historian Walter Muir Whitehill is wonderful not only for his vast knowledge, but for his "proper" Bostonian accent. There's also a little sound-and-light show about Boston in 1775—with a 20-foot-tall topographical model of the city when all the hills were in place and Back Bay was its watery old self. ♦ Admission. Daily until 11PM. 200 Clarendon St (between St. James Ave and Stuart St). 247.1977

2 Copley Square Once called "Art Square" for the galleries, art schools, and clubs clustered around it, the plaza's modern name honors John Singleton Copley, Boston's great colonial painter. Originally an unsightly patch created by the disruption of Back Bay's grid by two rail lines, the square blossomed after the **Museum of Fine Arts** opened its doors there. (The museum stood at the site of today's **Copley Plaza Hotel** until the institution moved to its current address in Fenway and its old residence was demolished.) **Trinity Church** and the **Boston Public Library** were spectacular additions, and the presence of numerous ecclesiastical and academic institutions nearby, including the **Massachusetts Institute of Technology** and the **Harvard Medical School**, enhanced the square's reputation—in Bostonians' minds—as the "Acropolis of the New World." The plaza's latest look (created in 1989 by **Dean Abbot**) is pleasant, but fails to satisfy Bostonians' century-old dreams of a magnificent public space. ♦ Bounded by Dartmouth and Clarendon Sts, and Boylston St and St. James Ave

2 Trinity Church Approach Copley Square from any direction, and your eyes will be drawn to this grandiose French-Romanesque–inspired edifice (pictured below). A National Historic Landmark, it is one of the great buildings in America. The century and more that has passed since this church first graced the city has taken nothing from its power to fascinate. Like a wise and tolerant elder, it offers a model of urbane dignity and grandeur that has never been equalled in Boston. The church converses most with the old **Boston Public Library** across the way, another handsome building.

Henry Hobson Richardson was at the summit of his career when he designed this ecclesiastic edifice in 1877. In the 1860s its leaders decided to move the parish from Summer Street (downtown) to the Copley Square site. In retrospect their decision seems prescient; one of Boston's great conflagrations destroyed the Summer Street building in November 1872. In March of that year, six architects had been invited to submit designs for the new structure. Thirty-four years old at the time and a New York City resident, **Richardson** had already contributed one admired piece to the emerging Back Bay fabric, the **First Baptist Church** (then called **New Brattle Square Church**) under construction on Clarendon Street.

The cruciform church's fluid massing is an inimitable **Richardson** tour de force, especially the leaping exterior colonnade. To contend with the awkward triangular site, he designed the great square tower as the central element. Assisting **Richardson** with the tower

Trinity Church

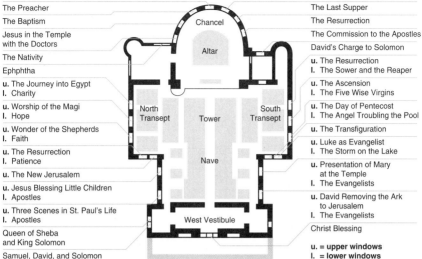

The Preacher

The Baptism

Jesus in the Temple with the Doctors

The Nativity

Ephphtha

u. The Journey into Egypt
l. Charity

u. Worship of the Magi
l. Hope

u. Wonder of the Shepherds
l. Faith

u. The Resurrection
l. Patience

u. The New Jerusalem

u. Jesus Blessing Little Children
l. Apostles

u. Three Scenes in St. Paul's Life
l. Apostles

Queen of Sheba and King Solomon

Samuel, David, and Solomon

Chancel

Altar

North Transept

Tower

South Transept

Nave

West Vestibule

The Last Supper

The Resurrection

The Commission to the Apostles

David's Charge to Solomon

u. The Resurrection
l. The Sower and the Reaper

u. The Ascension
l. The Five Wise Virgins

u. The Day of Pentecost
l. The Angel Troubling the Pool

u. The Transfiguration

u. Luke as Evangelist
l. The Storm on the Lake

u. Presentation of Mary at the Temple
l. The Evangelists

u. David Removing the Ark to Jerusalem
l. The Evangelists

Christ Blessing

u. = upper windows
l. = lower windows

was apprentice **Stanford White**—later of **McKim, Mead & White,** the **Boston Public Library** architects. The church's ageless vitality comes from the tension between **Richardson**'s powerful vision of the whole and his spirited treatment of its parts. Elegant bands of red sandstone hold the coarse granite's brute force in check. Inside and out, the church is richly polychromatic in wood, paint, glass, and stone—another **Richardson** signature. With the aid of six assistants, most notably young Augustus Saint-Gaudens, John La Farge decorated the majestic interiors. Look for his 12 oil paintings in the arches beneath the vaulted ceilings below the tower, 103 feet above the nave. La Farge orchestrated production of the stained-glass windows (see the diagram above), among them vividly glowing creations of his own— look for the lancet windows on the west wall in particular—and some jointly executed by Edward Burne-Jones and William Morris and Company. The interior resembles a gigantic tapestry woven in intricate patterns of opulent gold and medieval tones. The most wonderful time of the year to visit this site is Christmas, when the church is filled with candlelight and carols during the special annual service.

Outside, Saint-Gaudens added a fine flourish: on the church's northeast corner stands his dramatic depiction of *Phillips Brooks,* the Copley Square Trinity's first rector, the Episcopal Bishop of Massachusetts, and author of *O Little Town of Bethlehem.* A somber, shrouded Christ stands behind the orating preacher. It was daring Brooks who convinced his congregation to move to the new frontier of Back Bay. Saint-Gaudens died before his design was sculpted; assistants completed the statue in 1910, and it was set into a marble canopy by **McKim, Mead & White.** Step into the cloistered colonnade to your left that overlooks a pretty enclosed garden with its much humbler statue of *St. Francis of Assisi.* Free half-hour organ recitals are offered on Friday. ♦ Tours available by arrangement. 206 Clarendon St (at Copley Sq). 536.0944 &

3 Copley Plaza Hotel $$$$ The empress dowager of Boston's hotels enshrines the mature, full-flowered Back Bay. It not only draws business and international guests, but also lovers of grand epochs gone by. Designed in 1912 by **Clarence Blackall** and **Henry Hardenbergh** (the latter was the architect of the Plaza Hotel in New York and the Willard Hotel in Washington, DC), this Italian Renaissance Revival structure has endured well. A pair of gilded lions guard the entrance. Take a walk through the glittering lobby with its mirrored walls and the painted sky hovering over the registration desk— glorious overkill. All 393 rooms have been renovated in period style. Every June the fabulous ballroom becomes a fantasyland for the debutante cotillion. Corner suites overlook Copley Square and **Trinity Church.** Rooms for nonsmokers and 15 rooms designed for people with disabilities are available. There's also a multilingual staff and room service. Pets are allowed. ♦ 138 St. James Ave (between Trinity Pl and Dartmouth St). 267.5300, 800/225.7654; fax 247.6681 &

Within the Copley Plaza Hotel:

Plaza Dining Room ★★★$$$$ Dine in British Empire magnificence under a barrel-vaulted ceiling, attended by a well-trained battalion of captains, waiters, and busboys. US presidents John F. Kennedy and Jimmy Carter ate here; so have many movie stars. This unabashedly opulent dining room is gilded, polished, and stately, and under the gifted French chef Gerard Thabius, the costly

European cuisine has finally attained the heights of its setting. The encyclopedic wine list is one of the city's finest. Piano music streams in from the foyer. ♦ French ♦ Tu-Sa dinner. Reservations and jacket and tie required. Valet parking. 424.0196 ♿

Plaza Bar ★★★$$ Collect yourself on posh leather lounges under this Edwardian bar's handsome coffered ceiling, and enjoy jazz piano played from 8PM on. Hors d'oeuvres can be ordered from 5PM to 6PM. ♦ M-Sa. 267.5300 ♿

Copley's Restaurant and Bar ★★$$ This atmospheric, clubby place serves reasonably priced cuisine with a New England accent. There's a bar lounge at the back. On a cold afternoon, retreat to this wonderful high-ceilinged setting, where enormous draped windows overlook Copley Square. ♦ American ♦ Daily breakfast, lunch, and dinner. 267.5300 ♿

Tea Court ★$ At the heart of the bustling lobby, yet curiously sedate, this pretty cafe serves light fare throughout the day and one of Boston's tastiest teas. ♦ American ♦ Daily breakfast, lunch, and dinner. 267.5300 ♿

4 Boston Public Library To fully justify its title, the "Athens of America," Boston demanded a splendid public library that would set an example for the nation. After all, America's first free municipal library supported by public taxation opened in Boston in 1852; today, serving over two million people yearly, it's the second-largest library in the country. In its every detail, architect **Charles Follen McKim**'s coolly serene Italian Renaissance Revival edifice, which was built in 1895 and is on the National Register of Historic Places, enshrines and celebrates learning. A "Palace for the People" was what the library's trustees had in mind, and that's precisely what **McKim**'s firm (**McKim, Mead & White**) achieved. The library's decoration and design brought together the most magnificent crew of architects, artisans, painters, and sculptors ever assembled in the US until that time. Materials alone reflect the nothing-but-the-best attitude of its creators; for instance, a palette of more than 25 different types of marble and stone was used. Although years of neglect have diminished much of the beauty, a massive $50-million restoration is underway to return the building to its original glory by the end of the century. Meanwhile, parts of the library may be temporarily closed.

Flanking the Dartmouth Street entrance are Bela Pratt's huge 1911 bronzes of two seated women personifying *Art* and *Science,* their pedestals carved with the names of artists and scientists. Prickly wrought-iron lanterns bloom by the doorways—startlingly Halloweenish. Look at the library parapets carved with the names of important people in the history of human culture. There are 519 names in all; the carvers mistakenly repeated four. When one local newspaper reported that **McKim, Mead & White** had amused themselves by working the firm's name into the first letters in three of the panels, enough taxpayers were incensed that the architects had to erase their clever acrostic.

Pass through the bronze portals and enter the main entrance hall. Everywhere you turn there are more inscriptions, dedications, and names of the forgotten great and zealous benefactors. Brass intarsia of the zodiac signs inlay the marble floor; also look up at the intricate mosaic ceilings. Climb the grand staircase of tawny sienna marble past the noble pair of lions to the enormous contemplative Arcadian allegories by Puvis de Chavannes (artist of the poetic murals in the Hôtel de Ville in Paris), which decorate the second-floor gallery. Adjacent is **Bates Hall,** a cavernous reading room 218 feet long with a barrel-vaulted ceiling 50 feet high. To the right is the former **Delivery Room,** where Bostonians waited for their requested books to arrive, transported from the stacks by a tiny train hidden from view.

In the library's remotest reaches on the third floor resides one of Boston's forgotten treasures: the **Sargent Gallery.** Few people ever find their way up the gloomy stairs to this poorly lit place, yet John Singer Sargent considered this gallery the artistic apex of his career. He devoted 30 years to planning the historical murals—their theme is Judaism and Christianity—and designing the entire hall where they were placed. The gallery wasn't quite complete when he died in 1916. The somber murals are tragically faded, but nonetheless deserve attention. Also on the third floor is the **Wiggin Gallery,** which mounts frequent exhibitions of local artists, and the **Cheverus Room,** housing library treasures such as the *Joan of Arc Collection.*

The most satisfying way to end any trip to "the BPL"—the library's nickname—is to visit its peaceful central courtyard with reading in hand. (If you don't qualify as a borrower, bring your own.) Follow the example of other Bostonians and pull a chair between the sturdy stone columns of the cloister, modeled after the Palazzo della Cancelleria's in Rome. The landscaping is simple—just a few trees, a reflecting pool and fountain, and some plantings. Even on a rainy day this is a restful place to read. ♦ Free. M-Sa. One-hour tours depart from the lobby at the Dartmouth entrance. No tours on Friday. Dartmouth St (at Copley Sq). 536.5400 &

4 Boston Public Library Addition When the **Boston Public Library** outgrew **McKim, Mead & White**'s palatial structure, this annex was added in 1972. In materials and monumentality, **Philip Johnson**'s addition echoes the original structure, yet with a colder, starker feel. The interior connection between the new and old buildings is circuitous—you reach the old from the new by turning left just beyond the entry turnstiles and following a corridor past Louise Stimson's appealing dioramas to an innocuous door that leads back to the original building. Nevertheless, Bostonians use the "new" building like mad; here the stacks are open, so there's immediate access to the books. Exhibitions are held regularly in the lofty central space. In the basement is a comfortable theater, where a free film series offers weekly screenings and regular readings are held. Many homeless people frequent the library; it's one of the city's few places truly hospitable to all Bostonians.

The **Access Center** on the Concourse Level serves people with disabilities, offering special equipment and materials. There are large rest rooms in the basement here (a plus in a city with a dearth of public bathrooms), as well as telephones. ♦ M-Sa. 666 Boylston St (between Dartmouth and Exeter Sts). 536.5400 &

5 Westin Hotel, Copley Place $$$ One of Boston's many major chain hotels, this hostelry has 804 rooms and suites on 36 floors, with good views to be had above the 11th floor and two specialty suites on the 36th floor. There are floors designed for people with disabilities and others reserved for nonsmokers. Other amenities include 24-hour room service, a bilingual concierge, valet parking, a health club with an indoor pool, a car-rental desk, many stores, and several restaurants. Small pets are allowed. ♦ 10 Huntington Ave (at Dartmouth St). 262.9600, 800/228.3000; fax 424.7483

Within the Westin Hotel, Copley Place:

Turner Fisheries ★$$$ This softly lit, spacious restaurant is also *quiet*. You can enjoy conversation along with absolutely fresh, simply prepared seafood. The clam chowder has been elevated to the citywide annual Chowderfest's Hall of Fame. For a quick, light meal, there's an oyster bar, or sit in the lounge and order the smoked-bluefish appetizer. ♦ Seafood ♦ Daily lunch and dinner. Reservations recommended. 424.7425 &

6 House of Siam ★$ Though tucked in an inconvenient block across Huntington Avenue from the **Westin Hotel,** this little pink haven is worth seeking out as an inexpensive respite from Back Bay's complacent costliness. The duck and other standard dishes are excellent; try chicken or beef typhoon sautéed with bamboo shoots, minced hot chili peppers, garlic, and basil. ♦ Thai/Takeout ♦ M-Sa lunch and dinner; Su dinner. 21 Huntington Ave (between Exeter and Dartmouth Sts). 267.1755 &

7 Copley Square Hotel $$ One of Boston's oldest, this modest-size 1891 hotel is a Back Bay bargain and attracts an international clientele. It has a pleasantly low-key, informal European style—nothing fancy. All 143 rooms and suites—varying greatly in size—feature in-room coffeemakers, individual climate control, closet floor safes, and windows you can open. The nearby **Westin Hotel**'s health facilities are available to guests for a small fee. Dining options include the newly revived **Original Sports Saloon**—where the baby-back ribs are as famous as the athletes who occasionally drop in—and an inexpensive coffee shop. Other perks include rooms for nonsmokers, inexpensive adjacent parking, and an airport limo. ♦ 47 Huntington Ave (at Exeter St). 536.9000, 800/225.7062; fax 236.0351 &

Within the Copley Square Hotel:

Cafe Budapest ★★$$$ Serenaded by violin and piano, propose marriage, celebrate an anniversary, or toast true love in this intimate, Old European bar with alcoves for two. For almost 25 years this has been the most romantic restaurant in Boston—but be *sure* to request the tiny blue or pink dining room. Contrary to common opinion, lovers usually have perfectly good appetites—may even need extra fuel—and the Central European cooking is certainly rich, hearty comfort food, albeit elegant. Perennial favorites are the iced tart-cherry soup, *Wiener schnitzel à la Holstein* (sautéed veal topped with a fried egg and anchovies), veal *gulyas* (goulash), and sauerbraten. The homemade pastries include extraordinary strudels, of course, and Hungarian wines are served. The pianist and strolling violinist perform Tuesday through Saturday. ♦ Hungarian ♦ Daily lunch and dinner. Reservations recommended. Jacket and tie required. 266.1979 &

Restaurants/Clubs: Red	**Hotels:** Blue
Shops/ 🌳 Outdoors: Green	**Sights/Culture:** Black

8 Copley Place The largest private development in Boston's history, this complex covers 9.5 acres of land and air rights above the Massachusetts Turnpike. With 3.7 million square feet of space, it is the size of 2,500 average American homes, 822 football fields, or more than two **John Hancock Towers.** It includes two hotels, more than a hundred upscale shops and restaurants, an 11-screen cinema, four 7-story office buildings, 1,400 parking places, and 104 residences. In the central atrium, 1,000 gallons of water per minute cascade over Dimitri Hadzi's 60-foot-high water sculpture made of more than 80 tons of travertine and granite.

Needless to say, the genesis of this giant created a furor that hasn't entirely abated. Plunked down at one corner of Copley Square, unfortunately, the behemoth has become a formidable barrier to the neighboring South End. But as bland, anonymous, and prefab-looking as the exterior is, inside, it's marble, marble everywhere, and hardly a bench to sit on. You're meant to come with laden pockets, ready to empty them in shops identical to those in many other cities, with a few exceptions. By and large, stick to Newbury Street unless the weather is bad, because although prices are exorbitant there, too, it's much more genuinely Boston. ◆ Daily. 100 Huntington Ave (between Dartmouth and Harcourt Sts). 375.4400 (information desk) &

Within Copley Place:

Traveldays Bookshop Reminiscent of a cruise ship, this shop is decked out in Art Deco style with lighting fixtures that resemble portholes and gold-stenciled grillwork. The stock at this **Doubleday** offshoot covers travel only—there is a large section on Boston and New England, as well as an extensive inventory traversing the US and Europe. (Even if it's not a travel book you want, they will special-order any title, which takes one to seven days.) There are also maps, language tapes, "video visits," and a huge globe in the back that enables you to plot your route before you even leave the store. ◆ Daily. First floor. 247.2291. Also at: Prudential Center, 800 Boylston St (at Gloucester St). 536.2606; Heritage on the Garden, 99 Park Plaza (between Charles St S and Arlington St). 482.8453

Artful Hand Gallery Representing only US artists, the crafts featured here are contemporary, sophisticated, and eclectic, with a wide range of prices. On a $12 budget, you could take home handmade earrings, beeswax candles, a glazed ceramic mug, or a wooden letter opener. The prohibitively expensive glass sculptures by Orient and Flume are exquisite, as is the ceramic jewelry. ◆ Daily. First floor. 262.9601

9 Boston Marriott Copley Place $$$ This massive 38-story complex rode into town in the early 1980s with the **Copley Place** megadevelopment (so there's plenty of shopping and movies right next door). The highest-up of the 1,147 rooms and suites offer pleasing views; all the guest rooms are furnished in Queen Anne–style, with cable TV, and individual climate control. Many rooms are designed for people with disabilities; four floors are for nonsmokers. The two levels of executive rooms cost more, and include breakfast, a private lounge, and special concierge service. Look for the waterfall gushing in the four-story atrium. The hotel is also connected to the **Prudential Center** and **Hynes Convention Center** by an enclosed footbridge. There are three restaurants within the hotel: **Bello Mondo** (Northern Italian), **Gourmeli's** (American), and **Champions Sports Bar** (burger and sandwiches). Other features include 24-hour room service, valet parking, valet service, a travel agency, an indoor swimming pool, health facilities, barber and beauty shops, meeting facilities and business services, an exhibit hall, and Boston's largest ballroom. Though a tunnel insulates guests from noise and pollution, the hotel is directly above the Massachusetts Turnpike. ◆ 110 Huntington Ave (between Exeter and Harcourt Sts). 236.5800, 800/228.9290; fax 236.5885 &

10 Boylston Street Unlike human-scale Newbury Street with its continual retail diversions, or Commonwealth Avenue with its architectural attractions, this thoroughfare seems like a long walk from one end to the other. This once unkempt road bordering Boston's rail yards was recently revamped, and today is a fashionable stretch, with new shops and restaurants scattered among imposing historic, cultural, and religious institutions. ◆ From Arlington St to Massachusetts Ave

10 The Lenox Hotel $$ When this historic hotel opened in 1900 it stood alone in the midst of railroad tracks. That year the *Boston Sunday Post* said the edifice would "scrape the sky and dally with the gods." In its heyday, Enrico Caruso stayed here. Later, like its city, the hostelry fell on hard times. Having recently undergone a multimillion-dollar renovation, today it has all the luxury of a newcomer and all the charm of a European-style pension. The 222 classically decorated rooms line spacious corridors and feature high ceilings, hand-carved gilt moldings, separate sitting areas, and walk-in closets. The corner rooms with working fireplaces are definite favorites. Some floors are reserved for nonsmokers. Long popular with travelers on a budget, in recent times the establishment has raised its rates—but a genuine personal touch is still present. Amenities include an exercise room, valet service, valet parking, and baby-sitting. Pets are welcome. **The Lenox Pub & Grill** serves hearty, casual pub fare downstairs and grilled entrées upstairs. ♦ 710 Boylston St (at Exeter St). 536.5300, 800 225.7676; fax 267.1237 ♿

Within The Lenox Hotel:

Diamond Jim's Piano Bar All night long, it's one great big friendly, spontaneous sing-along; locals and visitors feel free to come in and pitch their pipes when they are in the mood and have the courage. Regulars are dubbed the **Lenox Singers.** On the second Wednesday of every month, there's a sing-off judged by local celebrities. Tom Selleck, Guy Lombardo, Tony Bennett, and assorted **Metropolitan Opera** stars have shown up here. No food is served—that would only vex the vocal chords. ♦ M-Sa. 536.5300 ♿

11 **J.C. Hillary's** ★$$ A little nondescript, but well established and nicer looking than the other Back Bay restaurants of its ilk, this place offers respectable burgers and bar food, seafood, and pasta at reasonable prices, as well as a bar. ♦ American/Takeout ♦ Daily lunch and dinner. Reservations recommended on weekends. Valet parking evenings. 793 Boylston St (at Fairfield St). 536.6300

11 **The Famous Atlantic Fish Company** ★$$ Long on selections and better priced than many seafood houses in Boston, this is a reliable choice for a casual meal. Fried-clam lovers will be particularly content. At lunchtime, your meal is guaranteed to arrive within 12 minutes after ordering or it's on the house, so there's always a crowd of time-is-money professionals. ♦ Seafood ♦ Daily lunch and dinner. 777 Boylston St (between Exeter and Fairfield Sts). 267.4000 ♿

12 **Buddenbrooks Booksmith**
This shop boasts that it's the only place in the world where you can buy the illustrated first edition of *Paradise Lost* and a mass-market edition at the same time—but you'll have to go upstairs to search them out. The first floor is now **Royal Discount Bookstore,** which features new titles and a healthy supply of remainders. Finds in the second-floor original shop may include first and early illustrated editions of children's books. Creaky wooden floorboards and disorderly displays add to the proper bookstore mood. ♦ Daily. 755 Boylston St (between Exeter and Fairfield Sts). 536.4433 ♿

12 **Boston Chicken** ★$ Queue up with the lunchtime crowds for stellar take-out chicken; it's roasted slowly in a brick-fired rotisserie to seal in a secret marinade. The result is well worth the wait. ♦ Fast food ♦ Daily lunch and dinner. 745 Boylston St (between Exeter and Fairfield Sts). 859.0015

13 **Morton's of Chicago** ★★$$$$ This restaurant's stock of tender, prime-grade dry-aged beef is flown in fresh daily from Chicago. One.of a chain of 18 restaurants, this place has a fabulous way with steak, especially the 24-ounce porterhouse, their hallmark. Come famished enough to eat a side of beef, a flock of chickens, or a school of fish—even the baked potatoes are behemoths. There are some smaller cuts of meat, but that's relative here. Crowds of businesspeople mean a lot of power eating is going on. It's located in what Bostonians have nicknamed "The Darth Vader Building," and you've never seen a modern building so awful. The architectural equivalent of a bad haircut, it's odd-looking and sticks out in the wrong places. ♦ Steakhouse/American ♦ M-F lunch and dinner; Sa-Su dinner. Reservations recommended. Valet parking. 1 Exeter Plaza (at Boylston St). 266.5858 ♿

13 **Glad Day Bookshop** The only one of its kind in New England, this bookstore stocks a comprehensive selection of gay and lesbian literature, including foreign-language titles. Magazines, cards, calendars, CDs, cassettes, and videos are also sold. Special orders are welcome. Just outside is a heavily used community bulletin board. Located on the second floor, the bookstore can be reached by the steps or a cramped elevator—too small for many wheelchairs. ♦ Daily. 673 Boylston St (between Dartmouth and Exeter Sts). 267.3010 ♿

14 **Geoffrey's Cafe-Bar** ★$ Casual and hectic, this bistro features specialty egg dishes, fresh soups, grilled luncheon sandwiches, and rotisserie and pasta entrées. Breakfast on homemade muffins and yogurt in the sunny front alcove. ♦ American ♦ Daily breakfast, lunch, and dinner. 651 Boylston St (between Dartmouth and Exeter Sts). 437.6400

Restaurants/Clubs: Red   **Hotels:** Blue
Shops/ 🌿 Outdoors: Green   **Sights/Culture:** Black

14 New Old South Church Yes, that's truly its name, and what would you expect in a city that's as full of odd monikers as Boston? The **Old South Church** moved here from its 18th-century meeting house, which still stands on Washington Street. The church's Northern Italian Gothic design—executed by **Cummings and Sears** in 1874-75 and now a National Historic Landmark—is pleasingly picturesque with its multicolored ornament, tall campanile, and copper-topped Venetian lantern (see the illustration below). On the entry portico's right wall, look for the tombstone remnant set in concrete that records the death of John Alden, congregation member and eldest son of John and Priscilla Alden of the Plymouth Colony. With a subway station entrance and newsstand located near its porte cochere, the church is always witness to lively comings and goings. Only the sanctuary and chapel are open to the public.♦ M-F; Su until 2PM. 645 Boylston St (between Dartmouth and Exeter Sts). 536.1970

Next to the New Old South Church:

Copley Square News Max has run this newsstand—where you can get periodicals in English, Spanish, French, Italian, and German, as well as flowers—for over 65 years. ♦ M-Sa 3AM-6:30PM. Boylston St (at Dartmouth St). 262.1477 (a pay phone; Max will answer)

15 Bromer Booksellers A stop on the treasure-seeking trail of the serious browser and buyer only, and *not* for casual page-thumbers, this impeccable second-floor gallery displays rare books of all periods. Earnest collectors themselves, Anne and David Bromer sell literary first editions, private press and illustrated books, books in finely crafted bindings, and rare children's books. The couple is internationally recognized as major dealers in miniature books—less than three inches in both dimensions—on all subjects, such as a minuscule *New Testament* written in shorthand and published in 1665, or *Mite,* a late-1800s English compendium of funny nonsense. ♦ M-F. 607 Boylston St (at Dartmouth St). 247.2818

16 Cafe La Poche ★★$$ This newcomer adds a touch of class to the neighborhood. Owner Jack DiCiaccio takes great pride in his food offerings—from gourmet coffees and delectable pastries at breakfast, to soups and salads and sandwiches at lunch, to delicious chicken dishes at dinner. The snappy international decor of tile and marble transports you to a European cafe; sidewalk tables complete the picture. ♦ Cafe ♦ Daily breakfast, lunch, and dinner. 575 Boylston St (between Clarendon and Dartmouth Sts). 267.9247

New Old South Church

16 Small Planet Bar and Grill ★$$ Almost any palate will be pleased by the wide range of dishes—from stir-fry to vegetable lasagna, paella to pizza—offered by his neighborhood bistro. Owner Frank Bell has kept his prices as appealing as his array of entrées. After dinner on a clear night, walk across Copley Square to the **Hancock Tower,** and ride up to the observatory to see illuminated Boston compete with the stars. ♦ International ♦ Daily lunch and dinner. 565 Boylston St (between Clarendon and Dartmouth Sts). 536.4477 ♿

16 Mr. Leung ★★$$$ A world apart from the Formica tabletops and slapdash service prevalent in Chinatown, this suave restaurant with its black-lacquer decor theatrically presents upscale Szechuan-Cantonese dishes to a well-heeled clientele. Taking center stage under tiny ceiling spotlights is a smashing rendition of Peking duck for two. You can order the old standbys here, too, *moo shu* pork and all, but they come quite dear. ♦ Szechuan/Cantonese ♦ Daily dinner. Reservations and jacket required. Valet parking evenings. 545 Boylston St (between Clarendon and Dartmouth Sts). 236.4040 ♿

17 500 Boylston Street Called "a sort of box covered with architectural clothes" by architect/*Boston Globe* architectural critic **Robert Campbell,** this 1988 building by **John Burgee** and **Philip Johnson** is an overblown, outscaled complex that houses fancy shops and offices. Its famous architects must have lost interest during the project—the building is unimaginative kitsch that turns a cold shoulder to its perennially inviting neighbor, **Trinity Church.** The bowling-ball spheres and urns along the parapets look ready to topple. **Johnson** was the architect of the **Boston Public Library Addition,** and **Johnson** and **Burgee** designed **International Place** near **South Station** in the Financial District, another graceless building that dismays many Bostonians. Local citizens tried to halt the construction of this building—to no avail. ♦ At Clarendon St

Within 500 Boylston Street (an entrance is also located on Clarendon St):

Skipjack's ★$$
This Art Deco and neon restaurant with an underwater motif looks like what it is: an upstart rival to

Boston's venerable seafood establishments.

The favorite seafood emporium of many younger Bostonians, it purveys 33 different types of seafood—including many Pacific varieties like Hawaiian mahimahi—that are not just broiled or fried, but in adventurous preparations, such as their signature coating of lemon, soy, and spice. This brash contender draws long lines and gets very hectic; if you feel daunted when you arrive, you can opt for a take-out dinner. Or phone in an order. They'll deliver to Boston, Cambridge, and Brookline. Live jazz accompanies the Sunday brunch. ♦ Seafood/Takeout ♦ M-Sa lunch and dinner; Su brunch and dinner. Valet parking evenings. Restaurant 536.3500, takeout 536.4949. ♿ Also at: 2 Brookline Pl (between Brookline Ave and Harvard St), Brookline. 232.8887; 5 Bennett St (at Eliot St), Charles Square, Cambridge. 876.9900

18 Hard Rock Cafe ★$ The crowds of tourists and teens piling up under a fake rock facade inscribed "Massachusetts Institute of Rock" should clue you in: here's Boston's rendition of the famous chain of restaurants where rock 'n' roll is family fare. There's no live music here, as anyone in the know knows—just eardrum-pummeling recordings of old hits and a menu of surprisingly good bar food starring burgers and barbecue. The rock 'n' roll theme plays itself out all over. The bar's shaped like a Fender Stratocaster guitar; stained-glass windows honor Elvis Presley, Jerry Lee Lewis, and Chuck Berry; and one wall is covered with bricks taken from the demolished Cavern Club in Liverpool, England, where the **Beatles** got their start. Like all of its siblings, the cafe overflows with its share of memorabilia: Roy Orbison's autographed Gibson, John Lennon's original scribblings for *Imagine,* an Elvis necklace, and a cavalcade of objects belonging to other stars. But really, why come here unless you like din with your dinner, or want to personally experience a legendary marketing coup, or have a young friend who's hot on the idea? ♦ American ♦ Daily lunch and dinner. 131 Clarendon St (at Stuart St). 424.7625 ♿

19 The Lyric Stage The oldest resident professional theater company in Boston now resides in spacious quarters within the **YWCA** and mounts such neglected classics as George Bernard Shaw's works. Led by artistic director Ron Ritchell, the company is one of the few non-university–sponsored theaters to warrant critical attention. ♦ 140 Clarendon St (between Stuart St and the Massachusetts Turnpike). 437.7172 ♿

20 Club Cafe ★★$$ Attracting a predominantly (though not exclusively) gay clientele, this sophisticated spot is ideal for a light meal. Chef Julia Brant's menu ranges from pizza to cold duck salad with jicama and endive. Also on the premises is **Club Cabaret,** an intimate setting for stellar (if sporadic) live musical performances. ♦ International ♦ M-Sa lunch and dinner; Su brunch and dinner. 209 Columbus Ave (at Berkeley St). 536.0966 &

BLUE WAVE

20 Blue Wave ★★$$ A lively pocket of California cuisine (read: healthy, eclectic, inventive), this popular spot is a curious blend of high-tech decor and warm vibes. Manager Bruce Ployer likes to showcase favored artists and is constantly shaking up the mix. Chef/owner Russ Berger reaches beyond the ordinary with such unique dishes as pan-seared tuna that is walnut-crusted and served with a passion fruit and orange juice reduction sauce. ♦ California/Takeout ♦ M-F lunch and dinner; Sa dinner; Su brunch and dinner. 142 Berkeley St (at Columbus Ave). 424.6711 &

GRILL 23 & Bar

21 Grill 23 & Bar ★★$$$$ A sea of white linen, mahogany paneling, banker's lamps, and burnished brass give this place a formal demeanor—the ideal setting for a festive but seemly occasion. During the week you'll see many more wheeling-and-dealing Boston professionals than tourists here. Famous for its savoir faire with red meat, especially the perfectly aged and charbroiled 18-ounce New York sirloin, the restaurant turns out splendid seafood and poultry, too. The old-fashioned American practice of topping off hearty fare with equally hearty sweets is bolstered in a dessert list that features good old apple pie and New York cheesecake. Be sure to come famished, but be forewarned: with few rugs on its wooden floors and an open kitchen, the cavernous dining room gets very noisy.

The restaurant is located in the renovated **Salada Tea Building,** which was designed by **Densmore, LeClear, and Robbins** in 1929. On your way out, be sure to look for the fantastic bronze doors at the Stuart Street entrance. Cast from Englishman Henry Wilson's design, they depict exotic scenes from the tea trade and won a silver medal at the 1927 Paris Salon. Elephants and solemn human figures protrude dramatically in bas-relief from the bronze doors and their carved stone setting. ♦ American ♦ Daily dinner. Reservations and jacket and tie recommended. 161 Berkeley St (at Stuart St). 542.2255 &

22 Houghton Mifflin Building Posh digs for Boston's venerable publisher (and several other tenants), this 22-story high-rise designed by **Robert A.M. Stern** (the entrance is pictured above) turns inward for luxury, unlike its ostentatious neighbor, **500 Boylston Street.** The outside is all clean, tasteful lines; the interior is creamy marble with a five-story "wintergarden," complete with splashing fountains. This is a secret retreat in the heart of downtown. ♦ 222 Berkeley St (at Boylston St)

Within the Houghton Mifflin Building:

Cottonwood Cafe ★★★$$ Haute Tex-Mex is the most appropriate rubric for this bountiful, robust fare, served in an evocative, pared-down setting that always seems to suggest the desert at sunset, even at high noon. You can indulge in the delicious Rocky Mountain lamb (mesquite-grilled, with raspberry chipotle sauce on one-half of the enormous platter, cilantro pesto on the other) in the cafe (more like a bar with some bar tables) or in the restaurant proper, where a booth is your best choice. Lunch is not served in the cafe, but otherwise the menu's the same, and both rooms are informal. The service is attentive but unintrusive, and the fresh-fruit margaritas here are just heavenly. ♦ Tex-Mex ♦ Restaurant: daily lunch and dinner. Cafe: daily afternoon snacks and dinner. Reservations recommended. 247.2225. & Also at: 1815 Massachusetts Ave (at Porter Sq), Cambridge. 661.7440

City Sports A popular local outfitter, this rapidly growing chain has chosen to decorate its flagship store with raw beams and exposed ducts, and somehow the stripped-away aesthetic is effective. The high-energy music pumping through doesn't hurt. ♦ Daily. 480 Boylston St (between Berkeley and Clarendon Sts). 267.3900 &

23 Berkeley Building Stand on the opposite side of the street to get a full view of this striking Beaux Arts–inspired office building, designed in 1905 by **Codman & Despredelle.** Look for its spectacular cornice and colorful banners waving above. Clad in enameled terra-cotta, the steel frame supports five-story towers of glass edged in sea-foam green. There's only one elegant embellishment of gilt—the facade is dressy enough. Parisian architect **Desiré Despredelle** taught design classes across the street, where the **Massachusetts Institute of Technology**

School of Architecture was once located.
♦ 420 Boylston St (at Berkeley St)

24 The Rattlesnake Bar & Grill ★★$
Oblivious to its high-rent neighbors, Gordon Wilcox's down-home joint claims to serve "food of the Americas," but really, anything goes at this whimsical joint—everything from quesadillas to duck confit and state-of-the-art Sauza Gold margaritas. Out back, there's an "Urban Canyon" patio with an Aztec-motif mural painted by David Omar White's class at the **Museum of Fine Arts.** With TVs blaring sports as young singles try to corral one another, brace yourself for bustle and din.
♦ Pan-American ♦ Daily lunch and dinner. 384 Boylston St (between Arlington and Berkeley Sts). 859.8555 ♿

24 Women's Educational and Industrial Union (WEIU) Floating above this local institution's decorative entry (the building was designed by **Parker, Thomas & Rice** in 1906, and restored in 1973 by **Shepley, Bulfinch, Richardson & Abbott**) is a gilded swan: it was chosen as a logo because the union was launched in 1877, the same year the **Swan Boats** settled in the **Public Garden**'s lagoon. A small group of women established the association to further employment and educational opportunities and to help the elderly, disabled, and poor. In 1891 Julia Ward Howe became the first president of the Traveler's Information Exchange, which began as a secret underground organization for women travelers, unaccompanied by men, to share information. Today men participate in all of the organization's programs. In 1926 Amelia Earhart found a job as a social worker through career services program here. Her application was noted "Has a sky pilot's license???"

The genteel retail shop run by this private social service organization is a favorite with Bostonians, particularly at holiday time. Staffed by friendly volunteers, the store is filled with handmade articles of all kinds, books and toys for children, knitting and craft supplies, stationery and wrapping papers, and a wealth of household treasures. Be sure to visit the antique consignment shop on the upper level where great finds often surface.
♦ M-Sa. 356 Boylston St (between Arlington and Berkeley Sts). 536.5651 ♿

25 Shreve, Crump & Low Since 1800, innumerable Brahmin brides have registered at this renowned institution, and countless marriages have been launched with jewelry, sterling, crystal, and china purchased from the city's jeweler of choice. You can also pick up your favorite new baby's little silver cup here, order personalized stationery, or peruse exclusive New England items. The illustrious antiques department displays 18th- and 19th-century English and American furniture and prints; China-trade furniture and porcelain;

and English, Irish, and American silver. Service here is assiduous and expert. ♦ M-Sa. 330 Boylston St (at Arlington St). 267.9100

26 Arlington Street Church, Unitarian Universalist This church's most striking feature is its shapely tower (pictured below), inspired by St. Martin's-in-the-Fields in London. The first building erected in Back Bay (completed in 1861), this simple brownstone structure by **Arthur Gilman** was quite conservative in style—as if unsure of its leadership role in storming the mud flats. The outspoken minister William Ellery Channing served here for years; his statue just across the way in the **Public Garden** keeps watch still. A staunch abolitionist, Channing invited Harriet Beecher Stowe and William Lloyd Garrison to address his congregation. During the Vietnam War, the church was active in the peace movement. Attendance skyrocketed

⊥ *Arlington Street Church, Unitarian Universalist*

COURTESY OF THE ARLINGTON STREET CHURCH, UNITARIAN UNIVERSALIST with the arrival of Reverend Kim Crawford Harvie—a woman—who still ministers here. Inside, look for the numerous Tiffany windows. ♦ 351 Boylston St (at Arlington St). 536.7050

26 The Parish Cafe ★$ Named for a fictional boîte in Gabriel García Márquez's *Love in the Time of Cholera*, this intentionally funky cafe—owned by Gordon Wilcox of **The Rattlesnake Bar & Grill** across the street— features sandwiches that pay homage to the great chefs of Boston: Lydia Shire, Chris Schlesinger, et al. ♦ American/Takeout ♦ Daily lunch and dinner. 361 Boylston St (between Arlington and Berkeley Sts). 247.4777 ᵔ

27 Harbridge House In 1893 Boston's grande dame and arts patron Mrs. J. Montgomery Sears combined 12 Arlington Street, a formidable five-story French and Italian–style mansion built by **Arthur Gilman** in 1860, with 1 Commonwealth Avenue, creating a small palace to house her famous art collection and music room. Pianist Ignace Paderewski and violinist Fritz Kreisler visited Mrs. Sears here, as did John Singer Sargent, who executed a portrait of his patron and her daughter at home. **Gilman** also designed **Arlington Street Church** down the block. ♦ 12 Arlington St (at Commonwealth Ave)

28 The Gibson House Facades can only reveal so much; here's your best chance to peer into private Back Bay life. Three generations of Gibsons lived in decorous luxury in this Victorian residence, one of Back Bay's earliest. It was built for Catherine Hammond Gibson and bequeathed nearly a century later to the Victorian Society in America by her grandson Charles to be made into a museum enshrining his family's life and times. Not much to look at on the outside, inside is a wonderful six-story repository of perfectly preserved Victoriana. The Gibsons' ghosts would be quite content to wander through their beloved, dim rooms (sunshine was considered common then), still crowded with the ornaments, overstuffed furniture, fixtures, keepsakes, and curios they amassed and passed down to one another. The tour takes you into the kitchen, laundry, and other service areas so you get a full portrait of daily life at the Gibsons's. ♦ Admission. W-Su afternoons May-Oct; Sa-Su afternoons Nov-Apr. Groups of 12 or more by appointment only. 137 Beacon St (between Arlington and Berkeley Sts). 267.6338

Fanny Merrit Farmer introduced modern measurements, such as the teaspoon, to American cooking. Her cooking school, founded in 1902, occupied 40 Hereford Street (now the site of condominiums in Back Bay) for years. Farmer's *Boston Cooking-School Cookbook* was a smash hit, and her books still grace kitchens all across America.

29 Goethe Institute, German Cultural Center New England's branch of the Munich-based institute inhabits an Italian Renaissance Revival building erected in 1901 by **Ogden Codman**. It was constructed for Boston financier Eben Howard Gay so that he could house his formidable Chippendale and Adams furniture collection, parts of which are now in the **Museum of Fine Arts,** where Gay donated the **Chippendale Wing.** The institute's library collection of more than 6,000 volumes and 40 periodicals and newspapers is open to the public, though only cardholders may check out materials. Language programs and film series, exhibitions, and other cultural events are also offered. ♦ Offices M-F; Library W-F, first Sa of every month. 170 Beacon St (at Clarendon St). 262.6050

30 Marlborough Street This peaceful, shady, residential street in the midst of urbane Back Bay is humbler than Commonwealth Avenue and has aged nicely. Many families live in the well-kept town houses adorned with tidy little gardens, and students share the blocks nearer Massachusetts Avenue. Every 14th of July this thoroughfare is blocked off near the **French Library** for the annual Bastille Day celebration, an evening of dining, music, and dancing that Bostonians enjoy with French flair—as if Lafayette had never left. ♦ From Massachusetts Ave to Arlington St

On Marlborough Street:

The French Library in Boston Ever since the dashing young Marquis de Lafayette won Bostonians' hearts, the city has had a special

fondness for all things French. Since it's founding in 1946, Boston's center for French language and culture (pictured on page 120) has grown quite a bit. Today it holds more than 45,000 books on many topics, and hundreds of cassettes, records, and periodicals (only members may borrow books). A special treat is its collection of *bandes dessinées* (comic books for mature readers) which offer a good workout in idiomatic and colloquial French. The library offers language lessons, lectures, exhibitions, concerts, children's activities, an annual Bastille Day celebration, and many other events. There's a cozy reading room and a theater where French films are regularly screened. Whether to ponder Sartre, flip through a travel guide, get a quick phrase translation, or ask anything at all about *La Belle France*, this is the place to come to. ◆ Tu-Sa; W-Th until 8PM. 53 Marlborough St (at Berkeley St). 266.4351

31 First and Second Church In 1968 **William Robert Ware** and **Henry Van Brunt**'s 1867 **First Church** burned down, but the confla-gration spared some remnants that **Paul Rudolph** ingeniously incorporated into this 1971 hybrid. **Rudolph** is best known for **Yale University's School of Art and Architecture** in New Haven, Connecticut. Even using coarse striated concrete—the brutal material that is his trademark—**Rudolph** creates poignant connections with the ruined fragments, particularly the square stone tower and rose window. ◆ M-F (call first). 66 Marlborough St (at Berkeley St). 267.6730 &

32 First Lutheran Church Entering from Berkeley Street, enjoy a quiet moment in the small landscaped courtyard nestled against this modest brick church, designed by **Pietro Belluschi** in 1959. ◆ 299 Berkeley St (at Marlborough St). 536.8851

33 Baylies Mansion In the early 1900s textile industrialist Walter C. Baylies moved to Boston, married into a wealthy family, and promptly metamorphosed into a full-fledged Brahmin. He tore down an 1861 house to build this showy Italianate mansion (designed by **Thomas and Rice** in 1912), adding a fabulous Louis XIV ballroom for his daughter's debut. A site for glittering society events, the room did its stint of civic service, too: during World War I bandages were rolled here. Since 1941 this has been the home of the Boston Center for Adult Education. Many of the mansion's original ornament and interior finishes remain untouched.
◆ 5 Commonwealth Ave (between Arlington and Berkeley Sts)

34 Commonwealth Avenue This expansive, ruler-straight street was the first major clue that the new Back Bay wouldn't resemble Boston's mazelike older districts. Modeled after the grand Parisian boulevards, "Comm Ave"—its undignified, unpunctuated nickname—was the first of its kind in America, setting a chic French example for the rest of Back Bay to follow; in fact the French Consulate is located at No. 3. The boulevard is 240 feet wide, with a 100-foot-long central mall that Winston Churchill deemed one of the world's most beautiful. The avenue is shaded with elm trees and planted with statues memorializing both the famous and forgotten. May visitors are lucky, arriving when the magnolias are in bloom. This Victorian promenade was once the place for the fashionable to stroll and be seen. Today a more casual collection of Bostonians ambles along, including plenty of dogwalkers and young matrons wheeling infants. The block after block of handsome buildings were once aristocratic town houses, but now boast luxury condos, apartments, and businesses. Unfortunately, a number of homes bear the indignity of having suburbanite roof decks and unsympathetic stories tacked on, ruining many a graceful roofline. The boulevard's northern, sunny side was the most desirable residential stretch in Back Bay, and many showplaces remain. Comm Ave starts to run out of charm when one nears Massachusetts Avenue and Kenmore Square beyond, however. So linger longest closer to the **Public Garden.** ◆ From Arlington St to Massachusetts Ave

35 First Baptist Church **Henry Hobson Richardson** was just starting to flex his creative muscles when he won the commission for this 1871 pudding stone church (originally called New Brattle Square Church) in a competition. Its marvelous campanile springs into the air to create one of Back Bay's most striking silhouettes. The belfry's frieze was modeled in Paris by Frédéric-Auguste Bartholdi, sculptor of the Statue of Liberty (Bartholdi had a way with drapery), and its scenes depict the sacraments of baptism, communion, marriage, and death. Some of the sculpted faces supposedly belong to famous Bostonians, including Hawthorne, Emerson, and Longfellow.

Protruding proudly from the corners, the angels' trumpets won them the irreverent nickname, "The Holy Bean Blowers." Come at sunset to admire their profiles etched crisply against a darkening sky. Unfortunately, the original congregation disbanded and funds ran out, so **Richardson**'s lofty plans for the church interior never came to be. ◆ M-F; service Su 11AM. 110 Commonwealth Ave (at Clarendon St). 267.3148

Restaurants/Clubs: Red   Hotels: Blue
Shops/ 🌳 Outdoors: Green   Sights/Culture: Black

36 Hotel Vendôme You'd think the marsh-bottomed Back Bay would sag under the weight of this magnificent monster, a hybrid of **William G. Preston**'s 1871 corner building and **J.F. Ober**'s main building, both renovated in 1975 by **Stahl Bennett**. For a hundred years, the hotel reigned as Boston's most fashionable hotel, the only place where Sarah Bernhardt would deign to lay her weary head. General Ulysses S. Grant, President Grover Cleveland, John Singer Sargent, Oscar Wilde, Mark Twain, and countless other worthies stayed here.

During its heyday, the hotel boasted unheard-of luxuries: It was the first public building in the city to have electric lighting, powered in 1882 by a plant Thomas Edison had designed. And every room had a private bathroom, fireplace, and steam heat. Inevitably, the hotel's glory days passed, and it became a run-down white elephant. In the 1970s the interior decor was obliterated during renovation, and a terrible fire destroyed portions of the roof and building. Now a condominium complex, the hotel has accepted its comedown as gracefully as possible. To the left at Dartmouth Street is **Preston's** original structure, forced to play a supporting role to **Ober**'s enormous addition on the right. The duo's conjoining marble facades ripple with opulent ornamentation.
♦ 160 Commonwealth Ave (at Dartmouth St)

Within the Hotel Vendôme:

Spasso ★★$$ Painted the color of butter, with lively prints and graffiti and a sunken patio on Commonwealth Avenue, this trattoria is jolly and appealing (its name means "fun"). Beyond such pasta dishes as "scallops *aromatica*" (fettuccine covered with scallops, pine nuts, black olives, and garlic) and pizzas topped with wild mushrooms and pine nuts, there are several substantial *secondi* (entrées), and an array of *dolci* (desserts), too. As the menu advises, "Mangia! Mangia!"
♦ Italian ♦ Daily lunch and dinner. Valet parking. 536.8656 ♿

37 William Lloyd Garrison Statue In Olin L. Warner's posthumous (1885) rendition, Boston's famed abolitionist looks as though he had been intently reading when the artist interrupted and asked him to pose. The statue suggests a man taut with energy, feigning relaxation, stretching back in his armchair with his books and papers hastily stuffed underneath. His profile is memorable. The fiery inscription "I am in earnest—I will not equivocate. I will not excuse. I will not retreat a single inch, and I will be heard!" expresses all of Garrison's unquenchable conviction and is from the inaugural manifesto of *The Liberator,* a journal he founded and edited.
♦ Commonwealth Mall (between Dartmouth and Exeter Sts)

38 Ames-Webster House This mansion was built by **Peabody and Stearns** in 1872 for railroad tycoon and US congressman Frederick L. Ames. Its massive pavilion and porte cochere were added 10 years later by **John Sturgis,** and the whole was renovated in 1969 by architectural firm **CBT** (**Childs Bertman Tseckares**). The exterior is impressive enough, with wrought-iron gates, a two-story conservatory, a monumental tower, and a commanding chimney. But inside is the extraordinary grand hall bedecked with elaborately carved oak woodwork.

The theatrical staircase ascends toward the skylit stained-glass dome, past murals by French painter Benjamin Constant. There's a compact jewel of a ballroom—decorated in celery green and gilt, and delicately proportioned, particularly its "heavens," the balcony where musicians played. Now housing private offices, unfortunately, the building is no longer accessible to the public.
♦ 306 Dartmouth St (at Commonwealth Ave)

39 Admiral Samuel Eliot Morison Statue In Penelope Jencks's statue, the sailor and historian is seated on a rock by the sea, binoculars in hand, dressed in oilskins with a jaunty yachting cap on his head. Notice the coppery lichen on his stony perch, and the sand crabs on the beach below. Smaller rocks are inscribed with such quotes from Morison's books as "Dream dreams then write them/Aye, but live them first." Just across the street is the exclusive **St. Botolph Club,** to which Morison belonged.
♦ Commonwealth Mall (between Exeter and Fairfield Sts)

40 Algonquin Club It would be hard to find a haughtier facade in the city than this one by **McKim, Mead & White,** with its overblown frieze and projecting pair of falcons. The Italian Renaissance Revival palace, which was built in 1887 for a private club, certainly catches the eye with its self-confident, flamboyant architectural maneuvers.
♦ 217 Commonwealth Ave (between Exeter and Fairfield Sts)

Restaurants/Clubs: Red   **Hotels:** Blue
Shops/ ♥ Outdoors: Green   **Sights/Culture:** Black

40 First Corps of Cadets Museum This place is for military history buffs. Established in 1726, the First Corps of Cadets is one of America's oldest military organizations. Members have served in most US wars and conflicts. The corps began as bodyguards to the royal governors of the Province of Massachusetts Bay. John Hancock served as colonel in 1774. The museum holds examples of most arms in existence, dating back to King George II. Many weapons and memorabilia were brought back from action by corps members. Also featured are flags, uniforms, drums, and paintings. ♦ Free. Two-hour tours by appointment only. 227 Commonwealth Ave (between Exeter and Fairfield Sts). 267.1726

41 267 Commonwealth $$ This intimate Victorian hotel is owned—and was restored—by Bob Vila, former host of "This Old House," a popular public TV series. An 1880 brownstone that was once a single-family residence, it is broken up into five one-bedrooms and four studios, with high ceilings, handsome woodwork, marble or hand-carved fireplaces, and kitchenettes. The studio rooms actually feel grander since they weren't divided to create sitting rooms. Room No. 7 was the master bedroom and overlooks Commonwealth Avenue and its mall, as does No. 5. The penthouse room is a contemporary addition with modern furnishings. About half the guests are corporate relocations; many are affiliated with hospitals. Opera, ballet, and music stars often stay here. Laundry facilities are in the building; weekly rates are available. ♦ Between Fairfield and Gloucester Sts. 267.6776

42 Nickerson House Architects **McKim, Mead & White**'s last Back Bay residence offers one monumental gesture in the sweep of its bulging granite bowfront. The 1895 building is a model of chilly restraint, but enjoyed a brief fling as the site of two of Boston's most lavish debutante balls, held by Mrs. Pickman, wife of the house's second owner, for her daughters. ♦ 303 Commonwealth Ave (between Gloucester and Hereford Sts)

In 1913, the nation's first credit union was opened by Boston's Women's Educational and Industrial Union.

43 Burrage Mansion Not all Bostonians were willing to surrender their highfalutin aspirations to fit Back Bay's decorous mold. Certainly not Albert Burrage; his theatrical 1899 limestone mansion simultaneously pays homage to the Vanderbilts' Fifth Avenue mansions and Chenonceaux, the French château on the Loire. A multitude of strange carved figures peer down from and crawl across the facade's excess of ornament. Burrage once cultivated orchids in the splendid glass-domed greenhouse at the rear. The mansion is now a rather luxurious retirement home. Peek inside to see how enthusiastically the interior competes with the exterior, particularly in the sculpted marble staircase and abundant embellishments. ♦ 314 Commonwealth Ave (at Hereford St)

44 Oliver Ames Mansion The original owner was head of the Ames Shovel Manufacturing Company, president of the Union Pacific Railroad, philanthropist, owner of the Booth Theatre in New York, and a Massachusetts governor. Clearly, a lion like Ames would command Back Bay's biggest mansion. **Henry Hobson Richardson** prepared a sketch for the house, but it was rejected and **Carl Fehmer** took over in 1882. Look at the frieze panels of putti and floral ornament portraying the activities that occurred in the rooms behind. Now an office building, the mansion served as the longtime headquarters of the National Casket Company. ♦ 355 Commonwealth Ave (at Massachusetts Ave)

45 Church Court Condominium In 1978 an up-and-coming young architect named **Graham Gund** caused a furor when he purchased the burnt-out shell of **Mount Vernon Church** for commercial development, but this elegant amalgam—with a clerestory topped by sculptor Gene Cauthon's ethereal bronze angel—set a brave standard for creative reuse. ♦ 492 Marlborough St (between Charlesgate E and Massachusetts Ave)

After graduating from Harvard College in 1859, Henry Hobson Richardson, a Louisiana native, launched into architectural studies at the Ecole des Beaux Arts in Paris. Returning to America seven years later, Richardson quickly advanced his individualistic style by creating works that were at once robust and monumental. He began his practice in New York, then moved to Boston after winning the Trinity Church commission. As Trinity's resplendent interior illustrates, Richardson liked to pull out all the stops, enlisting celebrated artists and sculptors to collaborate on the decoration of his houses, churches, schools, libraries, hospitals, bridges, and railroad stations. He even designed furniture like his predecessor—architect Charles Bulfinch—but won far greater fame.

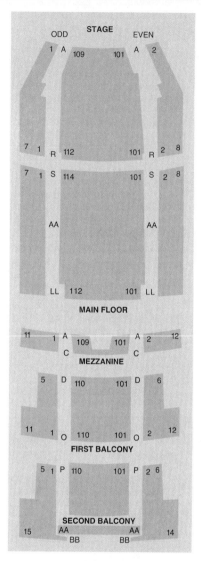

STAGE
ODD EVEN

1 A 109   101 A 2

7 1 R 112   101 R 2 8

7 1 S 114   101 S 2 8

AA   AA

LL 112   101 LL

MAIN FLOOR

11 1 A 109   101 A 2 12
C   C
MEZZANINE

5 D 110   101 D 6

11 1 O 110   101 O 2 12
FIRST BALCONY

5 1 P 110   101 P 2 6

SECOND BALCONY
15 AA   AA 14
BB   BB

46 Berklee Performance Center Associated with the highly regarded **Berklee College of Music,** this center (see the plan above) hosts popular performances of all types of contemporary music, especially jazz and folk. ♦ Admission. Box office M-Sa. No credit cards accepted. 136 Massachusetts Ave (at Boylston St). 266.1400, recorded concert information 266.7455

47 Sheraton Boston Hotel & Towers $$$ Here's where the sports teams stay, with one staffer solely dedicated to their needs and wants. The 1,250-room hotel abuts the **Hynes Convention Center,** which conventioneers can enter without ever going outdoors. A business service center handles word processing, copying, and other office functions. One of the 29-story twin towers offers four floors that are a mini-hotel-within-a-hotel, with quieter rooms, butler service, and a VIP lounge.

Every December the hotel sponsors the Bill Rodgers Jingle Bell Run—a fun run to benefit the Special Olympics—and about 4,000 people participate, wearing Christmas regalia. Get a room up high for good views of the **Christian Science International Headquarters** or the Charles River. A number of floors are dedicated to nonsmokers and people with disabilities. Small pets are allowed. Other amenities include 24-hour room service, an indoor/outdoor pool, a health club with a Jacuzzi, and a beauty salon and barber. ♦ 39 Dalton St (between Boylston St and Huntington Ave). 236.2000, 800/325.3535; fax 236.1702 ♿

Within the Sheraton Boston Hotel & Towers:

The Mass. Bay Company ★$$ Come here when you can't tolerate the lines or prices at Boston's higher-profile seafood houses. Specialties include award-winning clam chowder, salmon and trout smoked on the premises, and fish grilled over mesquite charcoal. ♦ Seafood ♦ Daily dinner. Reservations recommended. 236.8787 ♿

48 Back Bay Hilton $$$ A stone's throw from the **Hynes Convention Center,** this rather nondescript 25-story hotel caters assiduously to the business traveler. All 335 rooms are soundproofed, with small bathrooms, and decorated with calm, soothing decor. Many have balconies and bay windows you can open. Amenities include a year-round swimming pool; a health facility; 24-hour room service and parking garage; meeting and banquet rooms; and nonsmokers' floors. In addition to a lounge, there's an upscale nightclub. ♦ 40 Dalton St (at Belvidere St). 236.1100, 800/874.0663 ♿

Within Back Bay Hilton:

Boodle's of Boston ★★$$$ A sillier name for such an earnest grill room would be hard to find. The English decor is a little ponderous, but perfectly appropriate to the main business at hand: expertly grilling massive cuts of meat over hardwoods, including sassafras and hickory. Seafood and vegetables make many a pleasant turn on the grill here, too, and there are oyster dishes galore. You can dress up the entrées by choosing from 20 butters, sauces, and condiments. ♦ Steakhouse/American ♦ Daily breakfast, lunch, and dinner. Reservations recommended for dinner. 266.3537 ♿

49 Christian Science International Headquarters It's easy to overlook the little acorn from which this gigantic oak grew. **Franklin J. Welch's** original 1894 Romanesque **Christian Science Mother Church,** which founder Mary Baker Eddy called "our prayer in stone," is now dwarfed by a behemoth extension. The 1906 addition of **Charles E. Brigham** (with **Solon S. Beman, Brigham Coveney and Bisbee**) soars to a height of 224 feet. This Renaissance basilica bears the weight of its towering dome like giant Atlas holding the world upon his shoulders. Designed to seat 3,000, it boasts one of the world's largest working pipe organs, a 13,595-pipe Aeolian Skinner manufactured locally. Located on what was the outer edge of respectability, in the midst of tenements and crowded residential blocks, the old and new church clung together until 1973, when **I.M. Pei**'s master plan carved out a great swath of 22 acres, populating its core with monumental church administration buildings.

Strategically flanking the church like Secret Service agents are the 28-story **Church Administration Building;** the fan-shaped **Sunday School;** and the low-slung **Colonnade Building.** They surround a vast public space dominated by a 670-foot-long, 100-foot-wide reflecting pool rimmed with red granite, a pleasant feature with a hidden agenda: to cool water from the air-conditioning system. The circular fountain at one end is dull when shut off, but, gushing on hot days, it becomes a hectic playground and contributes a badly needed note of spontaneity to this austere, over-planned setting. With rows of manicured trees, flowerbeds, and water, the plaza is a popular lunchtime spot. But in the winter the wind can whip through here fiercely, treating the office tower as a sail.

To one side of the church is the **Christian Science Publishing Society** building, offices for the well-regarded *Christian Science Monitor,* founded in 1908. Inside, look up at the two extraordinary glass globe lanterns suspended from the lobby ceiling; one lights up to tell the time, the other the date. Follow signs to the fabulous *Mapparium,* a vividly colored stained-glass globe 30 feet in diameter, traversed by a glass bridge. Since glass doesn't absorb sound, you can stand at one end and send whispered messages echoing eerily across the way to a partner. Made of more than 600 kiln-fired glass panels, the *Mapparium* is illuminated from behind by 300 lights. Designed by the building's architect, **Chester Lindsay Churchill,** the globe was completed in 1932 and has not been altered since. It's outdated, but all the more interesting for its pre-World War II record of political boundaries. Ten-minute guided tours of the *Mapparium,* and guided tours of the original church and the extension are offered. ♦ Free. Mother Church Tu-Su; Mapparium Tu-Sa. Mother Church: 175 Huntington Ave (at Massachusetts Ave). Mapparium (within Christian Science Publishing Society Building): 1 Norway St (off Hemenway St, west of the Mother Church). General information 450.2000

50 Horticultural Hall Founded in 1829, the Massachusetts Horticultural Society sponsors the nation's oldest annual spring flower show. It is a spectacular event, but has bloomed too large for this exhibition hall (designed in 1901 by **Wheelwright and Haven** and now on the National Register of Historic Places), the society's headquarters. Unfortunately, the show was uprooted to the impersonal (and remote) **Bayside Exposition Center** in Dorchester. The Horticultural Society launched America's school-gardening movement, which now brings gardening studies into many Boston public schools and spreads the love of growing things via its traveling Plantmobile exhibits. In addition to operating the world's largest independent horticultural library, the society runs a shop selling seeds, books, and prints. You can even call for free advice. The society's decorative building—which it now shares with other organizations, such as *Boston* magazine—makes a striking couple with **Symphony Hall** across the street. ♦ Free. M-F; Sa until 2PM. 300 Massachusetts Ave (at Huntington Ave). 536.9280 ♿

51 Newbury Street With the third-highest rents in the US, tying with New York City's Fifth Avenue and coming in behind Beverly Hills's Rodeo Drive and Palm Beach's Worth Avenue, even the pavement on this thoroughfare aspires to commercial heights. Though it's less fashionable the closer you are to Massachusetts Avenue, nowhere else in Boston will you feel underdressed just strolling along. In addition to boutiques and galleries, there are dozens of hair "designers," tanning and facial salons, and modeling studios along this stretch. For those who seek beauty-to-go, there's art, literature, antiques, and costly geegaws galore, plus a thriving cafe society. ♦ From Massachusetts Ave to Arlington St

51 360 Newbury Street An early 1900s warehouse designed by **Arthur Bowditch** was metamorphosed into a dramatic iconoclast by architect **Frank O. Gehry** with the assistance of **Schwartz/Silver Architects** in 1989. The building towers over the Massachusetts Avenue end of Newbury Street. Viewed from the Massachusetts Turnpike and from many Back Bay angles, the structure is a challenging, alert, eye-catching presence—and, though critically lauded, not universally beloved. Its brash projecting struts, canopy, and cornice make it appear scaffolded and still in process, as if the building hasn't quite decided what it wants to be yet. Step into the bank-breaking splendor of the lobby on the Newbury Street side, and also check the wall next door for Morgan Bulkeley's surrealist mural *Tramount,* depicting—in odd little vignettes—the history of the city. ♦ At Massachusetts Ave

Within 360 Newbury Street:

Tower Records/Video Calling itself "the largest record store in the known world," this enormous multilevel emporium is one of a chain of almost 100 stores in the US, England, and Japan, and sells LPs, 45s, CDs and cassettes (including single recordings), and videos. It covers all the music bases, but this isn't the place to come for unconventional, hard-to-find recordings. You can purchase tickets to most concerts in person at the **Ticketmaster** counter. A lot of late-night socializing goes on here. ♦ Daily until midnight. 247.5900 &

52 The Capital Grille ★★$$$$ Top-grade steak—dry-aged in plain view on the premises—is this upscale restaurant's primary raison d'être. Some straightforward seafood is also served. The decor is modeled after an old-fashioned men's club: lots of dark paneling (lifted from a 16th-century Welsh castle), marble floors, and a long brass bar with private wine lockers. It attracts a prosperous crowd whose business image requires a certain show of conspicuous consumption. ♦ American ♦ Daily dinner. Reservations recommended. Valet parking. 359 Newbury St (between Massachusetts Ave and Hereford St). 262.8900 &

52 Johnson Paint Company Look for the famous sign with bright multicolored stripes and real gold leaf. The Johnson family's business has occupied this former carriage house—where horses owned by wealthy Back Bay residents once slept—for more than 50 years. In addition to selling good old-fashioned paint products—they've carried the same lines of paint since 1936—the store is a fixture in the fine arts community, stocking what the staff refers to as "fancy painting stuff"—brushes imported from five countries, easels, tables, pads, powdered pigments, and art books. If you have a tricky wall color to match, this is a good place to come. Renowned citywide, the color mixer has worked here for more than 30 years and is better than a computer at matching samples. Classes run continually on faux painting, glazing, gilding, and other techniques. You can even buy a T-shirt with the store's gaily colored emblem. ♦ M-F; Sa until 1PM. 355 Newbury St (between Hereford St and Massachusetts Ave). 536.4244 &

Restaurants/Clubs: Red   Hotels: Blue
Shops/ 🌳 Outdoors: Green   **Sights/Culture: Black**

53 Avenue Victor Hugo Bookshop Just a glance in the window reveals what a treasure trove this used bookstore is. Row upon row of nine-foot-tall bookshelves are crammed with used books in 250 subject areas, ranging in price from 25¢ paperback romances to $200 limited editions. Put yourself in a nostalgic mood browsing through the used periodicals dating from 1854 to the present. There's some new fiction, comic books, a great card and postcard selection, old maps, and vintage sheet music, too. Prowling the premises is Feet, the store's lordly cat. "All used bookstores should have one," says owner Vincent McCaffrey. ♦ Daily. 339 Newbury St (between Hereford St and Massachusetts Ave). 266.7746 &

53 The Ultimate Bagel Company This narrow storefront lives up to its boastful name, with the plumpest, tastiest bagels (including a healthful eight-grain wheat germ variety) and assorted cream-cheese spreads (some cholesterol-free), plus soups, salads, and sandwiches. Check out the rear-wall mural, a faux Florentine garden painted by Bopäs, the partnership of decorative painters Gedas Paskauskas and Robert Grady. ♦ Daily. 335 Newbury St (between Massachusetts Ave and Hereford St). 247.1010. & Also at: 1310 Massachusetts Ave (at Harvard Sq), Cambridge. 964.8990

53 Sonsie ★★$$$ Complete with bar and brick oven, this fashionable bistro offers bustling sidewalk tables or more quiet, elegant dining at inside booths. Not to be outdone for originality, chef Bill Poirer prepares a range of dishes that will satisfy any number of palates. Stunning pizza presentations include a tasty delight with spicy shrimp, peppers, ricotta, and leeks, and another topped with lime chicken, salsa, guacamole, and jack cheese. Entrées include sake-steamed salmon fillet with cucumber nori rolls and toasted sesame; white lasagna with chicken, eggplant, and sweet marjoram; and a vegetarian entrée of whole roast onion soup, wild mushroom tamale, *orecchiette* with broccoli and extra virgin olive oil, and vegetable mixed grill. Many of the dishes on the menu are designed to be low fat. Little or no dairy products are used, and special dietary preferences will be accommodated. ♦ International ♦ M-Sa breakfast, lunch, and dinner; Su brunch and dinner. 327 Newbury St (between Hereford St and Massachusetts Ave). 351.2500

54 Trident Booksellers & Cafe ★$
"Boston's alternative bookstore" sells some fiction, but is particularly strong in Jungian psychology, acupuncture, poetry, Eastern religions, and Buddhist, women's, and metaphysical works. Crystals, incense, scented oils, tarot cards, and bonsai trees are also on sale. The little cafe is a popular neighborhood meeting place for a broad spectrum of Bostonians, who come for its no-fuss, down-to-earth, tasty menu of homemade soups, sandwiches, bagels, croissants, and rib-sticking desserts like carrot cake, plus a variety of coffees. Readings are held every Sunday and are free (donations requested). ♦ Cafe ♦ M-Sa breakfast, lunch, and light dinner; Su lunch and light dinner. 338 Newbury St (between Hereford St and Massachusetts Ave). 267.8688

54 Newbury Comics This oddball store started as a comic-book outpost, then branched into anything music-related. They still sell comics, including some aimed at adult readers, but the eccentric inventory now encompasses independent label and import music in CDs and cassettes; music and comic T-shirts; music videos; music books; portable "music makers" and accessories; posters; biker-style jewelry; and bizarre novelties. College students flock here for hard-to-find recordings. ♦ Daily. 332 Newbury St (between Hereford St and Massachusetts Ave). 236.4930 ⴷ

54 John Fleuvog If your feet want to make a particularly eccentric fashion statement, don a pair of clunky Munster platforms fit for Frankenstein; or the Bump, a style for L'il Abner; or Doc Marten's incredibly blocky styles. English-made in plenty of leathers and colors, with crests and bows and buckles and tapestry, the shoes on sale here are all ready for action of some sort. ♦ Daily. 328 Newbury St (between Hereford St and Massachusetts Ave). 266.1079

54 The Nostalgia Factory
"The Eye Shall Never Rest" is the credo of this gallery bursting with old collectibles and ephemera. Owners Rudy and Barbara Franchi scour fairs, flea markets, and England to come up with their ever-changing assortment of rare posters, old postcards

and advertisements, political buttons, antique signs, soda-pop art, English royalty souvenirs, and memorabilia of all kinds. A browser's delight, yes, but the gallery also portrays more serious changing attitudes and trends: a fascinating display of magazine advertising from the 1920s through the 1950s chronicles products once considered safe and now banned or warned against, such as cigarettes, asbestos shingling, and lead paint. ♦ Daily. 324 Newbury St (between Hereford St and Massachusetts Ave). 236.8754

54 Boston Architectural Center (BAC) This bulky concrete block of a building is a 1967 exemplar of "Brutalism" by **Ashley, Myer & Associates,** the architectural firm that is now called **Arrowstreet.** The structure has turned out to be an unexpectedly amiable addition to Back Bay, but don't let the contemporary look fool you: It houses an architecture school, which began life in 1889 as a free atelier run by the Boston Architectural Club, where deserving youth were given drawing lessons. It is the only architecture school in the US that requires students to work full-time as fledgling architects while taking classes at night from an all-volunteer faculty. The inviting, glass-sheathed ground floor is a public space for student work and art and architectural exhibitions.

On the building's exterior west wall, New York artist Richard Haas painted one of his best murals in 1977. It has since become a Back Bay landmark. This six-story architectural trompe l'oeil is a cross-sectional view of a French Neo-Classical palace in the Beaux Arts style. Look for the mural's teasers: the shadow of a man against a corridor wall; a foot disappearing through a closing door; and a man appearing in a doorway on his way to the top of the rotunda. ♦ Gallery daily; M-Th until 11PM. 320 Newbury St (at Hereford St). 536.3170 ⴷ

55 Institute of Contemporary Art (ICA) and Engine and Hose House Number 33
A police station and firehouse shared this building (designed by city architect **Arthur H. Vinal**) in the 19th-century. The police eventually relocated next door (**Arrowstreet** performed the renovation in 1975) and the museum moved in after **Graham Gund Associates** handsomely restored its half in 1975. Inside the Romanesque-style shell are multilevel galleries and a 140-seat theater for mixed-media exhibitions, films, and performances in the visual arts. Established in 1936, the museum has no permanent collection and is famous for its eclectic, sometimes uneven, but always interesting array of work by known and unknown artists.

One-of-a-kind in Boston, the institute aims to be a research and development laboratory for new ideas. As you head over to the entrance, you'll see firefighters on the job, taking a break from time to time to watch the colorful crowd on the trendy art trail. And the ornate turret tower on the Hereford Street side is still used for drying fire hoses. ♦ Admission; free Wednesday-Thursday 5-9PM. W-Su. 955 Boylston St (at Hereford St). 266.5152 & (limited access, call first)

55 Division Sixteen ★$ Located in the former police station, this sleek Art Deco restaurant is a popular spot with students and youngish singles. At night there's inevitably a wait, and the horrendous din and clatter will drown out any conversation unless you insist on a booth in the back. But there is a reason to come here: monster portions of reasonably priced, decently prepared casual food, such as sandwiches, salads, omelettes, burgers, nachos, and the like. The shoestring fries are made from scratch. On a weeknight, better still a rainy one, this place goes well with an evening at one of the movie theaters nearby. ♦ American ♦ Daily lunch and dinner. 955 Boylston St (at Hereford St). 353.0870 &

56 John B. Hynes Veterans Memorial Convention Center Commonly called "the Hynes," this facility (pictured below) is ordinarily not open to the public. Cross to the opposite side of Boylston Street to study the impressive facade and ground-floor loggia, then peek inside at the magnificent main rotunda. A much admired structure, rebuilt in 1988 by **Kallmann, McKinnell & Wood Architects,** who also designed Boston's unusual **City Hall,** the center is so conciliatory toward its surroundings that it's easy to forget it can handle a convention of 22,000. Bankers, dentists, lumberers, and teachers—even the Association of Old Crows—have passed through its handsome portals. ♦ 900 Boylston St (at Gloucester St). 954.2000, recorded information 424.8585 &

57 Prudential Center Home of the insurance giant, "The Pru" is a dowdy complex, unloved by many and the worse for wear. It houses six million square feet of offices, apartments, hotels, and stores in a network of elevated blocky buildings and windy plazas, parts of which appear abandoned to the ravages of time. But when the sprawling 27-acre complex was plopped down here in the early 1960s by **Charles Luckman and Associates** and **Hoyle, Doran, and Berry,** it covered the unsightly **Boston & Albany** rail yards, introduced a new scale to Back Bay, and stirred high hopes for a rejuvenated modern Boston. It's worth a visit to grasp the radical 1960s concept of American urban renewal. The center recently underwent an overhaul, which entailed enclosing and modernizing the walkways.

Once the city's tallest skyscraper, the inelegant 52-story **Prudential Tower** has been outraced to the heavens by its rival, the sleek **John Hancock Tower.** Still, many Bostonians have grown fond of the homely smaller tower. Take an elevator up to the **Skywalk,** the observation deck on the 50th floor, and see what's happening for miles around. Or enjoy the view with a drink at the **Top of the Hub.** (Don't bother with a meal; the restaurant is just further proof that penthouse restaurants don't live up to their aerial heights.) At Christmastime, an enormous tree is illuminated on the plaza in front of the tower, facing Boylston Street. ♦ Admission to Skywalk. Daily. 800 Boylston St (at Fairfield St). 236.3318 &

58 The Cactus Club ★$ The American Southwestern motif has gotten so out of hand here, it must be parody (intense aqua galore, O'Keeffe-esque skulls, a buffalo over the bar); but as the big, high-ceilinged rooms fill up, the design assault recedes. Beneath this garishly cheerful disguise lurks a fern bar. The nouvelle Southwestern cuisine highlights ribs, grilled fish and meat, pastas, barbecue, and the like, with such welcome accents as fresh coriander and chipotle peppers. If you have a

John B. Hynes Veterans Memorial Convention Center

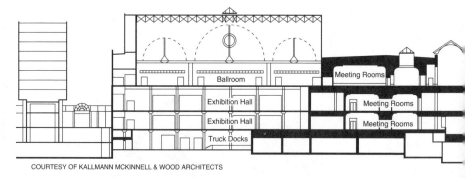

COURTESY OF KALLMANN MCKINNELL & WOOD ARCHITECTS

penchant for swimming in fishbowl-size glasses, you'll like the drinks. This has become a popular hangout for a youngish crowd. The restaurant inhabits the handsome **Tennis and Racquet Club** building (constructed in 1904), which has a splendid gate in its lobby that prevents access to upstairs offices after hours. ◆ Southwestern ◆ Daily lunch and dinner. 939 Boylston St (at Hereford St). 236.0200 ₺

59 Steve's Greek & American Cuisine ★$
Lots of locals, students, and conventioneers from the nearby **Hynes** come to this cheerful restaurant whose owner, Steve Kourtidis, says, "It's our pleasure to serve the people." On one side is the take-out operation, on the other the pleasant plant-entwined dining room overlooking Newbury Street. The menu features Greek and Middle Eastern favorites—moussaka, grape leaves, *baklava*, shish kebabs—and burgers and omelettes. This is not the place to come if cigarette smoke bothers you. ◆ Greek American/Takeout ◆ Daily. No credit cards accepted. 62 Hereford St (at Newbury St). 267.1817

60 L'Espalier ★★★$$$$ This refined and sophisticated establishment started Boston's restaurant revolution in 1978, yanking the city out of its doldrums into a new era of posh cuisine. Frank McClelland, acclaimed successor to the original owner, leans a bit more toward contemporary American cuisine and uses native products. But dinner here is as rarefied and highfalutin an event as ever. Set in a stately 1873 town house, the stunning dining rooms will satisfy your whim to experience Back Bay's heyday. The prix-fixe menu might include sautéed yellowfin tuna steaks, squab and fig salad, grilled partridge, or duck breast coupled with foie gras; every dish is tenderly treated and gorgeously presented in modest—sometimes overly so—portions. The service is exceedingly proper. ◆ French ◆ M-Sa dinner. Reservations required Friday-Sunday. Jacket and tie recommended. Valet parking. 30 Gloucester St (between Newbury St and Commonwealth Ave). 262.3023

"The Pledge of Allegiance" was written by Francis Bellamy, who lived at 142 Berkeley Street (now known as "The Pledge of Allegiance House").

60 Casa Romero ★$$$ The prices are steep, though there's compensation in the picturesque dining rooms brightened with hand-painted tiles and Mexican handicrafts. A number of dishes are outstanding: avocado soup, chicken with *mole poblano* (in a rich garlic, onion, chili peppers, and chocolate sauce), and *puerco adobado* (pork with smoked chilies) are a sampling. Enter from Gloucester Street at the side alley that runs between Commonwealth Avenue and Newbury Street. ◆ Mexican ◆ Daily dinner. Reservations recommended. 30 Gloucester St (between Newbury St and Commonwealth Ave). 536.4341

61 Miyako ★★$$ The former site of several trendy restaurants that lacked staying power has turned out to be the perfect setting for this elegant Japanese restaurant. It's a choice duplex corner spot with a roomy patio, and inside the decor is minimalist: gray walls with the odd extravagant floral display. All the better to focus on exquisitely delicate tastes. A sushi bar is tucked into the sub-street level, and the airy second floor features traditional tatami seating. ◆ Japanese ◆ Daily lunch and dinner. 279A Newbury St (at Gloucester St). 236.0222

61 Cafe Jaffa ★$ An inviting storefront with broad picture windows and bare brick walls, this modest cafe has been an instant hit with its authentic—and affordable—Middle Eastern fare: hummus, falafel, *schawarma* (ground roasted lamb or chicken), and the like. ◆ Middle Eastern/Takeout ◆ M-Sa lunch and dinner; Su lunch and dinner. 48 Gloucester St (between Commonwealth Ave and Newbury St). 536.0230 ₺

62 Culture Shock Wunderkind Patrick Petty is probably the most radical clothing designer working on Newbury Street, and his shop is decidedly the most daring. These are street styles with pedigrees: Vivienne Westwood, Moschino, BCBG. The clientele varies from Roxbury kids to suburban matrons, all equally energized by Petty's custom music mix. ◆ Daily. 286 Newbury St (between Gloucester and Hereford Sts). 859.7508

63 Dad's Beantown Diner ★$ So what if the 1950s decor (diamond-pattern aluminum paneling, glass bricks, turquoise banquettes, vintage photos) is a re-creation, not the real thing? Families nonetheless love the hearty food—"like Mom's!" boasts the menu—and reasonable prices, at least for this part of town. Meat loaf, pot roast, potpie—you can pile it on and still make room for Jello parfait. ♦ American/Takeout ♦ Daily lunch and dinner. 911 Boylston St (between Gloucester and Hereford Sts). 296.3237 &

64 Gyuhama ★★$$ One of Boston's best sushi bars is also the only place in town serving lobster sashimi. It's a spectacular presentation that's not for the fainthearted, since the lobster pieces may still be twitching when served! Less daring choices include delectable sukiyaki. The basement dining room is intimate, though a trifle seedy. There are always many Japanese diners, a testament to the fastidiously fresh and imaginatively prepared food. In fact, there are so many regulars that it can have a cliquey air. Dine early or be prepared for a wait. ♦ Japanese ♦ Daily lunch and dinner. 827 Boylston St (between Gloucester and Fairfield Sts), Basement level. 437.0188

65 Fine Time Vintage Watch Gallery The owners are experienced timepiece dealers and specialize exclusively in buying, selling, restoring, and appraising fine vintage wristwatches and antique pocket watches, such as Patek Philippe, Rolex, Vacheron, Hamilton Watch Company, Cartier, and Waltham. They even carry authentic Mickey Mouse alarm clocks. You won't find any reproductions here—just the splendid real ticktockers. ♦ Tu-Sa. 279 Newbury St (at Gloucester St). 536.5858

65 Nomad A one-stop shop for "folk art, jewelry, clothing in a global style," this pleasantly packed shop harbors a panoply of international finds—from Thailand hill-tribe garb to sparkly Frida Kahlo icon earrings. Enjoy the world-beat music while browsing. ♦ Daily. 279 Newbury St (at Gloucester St). 267.9677

The largest teddy bear in the world sits in front of FAO Schwarz on Newbury Street. The teddy is 12 feet high, weighs about two tons, and costs about $500,000.

Restaurants/Clubs: Red   **Hotels:** Blue
Shops/ 🌿 Outdoors: Green   **Sights/Culture:** Black

65 Davio's ★★$$$ This romantic, jewel-box restaurant, a favorite with Back Bay residents, features fine Northern Italian cuisine. The kitchen makes its own pastas and sausage, and lavishes attention on soups, seafood, venison, and veal. The wine list includes some costly Italian venerables. At the informal cafe upstairs, snack on fashionable pizzas and pastas at lower prices. There's a little terrace out back for fair-weather dining. ♦ Italian ♦ Dining room M-Sa lunch and dinner; Su dinner. Cafe daily lunch and dinner. Reservations recommended in dining room. Valet parking evenings. 269 Newbury St (between Fairfield and Gloucester Sts). 262.4810. Also at: The Royal Sonesta, 5 Cambridge Pkwy (at the Charles River Dam), Cambridge. 661.4810

66 Frontier Owner Mimi Packman has a knack for rounding up resonant retro artifacts, often adapting them to brave new uses. Old upholstery fabrics become charming dresses and jackets, vintage tablecloths, and comfy pillows. The stock is always evolving, but the white picket fence out front is a reliable sign of what you'll find inside. ♦ Tu-Sa. 252 Newbury St (between Fairfield and Gloucester Sts). 421.9858

66 Ciao bella ★★$$ Convivial singles like to lunch at the bar, looking out at Newbury Street. In the evening the dressy dining room draws a chic clientele. Dabble in the appealing selection of appetizers, like *involtini di melanzani* (stuffed eggplant), then turn to pasta or a simple meat dish like the *cotoletta di vitello* (veal cutlet). Dine alfresco on the patio in nice weather. ♦ Italian ♦ Daily lunch and dinner. Reservations recommended Friday-Sunday. Valet parking. 240 Newbury St (at Fairfield St). 536.2626

67 Eastern Accent Table- and desktop items, most imported from Japan, are displayed against a vivid chartreuse backdrop. Lovely glass pens, surrealist cutlery, cast-iron and concrete clocks, artful bowls and teapots, clever jewelry, and textured writing papers reflect the store's motto, "living with design," and the Japanese precept that the functional should be well made. Other straightforward materials include stainless, celluloid, and Bakelite, natural porcelains, silk, and anodized aluminum. ♦ M-Sa. 237 Newbury St (at Fairfield St). 266.9707

68 Vose Galleries of Boston The fifth generation of Voses now run this art gallery. Established in 1841, it's the oldest continuously run gallery in America. More than 30,000 paintings have passed through here since 1896. The family specializes in 18th-, 19th-, and early 20th-century American painting, and they've sold paintings to nearly every major American museum. They frequently show works by the Hudson River School, Luminists, American Impressionists (including Childe Hassam and John Henry Twachtman), and the Boston School. At the turn of the century a Vose agent returned from France with a full-length male nude by Géricault. High-minded Seth Vose decided to cut off the improper lower portion and sold the torso to the wife of the **Museum of Fine Arts'** president. Fifty years later Vose's descendants came upon the unseemly portion in their basement and gave it to the **MFA,** where it was joined to the previously donated upper portion, thus making the poor man whole again. ♦ M-Sa. 238 Newbury St (at Fairfield St). 536.6176

69 Emporio Armani Obviously no longer a fashion backwater, Boston has earned a third outpost of the infamous designers' coterie of stores. (The others are **Giorgio Armani** at 22 Newbury Street and **Armani A/X** at Copley Place.) This one claims 24,500 square feet in the rehabbed **United Business Services** office building. ♦ Daily. 210-214 Newbury St (between Exeter and Fairfield Sts). 262.7300 ♿

69 Armani Express ★★★$$$$; This elegant restaurant is, as you might expect from the shrewd Giorgio, purely upscale Italian. The *ambiente* is impeccable: soft-toned woods, cream-and-yellow walls, pastel linens. Goose prosciutto and tuna carpaccio are but two of the sumptuous antipasti featured here. Other popular dishes include the ravioli *d'arigosta al marsala* (filled with lobster and ricotta cheese, and sautéed in a marsala, fresh tomato, and basil sauce), the *agnolotti d'anatra al pomodori secchi* (homemade ravioli with confit of duck meat, and sautéed with sun-dried tomatoes, white wine, and parmesan cheese), and the linguine *alle cozze e vongole* (with clams and black mussels in a garlic, olive oil, red chili, white wine, and fresh tomato sauce). For dessert, try the *sacripantina*—a sweet, crispy tart filled with *frangipane* cream and strawberries. There's

also a bustling cafe under the same name downstairs. ♦ Daily lunch and dinner. Jacket and tie required. 214 Newbury St (between Exeter and Fairfield Sts). 437.0909 ♿

70 Exeter Street Theatre Building This Victorian gem of granite and brownstone, the 1884 work of **H.W. Hartwell** and **W.C. Richardson,** was built as a temple for the Working Union of Progressive Spiritualists. It had a long run as a repertory movie theater, and suffered the indignity of having a greenhouse extension appended to its street level. **CBT (Childs, Bertman, Tseckares, Casendino)** was responsible for the 1975 renovation that resulted in **Friday's** (★$$, 266.9040), a schlocky—albeit popular—singles bar. ♦ 26 Exeter St (at Newbury St)

Within the Exeter Street Theatre Building:

Waterstone's Booksellers Perhaps the most civilized enclave on Newbury Street, this British shop offers three roomy floors of well-stocked shelves, with a reading area so you can skim before buying. The store's reading series—several events a week—attract stellar talents, and the quarterly newsletter, *Voices,* is at once witty and pithy. A frequent visitor calls the store "literal heaven." ♦ Daily. 859.7300

71 Nielsen Gallery Nina Nielsen has run this gallery for more than 25 years, and exhibits contemporary works by Joan Snyder, Jake Berthot, Harvey Quaytman, Jane Smaldone, and Porfirio DiDonna. Not a trend-chaser, Nielsen looks for artists—many young, awaiting their first break—whose work expresses highly personal viewpoints, often spiritual, whom she sticks with and nurtures. She will also show work by such famous 20th-century artists as Jackson Pollock and David Smith. Nielsen likes what she likes and has many clients who feel the same. She doesn't shy away from making one of her biggest interests apparent: the continuum of spiritual substance in art. Says Nielsen about purchasing art: "Buy for love after talking to knowledgeable people." ♦ Tu-Sa. 179 Newbury St (between Dartmouth and Exeter Sts). 266.4835 ♿ (with advance notice)

71 Marcoz Something splendid always graces the show windows here. The two handsomely preserved floors of a Victorian town house make a divine setting for decorative merchandise from the 18th to the early 20th century. The hard-to-find accent pieces are imported from England or France, or purchased from New England estates. Knowledgeable and friendly, Mr. Marcoz will tell you all about whatever strikes your fancy, be it the 17th-century Madonna and Child processional figures, a 19th-century French *boule de petarque* (boccie-style ball), exquisite engravings, ivorine and sterling-silver napkin rings, a desktop inkwell, a pocket watch, furniture, or other singular finds. ♦ M-Sa. 177 Newbury St (between Dartmouth and Exeter Sts). 262.0780

71 The Society of Arts and Crafts Stop in here for a special handmade, one-of-a-kind something. The oldest nonprofit craft association in America, operating since 1897, the society promotes established and up-and-coming artisans by putting their wares before the public. All work is selected by jury: jewelry, ceramics, glass, quilts, weaving, wood, collages, leather, clothing, accessories, and furniture (always especially noteworthy). Themed exhibitions are held on the second floor. ♦ Daily. 175 Newbury St (between Dartmouth and Exeter Sts). 266.1810. Also at: 101 Arch St (at Summer St). 345.0033

71 Pucker Gallery More than 20 years in the business, this gallery displays local and international contemporary artists' graphics, paintings, sculptures, and porcelains. It also carries modern masters such as Chagall, Picasso, and Hundertwasser. Israeli art is a gallery specialty, with works shown by Samuel Bak and David Sharir. ♦ M-Sa. 171 Newbury St (between Dartmouth and Exeter Sts). 267.9473

72 La Ruche The perfect source for whimsical house gifts, this shop owned by Maria Church and Apple Bartlett (the daughter of legendary designer Sister Parrish), is best known for trompe l'oeil and painted furniture and lampshades, as well as Italian and French faience. They also carry flora- and fauna-shaped mugs, teapots, and jars; lovely French ribbon; garden ornaments; unusual glasses; linens; lamps; tapestry pillows; and other decorative wares. Potpourri scents the air. ♦ M-Sa. 168 Newbury St (between Dartmouth and Exeter Sts). 536.6366

72 The Copley Society of Boston The oldest art association in America, this nonprofit society was founded in 1879 to promote access to art, particularly new European trends, and to exhibit the work of its members and other artists of the day. Members John Singer Sargent and James McNeill Whistler showed their work in galleries run by this society. In 1905 the organization mounted Claude Monet's first American exhibition, a controversial event, and in 1913 Marcel Duchamp's *Nude Descending a Staircase* was shown here, creating an enormous furor. Today the society has more than 800 committee-selected members from around the world, though most come from New England. It operates two floors of galleries, with individual artists renting space upstairs and an ongoing members' show downstairs. The society has become somewhat mired in tradition and is no longer in the vanguard; in addition, its shows are uneven in quality. However, works by noted and rising artists are

often on view, so it's worth investigating. ♦ Tu-Su. 158 Newbury St (between Dartmouth and Exeter Sts). 536.5049

73 Kitchen Arts At this wonderful resource for cooks, both expert and far-from, you can pick up any kitchen tool your culinary sleight-of-hand requires. The emphasis here is on performance, not pretty-to-look-at gifts; these wares are ready to go to work immediately—slicing, dicing, decorating, coring, chopping, cracking, grinding, whatever. Kitchen cutlery and knife sharpening are subspecialties. ♦ Daily. 161 Newbury St (between Dartmouth and Exeter Sts). 266.8701

73 Du Barry $$ Don't expect French cooking worthy of accolades here. Nonetheless, this quiet, old-fashioned restaurant is a Back Bay landmark, family owned and operated since 1936—locals are loyal to this place, and it attracts its share of both students and celebrities. The owners are French, and their son is responsible for the classical and provincial cuisine. Dine out back on the terrace. Be sure to peruse Josh Winer's amusing faux-facade mural along the side of the building for a roster of nobs local and far-fetched (everyone from Paul Revere to Babe Ruth puts in an appearance). ♦ French ♦ M-Sa lunch and dinner; Su dinner; closed Sunday July–mid-September. Reservations recommended for parties of four or more. 159 Newbury St (between Dartmouth and Exeter Sts). 262.2445 ♿

74 Boston Art Club This artful 1881 assemblage is the work of Ralph Waldo Emerson's clever nephew, **William Ralph Emerson,** also creator of the fascinating **House of Odd Windows** on Beacon Hill. **Emerson** let loose his entire artillery of architectural forms and ornament on the Queen Anne–style facade: from every angle, there's something peculiar or interesting to see. An alternative high school now occupies the building. ♦ 270 Dartmouth St (at Newbury St)

75 Papa Razzi ★★$$ This inviting, busy Italian trattoria, complete with a wood-burning pizza oven, has a menu that leans toward rustic Northern Italian dishes with California overtones. Chef Tim Conway's hearty fare includes an array of splendid crispy-crust pizzas, polenta with grilled Italian sausages, and bountiful antipasti and pastas. ♦ Italian ♦ Daily lunch and dinner. 271 Dartmouth St (between Newbury and Boylston Sts). 536.9200

76 GBS Geoffrey B. Small is one determined designer. Having launched his business from his mother's suburban attic with some strategic—and costly—full-page ads in *Vogue,* he made the leap to Newbury Street. He turns out "bespoke" clothing for men and women: custom-made, from the fabric chosen through several computer-aided fittings. For true individualists, it's the only way to go. ♦ By appointment only. 129 Newbury St (between Clarendon and Dartmouth Sts). 536.6393 &

76 Autrefois Antiques The name means "yesteryear" in French, and 18th- and 19th-century France is captured here in fine imported hardwood furnishings, such as armoires, tables, chairs, chandeliers, and mirrors. Other epochs and origins also slip in, with the biggest shipments of new merchandise arriving in the spring and fall. The expert owners, Charles and Maria Rowe, will do on-site restoration and adapt old furnishings for modern needs. Updating lighting is their specialty. ♦ M-Sa. 125 Newbury St (between Clarendon and Dartmouth Sts). 424.8823. & Also at: 130 Harvard St (at Beacon St), Brookline. 566.0113

SERENELLA

77 Serenella Women come to this small, friendly boutique to invest in luxurious, classic, timeless clothes that will serve them well for years. The emphasis is on European designer daytime wear, with some accessories and shoes. Owner Ines Capelli does all the buying, and is always on the lookout for styles that are just right for her regular customers. ♦ M-Sa. 134 Newbury St (between Clarendon and Dartmouth Sts). 262.5568 &

RICCARDI

77 Riccardi The latest exemplars of European fashion rendezvous here. All of the clothing, for men and women, is made in Italy, but designs and influences come from throughout Europe. Even the store's facade looks Italian. Designers include Ann Demeulemeester (Belgium), Comme des Garçons (Japan), and Dolce e Gabbana and Romeo Gigli (Italy). The shoes and accessories are multinational, too. An entire department is devoted to sporting wear. The staff is always up-to-date and informative on fashions. This is certainly one of Boston's most worldly shops; they even accept JCB, the Japanese credit card. ♦ M-Sa. 128 Newbury St (between Clarendon and Dartmouth Sts). 266.3158

77 Rebecca's Cafe ★$ Everything is made fresh daily at this gourmet take-out place. Lines form all day long for homemade muffins and scones, fresh salads, hot entrée specials, and the spectacular desserts and pastries that this cafe's progenitor in Beacon Hill made famous. The chocolate-mousse cake and the fresh-fruit tarts are pure pleasure. There are a few tables at the back. ♦ Cafe/Takeout ♦ Daily breakfast, lunch, and dinner. No credit cards accepted. 112 Newbury St (between Clarendon and Dartmouth Sts). 267.1122

78 Bargain Box Many a discarded treasure is discovered at this quality thrift shop. It's run by the Junior League of Boston, Inc., a nonprofit women's organization dedicated to promoting community volunteerism. ♦ M-Sa. 117 Newbury St (between Clarendon and Dartmouth Sts). 536.8580

78 Cuoio For women only, this store showcases fashionable leather boots and shoes (the name means "leather" in Italian), lots imported from Italy, and such accessories as jewelry, hats, and fabulous hair ornaments. Many of these smart styles aren't available elsewhere in the city. ♦ Daily. 115 Newbury St (between Clarendon and Dartmouth Sts). 859.0636. & Also at: 170 Faneuil Hall Marketplace. 742.4486

79 David L. O'Neal Antiquarian Booksellers, Inc. Specializing in antiquarian books for more than 25 years, the focus here is on fine and rare books from the 15th century to present, including first editions in literature, many with superior bindings or leatherbound in sets. A large number of the works sold here have remarkable printing, typography, and illustrations. Original, historical, and decorative American and European prints from the 16th to the 19th century are also displayed. First-edition Jane Austen works; Nathaniel Bowditch's wonderful navigation book; James Fenimore Cooper's rare, anonymous first novel; Cotton Mather's *Psalter;* and Shelley's *Prometheus Unbound* represent a mere sampling of what many come to covet. An illustrated catalog is also available. ♦ M-Sa. Appointments are encouraged. 234 Clarendon St (between Newbury St and Commonwealth Ave). 266.5790 &

79 ōkw̄ Irene Kerzner and Henry Wong (the "o" in ōkw̄, pronounced *oh*-koo, stands for a departed partner) are the designers of choice for prominent businesswomen and socialites too distinctive to buy off the rack. Their creations are impeccably crafted of opulent fabrics and compellingly playful. ♦ By appointment. 234 Clarendon St (between Newbury St and Commonwealth Ave). 266.4114 &

80 Trinity Church Rectory The massive arched entry bellows the name of the 1879 rectory's masterful architect, **Henry H. Richardson,** who designed its parent **Trinity Church** at Copley Square. The building is now on the National Register of Historic Places; look at its surface, vigorously alive with twisting flowers and ornament. A third story was, unfortunately, added by **HHR**'s successor firm after his death. ♦ 233 Clarendon St (between Newbury St and Commonwealth Ave)

Restaurants/Clubs: Red	**Hotels:** Blue
Shops/ ♥ Outdoors: Green	**Sights/Culture:** Black

81 New England Historic Genealogical Society Many an aspirant to the lofty branches of some illustrious Yankee family tree has zeroed in on this private, nonprofit research library, the oldest of its kind in the nation and the first in the world. The mission: to plumb the past, to root out those roots. Housed in a former bank and founded in 1845, the society now holds 200,000 volumes and more than a million manuscripts dating to the 17th century. The organization's dedication to the study and preservation of family history has resulted in records and histories for all US states and Canadian provinces, plus Europe. There's no better place to try to entangle one's heritage with that of the Adams, the Cabots, the Randolphs, and other American Olympians. What would caste-conscious Boston do without it? There are more than 13,000 members with access to the archives. Visitors pay a half- or full-day research fee. ♦ Tu-Sa; W-Th until 9PM. 101 Newbury St (between Berkeley and Clarendon Sts). 536.5740

82 John Lewis, Inc. Swinging in the window, wave upon wave of silver strands lure passersby into this serene 1876 brownstone, where veteran Newbury Street proprietors John and Louise Lewis design jewelry. Working with solid precious metals and natural stones, the couple turns out a glittering array of imaginative designs. Some are simple expressions of rich materials and careful artisanship. Others are more intricate, such as the Lewis's line of Victorian-inspired jewelry with its cherubim, scrolls, flowers, and bows. ♦ Tu-Sa. 97 Newbury St (between Berkeley and Clarendon Sts). 266.6665 &

82 Kakas This over-a-century-old furrier ("five generations of recognized integrity") gained some unwelcome notoriety when it was learned that erstwhile manager Charles Stuart used its safe to store the gun with which he shot his wife. It's still the source of the finest—and costliest—coats in the city. ♦ M-F. 93 Newbury St (between Berkeley and Clarendon Sts). 536.1858 &

82 Haley & Steele It's fun to rifle—gingerly, of course—through the flat files crowded with prints of all kinds. The gallery focuses on 18th- and 19th-century prints in scores of categories, including botanical, sporting, architectural, military, New England maritime, birds, historical, and genre. You're sure to find a print here that will add a handsomely proper accent to your decor. The custom-frame shop specializes in painting conservation and French line matting, and has served local artists since 1899. ♦ M-Sa. 91 Newbury St (between Berkeley and Clarendon Sts). 536.6339 &

82 Mirabelle ★★$$$ Owner Stephen Elmont, founder of the enormously successful catering firm Creative Gourmets, set up this neighborhood cafe and geared it to the admittedly affluent. Dominated by a mural of western Europe, this bistro aspires to thoughtful conversations and straightforward cuisine: "There will be no food with multiple syllables," Elmont promises. ♦ American ♦ Daily breakfast, lunch, and dinner. 85 Newbury St (between Berkeley and Clarendon Sts). 859.4848 &

82 Martini Carl The Ventola family's boutique stocks sophisticated European apparel for men and women ranging from very casual to very dressy, with all the requisite accessories. The designer and private labels emphasize rich fabrics and leathers, superb tailoring, and enduring styles. ♦ M-Sa. 77 Newbury St (between Berkeley and Clarendon Sts). 247.0441 &

83 Church of the Covenant R.M. Upjohn designed this 1867 Gothic Revival Tiffany treasure house. The largest collection of the stained-glass master's work in the world—43 windows, some 30 feet high, and clerestories, too—are found here. Especially noteworthy is the sanctuary lantern with seven angels. It was designed by Tiffany's firm for the Tiffany Chapel exhibited at the World's Columbian Exposition of 1893 in Chicago, then installed here. Also, look for the Welte-Tripp pipe organ, a five-keyboard, manual, 4,500-pipe instrument, which can be heard during the church's fall and spring organ recital series. The church has a long history of giving generously to the community; it also founded the **Back Bay Chorale** and the **Boston Pro Arte Chamber Orchestra,** which perform regularly here and at **Harvard University.** ♦ Tu-Sa; closed afternoons January-April and November-December. 67 Newbury St (at Berkeley St). 266.7480 &

Within the Church of the Covenant:

Gallery NAGA Director Arthur Dion mounts interesting exhibitions of contemporary painting, sculpture, photography, and prints by the known and unknown. He likes to bridge the division between fine art and craft, and shows furniture and glass. Exhibits have included the work of Henry Schwartz, James Gemmill, and Irene Valincius; and furniture designers such as Tom Loesser and Judy McKie. The gallery occupies a generous swatch—1,400 square feet—in the church, whose progressive congregation gives art a boost by making a long-term space commitment to the gallery. ♦ Tu-Sa; closed mid-July–Labor Day. 267.9060

84 Louis, Boston Until the **New England Museum of Natural History** moved to its current site straddling the Charles River and changed its name to the **Boston Museum of Science,** it was jammed into this French Academic structure, designed in 1863 by **William Gibbons Preston.** The museum was one of Back Bay's pioneers. When it vacated, part of the moving-day chaos included lowering a stuffed moose from an upper-story window, a scene captured in a photograph that the museum now prizes. **Bonwit Teller** then resided here for decades until this astronomically priced clothier took over in 1987 and gave the building a much-needed restoration.

Three floors are dedicated to men's apparel and one to women's—everything's of exceptional quality. The building's splendid isolation makes it appear even more magnificent than it is. Inside, it's enjoyably spacious for browsing. ◆ M-Sa. 234 Berkeley St (between Newbury and Boylston Sts). 965.6100 &

Within Louis, Boston:

Cafe Louis ★★$$ The clothier's cafe deserves a special visit. High-ceilinged and furnished with lacquered bamboo chairs and tapestry banquettes, this pleasant nook echoes the store's sunny palette, but in a warm butterscotch. You can enter at the cafe's main entrance off the parking lot, but why not stroll through the store, past $1,000 sweaters and $200 scarves. The menu marries Italian and French flavors. Indulge in seductive pastries, smoked fish, or French toast ordered by the slice in the morning; antipasto for two or a sandwich handsomely composed and garnished for lunch; or a splendid slice of cake with tea in late afternoon. You can dine outdoors at tables on the cement landing, though the view of the parking lot and the **New England Life Building** across the way isn't exactly breathtaking. A small gourmet shop offers prepared and packaged treats of all kinds to go. The cafe's major flaw: it closes much too early. ◆ Cafe/Takeout ◆ M-Sa breakfast, lunch, and afternoon tea (dessert and takeout until 6PM). 266.4680 &

85 **Alan Bilzerian** The dramatic clothes in this store's striking display windows need few props; they speak for themselves. A native of Worcester, Mass, Bilzerian started out with a college student clientele more than two decades ago, then began selling to rock stars. Now his is the local name in fashion best known outside of Boston. In fact, New Yorkers with the fashion world at their feet still make special trips, and lots of celebrities drop in when in town—Cher and Mick Jagger among them. Featured are art-to-wear fashions, accessories, and shoes for men and women: the work of such European and Japanese designers as Yohji Yamamoto, Michele Klien, Issey Miyake, Katharine Hamnett, Rifat Ozbek, Jean Paul Gaultier, Azzedine Alaia, and Romeo Gigli, to name a few. Complementing the other collections, Bilzerian designs for men, and his wife, Bê, designs for women. Of course, outlandishly stylish wear commands outlandishly high prices. ◆ M-Sa. 34 Newbury St (between Arlington and Berkeley Sts).

536.1001 & (The staff will carry wheelchairs up the stairs; once inside, there's an elevator to the second-floor women's department.)

86 **Milano's Italian Kitchen** ★$ Wood-fired oven specialties enjoy ever-widening popularity in Boston, and they are as good here as anywhere. *Panini* (sandwiches), pasta, salads, and the antipasto are also worth a try. Start with the polenta cup (polenta shell filled with a ragout of vegetables covered with pesto sauce, and served with broccoli, peppers, and sun-dried tomatoes in a marinara sauce), or the popular *Antipasti Milano* (genoa salami, prosciutto, mozzarella, and marinated mixed vegetables drizzled with extra-virgin olive oil). Jugs of Chianti are placed on every table, and patrons are on the honor system to keep track of how many glasses they drink. ◆ Cafe/Takeout ◆ Daily lunch and dinner. 47 Newbury St (between Arlington and Berkeley Sts). 267-6150

86 **J.O.E.** Another local success story, Joseph Abboud has earned international renown for his ruggedly handsome men's clothes. His clothes are sensual, yet assertively masculine. ◆ M-Sa. 37 Newbury St (between Arlington and Berkeley Sts). 266.4200 &

86 **Romano's Bakery & Sandwich Shop** $ The Back Bay needs all the unpretentious, reliable spots it can get, and this small (40-seater), cafeteria-style eatery is one of the good places. It has won a dedicated clientele with its fragrant fresh muffins, bagels, Danish pastries, and croissants in the morning—the busiest time—and homemade soups, quiches, sandwiches, and tantalizing desserts later on. You can also get cappuccino and espresso. ◆ Cafe/Takeout ◆ Daily breakfast and lunch until 5PM. No credit cards accepted. 33 Newbury St (between Arlington and Berkeley Sts). 266.0770

86 **29 Newbury** ★★★$$ This perennially trendy bistro, a favorite with modeling, music, and media types, serves inventive cuisine that's considerably priced. Certain dishes sing, such as the wild mushroom ravioli in Madeira cream sauce, and even the burgers

are prepared exactly as they should be. The semi-subterranean dining room also doubles as an art gallery, and deep-set booths ensure privacy. More sociable types crowd around the bar or, in good weather, spill onto the sidewalk patio. Sunday brunch earns raves. ♦ American ♦ M-Sa lunch and dinner; Su brunch and dinner. Reservations recommended. 29 Newbury St (between Arlington and Berkeley Sts). 536.0290

87 Emmanuel Church Its uninspired rural Gothic Revival architecture (an 1862 effort by **Alexander R. Estey,** enlarged by **Frederick R. Allen** in 1899 and pictured above) doesn't do justice to this Episcopal church's lively, creative spirit. Dedicated since the 1970s to "a special ministry through art," the church organizes a variety of music and cultural events. A professionally performed Bach cantata accompanies the liturgy every Sunday from September through May. Jazz celebrations are held periodically. ♦ 15 Newbury St (between Arlington and Berkeley Sts). 536.3355 ⅙ (a portable ramp is available with advance notice)

Within Emmanuel Church:

Leslie Lindsey Memorial Chapel This 1924 Gothic chapel was commissioned by Mr. and Mrs. William Lindsey as a memorial to their daughter, Leslie, who with her new husband was bound for a European honeymoon on the ill-fated *Lusitania.* Some time after the boat sank, Leslie's body supposedly washed ashore in Ireland, still wearing her father's wedding gift of diamonds and rubies; they were sold to help pay for her memorial. The chapel is sometimes called the "Lady Chapel" for its marble carvings of female saints. Architects **Allen** and **Collens** were already nationally renowned for the Riverside Church in New York City when they designed the chapel.

88 Charles Sumner Great imported and American women's designer apparel by Donna Karan, Valentino, Louis Ferraud,

Missoni, Akris, and others, plus shoes, handbags, makeup, hosiery, jewelry, gloves, and hats are all carried at this head-to-toe boutique. The enthusiastic salespeople try hard to work with customers and make them feel at home. ♦ M-Sa. 16 Newbury St (between Arlington and Berkeley Sts). 536.6225. ⅙ Also at: Chestnut Hill Mall, Upper level. 244.6383.

88 Alpha Gallery The best free shows in town are often on display here. A family affair, the gallery is owned by Alan Fink, managed by his daughter Joanna, and often shows work by his wife Barbara Swan and son Aaron Fink—both of whom merit the attention. Also exhibited frequently are 20th-century and contemporary American and European painting, sculpture, and prints. Distinguished artists shown here include American painters Milton Avery, Bernard Chaet, and Fairfield Porter; Europeans Mimmo Paladino and Georg Baselitz; Massachusetts realist Scott Prior; and such gifted young artists as T. Wiley Carr. Over its 26-year history the gallery has mounted major exhibitions of work by John Marin, Max Beckman, and Stuart Davis, and Picasso's complete *Vollard Suite.* ♦ Tu-Sa. 14 Newbury St (between Arlington and Berkeley Sts). 536.4465

88 Barbara Krakow Gallery Don't pass by this fifth-floor gallery. That's hard to do anyway because there's an eye-catching marble bench carved with enigmatic messages by Jenny Holzer on the sidewalk out front. Now at its pinnacle, this gallery has been selling art for over 30 years. It is possibly Boston's most important gallery, and its prestige is directed to numerous worthy causes. Many of the most significant contemporary artists are shown here, among them Holzer, Agnes Martin, Cameron Shaw, Jim Dine, Donald Judd, and Michael Mazur. Despite the superstars on its walls, the gallery is a very hospitable, unpretentious place, combining sure taste with a willingness to take risks—showing work created by high-school kids, for example. ♦ Tu-Sa. 10 Newbury St (between Arlington and Berkeley Sts). 262.4490 ⅙

89 Cafe de Paris ★$ This is some kind of a fast-food joint, with velvet banquettes, burled paneling, and Deco sconces. The food is a cut above, too: from croissants and omelettes to true Parisian pastries. Grab a booth, or stock up and cross over to the **Public Garden** for breakfast in the park. ♦ French/Takeout

♦ Daily breakfast, lunch, and dinner. 19 Arlington St (at Newbury St). 247.7121

90 Domain It's fun to prowl through this mecca of home embellishments, a fantasy habitat for a menagerie of antique, traditional, and designer pieces, none commonplace or conventional. The aim here is to mass-market one-of-a-kind-looking furnishings. A multitude of quirky accessories crowd in with the beds, tables, and sofas. Textures, colors, patterns, and styles veer crazily in all directions. ♦ Daily (call for summer evening hours). 7 Newbury St (between Arlington and Berkley Sts). 266.5252 &

90 Ritz-Carlton Hotel $$$$ This nationwide hotel chain's reputation for luxury, elegance, and superlative service is exquisitely exemplified here at this, the oldest **Ritz-Carlton** in the country. Built in 1927 by **Strickland and Blodget,** and subtly expanded by **Skidmore, Owings & Merrill** in 1981, the hotel provides all the little niceties proper Bostonians love so well. The elevator attendants, for example, wear white gloves. The understated edifice perfectly expresses the fastidious courtesies and traditions of its inhabitant. There's nothing flashy or eye-catching about this building, except for its parade of vivid blue awnings, but it has become a timeless, steadfast fixture.

The 278 rooms and suites are simply and traditionally appointed in European style. Guest rooms have safes and locking closets, all windows open, and 41 suites have wood-burning fireplaces. Request a room with a view of the **Public Garden.** Rooms for nonsmokers and people with disabilities are available. You can bring your pet if it's leashed. There's a small health club, and guests have complimentary access to the fancy spa at **The Heritage** a block away. Other amenities are 24-hour room service, valet parking, same-day valet laundry, a multilingual staff, baby-sitting, a concierge, barber, and shoe-shine stand. If that's not enough, the staff "will provide anything legal." ♦ 15 Arlington St (at Newbury St). 536.5700, 800/241.3333; fax 536.1335 &

Within the Ritz-Carlton Hotel:

The Ritz Lounge ★★★$$ While a harpist thrums soothingly in the corner of this quiet, lovely drawing room on the second floor, sit in a high-backed chair and nibble tiny sandwich triangles, fruit tarts, and scones with jam, and sip perfectly brewed tea. A lobster buffet is held Friday and Saturday night, and there's dancing Thursday through Saturday evenings. ♦ Cafe/Tea ♦ Daily lunch and afternoon tea. Jacket and tie required evenings; no denim or running shoes allowed. 536.5700 &

The Ritz Bar ★★★$$ On a snowy evening, the gorgeous view of the **Public Garden** from this cozy street-level bar is out of a storybook. Inside, there's no entertainment, just plenty of welcome serenity and a crackling fire burning in the hearth. At lunchtime, there's upscale soups, club sandwiches, pasta dishes, and salads. The bar is famous for its perfect martinis; ask for the special martini menu, which featured 13 varieties at last count, including the "James Bond." Boston mystery writer Robert B. Parker's fictional sleuth Spenser has quaffed many a beer here. ♦ M-Sa lunch; daily cocktails. 536.7000 &

The Ritz Cafe ★★$$$ With its views of Newbury Street, quiet vanilla decor, and cordial service, this cafe offers respite during a hectic day. When you've had it with the world, come for a restorative touch of civility. Since you can't see the **Public Garden** from here, it's been reproduced in an honorary mural. Monday through Friday many of Boston's business heavy hitters breakfast here. At night the cafe also caters to the after-theater crowd. And children may order from a special menu. ♦ American ♦ Daily breakfast, lunch, and dinner. Reservations recommended at lunch. Jacket and tie required evenings; no denim allowed. 536.5700 &

The Ritz Dining Room ★★$$$$ New hub restaurants open every day—but there will *never* be another dining room like this. It's the hotel's showpiece, with cobalt-blue Venetian crystal chandeliers, gold-filigreed ceiling, regal drapery, and huge picture windows overlooking the **Public Garden.** There's no better place for wedding proposals, anniversaries, and other momentous occasions. Piano music and an occasional harpist add to the spell. Such timeless classics as rack of lamb and chateaubriand for two commune with a few more stylish offerings on the menu. But the chef introduces innovations very carefully; the old-guard patrons would rise up in arms if Boston cream pie and other old-time favorites were seriously challenged. Entrées low in sodium, cholesterol, and calories are available; as is a children's menu. Fashion shows are held here every Saturday, and chamber music accompanies the fabulous Sunday brunch. ♦ French ♦ Daily lunch and dinner. Reservations required. Jacket and tie required. 536.5700 &

For all Back Bay's French influences, its street names have remained Anglophile.

Kenmore Square/ Fenway

This side of Boston befuddles even Bostonians, who regularly scramble references to **Fenway Park** (the famous ballpark), **The Fenway** (a parkway), the **Fens** (part of the park system designed by Frederick Law Olmsted), and Fenway, the district containing all three. Kenmore Square is also a section of Fenway; it encompasses **Longwood Medical Area**, a dense complex of world-renowned medical and educational establishments that includes **Harvard Medical School**. A student mecca, Kenmore Square is practically a city unto itself. Unlike Beacon Hill or Back Bay, Fenway lacks a cohesive personality, and its indeterminate boundaries are a constant source of confusion to visitors and residents alike. But it's worth navigating the helter-skelter Fenway to explore its attractions: the **Museum of Fine Arts; Isabella Stewart Gardner Museum; Symphony Hall;** Olmsted's famous **Emerald Necklace;** and, of course, **Fenway Park**, home of the **Red Sox**.

Fenway was the last Boston neighborhood built on landfill, and only emerged after the noxious **Back Bay Fens** was imaginatively rehabilitated by Olmsted. Like the original Back Bay whose stagnant tidal flats metamorphosed into the city's most fashionable neighborhood, the Back Bay Fens

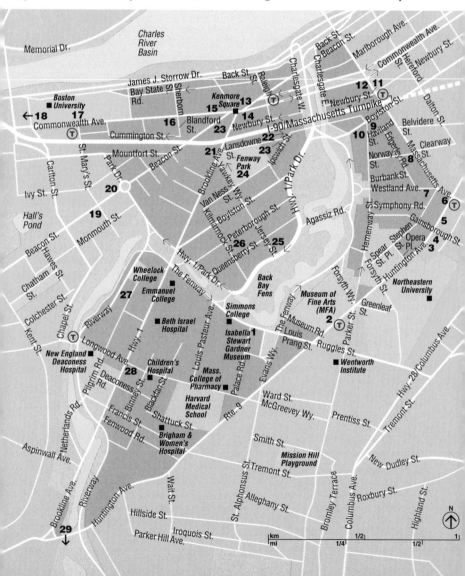

was considered an unusable part of town, a stinking, swampy mess that collected sewage and runoff from the **Muddy River** and **Stony Brook** before draining into the **Charles River.** The problem worsened after Back Bay was filled in and the Fens' unsanitary state became a concern for the city. A group of commissioners assembled to address its drainage problems and to simultaneously develop a park system for Boston, an idea that gained momentum in the 1870s. Co-creator of New York City's Central Park and founder of the landscape-architecture profession in America, Olmsted was called in as consultant and ultimately hired in 1878 to fix the Fens and create the Boston Park System. His ingenious solution involved installing a tidal gate and holding basin, and using mud dredged from the refreshed Fens to create surrounding parkland. Developers quickly recognized the neighborhood's new appeal, and it was "Westward-ho!" once again for overcrowded Boston.

The transformed Fens became the first link in Olmsted's **Emerald Necklace**, the most important feature in the Boston Park Department's plan for a city-scaled green-space network, and the first of its kind in the nation. Instead of a New York–style central park (inappropriate given Boston's topography), Boston wanted a system of open spaces throughout the city, offering breathing room to residents. This plan meshed perfectly with Olmsted's esthetic and social ideals for landscape architecture. He envisioned interconnected parks, recreation grounds, boulevards, and parkways that would not only beautify the environment and enhance public health and sanitation, but also direct urban expansion, population density, and the local economy. Boston and Olmsted were ideally matched: City officials appreciated not only his talents and civic-mindedness, but also his interest in solving practical problems through landscape design.

Olmsted's plan succeeded, as numerous cultural, medical, educational, and social institutions began relocating to the Fenway area. Boston's devastating downtown fire of 1872 and advances in public transportation also encouraged many to move. During the 1890s and early 1900s the **Massachusetts Historical Society, Symphony Hall, Horticultural Hall, New England Conservatory of Music, Simmons College, Museum of Fine Arts,** and **Harvard Medical School** were built. Another neighborhood pioneer was **Fenway Court**, the fashionable residence where Isabella Stewart Gardner installed the magnificent personal museum of art that now bears her name. Since then, other institutions have followed the same trail; **Northeastern University** and **Boston University** now dominate the district. Fenway's resident educational and medical institutions have played the largest role in shaping its contemporary character. Today, the Kenmore Square/Fenway area claims a huge concentration of college students and young adults. It has the lowest median age of all Boston neighborhoods and a transient feel. Originally an extension of prestigious Back Bay, with fine hotels, offices, and shops, Kenmore Square is now largely geared toward its student population, with plenty of fast-food joints and cheap-eats delis, good ethnic restaurants, clubs, music shops, and the like.

To get to the Back Bay side of this neighborhood, take the *Green Line* to the **Symphony** or the **Hynes Convention Center/ICA** subway stop. The **Kenmore Square** stop (also on the *Green Line*) puts you in the middle of the club and student scene. After **Kenmore**, the *Green Line* branches into three lines (*B, C,* and *D*) with different end points, so make sure you're on the right one. The *B Line* to **Boston College** makes frequent stops aboveground on Commonwealth Avenue (along **Boston University**'s campus), and the *C Line* to Cleveland Circle does the same on Beacon Street. The *D Line* (heading for Riverside) stops at **Fenway,** convenient to **Fenway Park,** and **Longwood,** near the **Longwood Medical Area.** For the **Museum of Fine Arts** and the **Isabella Stewart Gardner Museum,** you'll want to take the *E Line* (branching off at Copley, and headed for Arborway); get off at the **Museum** stop

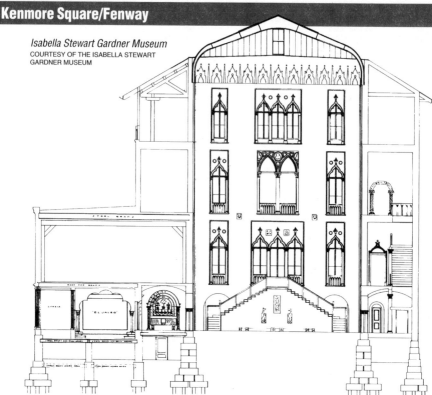

Isabella Stewart Gardner Museum
COURTESY OF THE ISABELLA STEWART
GARDNER MUSEUM

1 Isabella Stewart Gardner Museum

On New Year's Day 1903 Isabella Stewart
Gardner held a glorious gala-to-end-all-galas
to unveil her private art collection in its
opulent new **Fenway Court** home (pictured
above). No one could pass up this event,
including those who typically snubbed
flamboyant Isabella. Fifty **Boston Symphony**
musicians played a Bach chorale, and when
the crowd caught sight of the now-famous
flowering palace courtyard, a collective gasp
was followed by awed silence. Admirers and
detractors alike were wowed by Gardner's
resplendent array of paintings, sculpture,
tapestries, and objets d'art in their dazzling
setting. An admiring Henry Adams wrote: "As
long as such a work can be done, I will not
despair of our age. . . . You are a creator and
stand alone." Gardner herself described her
home, after 20 years of residence, as "very
nice, very comfortable, and rather jolly."

Upon her death in 1924, her will officially
turned the mansion into a museum (see the
plan at right) and stipulated the demanding
terms of its operation: all is to remain *exactly*
as it was upon her death, or else all shall be
sold and the proceeds given to **Harvard
University.** (That accounts for the
hodgepodge manner in which the works of art
are displayed—Gardner's preferences at work
into perpetuity.) Until recently the museum
director lived rent-free in Gardner's own lush
apartment; the most liberal reinterpretation of
her will to date was to transform these fourth-

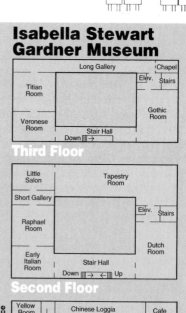

Isabella Stewart Gardner Museum

Third Floor

- Long Gallery
- Chapel
- Elev.
- Stairs
- Titian Room
- Gothic Room
- Veronese Room
- Stair Hall
- Down →

Second Floor

- Little Salon
- Tapestry Room
- Short Gallery
- Elev.
- Stairs
- Raphael Room
- Dutch Room
- Early Italian Room
- Stair Hall
- Down → ← Up

Ground Floor

- Entrance
- Exit
- Yellow Room
- Chinese Loggia
- Cafe
- Spanish Cloister
- Spanish Chapel
- East Cloister
- Sales Desk
- Wash Room
- Blue Room
- North Cloister
- Elev.
- Coat Room
- Court
- Administration
- MacKnight Room
- West Cloister ← Up

floor living quarters into office space, a controversial move. More recently, a tiny new gallery (17 x 22 feet) was reclaimed from storage space and deemed a "reasonable deviation" from the will. Museum curators have also initiated an artists-in-residence program (in the carriage house) to perpetuate Gardner's own predilections as patron.

For countless Bostonians and visitors, Gardner's museum has no equal, and many return again and again for another heady dose of her compelling creation. The museum's great appeal is in the total impression it creates. In a series of singular stage-set galleries—the **Veronese Room, Gothic Room, Dutch Room, Titian Room**—look for Botticelli, Manet, Raphael, Rembrandt, Rubens, Matisse, Sargent, Titian, La Farge, and Whistler. Nearly 2,000 objects are on display, spanning more than 30 centuries, with emphasis on Italian Renaissance and 17th-century Dutch masters. (Be sure to look for the **Blue Room** display of Gardner's correspondence with her distinguished friends.) Objects from different periods and cultures are liberally intermixed in the eclectic manner she favored. But on 18 March 1990, the most devastating day in the museum's history, terrible empty spaces were created on the walls. Thirteen uninsured paintings and artifacts valued at $200 million were stolen by two thieves disguised as policemen in what the *Boston Herald* dubbed "the Heist of the Century." The most famous work, *The Concert,* by Jan Vermeer, cost Gardner $6,000 at an 1892 auction in Paris; it is now priceless. The illustrious art historian Bernard Berenson, befriended by Gardner when he was a **Harvard College** student, sometimes advised her on what to buy, and counseled her to purchase two works by Rembrandt, *The Storm on the Sea of Galilee* (his only known seascape) and *A Lady and Gentleman in Black,* both stolen. In gentler times, Gardner often acted as her own security guard. The stolen paintings were never recovered, and today everything is insured.

With its soft light, cloudy pink walls, picturesque balconies, quiet fountain, and fragrant fresh flowers and plantings supplied by the museum's own greenhouse, the four-story courtyard is one of Boston's most serene and beloved places. It is composed of authentic architectural and decorative elements collected by Gardner throughout Europe and Egypt. From September through May, chamber or classical music concerts are held Saturday and Sunday in the **Tapestry Room** (fee in addition to admission).
♦ Admission; free Wednesday; members and children under 12 free; reduced admission for senior citizens and students. Tu-Su. Public guided tour Friday at 2:30PM; private tours require advance notice. 280 The Fenway (between Palace Rd and Evans Way). 566.1401, recorded concert information

734.1359 ♿ (limited because of narrow spaces; museum provides wheelchairs that fit everywhere)

Within the Isabella Stewart Gardner Museum:

The Cafe at the Gardner ★$$ Excellent lunches that include quiches, salads, sandwiches, and desserts are served at this cafe. Weather permitting, dine on the outdoor terrace overlooking the museum gardens.
♦ Cafe ♦ Tu-Su lunch 566.1088 ♿

2 **Museum of Fine Arts (MFA)** The first exhibitions under the auspices of this institution were displayed upstairs at the **Boston Athenaeum** on Beacon Hill; the works were moved in 1876 to the ornate Gothic Revival Copley Square quarters, since demolished. In 1909 the museum made the trek out to the newly fashionable Fenway area along with numerous other pioneering public institutions seeking more spacious sites than Boston proper could offer. This present residence is an imposing, if dull, Classical Revival edifice (designed by **Guy Lowell** in 1909) with a majestic colonnade on the Fenway side and a temple portico on the Huntington Street side flanked by two big wings, the newest designed in 1981 by **I.M. Pei & Partners.** Standing in the front courtyard is a statue of a mounted Indian gazing skyward, appealing for aid against the white man's invasion. Cyrus Edwin Dallin's *Appeal to the Great White Spirit* won a gold medal at the 1909 Paris Salon and attracted many admirers when erected here in 1913, but looks somewhat odd in this ordered setting today.

The museum's somber starkness ends abruptly indoors, where an embarrassment of riches begins, much of it acquired through the generosity of wealthy Victorian Bostonians committed to creating a cosmopolitan cultural repository. It is one of the country's greatest museums and deserves repeated exploration (see the plan on page 142). Begin with a dose of familiar sights and historic local names and faces in the American collections. More than 60 works by John Singleton Copley, including his portrait of Paul Revere and his famous silver *Liberty Bowl,* and paintings by local boy Winslow Homer, Gilbert Stuart, Edward Hopper, John Singer Sargent, Fitz Hugh Lane, Mary Cassatt, James McNeill Whistler, and Thomas Eakins are permanently on exhibit here. Holdings range from native New England folk art and portraiture to works by the Hudson River School, American Impressionists, Realists, Ash Can School, and New York's Abstract Expressionists. The Department of American Decorative Arts and Sculpture is particularly noteworthy for its pre–Civil War New England products, and includes furniture, silver, pewter, glass, ceramics, sculpture, and folk art. The collection progresses from the rustic functional creations of early colonial times to

The Museum of Fine Arts

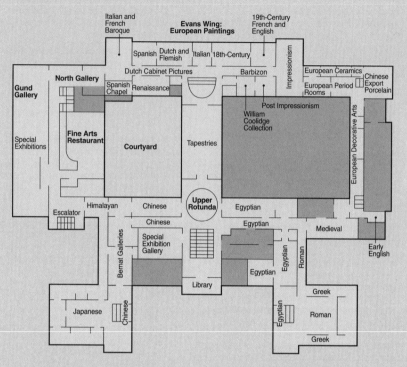

Second Floor

Evans Wing: European Paintings

- Italian and French Baroque
- Spanish
- Dutch and Flemish
- Italian
- 18th-Century
- 19th-Century French and English
- Impressionism
- Dutch Cabinet Pictures
- Barbizon
- European Ceramics
- European Period Rooms
- Chinese Export Porcelain
- North Gallery
- Spanish Chapel
- Renaissance
- Gund Gallery
- Special Exhibitions
- Fine Arts Restaurant
- Courtyard
- Tapestries
- Post Impressionism
- William Coolidge Collection
- European Decorative Arts
- Himalayan
- Chinese
- Upper Rotunda
- Egyptian
- Escalator
- Chinese
- Egyptian
- Medieval
- Bernat Galleries
- Special Exhibition Gallery
- Egyptian
- Roman
- Early English
- Egyptian
- Library
- Greek
- Japanese
- Chinese
- Egyptian
- Roman
- Greek

First Floor

Evans Wing: American Paintings

- 20th-Century American and European
- Ladies Committee Gallery
- American Folk Paintings
- Japanese Garden
- American Impressionism
- American Masters
- 19th-Century Landscape and Genre
- Copley and His Contemporaries
- American Federal
- Foster Gallery
- Special Exhibitions
- 20th-Century Works on Paper
- Karolik Collection
- Oak Hill Rms
- 19th-C. American
- Seminar Room
- Early 20th-C. American
- Watercolors
- American Neoclassicism and Romanticism
- 18th-C. European
- English Silver
- Remis Auditorium
- Museum Shop
- Courtyard
- American Modern
- 18th-C. Boston
- Forsyth Wickes Collection
- 18th-C. French Art
- Cafe
- WEST WING ENTRANCE
- Escalator
- C. Brown Gallery
- Carter Gallery
- Lower Rotunda
- Mummies
- 18th-Century American Furniture
- Islamic
- Members' Room
- Torf Gallery
- Pre-Columbian
- American Silver
- Slide Library
- Information Center
- Prints
- Prints Drawings Photography
- Musical Instruments
- Egyptian
- Indian
- Nubian
- Near Eastern
- S.E. Asian
- Japanese
- HUNTINGTON ENTRANCE
- Greek
- Korean
- Etruscan

Areas closed to the public

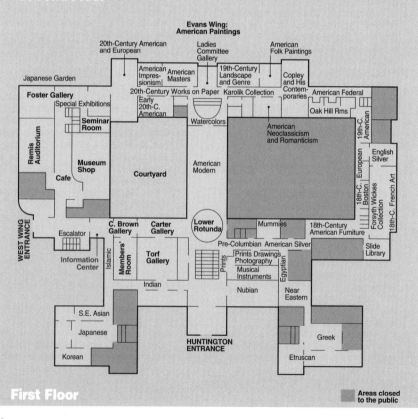

the elegant pieces popular in the increasingly prosperous colonies. The Department of Twentieth-Century Art is a Johnny-come-lately, emphasized only since the 1970s, but includes Jackson Pollock, David Smith, Robert Motherwell, Helen Frankenthaler, Morris Louis, Joan Miró, and Georgia O'Keeffe.

The museum owns superb works from all major developments in European painting from the 11th to the 20th centuries, with a particularly rich representation of 19th-century French works. Victorian Bostonians loved French painting, eagerly exhibiting the Impressionists who were still awaiting acceptance in their own country. On display in the **Evans Wing** galleries are many of the museum's 38 Monets and more than 150 Millets, including his best-known painting, *The Sower,* as well as works by Corot, Délacroix, Courbet, Renoir, Pissarro, Manet, van Gogh, Gauguin, and Cézanne. Other celebrated artists shown in this wing are van der Weyden, Il Rosso, El Greco, Rubens, Canaletto, Turner, and Picasso. The extraordinary assembly of Asiatic art—the largest under any one museum roof—features one of the greatest Japanese collections in existence, and important objects from China, India, and Southeast Asia. (Before you leave the grounds, be sure to visit **Tenshin-en-Garden of the Heart of Heaven,** on the museum's north side—a contemplative Japanese garden designed by garden master Kinsaku Nakane.) The Egyptian and Ancient Near Eastern Art galleries are a favorite with kids—they love the mummies—and are also treasure troves of jewelry, sculpture, and other objects from throughout Asia's western regions. The array of Old Kingdom sculpture is equaled only by the Cairo Museum; the **MFA** cosponsored excavations in Egypt for 40 years with **Harvard University.** And it is apt that the "Athens of America" boasts a superb representation of ancient Greek, Roman, and Etruscan objects, including bronzes, sculpture dating from the 6th to the 4th centuries BC, and vases painted with fascinating figures and vignettes by some of the greatest early Greek artists.

Another highlight is the Department of European Decorative Arts, which features a collection of antique musical instruments that includes lutes, clavichords, harps, and zithers, replicas of which are often played in special concert programs. The Department of Textiles displays an international collection of tapestries, batiks, embroideries, silk weavings, costume materials, and other textiles. The Boston area was the capital of the textile industry in the late 19th century, and this was the first museum in America to elevate textiles to the status of art. Its collection ranks among the world's greatest. Spanning the 15th century to today, the Department of Prints and Drawings has particularly outstanding 15th-century Italian engravings and 19th-century lithography, many works by Dürer, Rembrandt, Goya, the Tiepolos, and the German Expressionists, Picasso's complete *Vollard Suite,* the M. and M. Karolik Collection of American Drawings and Watercolors from 1800 to 1875, a growing collection of original photographs, and still more.

Special exhibitions are mounted in the modern light-filled **West Wing,** where you'll find the **Fine Arts Restaurant, Galleria Cafe, Cafeteria,** and **Museum Shop.** Many Bostonians make special trips just to visit the latter for its wonderful selection of books, prints, children's games, cards and stationery, reproductions of silver, jewelry, glass, textiles, and other decorative items aplenty. Excellent film, concert, and lecture series are held in the **West Wing**'s **Remis Auditorium.** Also in the neighborhood is the **School of the Museum of Fine Arts** and the **Massachusetts College of Art,** both of which maintain galleries.
♦ Admission; free Wednesday 4PM-9:45PM, except for the Graham Gund Gallery; reduced admission when only the West Wing is open; members and children under six free; reduced admission for students and senior citizens. Tu-Su; W until 10PM; West Wing only Th-F 5-10PM. Free guided tours. Free introductory walk in Spanish the first Saturday of every month. Paid parking available on Museum Rd. 465 Huntington Ave (at Museum Rd). 267.9300, daily schedules 267.2973; TTY/TDD 267.9703, concerts, lectures, film information 267.9300, ext 300 ♿ (parking for people with disabilities near West Wing entrance)

Within the Museum of Fine Arts:

Fine Arts Restaurant ★★$$ The food is unexpectedly good, with special themed menus playing off the current high-profile exhibition. For *The Age of Rubens,* an entrée called "lamb Flemish style" (garlic- and sage-seared leg of lamb with wild mushrooms, braised endive, and herb ravioli) was among the offerings. This is a popular destination for lunch—even with those who aren't in the mood for pictures or an exhibition. ♦ American ♦ Tu-Su lunch; W-F dinner. 266.3663 ♿

Galleria Cafe ★$ Refuel for another foray through the galleries over a cappuccino or a glass of wine, and a light meal, fruit, cheese, or dessert at this informal open cafe. ♦ Cafe ♦ Tu-Su breakfast, lunch, and dinner. 267.9300 ♿

Cafeteria $ If you're on a budget, this is the best option for a quick meal, and there's rarely a wait. ♦ American ♦ Tu-Su breakfast and lunch; W-F dinner. Lower level 267.9300 ♿

Restaurants/Clubs: Red   **Hotels:** Blue
Shops/ 🌲 Outdoors: Green   **Sights/Culture:** Black

143

3 Greater Boston YMCA $ Mainly students and tourists stay here at the first of this nationwide associations' outposts, founded in 1851. There's a 10-day maximum visit, and you must be at least 18 years old with a picture ID and luggage to stay. Two of the three floors are for men, and the other is coed. There are 50 single and double rooms including one suite; all share baths (except the suite). Children can stay with a parent. Breakfast is free, as is use of the gym, indoor track, pool, and sauna. There's a cafeteria-style restaurant and laundry facilities on the premises. Smoking is allowed only in the rooms. A modest key deposit is required. Reserve two weeks in advance by mail; walk-ins are accepted daily after 12:30PM. ♦ 316 Huntington Ave (between Gainsborough St and Opera Pl). 536.7800 ♿

4 Jordan Hall at the New England Conservatory of Music (NEC) Like **Symphony Hall**, only smaller and more intimate, this hall—designed in 1903 by **Wheelwright and Haven**—is an acoustically superior concert space, ideal for chamber music. The conservatory was established in 1867 as the first music college in the country and is internationally renowned today for its undergraduate and graduate music programs. In addition to 400 concerts, most free and held during school months, a number of musical groups, including the **Juilliard Quartet, Tokyo String Quartet, Boston Symphony Chamber Players, Cantata Singers,** and the **Boston Chamber Music Society** perform here. The hall was funded by Eben Jordan, founder of the **Jordan Marsh** department stores. ♦ Box office M-Sa. No reservations by telephone or mail. 30 Gainsborough St (at Huntington Ave). Program information 536.2412, box office 262.1120 ♿ (call in advance)

5 Boston University Theatre Acclaimed **Huntington Theatre Company (HTC),** the professional company-in-residence, puts on five plays annually at this charming 1925 Greek Revival theater, which seats 850. The focus here is both classic and contemporary, ranging from Shakespeare and musicals to new plays. Discounts are offered for senior citizens, students, and groups; subscriptions are also available. ♦ 264 Huntington Ave (between Gainsborough St and Massachusetts Ave). Ticket information 266.0800 ♿ (call in advance)

Socialite and art collector Isabella Stewart Gardner delighted in shocking staid Boston—among other affronts, she wore diamonds mounted on wires like antennae in her hair and walked her two pet lions on Beacon Street. Soirees at her Fenway palazzo featured her favorite refreshments: champagne and doughnuts.

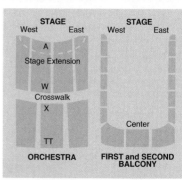

6 Symphony Hall Deep-pocketed Brahmin philanthropist and amateur musician Henry Lee Higginson, who founded the **Boston Symphony Orchestra (BSO)** in 1881, wanted his creation's new home to be among the world's most magnificent, so he commissioned **McKim, Mead & White** as architects. The building, completed in 1900, is on the National Register of Historic Places. The hall's enduring fame stems not from its restrained Italian Renaissance style, however distinguished, but rather from its internationally distinguished acoustics, which have earned it the nickname "Stradi varius" among concert halls (see the plan above). It was the first concert hall in the world to be built according to an acoustical formula, the work of Wallace Sabine, an assistant professor of physics at **Harvard University,** who probed the scientific basis of acoustics. The 2,625-seat hall is basically a shoebox-shaped shell built to resonate glorious sound to astound the ears; the eyes matter less (physical comfort, too; the seats are rather hard).

Directed by Seiji Ozawa, the **BSO** remains one of the world's preeminent orchestras. It is in residence here from October through April; in July and August it performs at Tanglewood, an open-air facility in western Massachusetts. The hall is also home to the beloved **Boston Pops.** Conducted by Hollywood composer and Oscar-winner John Williams, this beloved orchestra performs at home from May to mid-July. (The seats are removed from the main floor, replaced by tables and chairs, and food and drink are served. No one should miss the chance to experience the orchestra and hall together, a delight music-loving Boston has always cherished. The **Handel & Haydn Society,** America's oldest continuously active performing arts organization, performs here, too, as do many other local, national, and international groups. The hall also boasts a magnificent 5,000-pipe organ. ♦ Box office M-Sa. To reserve and charge seats for BSO or Pops performances, call Symphony-Charge at 266.1200. Same-day, one-per-customer discounted seats for BSO performances are available on Tuesday, Thursday, and Friday. The line forms near the box office Tuesday and Thursday from 5PM, and from 9AM on Friday. 301 Massachusetts Ave (at Huntington Ave). 266.1492 &

7 Thai Cuisine ★$$ After a concert at **Symphony Hall** or a foreign film at the **MFA,** dine on good Thai dishes—fiery or delicate—in this little 30-seater behind the hall. The owner has opened several other Thai restaurants in Greater Boston, all highly regarded. Go the spicy route with *kang liang* (peppered shrimp soup) or *gai pud gra prao* (chicken, onion, and chilies), or try more subtle tastes like *tom you koong* (soup with shrimp, lemongrass, lime, and chilies), steamed whole fish, Thai seafood combination, or the selection of curry dishes. The service is sometimes rushed. ♦ Thai/Takeout ♦ Daily lunch and dinner. 14A Westland Ave (at Massachusetts Ave). 262.1485 &

8 Bangkok Cuisine ★$ A favorite with students and people working nearby, Boston's oldest Thai restaurant is still turning out great beef and chicken *satay* (marinated, skewered, and grilled or broiled), *duck choo chee* (curry), *pad Thai* (thin noodles served with shrimp, egg, bean sprouts, and peanut sauce), whole fried bass with chili sauce, and Thai bouillabaisse, which features assorted tender seafood served in a puffed pouch. The long, narrow dining room empties and fills quickly, but service is sometimes desultory, so allow extra time if you have a concert or movie ahead. ♦ Thai/Takeout ♦ M-Sa lunch and dinner; Su dinner. 177A Massachusetts Ave (at Norway St). 262.5377 &

9 Boston International American Youth Hostel (AYH) $ There's no cheaper lodging available in the city, and it's near the **Museum of Fine Arts.** Offering 150 beds in the winter and 220 in the summer, the hostel accommodates men and women of all ages in dormitory style, with six bunks per room, separated by sex. Every floor has showers and bathrooms, and the building houses laundry facilities plus two kitchens with utensils. Sleeping bags are not allowed; you can rent a sleep sheet for a modest fee and deposit. The hostel fills up quickly from May until fall. The fee is lower if you're a member, and you can join on the spot—summer bunks are reserved for members only. Bikes and packs can be stored securely on the premises. No alcohol is allowed, there is no smoking except in one public room, and there's a four-night limit per 30-day period. You can reserve by phone if paying with MasterCard or Visa; walk-ins accepted nightly for 25 percent of the beds. ♦ 12 Hemenway St (at Haviland St). 536.9455

The Boston Red Sox, originally called the Pilgrims, were renamed for the color of the players' stockings by owner John Taylor in 1907.

9 Looney Tunes This music emporium is a good source for serious and dilettante collectors of used and out-of-print jazz, classical, and rock records, some rare. The shop also sells movie and Broadway sound tracks, comedy, country, blues, and opera LPs and 45s, plus "cut-outs" (discontinued recordings), CDs, cassettes, and videos. They carry a few new items, too, and also buy and trade. ♦ Daily. 1106 Boylston St (at Hemenway St). 247.2238. & Also at: 1001 Massachusetts Ave (between Dana and Ellery Sts), Cambridge. 876.5624

9 Counterpoint Cafe ★$ Inexpensive fare served in a stylish setting is what you'll find here. Try the omelettes, fresh muffins, and steamed hot chocolate for breakfast; smoked turkey and avocado on homemade mini-baguette, Green Goddess salad (topped with prosciutto, swiss cheese, and sliced turkey), or tasty daily specials for lunch. This is an ideal spot for a light pre-concert bite. ♦ Cafe ♦ M-F breakfast and lunch until 6PM; Sa-Su breakfast and lunch until 2PM. 1124 Boylston St (at Hemenway St). 424.1789

10 The Massachusetts Historical Society The first historical society founded in the New World (in 1791) is housed in an 1899 National Historic Landmark designed by **Edmund March Wheelwright.** It largely operates as a research center for the study of American history and is only surpassed by the Library of Congress. The focal point is the library, which contains some 3,200 collections of manuscripts and several hundred thousand books, pamphlets, broadsides, maps, early newspapers, and journals, including Governor John Winthrop's and the Adams family's papers, Paul Revere's accounts of his famous ride, two copies of the Declaration of Independence—one written in John Adams's hand, the other in Thomas Jefferson's—and a staggering quantity of other such treasures.

The society's rare-books collection includes most of the important early books printed in America, or about the US's discovery and settlement. Government, politics, women's history, slavery, the China trade, railroads, science, and technology—the breadth of topics addressed is immense. The society also owns prints, engravings, furniture, antique clocks, personal belongings, and several hundred works of art. The first map produced in British North America, an 18th-century Indian archer weather vane by Deacon Shem Drowne (maker of **Faneuil Hall**'s grasshopper weather vane), a list of Americans killed in the Battle of Concord, and Jefferson's architectural plans for Monticello are among the items it preserves. All these virtues not withstanding, here's the catch: to use the library, a form demonstrating that you are a "serious" person with a "worthy" pursuit must be filled out and submitted ahead of time. ♦ Free. M-F. Free guided tours are given if requested in advance. 1154 Boylston St (at Charlesgate E). 536.1608 ♿

11 The Other Side Cosmic Cafe ★$ The "other side" refers to the extension of Newbury Street (past Massachusetts Avenue) that most people don't even know is here, and "cosmic" alludes, one presumes, to its atmospheric aspirations. Whatever—this "Seattle-style coffeehouse/cafe," with its classical/industrial decor (cast-iron railings, red-velvet drapes) and standard fare (soups, salads, and sandwiches), is just the ticket for the young throngs tipping the balance of trade to the "downscale" end of the street. It's handy, too, for the concert-bound. ♦ Coffeehouse/Cafe ♦ Daily breakfast, lunch, and dinner. 407 Newbury St (at Massachusetts Ave). 536.9477 ♿

11 Oceanic Chinese Restaurant ★$ It would take hundreds of visits to exhaust this versatile restaurant's enormous menu. In addition to unadventurous old favorites like spareribs and spring rolls, unusual specialty seafood items are served here, including shark's fin and shredded duck soup, whole fried sole, abalone with tender vegetables, clams with black-bean sauce, and various seafoods with ginger and scallions. Treats that don't hail from the sea are crisp roasted duck, spicy Szechuan dishes, and sizzling hot pots. The restaurant is a trifle fancier than the average Chinatown choice, but it replicates that neighborhood's estimable authentic cuisine—for that's where the owners and staff started out. ♦ Chinese/Takeout ♦ Daily lunch and dinner. 91 Massachusetts Ave (between Commonwealth Ave and Newbury St). 353.0791 ♿

12 The Eliot Hotel $$ Located on the edge of Back Bay, this all-suite hotel built in 1925 (and extensively renovated in 1993) is a convenient place to stay. It's minutes from **Symphony Hall** and the **Museum of Fine Arts,** and a five-minute walk from **Fenway Park** and the **Public Garden.** There used to be a pack of historic hotels along Commonwealth Avenue—the **Vendome**, the **Tuilerie**, and the **Somerset,** to name a few. This hostelry is the sole survivor, with 90 rooms on nine floors. All the guest rooms are swathed with traditional English-style chintz fabrics, authentic botanical prints, antique furnishings, and lovely French doors separating living rooms from bedrooms. Amenities include Italian marble baths; two televisions with a free movie channel; and a stocked mini-bar, coffeemakers, and microwaves in the personal pantries. The privately owned hotel attracts international visitors, conventioneers, and visiting professors mostly, and is one of the city's best buys. The overall ambience is quiet and luxurious, with the old-fashioned intimacy of a European hotel. Continental and full breakfasts are served in the dining room. Nonsmoking rooms and pay parking are available. ♦ 370 Commonwealth Ave (at Massachusetts Ave). 267.1607, 800/44ELIOT; fax 536.9114

Within The Eliot Hotel:

The Eliot Lounge and Cafe $ The famous sports bar, presided over by gregarious bartender and running guru Tommy Leonard, is unofficial headquarters for the **Boston Marathon.** This comfortable, friendly bar attracts all kinds, and students flock in for once-a-week DJ dancing. The cafe serves down-to-earth fare like chili, pizzas, sandwiches, and hamburgers. ♦ American/Takeout ♦ Cafe: M-F dinner; Sa-Su lunch and dinner. Bar: daily until 2AM. Enter from Massachusetts Ave. 421.9169, 262.1078

13 The B.U. Bookstore You won't have any trouble locating this store— blinking away atop it is Kenmore Square's famous landmark, the **Citgo Sign. Boston University**'s bookstore is one of the largest in New England, with three floors of books to browse among. In addition to textbooks, there's a great selection of current and backlist hardcover and paperback books: best-sellers, cookbooks, children's books, classics, hobbies, gardening, law, women, history, politics—the works. The store sponsors frequent events, including author signings and children's story readings. And beyond books, this six-story department store includes specialty shops selling clothing and accessories, chocolates, stationery, housewares, office supplies, flowers, electronics and cameras, and more. There's even a travel agent. If you're in the square with time to spare before a **Red Sox** game, this is the place to dawdle. ♦ Daily. 660 Beacon St (at Commonwealth Ave). 267.8484 ♿

Within The B.U. Bookstore:

Cafe Charles ★$ There are plenty of places to grab a quick bite in Kenmore Square, but few are as serene as this pretty cafe. Soups, sandwiches on French bread, muffins, cappuccino, and desserts, including an excellent hazelnut torte, are served. Bring a book and relax at a table, or watch the

nonstop activity on the streets below from the windowside marble counter. The cafe overlooks the last mile marker for the **Boston Marathon.** A good place for conversation, it attracts university students, faculty, and president—as well as local residents—but most Bostonians haven't discovered it.
♦ Cafe/Takeout ♦ M-Sa breakfast and lunch until 6PM; Su lunch until 5PM. Second floor. 267.8484 ☐

Atop The B.U. Bookstore:

Citgo Sign The 60-square-foot, double-sided sign with its two miles of red, white, and blue neon tubing—its pulsating delta is controlled by computer—dates from 1965. An immediate Pop Art hit, the sign inspired one filmmaker to create a short film called *Go, Go Citgo,* in which the sign did its off-and-on routine to music by the **Monkees** and Ravi Shankar, an Indian sitarist. But the sign was turned off during the energy crisis of the 1970s, and almost torn down in 1982. However, its fans came to its defense: Arthur Krim, a Cambridge resident, college professor, and member of the Society for Commercial Archaeology (which works to preserve urban and roadside Americana such as neon signs, diners, and gas stations), helped lead the fight to save Kenmore Square's illuminated heartbeat from the scrap heap. Oklahoma-based Citgo agreed to keep the sign plugged in and maintained.

14 Nuggets This was the first store in the area to sell new, used, rare, and out-of-print records, CDs, tapes, and 12" dance singles, as well as related posters, T-shirts, and magazines. You can find jazz, reggae, blues, and more. ♦ Daily; M-Sa until 1AM. 486 Commonwealth Ave (between Raleigh St and Brookline Ave). 536.0679. Also at: 1354A Beacon St (at Harvard St). 277.8917

14 Cornwall's ★$ Hearty food, games, and magazines up for grabs, and, above all, a great assortment of esoteric brews on tap explain the appeal of this tiny shoebox of a pub, which has fortified **BU** students for a decade. ♦ English/International ♦ Daily lunch and dinner until 2AM. 510 Commonwealth Ave (at Kenmore Sq). 262.3749

Restaurants/Clubs: Red   **Hotels:** Blue
Shops/ ☂ Outdoors: Green   **Sights/Culture:** Black

The House That Mrs. Jack Built

The larger-than-life Isabella Stewart Gardner (1840-1924) was a charismatic, spirited, and independent New Yorker who married into Victorian Boston's high society but never bowed to its conventions. (Her husband, John, was known as Jack to close friends, hence her nickname, "Mrs. Jack.") Though she became a prominent private art collector and flamboyant socialite, many proper Bostonians forever dismissed her as a brash outsider. But Isabella didn't give a hoot. A passionate woman, she loved the spotlight, so much so that she built a showcase mansion which is now a museum (see page 140) to enshrine her collections and to throw gala parties.

Gardner delighted in upstaging her critics and creating a stir with outrageous behavior, but with a regal awareness of her lofty social stature. Among her many pleasures were art, literature, and music, and she surrounded herself with the most fashionable talents of her time. However, most of her tremendous energy went toward acquiring fabulous art objects.

When their posh Back Bay mansion on Beacon Street became too small for her treasures, the Gardners started planning for a museum. After John's death in 1898, she built **Fenway Court,** a 15th-century Venetian-style palazzo that proudly towered alone in the unfashionable Fenway. While "Mrs. Jack's Palace" was under construction, Gardner was always on the scene directing and often got into the action—climbing on scaffolds to daub the paint to her liking on the courtyard walls. She was accompanied by a trumpeter who summoned workers when she wanted to confer with them: one note for the architect, another for the plumber, and so on. Anyone ignoring the summons was fired.

Gardner held court among her collections, blurring the distinction between residence and museum in an extraordinary, idiosyncratic way. Signs of her presence remain—a table is set for tea as if she were in the next room. Prevented by gender from the prestige and power for which she was suited by temperament, Gardner found in the museum the stage, cultural forum, artistic medium, and professional avocation denied her by her times. Look for the plaque she first affixed over the door in 1900, giving her home its official name. Then find the seal designed for her achievement—carved in marble and set into the museum facade's brick wall—which bears her motto, "*C'est mon plaisir*" (it is my pleasure), and a phoenix, a symbol of immortality. Henry James thought she resembled "a figure on a wondrous cinquecento tapestry." John Singer Sargent's portrait of Gardner started a scandal when it was first unveiled in 1888 at the private, then all-male **St. Botolph Club,** to which her husband belonged. Isabella had posed barearmed in a clingy décolleté gown, which so shocked proper Bostonians that her husband became infuriated, threatened to horsewhip any gossipers, and forbade the picture to be publicly displayed. But today you can see it through untitillated 20th-century eyes at Isabella's museum, where it finally found its niche in 1924.

14 Rathskeller (The Rat)/Hoo Doo BBQ ★$
One of the very few clubs in town serving good music and good food, **The Rat**'s not much to look at, to say the least, but it was Boston's first New Wave club. Many local groups got a boost here, and this was the first Boston club to headline the **Cars, Police, Talking Heads,** and **Go Gos.** The club books high-quality local and touring rock bands, up to four a night, three or four nights a week, and they usually go on at 9:30PM. On weekends you can listen for free to bands playing on the balcony. There are four bars serving cheap drinks, plus pinball, video, and a great jukebox.

A number of musicians—not to mention locals—have enjoyed chef Paul DelTrecco's ribs, chicken, crisp french fries and onion rings, salads, coleslaw, corn bread, and sweet-potato pie. Some struggling performers have even done stints in the kitchen. ♦ American/Barbecue ♦ Cover for club. Daily lunch and dinner. You must be 21 or older, unless a special all-ages show is scheduled. No credit cards accepted. 528 Commonwealth Ave (at Brookline Ave). 536.2750 ᴕ (Hoo Doo BBQ only)

15 Howard Johnson/Kenmore $$ Just beyond Kenmore Square on **Boston University**'s campus, this bustling stopover is convenient to **Fenway Park,** western Boston, and Back Bay. Lots of tour groups stay here. An older but well-kept hotel, it has 180 rooms on seven floors—including an executive section with larger rooms and VCRs, and complimentary coffee and newspaper—plus a restaurant, lounge, and indoor swimming pool. Nonsmokers' rooms and free parking are available. ♦ 575 Commonwealth Ave (between Beacon and Sherborn Sts). 267.3100, 800/654.2000; fax 267.3100 ext 40

16 Photographic Resource Center (PRC)
One of the few centers for photography in the country, this nonprofit arts organization leases space from **Boston University** and houses three galleries for exhibitions and a nonlending photography library. The building's intelligent, award-winning design (by **Leers, Weinzapfel Associates/Alex Krieger Architects** in 1985) evokes the mechanical process of photography, its manipulation of light—particularly in the architects' use of industrial materials and glass. The exhibitions emphasize new and experimental photography from the US and abroad; popular shows have included *The Emperor's New Clothes,* an exploration of censorship as it relates to art, pornography, and fashion. Check local papers or call to find out about frequent lectures/slide presentations; Chuck Close, Mary Ellen Mark, John Baldessari, and William Wegman have all spoken here. Everything is open to the public. The organization publishes a monthly newsletter and the trimesterly journal *VIEWS,* and offers educational programs. Call in advance to arrange a tour. ♦ Admission. Tu-Su; Th until 8PM. 602 Commonwealth Ave (at Blandford St), Basement level . 353.0700 ᴕ

17 Mugar Memorial Library of Boston University Few outside the university community know about this library's marvelous and massive Department of Special Collections, dedicated to scholarly research but also open to the public. Owned and exhibited here are rare books, manuscripts, and papers pertaining to hundreds of interesting people, famous and not, from the 15th century onward (the 20th-century archives are particularly strong). The third-floor **King Exhibit Room** displays documents from the archives of alumnus Dr. Martin Luther King Jr.

The library also boasts a huge holding of Theodore Roosevelt's and Robert Frost's papers and memorabilia. The collections span journalists, politicians, mystery writers, film and stage actors, and musicians. Browse awhile and you'll encounter Frederick Douglass, Bette Davis, Florence Nightingale, Albert Einstein, Tennessee Williams, original cartoons of Little Orphan Annie and L'il Abner, Irwin Shaw, Arthur Fiedler, Eric Ambler, Walt Whitman, Michael Halberstam, Rex Harrison, Fred Astaire, and Abraham Lincoln. ♦ Daily; Special Collections: M-F. 771 Commonwealth Ave (at St. Mary's St). 353.3696, Tours 353.3710 ᴕ

18 Paradise Rock Club This club and adjacent **M-80** are beyond the neighborhood's borders, but shouldn't be overlooked because they are two of Boston's best places to dance and to see national and international groups in concert. Other than for scheduled performances, the **Paradise** is only open on Saturday night for dancing to DJ-spun records. New Wave and rock are the mainstays; but jazz, folk, blues, and country are also frequently booked. The **Buzzcocks,** Rickie Lee Jones, **U2, Tower of Power,** the **Scorpions,** and Nick Lowe have all appeared here. Get tickets in advance, since few if any are available for popular groups on the day of the shows. There's a full bar, and minimum age requirements vary by shows. By subway, take the *B Line* to the **Pleasant Street** stop. ♦ Admission. Box office M-Sa. Doors open at 8PM for shows; sometimes two are scheduled per night. Cash only at the door; credit cards accepted at box office and bar. 967 Commonwealth Ave (between Pleasant and Babcock Sts). Recorded information 351.2582; Ticketmaster 931.2000

18 M-80 DJs spin dance music at this European-style club. Many international exchange students seek it out, and it is jam-packed some nights. There's a full bar, but no food is served. ♦ Cover. W, F-Sa 11PM-2AM. You must be at least 21. No jeans or sneakers allowed. 969 Commonwealth Ave (between Pleasant and Babcock Sts). 351.2582

19 Savoy French Bakery One owner of this savory spot was trained by a French baker, so the goods are classic French. Go out of your way to sample the fantastic apple-and-almond, apricot, chocolate, plain, and other croissant varieties baked here. Equally delicious are the decorative fresh-fruit tartlets and minicakes such as hazelnut *frangipane* (layered torte), the assortment of cookies—try the traditional French *palmier,* nicknamed "elephant's ear," and the breads, including baguettes, *batards,* and *petit pain.* Truffles are also a taste treat. ♦ Tu-Su. No credit cards accepted. 1003 Beacon St (at St. Mary's St). 734.0214

20 Sol Azteca ★★$$ Dinner begins with some of the best piquant salsa and chips to be had in Boston, and progresses to marvelous Mexican fare like *chiles rellenos* (chili peppers stuffed with cheese), enchiladas *verdes* (in a green sauce), *camarones al cilantro* (shrimp seasoned with cilantro), and *puerco en adobo* (pork tenderloin with spicy red peppers). With the meal, enjoy excellent sangria or Mexican beer; afterward, try coffee flavored with cinnamon and the great coffee-flavored flan. The rustic dining rooms are gay and festive with hand-painted tile tables and handicrafts. ♦ Mexican ♦ Daily dinner. Reservations recommended Monday-Thursday, and Su. 914A Beacon St (between Park Dr and St. Mary's St). 262.0909 &

21 Boston Beer Works ★$$ Yet another on-site brewery complete with gleaming tanks, this one is unusually well situated, a stone's throw from the ballpark. The menu is surprisingly ambitious, with such interesting entries as onion-and-ale soup, barbecued Cajun andouille sausage, shark shish kebabs, and "beer-basted" burgers. Sunday brunch features a "make your own omelette" option. ♦ American ♦ Daily lunch and dinner. 61 Brookline Ave (between Lansdowne St and Yawkey Way). 536.2337 &

22 Avalon This mammoth dance club holds up to 1,500 people for a rotating roster of music. Thursday features international music, Friday high-energy dance tunes, Saturday Top 40 and progressive, and Sunday is gay/lesbian night. There's a full bar, but no food is served. Expect to wait; but barring late arrival, everyone gets in eventually. ♦ Cover. Th-Su until 2AM. You must be at least 21. No sneakers, jeans, or athletic wear allowed except Sunday and concert nights. No credit cards accepted. 15 Lansdowne St (between Brookline Ave and Ipswich St). 262.2424 &

22 Axis Music changes nightly and includes progressive, punk, funk, heavy metal, hard rock, live bands, alternative dance tunes, and DJ spins. Creative dress is encouraged; "When in doubt, wear black" is the club's advice. On Sunday, this smaller club (800 capacity) connects with its next-door neighbor for gay/lesbian night—enter through **Avalon.** ♦ Cover. Tu-Su until 2AM. Call for information on age minimums and shows. 13 Lansdowne St (between Brookline Ave and Ipswich St). 262.2437 &

22 Venus de Milo Look for her statue above the entrance, sporting three neon hula hoops. The club strives for a dark Gothic Renais-sance decor, its youngish urban crowd dancing to hip-hop, house, and funk music. Wednesday is gay night, Thursday is rave night, Friday features high-energy dance music, and Saturday's theme is Trash Disco. ♦ Cover. M-Sa until 2AM. You must be 21 or older except on 19-and-over nights. No athletic wear, baseball caps, or work boots allowed. No credit cards accepted. 7 Lansdowne St (between Brookline Ave and Ipswich St). 421.9595 &

22 Bill's Bar This small (250 maximum) 1950s-homage bar changes personas nightly for a 21-plus crowd. Monday is movie night, featuring offbeat films and music videos; Tuesday brings in a local band; Wednesday means jukebox tunes and no cover; Thursday, with a DJ, is college night; Friday and Saturday are low-key (again, no cover); and Sunday is live reggae. ♦ Cover. Call ahead for hours. 5½ Lansdowne St (between Brookline Ave and Ipswich St). 421.9678 &

22 Jake Ivory's Audience participation is prized, what with dueling pianos and regular sing-alongs after every **Red Sox** game. "If you don't have a good time here, it's your own fault," says the *Boston Globe.* ♦ Cover. W-Sa until 2AM. 1 Lansdowne St (at Ipswich St). 247.1222 &

23 Jillian's Billiard Club Get behind the eight ball at one of 50 tournament-quality billiard, pocket billiard, and snooker tables. You'll find darts, shuffleboard, a batting cage, Ping-Pong games, video games, and wide-screen TVs, too. Cafe fare, beer, and wine are served. ♦ Fees are prorated by the minute. Daily. Only those 18 and over are admitted after 8PM. No hats, tank tops, sweats, or cutoffs allowed. 145 Ipswich St (at Lansdowne St). 437.0300

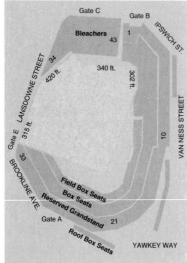

24 Fenway Park Fans are thrillingly close to the players at the country's smallest major-league ballpark—it has a 34,000-person capacity (see the plan above). Carl Yastrzemski, Ted Williams, Dwight Evans, and Roger Clemens have all dominated the diamond. Babe Ruth made his debut as a **Red Sox** pitcher here on 11 July 1914. He was later traded. Built in 1912 and rebuilt in 1934, the park is a classic, with plenty of quirks that enhance its battered charm. It still has real green grass, and its idiosyncratic shape is the result of an awkward site, since the surrounding lots weren't for sale when the ballpark was embedded in the city. Even if baseball leaves you unmoved, come for the show—just sitting among Boston's demanding, impassioned, extremely vocal fans is fun.

The ballpark opens one-and-a-half hours before game time. Tickets are available on a first-come, first-served basis to an alcohol-free reserved zone. Ask about special youth, senior citizen, and family discounts available for designated dates. Souvenirs are sold on all sides of the park (look for the amazing **Souvenir Shop** across from the ticket office). Before and after the games, crowds flock to the **Cask 'n Flagon** sports bar (62 Brookline Avenue, 536.4840), among other neighborhood watering holes. ♦ Ticket office:

M-F. 4 Yawkey Way (between Lansdowne and Van Ness Sts). Tickets 267.1700, recorded information 267.8661 & (special section)

25 Buteco Restaurant ★$ Don't be put off by the shabby facade; good food lurks inside. With Latin music pulsing in the background (a live band plays Mondays), a diverse, youngish clientele packs the tiny dining room. Plates get piled with such spicy Brazilian dishes as: *mandioca* (fried cassava root with carrot dipping sauce), hearts of palm salad, black-bean soup, *picadinho a carioca* (beef stew with garlic), *vatapá a Baiana* (sole baked in coconut milk and served on shrimp with peanut paste), and *churrasco* (mixed grill). On weekends order *feijoada*, the Brazilian national dish—a hearty stew with black beans, pork sausage, beef, collard greens, and orange. ♦ Brazilian ♦ M-F lunch and dinner; Sa-Su dinner. Reservations recommended Saturday and Sunday. 130 Jersey St (between Queensberry St and Park Dr). 247.9508. & Also at: 57 W Dedham St (between Tremont St and Shawmut Ave). 247.9249

26 Thorntons Fenway Grill ★★$ Though there are many grilled dishes on the menu, this place is known for its generous sandwiches and super salads. Come to this sprawling corner restaurant for a summer supper and some beer or wine before or after the **Red Sox** play. ♦ American ♦ M-Sa breakfast, lunch, and dinner; Su brunch and dinner. 100 Peterborough St (at Kilmarnock St). 421.0104 &

26 Wheatstone Baking Company Through picture windows, watch as bakers whip up the croissants, muffins, sticky buns, coffee cakes, and breads available for sale at the counter. This is primarily a wholesale bakery, with four little cafe tables, but breakfast treats don't come any fresher. ♦ Bakery/Takeout ♦ Daily. 86 Peterborough St (between Kilmarnock and Jersey Sts). 247.3566 &

26 Sorento's ★★$$ The decor is pretty dramatic for a neighborhood pizza place: all black-and-white contrast, including the harlequin tile floor. But this is no ordinary pizza, either, not with toppings like imported prosciutto, fried eggplant, and fontina cheese. Try the chicken *à la Abruzzi* (pâté sautéed with basil and spinach and served over cappellini). It's just one of a full array of luscious pasta dishes that share star billing here. ♦ Italian/ Takeout ♦ Daily lunch and dinner. 86 Peterborough St (between Kilmarnock and Jersey Sts). 424.7070 &

27 Wheelock Family Theatre Boston's only Equity theater company serving younger audiences staunchly upholds a nontraditional casting policy and mounts ambitious, polished productions, ranging from musicals to drama. It seats 650. ♦ 180 Riverway (between Park Dr and Longwood Ave). 734.4760 &

28 The Best Western Boston $$ Smack dab in the middle of the **Longwood Medical Area,** this 152-room economical hotel attracts many guests connected with the center. In addition, the **Museum of Fine Arts** and **Isabella Stewart Gardner Museum** are nearby, and it's just 15 minutes to Back Bay via the *Green Line.* Rooms for nonsmokers and for people with disabilities are available; and there is a restaurant as well as room service. The hotel is connected to a galleria of fast-food shops, a health club, and other services. ♦ 342 Longwood Ave (at Brookline Ave). 731.4700; fax 731.6273 &

29 The Arnold Arboretum of Harvard University Built on the old Benjamin Bussey farm, this arboretum has more than 4,000 woody plants, trees, shrubs, and vines collected on expeditions throughout the world. Olmsted interlaced its acreage with walks and drives offering a pleasant progression through meticulously sited plantings. Rare finds from China, Tibet, Borneo, Japan, and the Americas are in bloom everywhere. The arboretum is the focal point of a favorite annual event, Lilac Sunday. Azaleas, magnolias, and fruit trees burst forth in full glory, too. Along the Chinese Path, some rarer older Asian specimens are planted, including the Dove Tree from China, a magical sight in spring when its creamy white bracts flutter like wings. Wind your way up to one of several promontories for splendid views. The **Hunnewell Visitor Center** offers year-round events, workshops, classes, and exhibitions. The shop offers New England's largest selection of books on horticulture and other items. ♦ Free (donations welcomed). Arboretum: daily. Shop: Tu-Su. Guided walking tours or bus tours can be arranged for a fee. Driving permits for senior citizens and disabled persons available for slow-speed

touring. 125 Arborway (between Hyde Park Ave and Centre St), Jamaica Plain. 524.1718 (plant questions answered M-Tu 1-3PM), recorded information on what's in bloom 524.1717 &

29 Franklin Park Zoo Renovated in 1989 by **Huygens, DiMella, Shaffer and Associates,** the prime attraction of this 70-acre zoo (see map below) is the domed **African Tropical Forest Pavilion,** the largest in North America, with sculpted cliffs and caves, waterfalls, wooden footbridges, and lush African vegetation. The three-acre environmental exhibit is home to gorillas, leopards, forest buffalo, bongo antelopes, dwarf crocodiles, three-inch-long scorpions, and exotic birds. One of the stars is 20-year-old Camille, a shy 500-pound pygmy hippo. There are 75 species and 250 specimens in all, with no cages and almost imperceptible barriers between the looked-ons and onlookers. Exhibits educate on the international crisis of human destruction of African and South American rain forests. When it's cold outdoors, come soak up some warm tropical mist. The exhibit's ecosystem creates periodic rainstorms and rainbows. The zoo also features a **Children's Zoo** with a petting barn, where kids learn about New England farm animals. The **Hooves and Horns** section stars zebras and camels, including Boomer the dromedary. In **Birds' World,** you can see and touch more than 50 species of birds in a Chinese-pagoda birdhouse and free-flight cage, which dates from the zoo's 1913 opening. At press time, plans were afoot to add a lion pavilion. ♦ Admission; children three and under free; discount for senior citizens, uniformed military, children four to 11. Daily. Franklin Park Rd (off Blue Hill Ave). 442.4896, 442.2002 &

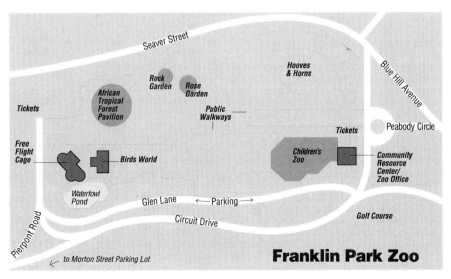

Franklin Park Zoo

The Emerald Necklace

Ponds and parks strung together by parkways form Boston's prized **Emerald Necklace,** which, when charted on a map, looks like it's dangling from Boston Harbor like a chain around a slender neck. Executed for the Boston Park Commission in 1895, Frederick Law Olmsted's design for an interconnected park system totaled more than 2,000 acres of open land, its main artery the five-mile-long **Emerald Necklace.** (When Olmsted found his professional niche at age 35, the notion of creating public parks was still novel. Today he is lauded as the creator of landscape architecture as a profession and an art in America.)

The largest continuous green space through an urban center in the country, the **Necklace** traverses a number of communities and is adorned with five major parks—**Back Bay Fens, Muddy River Improvement, Jamaica Park, Arnold Arboretum,** and **Franklin Park**—all connected by parkways. Olmsted's **Necklace** was further embellished by joining the **Boston Common** and the **Public Garden.** The **Charles River Esplanade** is often considered an additional strand, although it wasn't built until 1931, long after Olmsted's death. The **Necklace** has missing links (which the city promises to eventually fix), most importantly the never-realized Columbia Road extension by which Olmsted intended to connect **Franklin Park** with **Marine Park** in South Boston. At press time such improvements were on hold until 2000 at the earliest. The only way to see the entire **Emerald Necklace** at one time is to drive its length along the parkways, but the twisting route will offer fleeting glimpses of greenery and water, not at all the restful communion with nature Olmsted had in mind. Instead, pick a fair-weather day and jog, bicycle, walk, or ride a horse through a segment of the park system. The **Necklace** is dotted with benches, fields to sun in, and shady meadows.

The **Emerald Necklace** starts at the **Boston Common (1)**, proceeds through the **Public Garden (2)**, then continues along **Commonwealth Avenue Mall (3)** to **Charlesgate (4)**, the original connection forged between the mall and the **Back Bay Fens (5)** where the Muddy River entered the **Charles River Estuary**. But **Charlesgate**'s open wetlands were largely destroyed when elevated overpasses to Storrow Drive were built during the 1960s. The **Necklace** still joins tenuously with the **Back Bay Fens,** Olmsted's first contribution. Named after the marshlands of eastern England, the **Fens** originally embodied its designer's love for idyllic English rural landscapes. Dredging, draining, and landscaping rescued the **Fens** from its reeking muddy past and made way for tranquil salt-marsh meadows. The damming of the Charles River in 1910 changed the water from salt to fresh, destroying Olmsted's original scheme. Years of neglect have also taken their toll. Yet the park is still a pleasant spot to wander among willows, dogwoods, lindens, and hawthorns. The **Victory Gardens** planted during World War II and the spectacular **Rose Garden** behind the **Museum of Fine Arts,** as well as an athletic field, have settled in to stay. And the pudding stone bridge where Boylston Street crosses the river is a poetic charmer,

designed in 1880 by Olmsted's friend **Henry Hobson Richardson.** A cautionary note: Don't linger in the **Fens** after dark, and never stray into the stands of debris-laden tall reeds.

The **Muddy River Improvement (6)** is the next ornament, although its connection to the **Fens** via the Riverway was obliterated by construction of the former **Sears Roebuck** building. A little perseverance returns you to a meandering riverside park with bridle, walking, and running paths; graceful bridges; placid ponds; and lush plantings. The **Improvement**—unpoetically named for the spruce-up job it accomplished—widens at a section now called **Olmsted Park,** where **Leverett, Willow,** and **Wards Ponds** are located. And then one arrives at **Jamaica Park (7)**, its centerpiece the largest freshwater pond in Boston. Fringed by a tree-shaded promenade lit by gas lanterns, **Jamaica Pond** is popular for sailing, rowing, walking, jogging, and fishing. **Edmund Wheelwright** designed the decorative 1913 boathouse and gazebo where refreshments are sold.

From Jamaica Pond the Jamaicaway leads to the world-renowned **Arnold Arboretum (8)** (details on page 151), which belongs to the Boston Park System, but is administered by **Harvard University.** Charles Sprague Sargent, a landscape gardener and the arboretum's first director for more than half a century, collaborated with Olmsted in 1878 to design this living museum of trees, named for its first big donor, a merchant and amateur horticulturist. Both Olmsted and Sargent envisioned a scientific outdoor museum that would also be a delightful, picturesque park.

Linked to the arboretum by the Arborway, the **Emerald Necklace**'s massive pendant is **Franklin Park (9)**, named for Benjamin Franklin. One of Olmsted's three greatest parks, its design expresses his precept that the natural world offers the ideal antidote to the dehumanizing quality of urban living. Within this 500-acre tract straddling **Dorchester, Jamaica Plain,** and **Roxbury,** Olmsted preserved and enhanced existing natural features. **Franklin Park** is a great green swath of rolling hills and broad fields and meadows, with hickory, hemlock, locust, oak, tulip trees, and myriad other plantings, and enormous boulders and park ornaments fashioned from Roxbury pudding stone. But because the park is four miles from the heart of Boston and tricky to reach, it never got the popularity it deserved, and languished from the 1940s until recently. And like the **Fens,** changes have been made that spoil the integrity of Olmsted's original plan. But if **Franklin Park** is not a perfect emerald, it's still a gem, a sanctuary from the city where one can walk, jog, picnic, bird-watch, play golf or baseball, watch the annual September Kite Festival, attend festivals such as the August West Indian Carnival, visit the zoo, and generally let loose a little. The 18-hole golf course does not emit a private country-club atmosphere—residents come together to play on the par-70 course, the country's second-oldest municipal golf course. Although it will take time for **Franklin Park** to shake its unfair poor reputation, it is actually one of the city's safer parks.

Don't linger after dark or stray into the overgrown areas, but do enjoy an oasis that Bostonians have begun to appreciate anew.

The **Necklace** breaks after **Franklin Park,** but it should have led via **Columbia Road** through **Upham's Corner** and on to **Marine Park (10).** (A lack of funds kept Columbia Road from becoming the spacious green boulevard Olmsted intended.) Eclipsed long ago by suburban beaches, **Marine Park** no longer draws crowds, but the sea breezes and harbor views are worth an outing, and this is where you can look at the shiny bellies of the big jets as they descend to **Logan International Airport.** It's best to drive here; there's always plenty of parking.

Now missing from the **Emerald Necklace, Charlesbank** was a pioneering neighborhood park (designed by Olmsted in the 1890s) that bordered the Charles River near **Massachusetts General Hospital.** The park was intended to alleviate the overcrowding suffered by residents of the **West End,** a neighborhood largely wiped out by urban renewal in the 1960s. **Charlesbank** featured the city's first

playgrounds and America's first sandboxes, called "sand courts." Today **Charlesbank** is mostly buried under a tangle of roadways.

Boston's Park Rangers direct all kinds of activities throughout the Boston Park System: historical strolls and tours, children's learning activities such as "Horse of Course" (about a day in the life of a park ranger horse), nature walks through the **Arnold Arboretum,** bird watching along the Muddy River, fishing on Jamaica Pond, an architectural exploration of **Commonwealth Avenue,** and more. Some events require reservations; all are free. For information, call the **Boston Parks and Recreation Department** (635.4505) or the **Boston Park Rangers** (522.2639).

Additional recreational and educational programs are planned for kids during the summer, including golf clinics at **Franklin Park,** "Sox Talk" with **Red Sox** players, and sailing on Boston Harbor and Jamaica Pond. Call the **Parks and Recreation Activities Eventline** (635.4006) for daily updates on what's going on. Boston parks are officially closed from 11:30PM to 6AM.

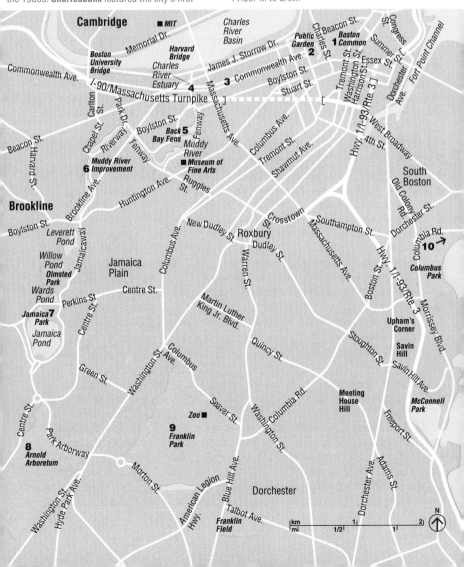

South End

This part of Boston is not a destination for sightseers, but rather for urban explorers who like to stray from the tourist tracks and make their own discoveries. Enticements include block after block of undulating Victorian bowfronts, intimate residential parks, vibrant street life, out-of-the-ordinary shops, and unusual restaurants of excellent quality—equal to those of Back Bay. Yet the South End is often overlooked, in favor of neighboring Back Bay for its **Copley Place** and **Prudential Center** developments.

The South End is one of Boston's most diverse neighborhoods—racially, economically, ethnically, and religiously. Within this scant square mile is the largest Victorian row-house district extant in the US, listed on the National Register of Historic Places. After a brief flowering as a genteel enclave, the neighborhood became home to Boston's immigrant populations. Today it still exudes port-of-entry flavor: various blocks are predominantly Lebanese, Irish, Yankee, Chinese, West Indian, African-American, Greek, or Hispanic. Boston's largest gay population resides here, too. Over the past 25 years young middle-class professionals have moved in, gentrifying patches of this crazy quilt. The neighborhood also has a bohemian side, attracting visual artists, architects, writers, performers, designers, craftspeople, and musicians.

Like Back Bay, the entire South End rests on landfill. The neighborhood was originally marshland bordering **Washington Street,** which was once a narrow neck that linked the peninsula to the mainland. By the mid-19th century upwardly mobile Bostonians wanted fashionable new quarters. From 1850 to 1875 the South End emerged as speculators filled in blocks of land and auctioned them off. Unlike Back Bay, there was no grid or grand plan. And while Back Bay is French-inspired and cosmopolitan in style, the South End follows more traditional English patterns. To attract buyers, developers created London-style residential parks such as **Worcester** and **Union Park Squares,** oases loosely linked by common architecture. Although less haphazard in plan than Boston's oldest neighborhoods, the South End still has a transitional, unpredictable feel.

The South End rose and fell from grace in less than a decade, eclipsed by glamorous Back Bay and the allure of streetcar suburbs. **Boston City Hospital** was founded in the 1860s; it is the oldest institution on **Hospital Row,** a dense cluster of university and municipal medical buildings located near the Roxbury border. By 1900 prosperous Bostonians had abandoned their handsome row houses, which were then divided into multiple units and lodging rooms to accommodate waves of immigrants and working-class families. Industries and businesses sprang up. The South End also became the largest lodging-house district in the country, gaining a reputation for dens of vices and unsavory pursuits. Finally declared a federal urban renewal area in 1965, the South End was torn apart, setting the stage for development and gentrification in the 1970s and 1980s.

The neighborhood endures, changeable and fascinating as ever. Residents and community groups take active parts in healing old wounds—the **Southwest Corridor Park** is but one attractive result. Although the neighborhood fabric has been neglected by insensitive institutions and individuals, many buildings and blocks are being recycled and renewed. Visit in the late morning or early afternoon, when the streets are safest and liveliest. Explore **Columbus Avenue** and **Tremont Street** for the greatest concentration of good shops and restaurants. Take a walk through tiny **Rutland Square** or tranquil Union Park Square, both hugged by carefully restored residences. Stroll along **Chandler, Lawrence,** and **Appleton Streets,** lined with appealing, smaller-scale brick houses. From block to block, the architecture changes from down-in-the-dumps to resplendently restored. And with each block you'll sense the presence of different populations, such as the African-American community to the south, and Middle Easterners and Armenians along **Shawmut Avenue** to the east.

A cautionary note: The South End's changeable nature means that many shops and restaurants come and go, and those that stay often keep ad hoc hours. The best approach is to call ahead when possible, be prepared for occasional disappointments, and be alert to interesting new finds.

The subway stops most convenient to the South End are the **Back Bay/South End** and **Massachusetts Avenue** stations (both on the *Orange Line*). The **Copley, Prudential,** and **Symphony** stops (all on the *Green Line*) are beyond the neighborhood's borders but are mere minutes away on foot. Amtrak also stops at **Back Bay/South End,** as well as at **South Station.**

1 Southwest Corridor Park Where an ugly gash once slashed the South End, a ribbon of attractive parkland now curls. In the early 1970s more than a hundred acres of housing in the South End and adjoining Roxbury and Jamaica Plain were demolished to make way for a highway project. Community protests killed that plan, but the blight remained, a sore spot awaiting healing. In 1977, 52 acres of this area were reclaimed for parkland to reknit divided neighborhoods. More than a decade in the making, the park—landscaped by Roy B.

Mann—has become a valued part of the city. Twenty-three architectural and engineering firms worked with more than 15 community groups to chart the course of the new green trail. The result: 4.7 miles of walkways and bike paths dotted with tot lots, street-hockey rinks, and basketball and tennis courts, and graced with young trees and plantings. An adjunct project, the community-run Southwest Corridor Farms, manages 13 acres, providing plots and training to urban gardeners. The lauded fingerlike park is as narrow as 60 feet in spots and as wide as a quarter mile in others, and points all the way to **Franklin Park,** the **Arnold Arboretum,** and **Forest Hills Cemetery.** Starting behind **Copley Place,** stroll as far west as your fancy takes you, and see how intensely used the well-loved park has become by all ages, all races, all economic groups. You can even read your way along, following the chiseled words of 18 local writers located near **T** stops along the **Corridor.**

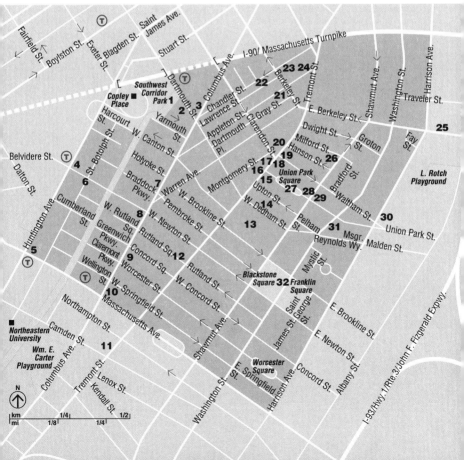

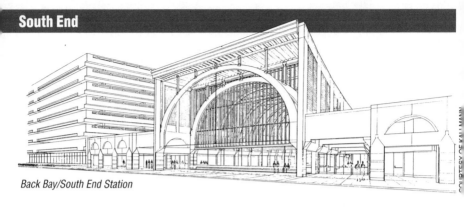

Back Bay/South End Station

The park is just one piece of the controversial, enormous, $750-million–plus Southwest Corridor Project still under way, which also involved relocating and depressing Boston's old elevated **MBTA** *Orange Line* and constructing nine new rapid transit stations. Two are in the South End. Pictured above, the **Back Bay/South End Station** is a well-crafted structure designed by **Kallmann, McKinnell & Wood Architects,** extending from Dartmouth Street across from the park's beginning to Clarendon Street. In its heroic navelike concourse, vaulted by huge wooden arches and illuminated by clerestory windows, the station recalls the grandeur of Victorian railway stations. The **Massachusetts Avenue Station,** by **Ellenzweig, Moore and Associates,** is a sleek, sinuous brick, glass, and aluminum structure located where the park intersects Massachusetts Avenue. The Southwest Corridor Project is also creating development parcels that are intended to revitalize neglected Boston neighborhoods by providing employment and development opportunities for those communities. At press time, a Registry of Motor Vehicles, a city police department, and a shopping mall were earmarked for construction along this route. ♦ Off Dartmouth St (between Huntington and Columbus Aves)

2 Moka ★$ A breezy "California-style cafe," this deli-counter establishment with an outdoor patio suggests summer whatever the season, thanks to Paula Carlton's surf's-up mural. The grazing's good right into the evening with salmon-and-black-bean burritos; roast turkey with apple butter, sharp cheddar, tomato, and romaine on homemade focaccia; and polenta pizza (topped with pieces of polenta, peppers, and onions). Desserts are equally imaginative and irresistible. There's a different cheesecake every day—look for the orange-almond version. For those a little more health conscious, fruit smoothies in a base of orange juice or milk are made to your specifications. Breakfast also warrants a visit, when Belgian waffles and homemade granola are some of the attractions. ♦ American/ Takeout ♦ Daily breakfast, lunch, and dinner. 130 Dartmouth St (between Huntington and Columbus Aves). 424.7768 &

2 Tent City The construction of affluent **Copley Place** across the way was the catalyst that brought African-American community activists to this site to protest the South End's gentrification. This forced Boston to alter plans for a parking lot and to build affordable housing instead. The result—designed by **Goody, Clancy & Associates** in 1988—is a gentle addition to the neighborhood. One-quarter of the units in the cheerful patterned-brick complex of apartments and row houses are market-rate, one-quarter are for low-income residents, and one-half are for moderate-income residents. The biggest surprise is the name, which preserves the political moment when the activists set up tents here, an early episode in the wave of tent cities that spread across the country as the homelessness crisis worsened. ♦ Dartmouth St (between Huntington and Columbus Aves)

3 The Claddagh ★$ This Irish pub offers just the sort of filling, unfussy food you'd expect to find in a neighborhood bar. You're best off with burgers, chicken, stews, and other straightforward items. The walls are adorned with Irish family crests. It becomes boisterous on weekends, often hosting sing-alongs; one room was renovated for live music. ♦ Irish-American/Takeout ♦ Daily lunch and dinner. 335 Columbus Ave (at Dartmouth St). 262.9874

4 The Colonnade Hotel $$ This 280-room hotel's amenities include a restaurant, bar, outdoor rooftop pool, fitness room, indoor parking, a multilingual staff, 24-hour room service, same-day valet service (for a fee), and foreign currency exchange. Rooms for people with disabilities and for nonsmokers are available. ♦ 120 Huntington Ave (at W Newton St). 424.7000, 800/962.3030; fax 424.1717 &

Restaurants/Clubs: Red	**Hotels:** Blue
Shops/ 🌳 Outdoors: Green	**Sights/Culture:** Black

5 The Midtown Hotel $$ A well-kept secret, this two-story, 159-room hotel is older and far less fashionable than the numerous luxury hotels located nearby, and also much less expensive. It's frequented by families, tour groups, and businesspeople. The rooms are spacious, and there's free parking, an outdoor pool with a lifeguard (in season), and a multilingual staff. Children under 18 stay free with parents. Winter packages are available on request. **Seiyoken,** a Japanese restaurant, is located on the premises. ◆ 220 Huntington Ave (at Massachusetts Ave). 262.1000, 800/343.1177; fax 262.8739 ᵫ

6 St. Botolph Street Stroll down this pleasant stretch of street, which New York City's Ash Can School painter George Benjamin Luks portrayed in *Noontime, St. Botolph,* on view in the **Museum of Fine Arts.** Look for the **Musician's Mutual Relief Society Building** at No. 56, an 1886 commercial hall designed by **Cabot and Chandler** that was renovated and suitably ornamented for the society's use in 1913 (it now houses apartments). Separated by stone lyres beneath the cornice are composers' names. At the Cumberland Street intersection is an attractive schoolhouse dating from 1891, converted to condominiums in 1980 by **Graham Gund Associates.** ◆ Between Harcourt and Gainsborough Sts

6 St. Botolph Street Restaurant ★$$$ This neighborly two-story restaurant in a rehabbed 19th-century town house is a good choice for Sunday brunch: a four-course prix-fixe feast featuring a Bloody Mary or screwdriver, muffins, an appetizer, entrée, coffee, and dessert. The casual street-level cafe—complete with bar and jukebox—offers bistro fare, with a full range of appetizers, grilled pizzas, sandwiches, pastas, risottos, soups, and salads; dinner is served in the upper level, an airy loft. The daring renovation of this turreted building, which seemed clever and cutting-edge in the 1970s, is looking rather crude and gauche in retrospect. ◆ American/Takeout ◆ Cafe: daily lunch and dinner; main dining room: daily dinner. Reservations recommended for dinner. 99 St. Botolph St (at W Newton St). 266.3030

7 Charlie's Sandwich Shoppe ★★$ Christi Manjourides stays up all night, baking pies and muffins. At 5AM sons Chris and Arthur arrive and get ready for a day at the grill. Regulars begin drifting in after sunrise, anticipating a gentle morning start with counter conversations over coffee and such famous breakfast platters as cranberry pancakes or a Cajun omelette with spicy sausage.

Family run for more than 50 years, this unpretentious luncheonette is a melting pot, attracting anyone with an appetite for hearty breakfasts and lunches. At communal tables, designer suits mingle with blue jeans and work boots, and celebrities mix with folks struggling to get by. Relax among the awards, accolades, and smiling photos taken since opening day in 1927. Stoke up on blueberry French toast, cheeseburgers, Greek salad, turkey hash, frankfurters and beans, fried clams, hot pastrami on a bulky roll, sweet-potato pie, and more. It's pleasant to linger here—that is, if you can ignore the lines of people waiting impatiently for a table. Duke Ellington and other famous African-American musicians were welcomed here in the 1940s, a period when people of color were barred from most Boston restaurants. ◆ American ◆ M-F breakfast and lunch; Sa breakfast, lunch, and dinner. No credit cards accepted. 429 Columbus Ave (between Braddock Pkwy and Holyoke Sts). 536.7669

8 Union United Methodist Church Designed by **A.R. Estey,** the architect of **Emmanuel Church** in Back Bay, this 1877 Gothic Revival creation has the gracious proportions and picturesqueness of a rural parish church. Its demure size makes it all the more friendly and inviting. ◆ 485 Columbus Ave (at W Newton St)

9 Jae's Cafe and Grill ★$ The healthful Korean fare served in this crowded, bustling storefront has attracted the trendies; there's almost always a line. A full array of sushi and sashimi await, along with soups, *satays* (skewered meat or poultry with various sauces), and "rice specials" such as *Yuk Hai Bi Bim Bab* (shredded raw beef marinated in seasoned sesame oil). ◆ Korean ◆ Daily lunch and dinner. Valet parking. 520 Columbus Ave (between Worcester St and Concord Sq). 421.9405

9 Divine Decadence Taking its name from the movie *Cabaret,* this shop offers a delightfully diverse array of American and European home furnishings and accessories dating from 1900 to today, with occasional earlier pieces. The focus is on unusual investment-quality items that epitomize their era—whether a kicky shoe-shaped 1920s chair from a defunct Boston shoe store, a fully functioning 1940s jukebox, or an 1980s desk with neon legs. Some collectibles are commonplace items that have become treasures with time, while others are the work of renowned designers like Charles Eames. It's always fun to come back, since you never know what owner Richard Penachio will chance upon next. The prices range widely, because there are lots of wonderful small items like clocks, tableware, and mirrors. Penachio updates and combines some items into artful new creations. When you leave the store, look up Claremont Parkway for a nice view of the **Christian Science Mother Church**'s dome. ♦ Tu-Sa. 542 Columbus Ave (at Worcester St). 266.1477

10 Harriet Tubman House Named for the "Moses of the South," who was herself a runaway slave and Underground Railroad organizer, this iconoclastic complex greets the street with spirit and purposefulness. It's home to the United South End Settlements, a social service organization responsible for vital community programs. The architect, **Don Stull Associates,** deserves applause for doing a lot with a little budget. Incidentally, the house stands on the site of one of Boston's famous jazz clubs, **The Hi Hat,** which burned down. ♦ Daily. 566 Columbus Ave (at Massachusetts Ave). 536.8610 ♿

COURTESY OF THE BOSTONIAN SOCIETY

11 Piano Craft Guild When new in 1853, the Chickering piano factory (pictured above) was reputedly the second-largest building in the country, dwarfed only by the US Capitol Building. The surprisingly graceful industrial structure is enlivened by a sprightly octagonal tower, and was renovated in 1972 by **Gelardin/Bruner/Cott** with **Anderson, Notter Associates** for artists' studios and living spaces.

Visit the two-story gallery showing works by residents. This was one of the first and largest mill conversions in the state, an early example of the creative lengths local artists have gone to obtain affordable housing. ♦ Call for hours. 791 Tremont St (between Camden and Northampton Sts). Recorded information 437.9365

12 Rutland Square One of the South End's most intimate oases is this shady, slim, elliptical park bracketed by two rows of three-story bowfronts. A number of facades break from the neighborhood pattern of warm redbrick, and instead are prettily painted and detailed in light colors. Only one block long, the square is a lovely sliver of green. ♦ Rutland St (between Tremont St and Columbus Ave)

13 Villa Victoria Built in 1976 by **John Sharratt Associates,** this housing complex is a local success story. A largely Puerto Rican community not only participated in every stage of its development, but also collaborated with the architect so that residents' cultural values and traditions would be expressed with dignity. While the complex is by no means beautiful, given limited funds, it has developed its own strong identity. ♦ Bounded by Tremont St and Shawmut Ave, and W Brookline and W Dedham Sts

14 Buteco II ★$ This easygoing hole-in-the-wall (its name is Portuguese slang for "joint") serves authentic Brazilian dishes like *mandi-oca frita* (fried cassava root with carrot sauce), *moqueca de peixe* (fish in spicy coconut sauce), and—Saturday and Sunday only—the popular *feijoada* (black-bean stew with sausage, dried beef, pork, rice, collard greens, and orange). Some traditional Spanish dishes are offered, too. The lively restaurant attracts an appreciative South American clientele. ♦ Brazilian/Spanish ♦ M-Sa lunch and dinner; Su dinner. Reservations recommended for five or more. 57 W Dedham St (between Tremont St and Shawmut Ave). 247.9249. ♿ Also at: 130 Jersey St (between Queensbury St and Park Dr), Kenmore Square. 247.9508

15 Tremont Ice Cream ★$ Just the kind of place everyone wants in their own neighborhood, this casual and cheap diner serves home-style food made on the premises. Sidle up to the six-stool counter or grab a booth. A great choice for breakfast is pancakes and French toast; the restaurant also serves clam chowder and makes soups fresh daily, plus basic sandwiches and salads. The ice cream comes from a dairy in Middleton, Massachusetts. ♦ American/Takeout ♦ Tu-Su breakfast, lunch, and dinner until 6PM. No credit cards accepted. 584 Tremont St (between Clarendon and Dartmouth Sts). 247.8414

16 Garden of Eden ★★$ All the fixings for a proper tea are prettily presented at this tiny basement shop. And at press time, owners Kelly Brown and Oliver Desnain had plans to add tables so that more than just counter-hangers could eat inside amid the dried flowers and garden statuary. They'll still carry top-notch teas, coffees, and jams, and such stellar baked goods as hearty whole-wheat loaves, rosemary focaccia, fruit tarts, and a full range of authentic French pastries. Only now those superb pastas, soups, and salads that have been going home with hungry Bostonians will be available to eat on-site. Try the garlic-parsley-basil pasta tossed with sundried-tomato–basil sauce and fresh pine nuts, or the *haricots verts* (thin string beans) tossed in a traditional French mustard-vinaigrette dressing. The most popular summer soup is the creamless cream of asparagus soup, thickened with puree of white rice. You won't find any canned ham or iceberg lettuce here. Sandwiches are topped with endive, watercress, romaine, or radicchio, and the meats are imported by truck once a week from New York City. It's the perfect place to grab a meal-on-the-run or to linger and stock a larder. ♦ Continental ♦ M-F breakfast, lunch, and dinner; Sa breakfast and lunch; Su breakfast and lunch September-June, breakfast only June-September. 577 Tremont St (between Dartmouth and Clarendon Sts). 247.8377

ST CLOUD

17 St Cloud ★★★$$$ A perennial favorite among the artistic and fashion crowds, this sophisticated spot looks out unabashedly onto the South End street scene, with picture windows on three sides. The interior draws attention, too, with intriguing murals and subdued lighting. The bar attracts an attractive mix; the dining room, upscale bistro-fanciers. The menu changes seasonally, but is distinguished by well-thought-out combos, such as grilled veal T-bone steak with corn soufflé and red-pepper fondue. Happily, the restaurant stays open later than most in town, and the bar is a lively late-night rendezvous. ♦ American ♦ M-Sa dinner; Su brunch and dinner. Reservations recommended. Valet parking after 5:30PM and for Sunday brunch. 557 Tremont St (at Clarendon St). 353.0202 &

18 Azita Ristorante
★$$$ First, a survival tip: Don't fall for the server's generous offer of "tap water or mineral water." The latter will cost you $2 per minimalist pop, or $7 a liter, and these prices won't be mentioned unless you think to ask. Nonetheless, the *primi piatti* (first courses), including the *farfalle* (butterfly pasta) with smoked salmon, vodka, and cream, are sublime. If the management doesn't quit nickel-and-diming, this pretty spot—with its ice-cream pink walls and whitewashed tin ceiling—could go begging. ♦ Italian ♦ M-Sa lunch and dinner. 560 Tremont St (between Waltham St and Union Park Square). 338.8070

19 Addis Red Sea Ethiopian Restaurant
★★$ Adventurous diners sit around a *mesob* (woven table) and use bits of *injera* (crepelike bread) to snatch up morsels of chicken, lamb, beef, or vegetables. There are two basic

preparations to choose from: *watt* (spicy) dishes are infused with *berbere* (cayenne pepper) sauce; the *alicha* (yellow pepper) variation tends to be a bit milder. Wash your dinner down with Ethiopian beer or wine. ♦ Ethiopian ♦ M-F dinner; Sa-Su lunch and dinner. 544 Tremont St (between Waltham and Hanson Sts). 426.8727

20 Boston Center for the Arts (BCA) Since 1970, the city has subsidized art and cultural events at this three-acre complex. In addition to providing studio space for some 60 artists chosen by their peers (one of the more noteworthy current tenants is playwright David Mamet), there is office and performance space for various theater and dance groups. One of the complex's many converted buildings is the **Cyclorama,** a beautiful, shallow, steel-trussed dome built by **Cummings and Sears** in 1884. Its original raison d'être was to house a novel tourist attraction: a 400-by-50-foot circular mural of the *Battle of Gettysburg* by Paul Philippoteaux, which is today exhibited in Gettysburg. Subsequently, the building served as a skating rink; a track for bicycle races; a gymnasium and workout ring for boxers, where Boston's famous prizefighter John L. Sullivan fought; Alfred Champion's garage, where he invented the spark plug; and a flower market from 1923 to 1968. The **Cyclorama** currently hosts three theaters, the annual art and antiques shows, flea markets, and other large events. The theaters, (the **BCA Theater, The Black Box,** and the **Leland Center**) have been used by more than 30 different performing arts groups from the Greater Boston area to present new, as well as classical, works. The attractive kiosk out front was originally a cupola atop a Roxbury building designed by **Gridley J.F. Bryant**—architect of the **Old City Hall,** the original **Boston City Hospital** building, and other Boston landmarks. ♦ 539 Tremont St (between Berkeley and Clarendon Sts). 426.5000 &

Within the BCA:

Mills Gallery Run by the **BCA**, this nonprofit gallery mounts far-ranging group shows by regional contemporary artists working in various media. Some performance pieces and installations are also shown. ♦ Th-Sa. 549 Tremont St (between Berkeley and Clarendon Sts). 426.8835 & (staff will assist)

Boston Ballet Corps of future (and present) ballerinas leapt for joy when work was completed in 1991 on this splendid and spacious dance center—the largest in New England—designed by **Graham Gund.** The foyer itself is like a stage set, with a grand pair of bifurcating staircases. The largest of the studios duplicates the dimensions of the **Wang Center** stage, so that *The Nutcracker*—the most popular rendition in the world—can be rehearsed right at home. ♦ Tours W, Sa. 19 Clarendon St (at Warren Ave). 695.6950 &

Hamersley's
BISTRO

Hamersley's Bistro ★★★★$$$
Ambitious in cuisine, modest in decor, Gordon and Fiona Hamersley's restaurant is one of the most appealing in Boston. In the exposed kitchen Gordon and his crew don baseball caps and deftly turn out favorites inspired by French country cooking—golden roast chicken, sirloin with mashed potatoes, bouillabaisse, cassoulet—as well as more adventurous flights of fancy like roasted salmon with oysters, bacon, and hollandaise sauce, or a marvelous grilled mushroom-and-garlic sandwich on country bread. Sunday is a day of rest for Gordon, with a slightly more casual and lower-priced evening menu. The cozy dining rooms are filled with an interesting assortment of neighborhood people, suburban visitors, artists, actors, musicians, architects, and the like. ♦ French ♦ Daily dinner. Reservations recommended. Valet parking. 553 Tremont St (at Clarendon St). 423.2700 &

21 Berkeley Residence Club $ Run by the YWCA, this 200-room residence for women combines features of a hotel, dormitory, and old-fashioned rooming house. The clientele is an interesting mix: tourists, students, and working and professional women, some settled in long-term. The rooms are tiny—just the basics—with some doubles available. Each well-kept bathroom is shared by 13 to 16 women. Stay the night or longer, paying by the week. There's a library, sitting room, laundry room, TV room, and pretty outdoor courtyard. The dining room serves two full meals a day (extra charge), with takeout available. Conveniently located, the residence is affordable and secure. Inquire about the rules, which aren't excessive and protect residents. The second floor has a less restrictive policy on gentlemen callers. In addition to weekly rates, there's a nominal fee for temporary membership. ♦ 40 Berkeley St (at Appleton St). 482.8850 &

22 The Terrace Townehouse $$ This 1870 bowfront bed-and-breakfast has only four rooms, but they're pips: spacious and luxuriously appointed, with private baths. You'll be coddled by owner Gloria Belknap, who's up on all the sights and restaurants, and brings fresh-baked breakfast to your room. ♦ 60 Chandler St (between Clarendon and Berkeley Sts). 350.6520

23 Chandler Inn Hotel $ Although a bit drab, this place is clean, safe, and a steal. The 56 rooms boast all the basic amenities, including air-conditioning. This so-called "gay-friendly" hotel is in fact genial to all, especially the budget-conscious traveler. ♦ 26 Chandler St (at Berkeley St). 800/842.3450

24 Icarus ★★$$$ The mood is muted and relaxed; the decor and cuisine, eclectic. A statue of winged *Icarus* beneath a cool ceiling band of neon surveys the two-tiered dining room, where a diverse clientele enjoys chef/co-owner Chris Douglass's seasonal inspirations, such as polenta with wild mushrooms and thyme, lobster in ginger-cream sauce on homemade noodles, grilled tuna with wasabi and sushi, pork loin with mango and jalapeño salsa, caramel-apple tart, and cherry-chocolate-chunk ice cream with icebox cookies. The lengthy wine list is superb. ♦ International ♦ M-Sa dinner; Su brunch; closed Sunday in summer. Reservations recommended Friday-Sunday. Valet parking Wednesday-Sunday. 3 Appleton St (between Berkeley and Tremont Sts). 426.1790

24 Appetito ★★$$ Northern Italian cuisine is Chef Richard Ansara's pride and joy. His spring menu features rigatoni *con pollo* (with grilled chicken and sun-dried cranberries in a spinach-brandy–cream sauce), *filetto di manzo* (beef tenderloin in a mushroom, marsala, plum-tomato sauce), and *gabbiano pizza* (brick-oven pizza with shrimp, fresh garlic, tomato, and mozzarella). The enticing cuisine is matched by a daring color scheme of rich purple (bar and tables), deep red (columns), and rich amber (walls). ♦ Northern Italian ♦ Daily dinner. 1 Appleton St (at Tremont St). 338.6777 &

25 Medieval Manor $$$$ What to say about this inexplicably popular and long-running themed theater/restaurant? Well, simply this: an evening here involves a three-hour, gargantuan, eat-with-your-fingers, fixed-price feast of sorts, and bawdy musical comedy starring singing wenches, oafs, strolling minstrels, and a sexist "Lord of the Manor." More than enough said. The whole thing's participatory, which means you can get into the action if you so choose—joined by many others from the typically vocal audience. Students pack the place. Believe it or not, vegetarians can join the orgy, too, with 48 hours' advance notice. Parties of four to eight are recommended, and no party of more than 10 is accepted if all male, all female, or all Harvard. There are more numbers-related rules; call to inquire. The best—possibly only—way to get here is by car: take the Southeast Expressway south to the Albany Street exit; then turn right onto East Berkeley Street. ♦ Admission. Call for show times. Reservations required. 246 E Berkeley St (at Albany St). 423.4900 &

26 Cedars Restaurant ★$ This is an informal place, where all the food is cooked by owner Elias Aboujaoude, who also lives in the building. And he sure knows how to prepare a meal. Featured are such Mediterranean standards as garlic-chicken on a skewer, hummus, tabbouleh, and kibbe. ♦ Lebanese/

Takeout ◆ Daily dinner. Reservations required for 10 or more. No credit cards accepted. 253 Shawmut Ave (at Milford St). 338.7528 ⓑ

27 Union Park Square The first square to be finished in the South End remains one of its most special places. The elliptical park (designed in the 1850s) enclosed by an iron fence is lush and shady, with fountains and flowers. It's bordered by big brick town houses dating from the neighborhood's brief shining moments before Back Bay became *the* place to lay one's welcome mat. The handsome houses and perfect park commune harmoniously in their own little world. Regrettably, gauche modern hands have tacked on unsightly extra stories here and there, marring an otherwise splendid composition. ◆ Off Union Park St (between Tremont St and Shawmut Ave)

28 On the Park ★★$$ A sunny, friendly spot with windows all around, this cafe is a few strides away from the South End's prettiest greenery—**Union Park Square.** It serves homemade breads and satisfying rustic dishes running the gamut from Southeast Asian to Latin American. Sunday brunch with Bellinis (champagne and peach-nectar drinks) is a neighborhood event. The ever-changing art on the walls comes from local artists and Newbury Street galleries. Regulars and word-of-mouth keep the cafe's 34 seats filled. ◆ International ◆ Daily dinner; Sa-Su breakfast and lunch. Reservations required for groups of six or more. 315 Shawmut Ave (at Union Park St). 426.0862

east meets west

29 East Meets West To Go This is a marvelous bakery for breads, muffins, pastries, and such desserts as the ultrarich chocolate crater cake and chocolate chubby cookies (ignore the name and chomp away). Geared mainly for takeout, the bakery does have a couple of tables and sells some lunch items, coffee, and sodas. Cakes can be made to order, too. ◆ Bakery ◆ Daily. No credit cards accepted. 312 Shawmut Ave (at Union Park St). 482.1015 ⓑ

30 Ars Libri Hidden away on the third floor in a nondescript converted factory now occupied by architects, designers, and dancers is a quiet shop renowned internationally for the country's largest comprehensive inventory of rare and out-of-print books and periodicals about the fine arts (including architecture and photography). Here's where one might be likely to encounter: all of Francisco de Goya's *Los Caprichos;* drawings by Albrecht Dürer; a complete set of *Pan,* the stunning journal of the German *Jugendstil;* an extremely rare edition of *La Prose du Transsibérien,* an extended poem illustrated by Sonia Delaunay; or

any number of other cherishable works. The owners buy and sell out-of-print and rare scholarly works, exhibition catalogs, print portfolios, and books with original graphics dating from the 16th century onward. Chances are you'll be pretty much alone here with plenty of time to savor the treasures, since most business is conducted via subject-oriented catalogs sent to universities, libraries, museums, and individuals. **Machado Silvetti** designed this collector's sanctuary. ◆ M-Sa. No credit cards accepted. 560 Harrison Ave (at Waltham St). 357.5212 ⓑ

31 Cathedral of the Holy Cross An unexpected sight along a sadly run-down stretch of Washington Street is this heroic Gothic Revival elephant, which was completed in 1875 by **Patrick C. Keely.** New England's biggest church, and the largest Catholic church in the country when it was built, the cathedral recalls an era when Irish Roman Catholic immigrants were a dominant presence in the South End. (The needs of this burgeoning population had already resulted in a prior **Keely**-designed church, the imposing white granite **Church of the Immaculate Conception** at Harrison Avenue at East Concord Street, an incredible design worth a look.) The Roxbury pudding stone cathedral seats 3,500 and accommodates 7,000, when you include standing room. It's still the principal church of the Archdiocese of Boston but is now used mainly for special occasions, such as when the Pope came to call in 1979. The front vestibule's arch contains bricks rescued from a Somerville (then called Charlestown) convent burned during anti-Catholic rioting in 1834. As is true of so many Boston ecclesiastical edifices, the intention was to surmount the two towers with spires, but that never happened. ◆ Washington St (at Union Park St)

32 Blackstone and Franklin Squares Divided by Washington Street, both squares were built in the 1860s but originated in an 1801 plan to which **Charles Bulfinch,** then chairman of Boston's Board of Selectmen, was a major contributor. Although they have lost a lot to time, the squares' original grandeur remains palpable. Look for the brownstone houses overlooking the square on West Newton Street. These exemplars of old-world architectural elegance will project you into the neighborhood's genteel past.

At 11 East Newton Street (between St. James and Washington Streets) stands the **Franklin Square House** apartments for the elderly. Built as the **St. James Hotel** in 1868, the lumbering French Second Empire building—equipped with two steam-powered elevators—was considered the South End's poshest hotel. At the height of the hotel's brief eminence, President Ulysses S. Grant stayed there. ◆ Washington St (Blackstone Sq at W Newton St; Franklin Sq at E Newton St)

Charles River Basin

Paths, playgrounds, lagoons, and lawns lace the Charles River Basin and its esplanade. Together, they form a lovely urban water park and the most spectacular section of the **Charles River Reservation.** Of all Boston's landmarks, this waterway is the most visually striking, with the Boston skyline on one side and **Cambridge** on the opposite. In this majestic, romantic setting, Bostonians congregate for promenades, outdoor concerts, picnics, jogging, bicycling, games, sailing, sculling, canoeing, and feeding the hungry ducks made famous in Robert McCloskey's 1941 children's book *Make Way for Ducklings.* In fall and winter the riverside is still and quiet, and the Cambridge shoreline seems far away. But in spring and summer the two-mile-long esplanade brims with activity from **Beacon Hill** to **Boston University,** and the river sparkles with white sails. As the days heat up, free evening concerts and dance performances draw enormous crowds; the pièce de résistance is the traditional Fourth of July **Boston Pops** concert, which attracts hundreds of thousands.

The lazy brown-green Charles casually zigs and zags, coiling left and right, even appearing at times to change its mind and turn back, before traversing an 80-mile course from Hopkinton to **Boston Harbor**—a distance of less than 30 miles as the crow flies. In general, the sluggish Charles is not an impressive river, shrinking to a mere stream in some places. But the Charles River Basin is the splendid lakelike section nine miles long that progresses from **Watertown,** past **Harvard University** and the **Massachusetts Institute of Technology (MIT),** and on to the Atlantic Ocean. Here the Charles has been sculpted into a splendid urban waterway.

The river got its name 15 years before the Puritans arrived, when explorer Captain John Smith sent early maps of New England home to 15-year-old Charles Stuart, the future King Charles I, and asked him to give its prominent features good English names. The river has always been a vital economic asset. Throughout the 18th and 19th centuries, industries fueled by the Charles included gristmills, sawmills, spinning and weaving companies, and manufacturers of paper products, leather, and chocolate. But intense industrialization polluted the river, and its estuary shrank from incessant landfilling. At low tide, the Charles was a malodorous eyesore bordering wealthy Back Bay, which is why that district appears to turn its back to the river.

In the early 1900s a long crusade to make the lower Charles healthy and attractive gained momentum. Prominent Boston and Cambridge residents, including landscape architect Charles Eliot (a colleague of Frederick Law Olmsted and founder of the Trustees of Reservations, a nonprofit conservation group) and philanthropists James J. Storrow and Henry Lee Higginson (founder of the **Boston Symphony Orchestra**) led the drive to build the **Charles River Dam** in 1908. This created the freshwater basin, with an embankment extending from **Charlesgate West** (where the **Back Bay Fens** meets the river) to the old **West End.** In the early 1930s Arthur A. Shurcliff, landscape architect of colonial Williamsburg, greatly embellished the embankment, designing the picturesque esplanade and its lagoons with funding provided by Storrow's widow, Helen Osborn Storrow. In 1951 Boston's **Museum of Science** took up residence astride the Charles River Dam on the Boston-Cambridge boundary. In the early 1950s, **Storrow Drive,** the frenetic autoway, was built on the original embankment and, ironically, named for James Storrow, the avid supporter of the park it shouldered aside; Storrow Drive's counterpart, on the Cambridge side of the river, is **Memorial Drive.**

On the Boston side of the river, the subway stop handiest to the esplanade is the **Charles** stop (*Red Line*). But within easy walking distance (only five or six blocks) are the **Arlington, Copley,** and **Hynes Convention Center/ICA** stops (all *Green Line*); and the **Back Bay/South End** stop (*Orange Line*). On the Cambridge side, the **Harvard Square, Kendall Square** (both *Red Line*), and **Science Park** (*Green Line*) stops are nearest the river.

THE PUBLICK THEATRE INC.

1 The Publick Theatre Inc. Boston's oldest resident professional theater company has been staging performances under the stars for more than 20 years, in cooperation with the Metropolitan District Commission (MDC). The company has put on classical plays and musicals—including Shakespeare, Gilbert & Sullivan, and *Man of La Mancha*—and new shows, too. The company's season runs from late May to early September, with subscriptions available and special discounts for families. Purchase tickets at the on-site outdoor box office after 7PM on performance nights, or charge by phone; tickets are also available at **Bostix** and **Out of Town Ticket Agency.** The theater seats 200, and there is free parking and picnic facilities. ♦ Shows W-Su 8PM, weather permitting. Christian A. Herter Park (between Soldiers Field Rd and the Charles River, across from the WBZ station), Brighton. 782.5425 &

2 Guest Quarters Suite Hotel Boston/Cambridge $$$ The site is inauspicious, right by the Cambridge/Allston exit on the Massachusetts Turnpike, but the 310 accommodations on 16 floors are all two-room suites, most with good views—request one facing the river. Each suite has two TVs, a wet bar and fridge, a fold-out sofa bed in the living room, and a king-size bed in the bedroom. Some bi-level suites are available on upper floors. Complimentary van service is provided to downtown Boston and Cambridge; there's an indoor pool, sauna, whirlpool, and exercise room, and reasonably priced on-premises parking. Suites for people with disabilities and for nonsmokers are also available. Ask about the hotel's special weekend rates (subject to availability). ♦ 400 Soldiers Field Rd (at the River St Bridge), Brighton. 783.0090, 800/424.2900; fax 783.0897 &

Within the Guest Quarters Suite Hotel Boston/Cambridge:

Scullers Jazz Club/Scullers Grille ★$$
If you're seeking jazz and light fare, such as pâté and smoked salmon, then this comfortable listening room will fit the bill. Local and national jazz and cabaret acts are booked here, with an emphasis on vocalists, and the crowd generally ranges in age from 28 to 45. For a more sumptuous feast sans music, try the restaurant for great bouillabaisse and other seafood specialties, and a marvelous river view. ♦ Jazz Club/Seafood ♦ Cover. Club: Tu-Sa; shows: Th-Sa; grille: M-Sa breakfast, lunch, and dinner; Su breakfast and dinner. Reservations recommended Thursday-Saturday. Jacket required; no jeans allowed. Only those 21 and older are admitted. On-premises parking for a fee. Second floor. 783.0811 &

Building Blocks: How Charles Bulfinch Shaped the City

For his enduring stamp on Boston buildings and topography, **Charles Bulfinch** (1763-1844) deserved to have many more places in the city named after him; after all, painter John Singleton Copley's name appears all over, and that Anglophile left America for good on the eve of the Revolution. No matter; this architectural genie didn't hanker after fame and fortune.

The first Bostonian to take up architecture as a profession, he was a creative dynamo who began life in a notable Boston family, then skirted poverty throughout his adulthood because he was a poor businessman and gave too much free architectural advice. A patriot through-and-through, **Bulfinch** nonetheless emulated English architecture, infusing his concern for harmony, hierarchy, public order, and propriety—he was Boston's police chief, after all, and head selectman for many years. **Bulfinch** didn't stop at buildings, either; he had grand visions for entire city segments. A pioneer urban designer, he was one of the Mount Vernon Proprietors engineering the shaping of **Beacon Hill.** With entire streets and scores of houses, public buildings, banks, churches, hospitals, offices, and schools to his credit, it was **Bulfinch** who turned an 18th-century town into a 19th-century city. A happier chapter of **Bulfinch**'s life was spent in Washington, DC, where he felt much more appreciated—well-paid at last—and contributed to the design of the US Capitol.

Restaurants/Clubs: Red		**Hotels:** Blue
Shops/ 🌳 Outdoors: Green		**Sights/Culture:** Black

The **Northwestern University Boathouse,** a deep-orange shingled structure, pays architectural homage to the river's older boathouses, especially Harvard's two from the turn of the century. Designed by **Graham Gund Associates,** the building has playful touches, such as oar-shaped balusters.

On Sunday during daylight-saving time, **Memorial Drive** on the **Cambridge** side of the river is closed to traffic from **Western Avenue Bridge** to **Eliot Bridge,** creating what is called **Riverbend Park.**

On the **Cambridge** side of the river near **Harvard University,** it's only a few minutes stroll up JFK Street to **Harvard Square**'s restaurants and shops.

Harvard's picturesque **Weld Boathouse,** designed by **Peabody and Stearns,** was built in 1909.

John W. Weeks Bridge is a graceful footbridge and the best place to watch the Head-of-the-Charles regatta in October.

Harvard University's first permanent boathouse, **Newell Boathouse,** with red-slate walls and delicate finials, dates from 1900 and was designed by **Peabody and Stearns.** The boathouse is dedicated to varsity teams, who often train for the US Olympic team or England's famed Henley Royal Regatta. Harvard's famous passion for rowing began with the founding of the country's first boat club in the 1840s. The oldest intercollegiate crew meet in the country is the annual Harvard-Yale competition, first held in 1854.

In 1911 a special act of Congress closed the Charles River to navigation so the **Anderson bridge** could be built without a drawbridge. "To a father by a son," a tablet reads; Lairz Anderson, US ambassador to Belgium, gave the bridge in memory of his father, Nicholas Longworth Anderson, also a Harvard graduate. Oddly, locals usually refer to the bridge by the son's name, not the father's

Above **Watertown,** about eight mils upstream from the Harvard Bridge, the river is rated Class B (okay for swimming and fishing). But below Watertown, the basin is NOT swimmable.

Radcliffe College

Fogg Art Museum

Memorial Dr.

JFK St.

Harvard University

1

Eliot Bridge

■ Soldiers Field

Anderson Bridge

Weeks Bridge

Harvard Stadium ■

Harvard University

Western Ave.

Hoyt Field

Western Ave. Bridge

Soldiers Field Rd.

River St.

River St. Bridge

2

Cambridge St.

3

■ Bath House

Magazine Beach

Boston Univ. Bridge

BOSTON

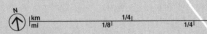

N

km
mi   1/4   1/2
     1/8   1/4

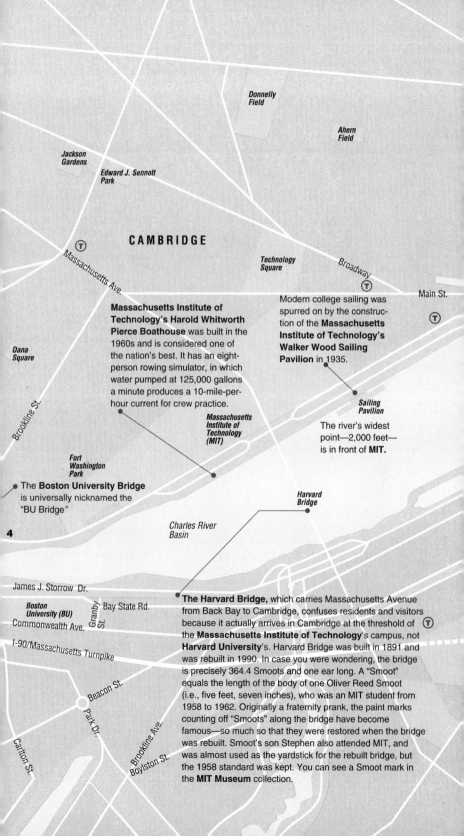

Donnelly Field

Ahern Field

Jackson Gardens

Edward J. Sennott Park

CAMBRIDGE

Technology Square

Broadway

Main St.

Massachusetts Institute of Technology's Harold Whitworth Pierce Boathouse was built in the 1960s and is considered one of the nation's best. It has an eight-person rowing simulator, in which water pumped at 125,000 gallons a minute produces a 10-mile-per-hour current for crew practice.

Modern college sailing was spurred on by the construction of the **Massachusetts Institute of Technology's Walker Wood Sailing Pavilion** in 1935.

Dana Square

Brookline St.

Massachusetts Ave.

Massachusetts Institute of Technology (MIT)

Sailing Pavilion

The river's widest point—2,000 feet—is in front of **MIT**.

Fort Washington Park

The **Boston University Bridge** is universally nicknamed the "BU Bridge"

4

Harvard Bridge

Charles River Basin

James J. Storrow Dr.

Boston University (BU)

Granby St.

Bay State Rd.

Commonwealth Ave.

I-90/Massachusetts Turnpike

Beacon St.

Park Dr.

Carlton St.

Brookline Ave.

Boylston St.

The Harvard Bridge, which carries Massachusetts Avenue from Back Bay to Cambridge, confuses residents and visitors because it actually arrives in Cambridge at the threshold of the **Massachusetts Institute of Technology**'s campus, not **Harvard University**'s. Harvard Bridge was built in 1891 and was rebuilt in 1990. In case you were wondering, the bridge is precisely 364.4 Smoots and one ear long. A "Smoot" equals the length of the body of one Oliver Reed Smoot (i.e., five feet, seven inches), who was an MIT student from 1958 to 1962. Originally a fraternity prank, the paint marks counting off "Smoots" along the bridge have become famous—so much so that they were restored when the bridge was rebuilt. Smoot's son Stephen also attended MIT, and was almost used as the yardstick for the rebuilt bridge, but the 1958 standard was kept. You can see a Smoot mark in the **MIT Museum** collection.

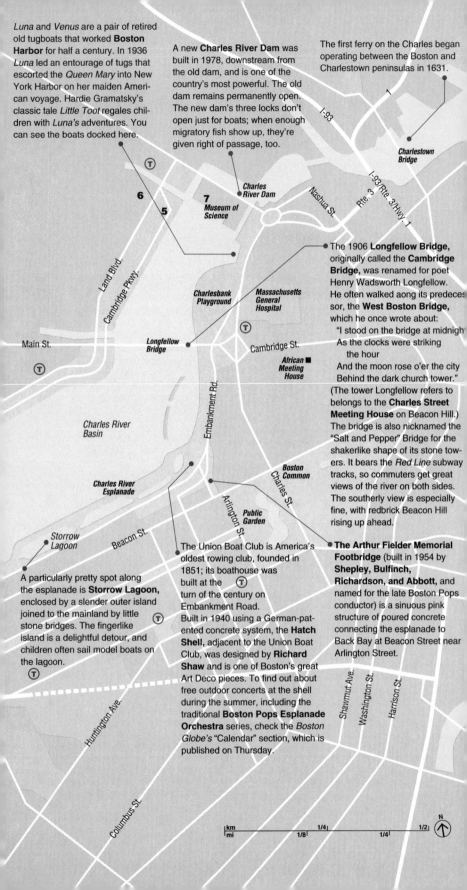

Luna and *Venus* are a pair of retired old tugboats that worked **Boston Harbor** for half a century. In 1936 *Luna* led an entourage of tugs that escorted the *Queen Mary* into New York Harbor on her maiden American voyage. Hardie Gramatsky's classic tale *Little Toot* regales children with *Luna's* adventures. You can see the boats docked here.

A new **Charles River Dam** was built in 1978, downstream from the old dam, and is one of the country's most powerful. The old dam remains permanently open. The new dam's three locks don't open just for boats; when enough migratory fish show up, they're given right of passage, too.

The first ferry on the Charles began operating between the Boston and Charlestown peninsulas in 1631.

Charlestown Bridge

I-93

Nashua St.

Rte. 3

I-93/Rte. 3/Hwy. 1

Charles River Dam

7
Museum of Science

6

5

Land Blvd.

Cambridge Pkwy.

Charlesbank Playground

Massachusetts General Hospital

The 1906 **Longfellow Bridge**, originally called the **Cambridge Bridge**, was renamed for poet Henry Wadsworth Longfellow. He often walked aong its predecessor, the **West Boston Bridge**, which he once wrote about:
"I stood on the bridge at midnight
As the clocks were striking the hour
And the moon rose o'er the city
Behind the dark church tower."
(The tower Longfellow refers to belongs to the **Charles Street Meeting House** on Beacon Hill.) The bridge is also nicknamed the "Salt and Pepper" Bridge for the shakerlike shape of its stone towers. It bears the *Red Line* subway tracks, so commuters get great views of the river on both sides. The southerly view is especially fine, with redbrick Beacon Hill rising up ahead.

Main St.

Longfellow Bridge

Cambridge St.

African Meeting House

Embankment Rd.

Charles River Basin

Charles River Esplanade

Boston Common

Charles St.

Arlington St.

Public Garden

Storrow Lagoon

Beacon St.

A particularly pretty spot along the esplanade is **Storrow Lagoon**, enclosed by a slender outer island joined to the mainland by little stone bridges. The fingerlike island is a delightful detour, and children often sail model boats on the lagoon.

The Union Boat Club is America's oldest rowing club, founded in 1851; its boathouse was built at the turn of the century on Embankment Road. Built in 1940 using a German-patented concrete system, the **Hatch Shell**, adjacent to the Union Boat Club, was designed by **Richard Shaw** and is one of Boston's great Art Deco pieces. To find out about free outdoor concerts at the shell during the summer, including the traditional **Boston Pops Esplanade Orchestra** series, check the *Boston Globe's* "Calendar" section, which is published on Thursday.

The Arthur Fielder Memorial Footbridge (built in 1954 by **Shepley, Bulfinch, Richardson, and Abbott,** and named for the late Boston Pops conductor) is a sinuous pink structure of poured concrete connecting the esplanade to Back Bay at Beacon Street near Arlington Street.

Shawmut Ave.

Washington St.

Harrison St.

Huntington Ave.

Columbus St.

km
mi

1/8   1/4

1/4   1/2

N

Charting the Charles

The **Charles River** has been steadily rebounding from severe abuse and pollution since the late 1970s. The Massachusetts Audubon Society's **Broadmoor Wildlife Sanctuary** is a 600-acre tract along the Charles in **Natick** and **Sherborn,** and this is where you can see the river environment in its most protected natural state (280 Eliot St, off Rte 16, South Natick, 508/655.2296.)

Many people run, skate, and bicycle along the banks of the Charles, or canoe to the wildlife sanctuary, where many say the waterway is its prettiest. The river's wetlands are home to wood ducks and mallards, great blue herons, great horned owls, wood warblers, ospreys, red-tailed hawks, white-tailed deer, red foxes, river otters, muskrats, minks, snapping turtles, and 30 or so fish species, including carp, northern pike, and large-mouth bass.

Sailing vessels bearing passengers and freight once plied the river, and later tugboats, tankers, and barges, but today recreational craft rule: canoes, rowboats, sailboats, and powerboats. The river is dotted with numerous boathouses and yacht clubs, many dating from the turn of the century, that offer rentals and classes and sponsor competitions.

Sailing Community Boating (21 Embankment Rd, 523.1038; TTY 523.7406 ♿) is a nonprofit organization that offers sailing tours and instruction for everyone at the lowest possible prices. Located behind the **Hatch Memorial Shell** (at the Charles Street footbridge), its fleet includes more than 150 sailboats, plus Windsurfers. America's oldest and largest public sailing program, it offers monthlong and summer memberships, two- and seven-day visitor packages, and discounted programs for senior citizens and youths. All kinds of special events and trips are scheduled regularly.

Canoeing and Rowing More than 60 of the Charles River's 80 miles can be explored by canoe, although a few portages are required. The **Charles River Watershed Association** (527.2799), a private, nonprofit conservation group founded in 1965, publishes a *Charles River Canoe Guide;* on the last Sunday in April, it sponsors popular races called Run of the Charles, with contestants furiously paddling and portaging canoes around dams.

You can rent canoes, kayaks, and rowing shells at the **Charles River Canoe and Kayak Center** at the Metropolitan District Commission (MDC) building (2401 Commonwealth Ave, Newton, 965.5110). The center offers canoeing, kayaking, and rowing classes for all levels. Better still, begin your journey farther up the river and rent your canoe at **Tropicland Marine and Tackle** (100 Bridge St, Dedham, 329.3777).

Rowing and the Charles have a long, romantic liaison. A single figure sculling gracefully over the river's surface is a common early morning sight. So, too, are "eights," crew boats with exhorting coxswains, which skim past and then disappear beneath the next bridge. The annual Head-of-the-Charles regatta (call 864.8415 for more information)—held on the next to the last Sunday in October—is the world's largest single-day regatta, the oldest head-style racing event

in the US, and an amazing spectacle. More than 4,000 male and female athletes from all over the world in almost 1,000 boats represent 200-plus colleges, clubs, high schools, and other organizations, or just themselves. The course extends upstream from the **Boston University Bridge** to a half-mile above **Eliot Bridge.** This is not a head-to-head competition; it's computer-timed, with boats departing at 10- to 12-second intervals.

For group or private rowing instruction, investigate **Community Rowing** at **MDC Daly Ice Rink** (Nonantum Rd, Newton, 455.1992). Open to the public from April through October, with very reasonable fees charged on a monthly basis, **Community Rowing** also organizes adaptive rowers' groups for people with disabilities.

Running, Roller Skating, In-Line Skating, and Skateboarding The favorite places to run and bicycle in Boston are the paths on both sides of the Charles. Roller and in-line skating, and skateboarding are popular here, too; skates and boards can be rented from **Beacon Hill Skate Shop** (135 Charles St S, Theater District, 482.7400). For more information on bicycling, see "Boston by Bike: Plum Paths for Pedal Pushers" on page 170.

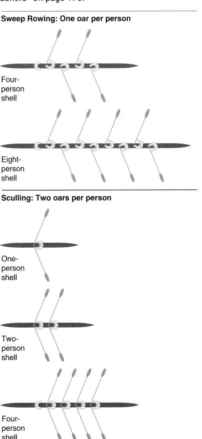

Sweep Rowing: One oar per person

Four-person shell

Eight-person shell

Sculling: Two oars per person

One-person shell

Two-person shell

Four-person shell

3 Howard Johnson Cambridge $$ Most of the rooms (202 in all) in this modern high-rise have lovely views—ask to overlook the river, although the Cambridge skyline is nice, too. It has an indoor pool, free parking, the **Bisuteki Japanese Steakhouse** and two other restaurants, and it's about a 15-minute walk along the Charles (best by day) to Harvard Square. Rooms for nonsmokers are available, and pets are welcome. ♦ 777 Memorial Dr (between the River St and B.U. Bridges), Cambridge. 492.7777, 800/654.2000 ⴲ

4 Hyatt Regency Cambridge $$$ A glitzy, glassy ziggurat-shaped structure nicknamed the "Pyramid on the Charles," the hotel has 469 rooms, some with outdoor terraces overlooking the river and Boston. The atrium rises 14 stories, with balconies, trees, fountains, even glass-cage elevators. The skylit health spa has an indoor pool, sauna, whirlpool, exercise room, and sundeck, plus a retractable ceiling and walls. There's also an outdoor basketball court. The hotel has adult's and children's bicycles for rent, so you can take a leisurely riverside journey. Accommodations for people with disabilities and for nonsmokers are available. The hotel is popular with families—there's a special rate for a second room when traveling with children—and locals seeking a little weekend luxury, as well as the ubiquitous business and convention crowds. Choose between valet or self-parking, and a free van shuttles guests to Harvard Square, Kendall Square, **Faneuil Hall,** the **Boston Common,** and **Copley Place.** ♦ 575 Memorial Dr (between the Harvard and B.U. Bridges), Cambridge. 492.1234, 800/233.1234; fax 491.6906 ⴲ

Within the Hyatt Regency Cambridge:

Spinnaker Italia ★$$ Boston's one and only revolving rooftop lounge and restaurant lets you gaze upon the city's twinkling night skyline, stretching from the Financial District and Beacon Hill to Back Bay and the **Prudential Center.** Although the cuisine is not as spectacular as the views, the Northern Italian fare includes tasty pastas, gourmet pizzas, and *petti di pollo* (roasted chicken breasts sautéed with artichoke). ♦ Italian ♦ M-Sa dinner; Su brunch and dinner. Reservations recommended. No jeans, sneakers, or T-shirts allowed. Free two-hour parking. 492.1234 ⴲ

5 Royal Sonesta Hotel Boston/Cambridge $$$ Ask for a room facing the river and look across at the gold dome of the **State House** gleaming above Beacon Hill. The hotel has 400 rooms furnished in contemporary style on 10 floors, including rooms for nonsmokers and for people with disabilities. Vouchers for a free

narrated river tour are available from early June to mid-September. The hotel also provides guests with free ice cream, bicycles, and cameras during the summer. Hotel recreational facilities include an indoor pool under a retractable roof. A courtesy van provides transportation to Harvard and Kendall Squares and Boston. The hotel displays an excellent modern art collection with pieces by Frank Stella, Andy Warhol, and Robert Rauschenberg. ♦ 5 Cambridge Pkwy (near the Charles River Dam), Cambridge. 491.3600, 800/766.3782; fax 661.5956

6 The Sports Museum of New England Housed inside the **Cambridgeside Galleria** mall, this popular spot encapsulates "great moments in New England sports history." Holdings include more than a thousand hours of film and video highlights, star memorabilia, and "action-packed displays." ♦ Admission. Daily. 100 Cambridgeside Pl, East Cambridge. 787.7678 ⴲ

7 Museum of Science One of Boston's most familiar sights is this museum's funky 1950s silhouette above the Charles. Streams of families and fleets of school and tour buses arrive all day long. If you're with kids, you can be sure they'll have a great time. If not, you might wish the crowds would thin and the decibels lower, but you'll still squeeze past many interesting exhibits (see the plan on page 169). In the beginning, the museum was the **Boston Society of Natural History,** founded in 1830, then the **New England Museum of Natural History,** residing in an imposing French Academic edifice in Back Bay. In 1951 the museum moved to modern quarters on this site straddling the Charles River Dam and changed its name to reflect the forward-looking attitude that has made it so innovative. The **Exhibit Hall**'s 400-plus exhibits date from 1830 to this minute, covering astronomy, astrophysics, natural history, and much more. All-time favorites are the *Plexiglas Transparent Woman* with light-up organs, the chicken hatchery with its active eggs, the world's largest Van de Graaff generator spitting 15-foot lightning bolts, a space-capsule replica, and the 20-foot-high model of tyrannosaurus rex. Walk on the moon or fly over Boston at the **Special Effects Stage,** or see how an ocean wave is made.

The museum has three cafeteria-style restaurants, but the one to try is the **Skyline Room Cafeteria** (★$) for its captivating views—perhaps the city's best—of Boston on one side of the Charles, Cambridge on the other, and boats passing through the dam below and cruising upriver. Explore the unparalleled **Museum Shop,** which has a fantastic inventory of science-related projects, gadgets, toys, jewelry, books, and T-shirts. Under former director Bradford Washburn, a world-renowned explorer, mountaineer, and mapmaker, the pioneering museum embraced modern science and exacting high demands of today's sophisticated visitors. It became a flexible participatory place, providing exceptional educational programs to families, schools, and communities. Special events include the *Inventor's Weekend Exhibition,* when students' inventions—such as an automatic baseball-card stacker—are exhibited along with adults' creations.
♦ Admission; discounts for senior citizens and children four to 14; children under four free 1-5PM Nov-Apr; separate admissions charged for **Charles Hayden Planetarium** and **Mugar Omni Theater,** with combination discount

tickets available. Daily; F until 9PM; free Wednesday 1-5PM. Paid parking available. Science Park (at the Charles River Dam, between Land Blvd and Embankment Rd). 723.2500, TDD 227.3235 &

Within the Museum of Science:

Charles Hayden Planetarium A $2-million Zeiss planetarium projector and state-of-the-art multi-image system create enthralling programs on what's happening in the heavens: everything from the seasonal skies over Boston to phenomena like black holes and supernova. There are also special laser shows. ♦ Admission; discounts for senior citizens and children four to 14. Call for show times. Not recommended for children under four. 723.2500 &

Mugar Omni Theater In Massachusetts's only OMNIMAX theater, a tilted dome 76 feet in diameter and four stories high wraps around you, and state-of-the-art film technology makes you feel surrounded by the images on the screen. The regularly changing films project you into locales like the tropical rain forest, Antarctica, inside the human body, outer space, or on a roller-coasterlike tour of Boston. ♦ Admission; discounts for senior citizens and children four to 14. Daily; call for show times. Reservations recommended. Not recommended for children under four. 723.2500 &

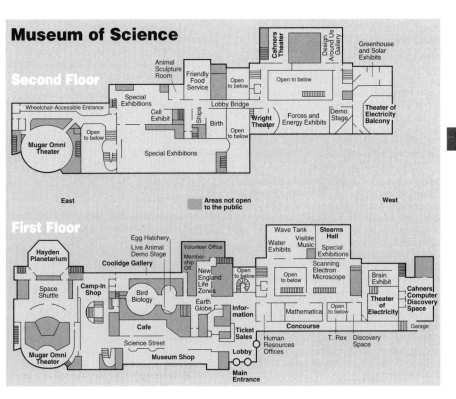

Museum of Science

Boston By Bike: Plum Paths for Pedal Pushers

Thanks to the many reckless drivers who dominate the city's streets, bicycling in Boston is more akin to navigating the Indianapolis 500 than it is a pleasurable pastime. But hope lingers on the horizon.

Over the past two decades, lobbying groups have made great strides toward making the city more welcoming to two-wheelers—primarily by promoting bike paths. The centerpiece is the **Dr. Paul Dudley White Charles River Bike Path,** a 14-mile loop that's increasingly bucolic the farther out you get. This trail hugs both banks of the **Charles** from the **Museum of Science** all the way to **Watertown Square.** Shorter in-town stretches include the **Southwest Corridor Linear Park Bike Path** (four miles in reclaimed **South End** parkland), the wooded **Riverway Bike Path** (from Boston's **Park Drive** to Brookline's **Brookline Avenue**), and the scenic **Jamaicaway Bike Bath** (landscape architect Frederick Law Olmsted's former bridle path along the **Muddy River**).

The latest thoroughfare is the **Minuteman Bike Path**—an 11-mile swath linking the **Alewife Station** in **Cambridge** (the outermost subway stop on the *Red Line*) to the towns of **Arlington, Lexington,** and **Bedford.** Congressman Joseph Kennedy, himself an avid biker, managed to eke out $1.2 million in federal funds to connect the Minuteman with the Dudley. He's also promoting a bill, which has been turned down and refiled twice, to dedicate three percent of federal highway funds to the development of bike and pedestrian routes.

Meanwhile, Boston's serious bikers—and they are legion—have grown adept at improvising patchwork itineraries. In many neighborhoods, such as student-packed **Cambridge,** no one will look askance if you cravenly stick to the sidewalk, as long as you're considerate. All subway lines except the *Green Line* (which is usually about as roomy as a sardine can) will accommodate bikes during nonpeak hours; call the **Massachusetts Bay Transportation Authority** (722.3200, 800/392.6100) for details.

To find out about other trails, including some to **Provincetown** on **Cape Cod,** contact the **Department of Environmental Management** (Division of Forests and Parks, Salstonstall Building, 100 Cambridge St, Boston, MA 02202, 727.3180). You can rent wheels at the **Community Bike Shop** (496 Tremont St, between Arlington and Berkeley Sts, South End, 542.8623) or **Back Bay Bicycles** (333 Newbury St, between Hereford and Massachusetts Aves, 247.2336). For general tips on bike trails, rules of the road, and rentals or repairs, call the **Boston Area Bicycle Coalition** (491.7433). Both the **American Youth Hostels** (1020 Commonwealth Ave, at Babcock St, 731.6692, Activities Hotline 730.8294) and the **Appalachian Mountain Club** (5 Joy St, between Mt. Vernon and Beacon Sts, 523.0636) organize cycling trips, too.

Bests

Robert Campbell
Architect and Architectural Critic

Lots of cities surpass Boston's food, architecture, and shopping, but none can top its streets and neighborhoods. Don't miss walking down **Beacon Hill,** along **Mount Vernon Street** to **Louisburg Square,** perhaps on Christmas Eve when the candles are in the windows and the carolers move from house to house.

Also walk through the **Public Garden,** on **Commonwealth Avenue,** along the **Charles River Esplanade,** or past the little shops of **Charles Street.**

Other streets where the city's karma seems to collect: **Union Park Square** in the **South End,** with sunlight falling through the trees on the bowfronts; **Marlborough Street,** the best proportioned and preserved of the streets of the **Back Bay**—easily the most successful "planned" residential neighborhood in American history; **Paul Revere Mall** behind **Old North Church** in the **North End,** Boston's only European-style "outdoor room"; **Harvard Yard** in November, the essence of austere Puritan New England—and so poignantly contrasted with **Harvard Square** next door, an explosion of punks and consumers; and **Newbury Street** in the **Back Bay,** a humanly scaled shopping street, with its stores tucked into three levels of what once were houses.

Art: The Fitz Hugh Lane seascapes at the **Cape Ann Historical Society** in **Gloucester**—America's greatest painter?—and his *View of Penobscot Bay,* which is in the **Museum of Fine Arts;** the *Robert Gould Shaw Memorial* by Saint-Gaudens in **Boston Common;** the Richard Haas mural on the **Boston Architectural Center;** and **Mount Auburn Cemetery** in **Watertown** in May, when the landscape is in bloom.

Food: The special pizza at **Bertucci's;** the brownies at **Rosie's Bakery & Dessert Shop** in Inman Square; **Locke-Ober,** an Edwardian survival; the tables outdoors at the **Harvest Restaurant** in Harvard Square; and a frank on a summer evening at **Fenway Park,** one of the last of the intimate ballparks and the home of a team that we know in our Puritan hearts will never win a world championship because of our guilt.

Buildings: **McKim, Mead & White**'s **Boston Public Library,** especially the old grand stair; the **Isabella Stewart Gardner Museum** (especially when there's a Sunday concert); the **Peabody Museum** in Salem, particularly the *South Seas* and *China Trade* exhibitions; the **Harvard Lampoon Castle** on Mount Auburn Street in Cambridge, a rare example of a funny building; and **Rowes Wharf,** approached from across the harbor on the **Airport Water Shuttle.**

Lovely New England villages such as **Stockbridge, Edgartown, Nantucket,** and so many more; the colony of miniature, brightly painted cottages—originally a religious encampment—at **Oak Bluffs** on **Martha's Vineyard;** and a tour of the mills of **Lowell.**

Jim Koch
Brewer and Founder, Samuel Adams Boston Lager,
Boston Beer Company

Le Meridien's chocolate buffet on Saturday afternoons—all the chocolate dessert you can eat.

Doyle's bar, on Washington Street in Jamaica Plain, offers a full range of beers from the Boston Beer Company, including experimental beers not available anywhere else, on draft.

Harvard Square on a Saturday night—watching the jugglers and listening to the musicians. Tracy Chapman started here.

Bike rides along the Charles River in summer and fall, from Watertown to the Science Museum along the Boston side then past Harvard and MIT on the Cambridge side.

Browsing for antique prints and books at Goodspeed's Book Shop on Beacon Hill.

Senate President Bulger's Saint Patrick's Day Breakfast and politician roast in South Boston (it's broadcast on cable). No one escapes unscathed, and Bulger has a wonderful singing voice.

Fresh oysters at Union Oyster House; prime rib and cornbread at Durgin-Park; and a three-pound lobster at Legal Sea Foods.

A walk in World's End, a beautiful park in Hingham—rolling meadows and a great view of Boston.

Saturday morning shopping at Haymarket, where bronze sculptures of garbage are cast into the sidewalk and street.

A Saturday afternoon tour of the Boston Beer Company Brewery.

Arthur Dion
Director/Art Dealer, Gallery Naga

After luxuriating in the city's great art galleries (the Institute of Contemporary Art, the Museum of Fine Arts, the Isabella Stewart Gardner, and the List), walk around Newbury Street and environs.

The King & I has the best Thai cuisine in town—classic pad thai, beautiful chicken basil.

Davio's, for haute Italian, irresistible homemade sausages, and supernal soups and sauces.

The amazing flower beds in the Public Garden.

The lights in the trees of the Public Garden and the Boston Common on a winter night.

Storrow Drive or Memorial Drive day or night, from the Museum of Science through Cambridge, it's almost worth renting a car.

Ice skating on the Swan Boat pond in the Public Garden (I've never done it, but it looks great).

The Charles River Esplanade is just gorgeous, especially if it's the first Sunday in June and you've just finished the 10K From All Walks of Life, which raised millions of dollars for AIDS care and research.

For the energetic, the adventurous, and the bold:

Fort Hill in Roxbury and Larz Anderson Park in Brookline, for great spaces and views.

The Museum of the National Center of Afro-American Artists—a gem.

The Cyclorama at the Boston Center for the Arts is a huge, odd, wonderful exhibition space.

Spring and fall weekends the largest clusters of Boston's many thousands of artists' studios are open to all. (Check the paper or call a gallery for details.) Fort Point, the South End, and Vernon Street, to name only the biggest, are all primers to the city's art world.

Cynthia Hadzi
Exhibitions Coordinator, Harvard University's Carpenter Center for Visual Arts
Dimitri Hazdi
Sculptor/Professor Emeritus, Harvard University

Everything at the Museum of Fine Arts, especially the special Japanese wing and garden; weekend afternoon concerts at the Isabella Stewart Gardner Museum; the Institute of Contemporary Art (ICA), which has a lively exhibit program; the Fogg, Sackler, and Busch Museums at Harvard—fabulous collections; the Carpenter Center for Visual Arts (the only Corbusier building in the United States) for contemporary exhibits; and the incomparable film program of the Harvard Film Archive.

The art galleries along Newbury Street, as well as the bookshops, stores, and cafes.

The American Repertory Theatre at Harvard and the revitalized Hasty Pudding Theatre.

Free summertime concerts in Harvard's splendid Sanders Theatre.

The Boston Athenaeum, an utterly Bostonian private library, which occasionally offers exhibits that are open to the public.

The Charles River—winding through the city, its activity makes everything seem more human.

The fountain and landscaping at Post Office Square (the fountain is by Howard Ben Tre), an oasis in the middle of the city.

Boston Public Garden (and not just for Swan Boats or ducklings!).

Trinity Church and the other wonderful Henry H. Richardson buildings scattered around, plus the reflection of Trinity Church in the Hancock Building (from here, check the views over the city, too).

The renovated houses around the South End and in Charlestown.

Magnolias in spring along Marlborough Street.

Tapas at Dali; hamburgers at the Harvest Restaurant; fish at the Dolphin; a cup of espresso in the North End; anything at Hamersley's Bistro.

Walks around Walden Pond in Concord; the Ralph Waldo Emerson and Louisa May Alcott Houses.

And best of all: the feeling of being able to escape to the ocean or mountains when necessary, all in under two hours.

Cambridge

Across the **Charles River** is Boston's intellectual, self-assured neighbor, Cambridge. Both Boston and Cambridge are crowded with college campuses, but it's Cambridge that exudes a true Ivy-League ambience. Many identify Cambridge with **Harvard University**, which is as old as the city itself; others associate it with the prestigious **Massachusetts Institute of Technology (MIT)**, which moved here from Boston in 1916. The two giant institutions account for more than 28,000 students, hailing from nearly 100 nations. **Harvard** alone is the alma mater of six US presidents. Since World War II, **Harvard** and **MIT**, with government and industry support, have made Cambridge a world-renowned research center that focuses on military and aerospace industries, artificial intelligence, and genetic engineering. These partnerships have spurred the growth of related industries in Cambridge and other cities, creating Massachusetts's high-tech economy.

In 1630 **New Towne** village was founded by the Massachusetts Bay Colony, led by Governor John Winthrop. Eight years later the settlement was nostalgically renamed Cambridge, after the English university where many Puritans had been educated. That same year, the nation's first college, founded here two years earlier by the colony's Great and General Court, was named **Harvard College** to memorialize John Harvard, a young Charleston minister who bequeathed his 400-volume library and half his estate to the fledgling school. And in 1639 the New World's first printing press was established in Cambridge, publishing the first American document, *Oath of a Free Man*. No other settlement in the colony was permitted a press until 1674, so Cambridge became the earliest publishing center of the hemisphere, ensuring prominence as a place of ideas.

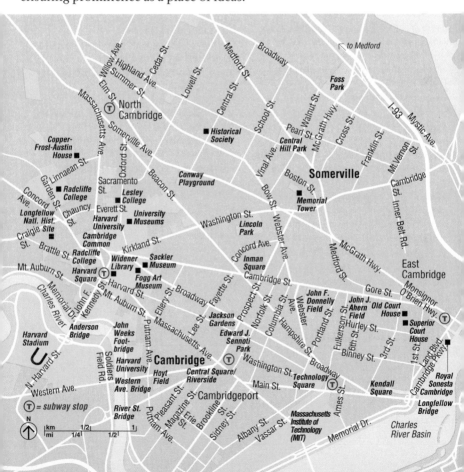

It is the engine of academia that drives the 6.25-square-mile city of over 95,000 "Cantabrigians" (as Cambridge residents are known), half of whom are affiliated in some way with the local universities. But that is by no means the whole story.

Cambridge has traditionally been a place for progressive politics and lawmaking, where generations of residents have embraced issues such as antislavery, women's rights, the antinuclear movement, environmentalism, opposition to the Vietnam War and US foreign policy in Central America, and many other concerns. Others dismiss Cambridge as an uppity enclave of eggheads and bleeding hearts, so strong is its reputation as a bastion of liberalism. But it's known for cultural diversity as well, for it is full of people from somewhere else. The cafes, bookstores, shops, and restaurants here reflect a multicultural persona—a mélange of Yankee gentry, blue-collar workers, conservatives, liberals, immigrant newcomers, and long-established ethnic groups. They live in **Brattle Street** mansions, crowded triple-deckers, chic condos, and subsidized housing.

In 1846 Cambridge officially became a city when **Old Cambridge** joined with the industrial riverside communities of **East Cambridge** and **Cambridgeport.** Today the city consists of distinctive neighborhoods, loosely defined as **Kendall Square**, East Cambridge, **Inman Square, Central Square,** Cambridgeport, **Riverside, Mid-Cambridge, North Cambridge, West Cambridge,** and the famous **Harvard Square. Massachusetts Avenue** runs the length of Cambridge, leading from the **Harvard Bridge** on the **Charles River** through **MIT**'s campus to Harvard Square and northward.

It would take months to fully comb Cambridge, so most visitors head directly to Harvard Square (commonly referred to as "the Square"), the city's centerpiece and the heart of Old Cambridge. Overdevelopment and the invasion of franchises have eroded some of its quirky charm, but you can still sit in cafes and browse in bookstores, pretending to read while overhearing amazing conversations among an extraordinarily eclectic group. On a warm afternoon sit at the **au bon pain** outdoor cafe and watch all of Cambridge stroll by. In summer the nighttime street life bustles, especially near **Brattle Square** (a tiny square-within-the-Square) where outdoor entertainers hold forth every few yards. Harvard Square boasts a galaxy of bookstores catering to every interest, and many stay open very late. Among the commercial landmarks are the **Harvard Coop, Out of Town News,** the **Tasty, Words-Worth,** and **Charles Square,** a hotel-and-shopping complex. Student-oriented "cheap eats" abound; as do vintage and avant-garde clothing boutiques, and housewares and furnishings stores. Experience the over-whelming aura of **Harvard Yard,** then walk up Brattle Street (formerly **Tory Row**) and visit lovely **Radcliffe Yard.** You'll see plenty of historic edifices and some interesting modern architecture. The square offers good theater, movies, and music in a variety of settings, plus **Harvard**'s great museums. Along with **MIT** and other local colleges and institutions, **Harvard** hosts a long menu of lectures, exhibitions, symposia, and cultural and sports events throughout the academic year.

Take the MBTA *Red Line* to get to Cambridge: the Kendall Square station is closest to MIT and it's near East Cambridge. (The Lechmere station on the *Green Line* is even more convenient to East Cambridge.) The Central Square station is a five-minute walk from Inman Square; the Harvard Square station is convenient to parts of North Cambridge; the Porter Square station is nearest to North Cambridge.

1 Harvard Square Not really a square at all, it's officially located where Massachusetts Avenue heading from Boston turns and widens into a big triangle, on which the landmark **Out of Town News** is located. On one side of this triangle is **Harvard University**; on the other two lie commerce. But to students and Cantabrigians, "the Square" always refers to the much larger area radiating from this central point, with most

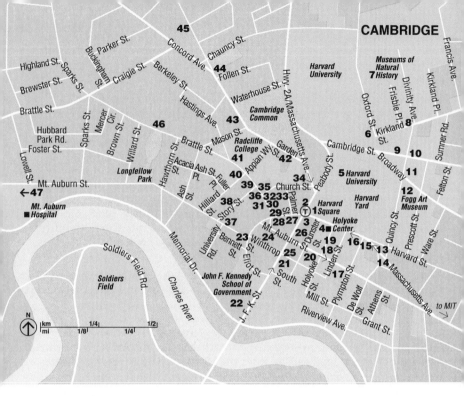

shops, restaurants, clubs, and services concentrated on Brattle, JFK, and Mount Auburn Streets, as well as on many small side streets like Church, Plympton, Dunster, and that whimsical pair, Bow and Arrow Streets. All around the Square, sidewalks are crowded with college students, professors, canvassers, protesters, businesspeople, and entertainers—in fact, you can safely assume you're heading beyond the Harvard Square area when the foot traffic around you starts to dwindle. ♦ Bounded by Peabody St, Harvard St, and Massachusetts Ave

In Harvard Square:

Cambridge Discovery Information Kiosk
Located near the subway station entrance (the main entrance is opposite the Harvard Cooperative Society) is an information kiosk where you can get bus and train schedules, maps, brochures, and a wealth of information on Cambridge, its universities, and the great self-guided walking tours to Revolutionary Cambridge, East Cambridge, and more. They sell a variety of guidebooks, too, highlighting architecture, restaurants, history, **Harvard University,** the Square, etc. Some of the materials are free and some are sold for modest fees to pay the overhead of the nonprofit Cambridge Discovery organization, which operates and staffs the kiosk.

The group provides information on the city to both tourists and residents, offering guided group tours for a fee (from late June to Labor Day; inquire at the booth for tour times), information packages, a newsletter, and school outreach programs. Many of the volunteers speak other languages and are ready for your questions. They also have information on local lodging. For more information, write Cambridge Discovery at PO Box 1987, Cambridge, MA 02238. ♦ Daily. 497.1630 &

Out of Town Newspapers Busy from opening to closing, this National Historic Landmark newsstand—universally called "Out of Town News"—sells newspapers from every major American city and many large cities worldwide, plus a huge array of magazines, maps, comic books, and **Harvard** T-shirts. Many a rendezvous is kept at the familiar ornate kiosk. If your craving for newspapers and mags isn't sated here, try **Nini's Corner** across the way, next to the **Harvard Coop,** where there's lots of souvenirs and postcards, too.

Also on this traffic island is sculptor Dimitri Hadzi's 21-foot-tall *Omphalos* (Greek for navel), signifying the center of the universe. Generations of **Harvard** students and Cantabrigians have considered the Square precisely that. ♦ Daily. No credit cards accepted. 354.7777 & (use the rear entrance)

Out of Town Ticket Agency Down the main entry to the **Harvard Square** station, look for the mezzanine-level window where you can purchase tickets to sports events, popular concerts, plays, special events, and anything going on at **Boston Garden,** from ice-skating shows to **Bruins** and **Celtics** games. ♦ M-F; Sa until 3PM. No credit cards accepted. 492.1900

2 Harvard Cooperative Society Universally known as "The Coop" (pronounced like the chicken abode), the society was founded in 1882 by students angered at local merchants' price gouging. Their enterprise sold goods to faculty and students, and gradually blossomed into a full-fledged collegiate department store. The store (pictured above) is owned by its members: **Harvard** and **MIT** students, faculty, employees, and alumni.

It's best known for its three floors of books, including best-sellers, paperbacks, nonfiction, remainders, and textbooks; New England's largest selection of posters; and anything and everything emblazoned with Harvard colors and the *Veritas* seal. The clothing and footwear selection for men and women may not be the height of fashion, but there's a little of everything and frequent sales. Also sold here are housewares, sports equipment, radios and TVs, luggage, computers, typewriters, small electronics, cameras and accessories, lots of stationery products, and just about anything else a student or faculty member might hanker for, including good snacks. Sidewalk sales are often set up in the rear alley, between the original building and its annex. You can also find rest rooms here, a relative rarity in the Square. ♦ M-Sa. 1400 Massachusetts Ave (off JFK St) 499.2000 &

3 The Tasty $ A dozen stools, a counter where doughnuts recline on pedestals under plastic covers, a grill that keeps the place warm winter and summer—that's all there's room for in this closet-size sandwich shop, open since 1916. A remnant of old Harvard Square before trendiness set in, it serves victuals round the clock. ♦ Coffeeshop ♦ Daily 24 hours. No credit cards accepted. 2A JFK St (at Massachusetts Ave). 354.9016 &

4 au bon pain ★$ The mass-produced croissants are surprisingly tasty; they also sell muffins, sandwiches, and soups. The real reason to come here is to relax outside on the large terrace in nice weather and watch the incessant tide of humanity flow to and from the Square. Students of human nature won't find a better vantage point or more varied collection of people in Greater Boston.

Singers, jugglers, and promoters of various causes often hold forth alongside the cafe. A local chess master regularly plays against the clock for a small sum at one of the cafe's chess tables, attracting aficionados. ♦ Cafe ♦ Daily breakfast, lunch, and dinner. No credit cards accepted. 1360 Massachusetts Ave (between Holyoke and Dunster Sts). 497.9797 &

5 Harvard University The first and foremost of the famed "Ivy League" schools was originally founded to train young men for the ministry. The university's seal (pictured at right) was adopted in 1643; *Veritas* is Latin for "truth." **Harvard College** gradually moved from Puritanism to intellectual independence, and became a private institution in 1865. In the mid-19th century the college became the undergraduate core of a burgeoning modern university, with satellite professional schools.

Today there are 10 graduate schools, including Arts and Sciences, Business Administration, Dental Health, Design, Divinity, Education, Government, Law, Medicine, and Public Health. With some 400-odd buildings on 380 acres of land in the Cambridge/Boston area, the university and its Cambridge surrounds are so entwined that it's hard to tell where town ends and gown begins. The current endowment of $5 billion (give or take many millions) represents the largest of any university in the world. **Harvard Houses,** where students live after their freshman year, dot the Square toward the river and include lovely Georgian-style brick residences with courtyards. Most memorable are the **River Houses,** best seen from the Charles.

The **Harvard University Information Office** is located on the ground floor of **Holyoke Center,** plainly visible from the street. Maps, pamphlets, self-guided walking tours, and other materials (some free, some sold) on the university and area events can be picked up here. Events tickets are sold here, too. Get a free copy of the *Harvard University Gazette,* which lists activities open to the public. Students also offer free one-hour tours (departing from the office) that give visitors a good general introduction to the university. ♦ Tours M-Sa during the academic year; daily in summer. Holyoke Center, 1350 Massachusetts Ave (between Holyoke and Dunster Sts). 495.1573 &

Cambridge has the highest concentration of bookstores per square mile in the country.

Restaurants/Clubs: Red   **Hotels:** Blue
Shops/ ♣ Outdoors: Green   **Sights/Culture:** Black

5 Harvard Yard Verdant and dappled with sun and shade, its great trees sentinels to the education of generations, this expanse (pictured above)—now on the National Register of Historic Places—exudes an aura of privilege and prestige, the essence of the institution. Anyone is welcome to relax on its grassy lawns, although when late spring arrives the air becomes thick with lawn fertilizer and noisy with machinery as the university starts sprucing for another commencement. Summer mornings are particularly tranquil here; early fall heralds the return of the students and faculty with their brisk, purposeful traffic to and from classes.

The university's oldest buildings date from the early 18th century; its newest were built yesterday. From **Holyoke Center,** cross Massachusetts Avenue and enter the gate, where you'll find the **Benjamin Wadsworth House,** an attractive yellow clapboard house, built in 1726, where **Harvard** presidents resided until 1849. It briefly served as General George Washington's headquarters when he took command of the Continental Army in Cambridge in 1775. Walk through the western side (considered the "Old Yard"); to the left is Early Georgian **Massachusetts Hall,** the oldest university building, dating from 1720, where the president's offices are now. Patriot regiments were once housed here and in several other buildings nearby. Opposite is **Harvard Hall** (built in 1766); between the two halls is Johnston Gate (erected in 1889), the main entrance, which was designed by **McKim, Mead & White.** Standing at attention by the gate is a bit of frippery, a tiny guard-house designed by **Graham Gund.** Next on the left is **Hollis Hall** (completed in 1763), where John Quincy Adams, Ralph Waldo Emerson, and Henry David Thoreau roomed. Beyond is **Holden Chapel** (built in 1742), a High Georgian gem, complete with a family coat of arms. Once called "a solitary English daisy in a field of Yankee dandelions," it is now tarnished through constant alterations. Next is **Stoughton Hall,** designed in 1805 by Harvard graduate **Charles Bulfinch.**

Opposite Johnston Gate on the right stands **University Hall,** designed by **Bulfinch** in 1815. It was this building that created the illusion of an academic enclave, instead of merely clusters of buildings facing outward. In front stands Daniel Chester French's 1884 statue of *John Harvard* (French also sculpted *Abraham Lincoln* in the Lincoln Memorial in Washington, DC). The statue is famous for the three lies set forth in its plaque stating "John Harvard, founder 1638." It is the image of an 1880s **Harvard** student, not of Harvard himself; Harvard was a benefactor, not a founder; and the college was founded in 1636. Nevertheless, the false John is nearly always surrounded by tourists and visitors. Although the light here is generally poor for photos, you'll probably have to swing wide of clusters of people posing. Every now and again, rival schools give the statue a decorative paint job.

Behind **University Hall,** in the "New Yard," is **Memorial Church** (constructed in 1932) with its soaring needle-sharp spire. By school regulations, the church's wonderful **University Choir** only performs during religious services here. Installed in the church is a glorious organ, a creation of the late C.B. Fisk of Gloucester and one of the greatest American instruments built according to Baroque principles. Many important international organists have vied to play it. Looming opposite is the massive **Widener Memorial Library.** (see below) which is across the grassy **Tercentenary Theatre,** where the university's commencements are held with every ruffle and flourish—even a Latin oration. As you head in that direction you'll pass Romanesque Revival **Sever Hall** on your left, designed by **Henry Hobson Richardson** in 1880, a National Historic Landmark and one of his greatest buildings. Study its brilliantly animated and decorative brickwork.

Alongside **Widener** are **Pusey Library,** located underground, where the university's archives and map and theater collections are stored, and **Houghton Library,** home to its rare books and manuscripts, including memorabilia and furnishings from Emily Dickinson's Amherst home, and the single book remaining from John Harvard's library. **Pusey** often exhibits selections from its theater collection on the first floor, and **Houghton** offers public displays of some of its treasures, with emphasis on fine bookmaking. Near **Lamont Library,** which is tucked in the corner, is a Henry Moore sculpture called *Four-Piece Reclining Figure.* ♦ Bounded by Massachusetts Ave and Cambridge St, Broadway, and Quincy and Peabody Sts

Within Harvard Yard:

Harry Elkins Widener Memorial Library
A more triumphal and imposing entrance than this would be hard to find, with its massive Corinthian colonnade and grand exterior staircase. Chilly gray and austere, this library (built in 1915) is the patriarch in Harvard's family of nearly one hundred department libraries campuswide. It was named for Harry Elkins Widener, who went down with the

Titanic; a plaque tells the story. The largest university library in the world, the collection of books found here is only surpassed by the Library of Congress and the New York City Public Library. It has 7.5 million volumes on more than five miles of bookshelves; the entire library system contains more than 12 million volumes, plus manuscripts, microforms, maps, photographs, slides, and other materials. The building is open to the public, but access to its stacks is limited to the fortunate cardholders with **Harvard** affiliation or to those with special permission. In the resplendent **Harry Elkins Widener Memorial Room,** bibliophile and collector Harry's books are on display, including a *Gutenberg Bible,* one of only 20 complete copies remaining, and a First Folio of Shakespeare's plays dated 1623, the first collected edition. Look for the dioramas depicting Cambridge in 1667, 1775, and 1936; and the John Singer Sargent murals in the main stair hall. ♦ Daily when school is in session; M-F during school vacations. 495.4166 ♿

6 Science Center The largest building on **Harvard**'s campus—built by **Sert, Jackson and Associates** in 1973—looks like a giant Polaroid Land camera, with a complex and multiterraced exterior. Science buff alert: on the center's lower level you'll find **Harvard**'s *Collection of Historical Scientific Instruments,* a repository for scientific apparatus used for **Harvard** teaching and research in astronomy, surveying, physics, geology, electricity, navigation, and other subjects since 1765. On view are telescopes, sundials, clocks, vacuum pumps, microscopes, early computing devices, and more, with additional devices donated to the university dating back to 1450. The *Tanner Fountain,* designed by sculptor Peter Walker, is a jet-misted cluster of rocks that's always alluring to children. On a sunny day, if you stand in the right place, you may see a brightly colored rainbow hovering over the fountain. There are occasional private exhibitions—call in advance. ♦ Free. Tu-F; closed June-September. Kirkland St (at Oxford St). 495.2779 ♿

Lobster Logistics

Indulging in your first lobster? Or anxious to perfect the cracking of this crafty crustacean? There's hardly a better place to learn than in Boston, where these critters are often caught and served the same day. Getting the meat out of the bright-red crustacean takes practice, patience, and a little perseverance. This guide to the art of lobster-eating should teach you the basics, but it's best to take an experienced lobster-cracking friend along for encouragement and coaching. And, despite how funny you may look, wear a bib—you're going to get more than a little messy.

1 Twist off the claws.

2 Crack each claw with a nutcracker.

3 Separate the tailpiece from the body by arching the back until it cracks.

4 Bend back the flippers and break them off of the tailpiece.

5 Insert a fork where the flippers broke off and push the meat out.

6 Unhinge the back from the body. This contains the tomalley (or liver), which some folks are known to consume. . . .

7 Open the remaining part of the body by cracking it sideways (the meat in this section is particularly good).

8 The small claws are excellent eating—just suck the meat out as illustrated here.

7 Museums of Natural History Sharing one roof are four separate **Harvard University** museums dedicated to the study of archaeology, botany, comparative zoology, and minerals. The most famous exhibition is the **Botanical Museum**'s *Blaschka Glass Flowers* collection, handblown by Leopold and Rudolph Blaschka in Dresden, Germany, using a process that was lost with their deaths. More than 840 plant species are represented, with a few irrevocably lost when shattered by sonic booms. Another odd exhibition is Rosalba Towne's 19th-century series of paintings depicting every plant and flower mentioned in the works of Shakespeare. Particularly wondrous is the **Mineralogical and Geological Museums**' collection of gemstones, minerals, ores, and meteorites. Look for the giant Mexican crystals.

The **Peabody Museum of Archaeology and Ethnology** is the oldest museum in this hemisphere dedicated to archaeology and ethnology, with treasures from prehistoric and historic cultures from all over the world. Founded in 1866 by George Peabody, many items in the museum's displays were brought back from **Harvard**-sponsored expeditions. The **Peabody**'s largest collections focus on North, Central, and South American Indian cultures. Visit the **Hall of the Maya,** and the **Hall of the North American Indian**'s exhibition of some 500 artifacts, which were blessed in 1990 by Slow Turtle, chief medicine man of the Wampanoag. The exceptionally comprehensive display includes objects from 10 or so different Indian cultures over five centuries, with a number of items brought back by the Lewis and Clark expedition, and features magnificent towering totem poles, peace pipes, a Plains Indian ceremonial outfit, warriors' long bows, and a bison skull with a symbol on its forehead representing the four winds.

Tracing the evolution of animals and man, the **Museum of Comparative Zoology** delights kids with its whale skeletons; a 180-million-year-old *Paleosaurus,* the 25,000-year-old **Harvard** mastodon; the giant sea serpent *Kronosaurus;* George Washington's pheasants; the world's oldest egg, 225 million years old; and the largest known fossilized turtle shell. The museum also displays the *Coelacanth,* a fish thought to have been extinct for 70 million years until fishers began to catch some live in 1938. Visit the museums' gift shop, a largely undiscovered treasure trove. The **Peabody** has a separate gift shop, also excellent. ♦ Admission (one fee for all four museums); free Saturday 9-11AM; children under five free; reduced for senior citizens, students, and children five to 15. Daily. 24 Oxford St (off Kirkland St). Peabody 495.2248, Botanical 495.2326, Mineralogical 495.4758, Zoology 495.2463. Recorded information 495.1910, admission information on all 495.3045 ♿ (inquire at admission desk)

7 Harvard Semitic Museum Founded in 1889, the museum participated in the first US archaeological expedition to the Near East that year, and the first scientific excavations in the Holy Land, from 1907 to 1912. The museum closed during World War II and reopened in 1982. It now presents special exhibitions drawn from its archaeological and photographic collections, which include 28,000 photographs of 19th-century life in the Near East. ♦ Admission. M-F. 6 Divinity Ave (off Kirkland St). 495.3123

8 Adolphus Busch Hall Named for the famous beer baron, this noble hall with its carved heroes and solemn inscriptions was formerly the **Busch-Reisinger Museum.** It is now occupied by **Harvard**'s Center for European Studies. Designed by a German architect and completed in 1917, the medievalesque edifice was built to house the university's Germanic collections. It was enormously expensive and is full of lavish detail. Originally lauding German culture, the hall and its purpose have been influenced by the world wars and changes in international opinion toward Germany. Much of the former museum's 20th-century German art was collected during the rise of Hitler, when the works were declared degenerate, banned by the Nazis, and shipped to the US.

The **Busch-Reisinger**'s Renaissance, Baroque, and modern holdings have been moved to the newer **Werner Otto Hall,** behind the **Fogg Museum** (see page 179). Still displayed in the hall are medieval statuary, stained glass, metal, and other works not needing a climate-controlled environment. Overlooking the wonderful courtyard garden are carved stone heads taken from Wagner's *Ring of the Nibelungen*. Evening concerts are given on the famous Flentrop organ as part of the **Fogg** music series; a small fee is charged. Across Kirkland Street from the hall is a Gothic Swedenborgian church, a little jewel. ♦ Courtyard M-F 11AM-3PM; collection 1-5PM second Sunday every month. 29 Kirkland St (at Quincy St). Concert information 495.4544

9 Memorial Hall Just north of Harvard Yard looms this Ruskinian Gothic giant (pictured above). Alive with colorful ornament, gargoyles, pyramidal roofs, and square tower, this cathedral-like hall has plenty of pomp and circumstance to spare. Designed in 1878 by two Harvardians, **Henry Van Brunt** and **William R. Ware,** the hall was built as a monument to university alumni who died in the Civil War—on the Yankee side, of course.

You can see their names inscribed in the transept inside. Some of the stained-glass windows were produced in the studios of Louis Comfort Tiffany and John La Farge. Innumerable momentous events—depending on one's perspective—have occurred here, from college registration and examinations to major lectures and concerts. ◆ Cambridge St (off Quincy St) &

Within Memorial Hall:

Sanders Theatre Celebrated painter Frank Stella and many other illustrious figures have lectured in the richly carved wooden theater, which seats 1,224. Also appearing here are such national performers as the **Beaux Arts Trio** and local music groups, including the **Pro Arte Chamber Orchestra of Boston, Cantata Singers, Cecilia Society,** and the **Cambridge Society for Early Music.** The festive Christmas Revels is an annual event. ◆ Admission for most events. Recorded information 495.2420 & (use the Kirkland St entrance)

10 George Gund Hall Home of the **Graduate School of Design,** this modern concrete building—completed in 1972 by **John Andrews**—is notable for the striking nighttime silhouette created by its stepped-glass roof, beneath which design students visibly toil at their drawing boards late into the night. Within this hall is the **Frances Loeb Library,** which has architecture and urban design collections. The first floor hosts changing architecture exhibits and a small **Charrette** art supply store. ◆ 48 Quincy St (between Kirkland and Cambridge Sts). 495.4731 &

11 Arthur M. Sackler Museum Across Broadway from the **Fogg Museum** is this relative newcomer to Harvard. Except for its brick stripes, interesting window arrangements, and touches of electric-lime paint, the chunky Postmodern building is quite ordinary-looking. It was designed in 1986 by British architect **James Stirling,** who aptly called **Harvard**'s campus "an architectural zoo." Exhibited here are ancient, Asian, and Islamic art, including the world's finest collections of ancient Chinese jades and cave reliefs and Chun-ware ceramics, and an exceptional selection of Japanese woodblock prints.

Special exhibitions are also mounted here, and the **Harvard University Art Museum Shop** is on the first floor. The very odd portal and pillar arrangement on the upper facade facing Broadway marks where a skyway was to connect this museum with the **Fogg,** but the plan was quashed by community opposition. ◆ Admission (includes Fogg Art Museum); free Saturday 10AM-noon; free for those under 18; reduced for senior citizens and students. Tu-Su. Free tours at 1PM. 485 Broadway (at Quincy St). 495.9400 &

12 Fogg Art Museum Founded in 1891, **Harvard**'s oldest art museum houses a comprehensive collection representing most major artistic periods in the history of Western art from the Middle Ages to the present. In this 1927 **Coolidge, Shepley, Bulfinch, and Abbot** design, art galleries on two levels surround an Italian Renaissance courtyard modeled after a 16th-century canon's house. The French Impressionists, British, and Italian holdings are especially strong; look for works by Whistler, Rossetti, Géricault, Fra Angelico, Rubens, Ingres, Beardsley, and Pollock, as well as Monet, Renoir, and Picasso, in the *Wertheim Collection* on the second floor.

Also on the second floor is **Harvard**'s first permanent gallery of decorative arts, which rotates treasures from the university's vast collection of furniture, clocks, chests, Wedgwood, silver vessels, and other household goods bequeathed by alumni and others over the past 300 years. Probably the most famous item is the *President's Chair,* a knobby, uncomfortable-looking triangular-seated chair made in England or Wales in the 16th century and brought to **Harvard** by Reverend Edward Holyoke, president from 1737 to 1769. Since Holyoke (a portrait of whom seated in this chair was painted by John Singleton Copley), the *President's Chair* has supported every **Harvard** president during commencement. The museum sponsors great concerts in the courtyard during the academic year, from Renaissance Italian composers to Gershwin. ◆ Admission (includes Sackler Museum); free Saturday 10AM-noon; free for children under 18; reduced for senior citizens and students. Daily. Free tours at 11AM. 32 Quincy St (at Broadway). 495.9400 &

12 Carpenter Center for the Visual Arts Coolly surveying **Harvard Yard** across the way, this sculptural edifice (pictured above) is the only structure designed by **Le Corbusier** in North America. It was built in 1963 and is now on the National Register of Historic Places. The iconoclastic concrete-and-glass form carries on an interesting dialogue with the sedate **Fogg Art Museum** next door and other conservative architectural neighbors. Orchestrated within this building, which contains the Department of Visual and Environmental Studies, are a rotating program of contemporary exhibitions in its two public galleries, lectures, and the wonderful *Harvard Film Archive* series. The center also houses a film archive, photography collection, and studios. ◆ Daily. 24 Quincy St (between Massachusetts Ave and Broadway). 495.3251, recorded information on film showings 495.4700 &

Restaurants/Clubs: Red **Hotels:** Blue
Shops/ 🌳 Outdoors: Green **Sights/Culture:** Black

Anatomy of a Town House

Although architectural elements vary from block to block and even from house to house in Boston, here's an illustrated guide to some typical permutations, as well as a lexicon unknown to most town-house dwellers themselves (at least until they run up against the need for renovations).

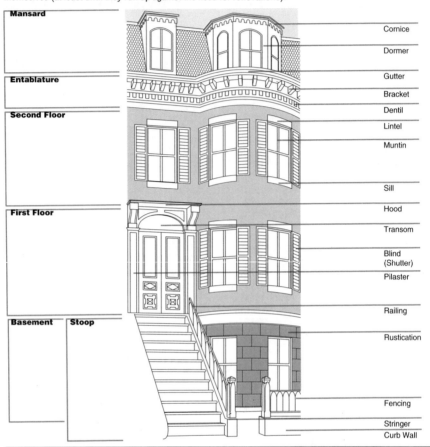

Labels (left side): Mansard, Entablature, Second Floor, First Floor, Basement, Stoop

Labels (right side): Cornice, Dormer, Gutter, Bracket, Dentil, Lintel, Muntin, Sill, Hood, Transom, Blind (Shutter), Pilaster, Railing, Rustication, Fencing, Stringer, Curb Wall

13 Inn at Harvard $$ **Graham Gund**'s 1992 design earned a "Worst New Architecture" award from *Boston* magazine: "looks like a plywood prop from Universal Studios and feels like an upscale hospital inside." Drop in and decide for yourself. There are 113 rooms plus one Presidential Suite. The four-story atrium—with its couches, tables, and shelves of up-to-date books (light meals and bar service are available here)—almost achieves the ambience of a "grand residential living room." It just needs a little breaking in. And they might reconsider the towering replicas of Baroque garden statuary, which look plain eccentric. ◆ 1201 Massachusetts Ave (at Harvard St). 491.2222, 800/528.0444 &

The building of bridges—particularly the West Boston Bridge of 1793 and the Craigie Bridge of 1909—turned Cambridge into a more viable city by opening direct routes to Boston.

Café Pamplona

14 Cafe Pamplona ★$ This is the most European of Cambridge cafes, a place where patrons linger comfortably for hours drinking espresso and writing, reading, or engaging in conversation from the mundane to the supremely esoteric. The tiny cafe is on the lower level of a snug red house, with an outdoor terrace where people hang about past midnight in the summer. The eclectic clientele leans toward highbrow. In addition to teas and coffees of all kinds (try the "mokka" drink), gazpacho, sandwiches, and specials, as well as flan, parfaits, chocolate mousse, and delightful little pastries are served. ◆ Latin ◆ Daily. No credit cards accepted. 12 Bow St (at Arrow St). No phone

15 Bartley's Burger Cottage ★$ A fixture in the Square since 1960, the Bartleys (and their son, Bill) have ushered several generations of ravenous college students through their undergraduate years. According to the owners, their roasted, marinated chicken is "a degree above the rest," but the real draw are the big juicy burgers—available in 30 variations, plus a dozen or so topical guises, such as The Madonna ("a naked burger stripped of its roll"). The place is chockablock with tiny tables and decorated with odd remnants of popular culture—e.g., a vintage ad with Reagan hawking cigarettes. For its many fans, it's the next best thing to home. ♦ American ♦ M-Sa lunch and dinner. 1246 Massachusetts Ave (at Plympton St). 354.6559 ♿

15 Harvard Book Store Open since 1932, this Cambridge institution and family business is a general-interest bookstore that emphasizes scholarly works and customer service. The bookstore (which puts out a monthly newsletter) is particularly strong in philosophy, literary theory and criticism, psychology, African-American and women's studies, classics, and books from university presses. People flock in for the great remainders selection and basement inventory of used paperbacks, hardcovers, and texts. Owner Frank Kramer also operates the extremely popular **Harvard Book Store Cafe** (190 Newbury Street, Back Bay, 536.0095), which has a more general-interest slant and serves good food to hungry book browsers. ♦ Daily. 1256 Massachusetts Ave (at Plympton St). 661.1515 ♿ (street level only)

15 The Grolier Poetry Book Shop Inc. This all-poetry bookshop was founded in 1927 as a rare-books store, then converted to its specialty in 1974 by poetry-loving owner Louisa Solano, who bought the shop because she couldn't afford to continue buying book after book. She has 15,000 poetry titles today, including books and cassettes on poetry, first editions, small-press publications, and little magazines. Solano cosponsors a poetry-reading series for unpublished poets, hosts autograph parties about once a week from September through May, and keeps a mailing list and bulletin board going, as well as a gallery of photographs of poets who are patrons. It's also a meeting place; lots of visiting poets use it as an information center and sounding board. ♦ Tu-Sa; closed noon-12:30PM. 6 Plympton St (between Massachusetts Ave and Mt. Auburn St). 547.4648, 800/234.7636

16 Briggs & Briggs Established in 1890, this distinguished shop is known for its stock of classical and popular sheet music and books. It also sells musical instrument accessories, stereo equipment, and a variety of classical, jazz, blues, folk, and world music on CDs and tapes. ♦ M-Sa. 1270 Massachusetts Ave (at Plympton St). 547.2007 ♿ (they offer assistance)

17 Harvard Lampoon Castle Cambridge's most whimsical building—designed by **Wheelwright and Haven** in 1909—is home to the *Harvard Lampoon* offices, an undergraduate humor magazine that inspired the *National Lampoon* (although there's no affiliation). "Poonies" have long been famous for their pranks, from stealing the **Massachusetts State House**'s *Sacred Cod* in 1933, to hiring an actress in 1990 to hold a press conference and pretend she was Marla Maples, Donald Trump's notorious girlfriend (now wife). Pick out the eyes, nose, mouth, and hat on the entrance tower. Atop is a statue of an ibis, frequently absconded by *Harvard Crimson* staffers. William Randolph Hearst, a former *Lampoon* business manager, donated the land. ♦ Mt. Auburn St (at Plympton St)

Within Harvard Lampoon Castle:

Starr Book Shop This academic bookstore purveys antiquarian sets and scholarly works in literature, philosophy, classics, history, biography, and general subject areas. They carry current reviewers' copies, too. Graduate and undergraduate students frequent the shop, which is owned and operated by Peter Starr. ♦ Daily. 29 Plympton St (at Mt. Auburn St). 547.6864

18 Pangloss Bookshop Peruse used, out-of-print, and rare scholarly monographs in the humanities and social sciences, as well as literary magazines. Book searches and special orders can be arranged here as well. ♦ M-Sa. 65 Mt. Auburn St (between Holyoke and Linden Sts). 354.4003

18 Elsie's Famous Sandwiches $ There was indeed an Elsie, who retired in the 1960s. Yet she'd probably find the food here quite familiar, for it never changes; young and old alike troop in for good fat sandwiches like the Turkey Deluxe, the Roast Beef Special, hot pastrami, and 30 or so other sandwiches and subs. You'll find salads, too, with dressings made right here, and bargain breakfasts in the AM. Munch away at a windowside counter, or brown-bag it and walk a few blocks to the river. **Harvard** alumni recall frequent trips to this popular spot. ♦ Sandwiches/Takeout ♦ M-Sa breakfast, lunch, and dinner; Su lunch and dinner. No credit cards accepted. 71A Mt. Auburn St (at Holyoke St). 354.8781

18 Delhi Darbar ★★$$ A recent addition to the Cambridge culinary collage, this place offers an unusually broad array of Indian cuisine. Try either the lamb and chicken tandoori specials, which take their name from the clay ovens used to cook with slow steady heat. Vegetarians should try the *shahl bhindi masala kadahi* (okra cooked with onions, ginger, tomatoes, and Indian spices).

♦ Indian/Takeout ♦ M-Sa lunch buffet and dinner; Su brunch and dinner. 24 Holyoke St (between Mt. Auburn St and Massachusetts Ave). 492.8993

19 The Hasty Pudding Building This rather ramshackle little theater is home to the undergraduate Hasty Pudding Theatricals, a dramatic society established in 1795 and renowned for its annual Hasty Pudding Awards to the Man and Woman of the Year. The celebrity recipients—Cher, Kevin Costner, and Jodie Foster are past winners—are honored with parades through Cambridge in February, accompanied by male club members in female attire. The guest is then treated to an irreverent performance and comedic roast, and presented with a ceremonial pudding pot. The theater is also used by the **American Repertory Theatre** (see the **Loeb Drama Center** on page 189) for its "New Stages" series; six months out of the year it's home to the **Cambridge Theatre Company,** a new venture stirred up from the ashes of the **Poets' Theatre** of the 1950s. ♦ 10 Holyoke St (between Massachusetts Ave and Mt. Auburn St). Box office 496.8400

Within The Hasty Pudding Building:

Upstairs at the Pudding ★★$$$ On the top floor, beneath high-vaulted ceilings and posters of old Hasty Pudding performances, amid forest green, crisp white, and romantic pink, enjoy a convivial repast away from the Square's commotion. This atmospheric restaurant offers such ambitious European dishes as grilled quail on gnocchi, clams Florentine, risotto with shrimp, rack of lamb with black-olive butter, venison steak, Queen Mother's cake, and Sicilian lemon cream with strawberry sauce. Many entrées are accompanied by a dramatic array of vegetables. The à la carte Sunday brunch is deliciously out of the ordinary. This is definitely not a student stomping ground, except perhaps when Mom and Dad come to town. ♦ Northern Italian/European ♦ M-F, Su lunch and dinner; Sa lunch. Reservations recommended. 864.1933 ⑆

20 Schoenhof's Foreign Books, Inc. Writer John Updike, **Harvard** economist John Kenneth Galbraith, and chef Julia Child have all shopped here. And soon after arriving in America, many of Boston's foreign residents and students immediately head to the understated shop in the basement of Harvard's Spee Club (a student organization). The reason: it's is the best foreign bookstore in the country, with more than 35,000 titles— original works, not translations—representing 200 languages (other than English). Founded

in 1856 by Carl Schoenhof to serve Boston's German community, this store's mission today is to bring together people and books of all nationalities. The sales staff are fluent in several languages and work together to choose books, with an emphasis on history, philosophy, literature, and literary criticism. The biggest selections are French, Spanish, German, Italian, and Russian. There's also a great department of references, records, and tapes for language learning; and children's books, too. The wholesale/retail store runs a worldwide mail-order service and is tenacious at tracking down even the most esoteric special orders—a French book on termites or a $5,000 German edition on Freud, for example. ♦ M-Sa; Th until 8PM. 76A Mt. Auburn St (between Dunster and Holyoke Sts). 547.8855

21 Iruña ★★$$ Despite **Harvard Square**'s international population, most of its restaurants have an Americanized style. Not this little cafe tucked down a short alley. The relaxed and simple European ambience and good food offered here for over a quarter-century has earned it a devout clientele. The Spanish specialties are moderately priced and good: try the gazpacho, garlic soup, paella, Basque chicken, or potato omelette, and wash your choices down with red or white sangria. Daily specials feature whatever's fresh. In warm weather, there's a small outdoor patio for dining, but it's actually more pleasant inside, especially if you dine early. ♦ Spanish ♦ M-Sa lunch and dinner. Reservations recommended Friday-Saturday. No credit cards accepted. 56 JFK St (between Winthrop and South Sts). 868.5633

22 John F. Kennedy Memorial Park Often nearly empty of people and very well maintained, this big, grassy park is wonderful for lounging. There's an interesting variety of trees, many still quite young, since the park was only completed a few years ago. It's behind the **John F. Kennedy School of Government** and **The Charles Hotel** (see below), with the river just across the street. Look for the fountain inscribed with JFK quotes. ♦ Bounded by JFK St and Memorial Dr ⑆

23 The Charles Hotel $$$ **Harvard University** guests, entertainment-industry folk, and business travelers who like to be near the late-night liveliness of the Square stay here, many on a long-term basis. The hotel is also popular with writers and sponsors readings. Part of the **Charles Square** complex, which features shops, condominiums, a health club, and restaurants, the 299-room, 10-story hotel offers many rooms overlooking the **John F. Kennedy Memorial Park** and the Charles River, with Shaker-style furniture, telephones and TVs in all bathrooms, and a patchwork down quilt on every bed. The King Charles minisuites have four-poster beds. Eighteenth-century quilts, New England antiques, and works by local artists enliven the hotel's main entry and halls. A concierge, a multilingual staff, a complimentary overnight shoe shine, 24-hour room service, valet parking, and special rooms for people with disabilities and for nonsmokers are just some of the amenities available. Guests have complimentary access to the neighboring **Le Pli Salon**'s (868.8087) exercise equipment and pool. Through special arrangement with nearby **Barillari Books,** you can order books by room service. The hotel and **Charles Square** jointly sponsor free jazz concerts in the courtyard on Wednesday from 6PM to 8PM (depending on the weather) from late June through September. ♦ 1 Bennett St (at Eliot St). 864.1200, 800/882.1818; fax 864.5715 ♿

Within The Charles Hotel:

Rarities ★★★$$$$ The subtle decor suits the sophisticated American cuisine served here, with soft piano music audible from the **Quiet Bar.** Named for a 1672 botanical book, the restaurant displays a collection of its prints. This is not a place to take dinner lightly; the food is too special and the wine list one of the best in town. The ambitious menu changes seasonally, with game and fresh seafood specialties. If you can handle it, the award-winning chocolate pâté dessert—a dense, rich, cakelike brownie served in slices and doused with sauces—will satisfy even the most intense chocolate craving. Sleek and chic it may be, but this place isn't too elitist to feature a good old banana split, too. A private dining room can be reserved for up to 16. ♦ American ♦ M-Sa dinner. Reservations recommended. Jacket and tie required. 661.5510 ♿

The Quiet Bar At the threshold to **Rarities,** pianists play softly here every night. Cozy and, yes, quiet, this is a nice change and a far cry from the noisy student bars that predominate in the Square. **Rarities'** desserts can be ordered here. There's no dress code, although the clientele generally has a well-heeled look. The bar offers very good wines. ♦ Daily 4PM-1AM. 661.5005 ♿

Bennett Street Cafe ★$$ This airy and open cafe overlooks a sunny courtyard. The menu ranges from simple offerings to complex regional cuisine with international twists and turns. Doodle away between courses with the crayons provided on the paper table covering. There are three seatings for the popular Sunday buffet brunch: 11AM, 1PM, and 2PM. Come back early on a week-day and enjoy a tasty continental breakfast before the Square wakes up. ♦ Regional American ♦ Daily breakfast, lunch, and dinner. Reservations recommended for six or more, and for Sunday brunch. 864.1200

The Regattabar The **Charles Hotel** pulled it off with panache: it gambled and launched a popular place to listen and dance to local and nationally acclaimed jazz acts. The **George Shearing Duo,** the **Milt Jackson Quartet,** Gary Burton, Herbie Hancock, Ahmad Jamal, Pat Metheny, Herbie Mann, and the **Four Freshmen** have all performed in this comfy venue. Tickets for Friday and Saturday sell out fast, so plan a week in advance. Jazzophiles drive up regularly from New York City to hear good jazz for reasonable prices. Hotel guests are admitted free to all shows Tuesday through Thursday and to any 11PM show; sign up with the concierge. All customers may purchase one-and-a-half tickets and stay for both shows on one night. ♦ Cover. Tu-Sa evenings. No jeans, tank tops, or sneakers allowed. 876.7777 ♿

23 The Shops at Charles Square This stark modern complex's numerous shops and restaurants include a branch of **Skipjack's Seafood Emporium** (★$$, 876.9900), the **Giannino Restaurant and Bar** (★★$$$, 576.0605), **Le Pli Salon** fitness center (868.8087), **Vilunya** (661.5753) for delightful folk art finds, and some national chains such as **Talbot's** (576.2278) and **Laura Ashley** (576.3690). Originally feared by locals as an unwelcome upscale intruder, this complex has proved very congenial—thanks in part to such public events as courtyard concerts, but mainly because the design is low-key and browser-friendly. The **Charles Square Parking Garage** is open 24 hours. ♦ Daily. 1 Bennett St (at Eliot St) ♿

24 The Spaghetti Club ★★$ The Cambridge cousin of Newbury Street's **Ciao Bella,** this subterranean dining spot opted for cheap chic: There are Italian comics and graffiti for the walls, *pizzette* and risottos for easy-on-the-wallet entrées. ♦ Italian ♦ Daily dinner. 93 Winthrop St (between JFK and Eliot Sts). 576.1210 ♿

24 Grendel's Den ★$ The food is nothing to flip over, but it's plentiful and cheap (many an impecunious student has subsisted on the refillable salad bar). With its high ceilings and wood paneling, this popular spot still has hints of its former grandeur as a university club. ♦ International ♦ Daily lunch and dinner. 89 Winthrop St (between JFK and Eliot Sts). 491.1160 ♿ (staff will assist)

Restaurants/Clubs: Red **Hotels:** Blue
Shops/ Outdoors: Green **Sights/Culture:** Black

Romantic Retreats

For a city that's briskly businesslike, Boston has hidden charms that deserve slower savoring. While everyone else goes about their appointed rounds, you and your loved one can meander at a private pace, enjoying your own sweet folie à deux.

Many of Boston's better hotels offer specially priced weekend packages, with amenities ranging from champagne and roses to spa privileges and limo service. The sexiest—simply because it's French—is **Le Meridien** (250 Franklin St, between Oliver and Pearl Sts, 451.1900, 800/543.4300), with stunning modern decor superimposed on a venerable old bank building. In its ornate but cozy bar, brass torchères cast a golden glow, and two splendid N.C. Wyeth murals lend a timeless air; the restaurant, **Julien,** offers outstanding French fare, luxurious service, and a degree of intimacy not matched elsewhere, thanks to comfy, encompassing armchairs. The area tends to shut down at night (all the better for focusing on each other) but by day is conducive to a number of interesting walks around **Beacon Hill, the North End, Fort Point Channel,** and the **Leather District.**

Traditionalism has its piquancy, too, and if that's more your style, try the **Ritz-Carlton Hotel** (15 Arlington St, at Newbury St, 536.5700, 800/241.3333), a bastion for Boston's old guard. Ask for a room overlooking the **Public Garden,** and with any luck you'll get a Childe Hassam–like landscape suffused with slanting light. The bar is a cosseting world unto itself, but the elegant dining room, alas, lacks culinary verve. Instead, head outside to explore. The restaurant **Biba** (300 Boylston St, at Arlington St, 426.7878) is nearby, for see-and-be-seen types who have the foresight to reserve well ahead.

Another popular restaurant, **29 Newbury** (29 Newbury St, between Arlington and Berkeley Sts, 536.0290) attracts a media and fashion crowd, but is coolly subdued; the banquetted alcoves are ideal for a tête-à-tête. Go for brunch at **Rebecca's** (21 Charles St, between Chestnut and Beacon Sts, 742.9747), plus a bit of sailboat-gazing along the **Charles River Esplanade;** browse the **Newbury Street** shops and galleries; or take in a courtyard concert at the **Isabella Stewart Gardner Museum** (280 The Fenway, between Palace Rd and Evans Way, 566.1401), always an indulgence for the senses.

Cambridge attracts couples intent on reliving—or prolonging—their youths. **The Charles Hotel** (1 Bennett St, at Eliot St, 864.1200, 800/882.1818) draws on the bustle of **Harvard Square,** while keeping just enough distance: It is calm, pampering, and pretty, with patchwork quilts on the pine beds, a super-spa **(Le Pli)** and even a premier jazz club, the **Regattabar.** The restaurant, **Rarities,** is a pared-down but Lucullan showcase for nouvelle cuisine; the atmosphere is properly worshipful, and no one will notice if you're mostly adoring each other. Another romantic venue is only a cab ride away: **Dali** (415 Washington St, at Beacon St, Somerville, 661.3254), a little-known but thoroughly charming Spanish hideaway. Street performers in **Harvard Square** range from balladeers to an oldies-by-request player piano, and the many cafes and bookstores (search out the **The Grolier Poetry Book Shop,** 6 Plympton St, between Mt. Auburn St and Massachusetts Ave, 547.4648, for love sonnets) collaborate to provide pensive pleasures. And don't forget, one of the best things to do is to stroll along the **Charles,** hand in hand.

24 Harvard Manor House $ In the heart of the Square, this low-key, friendly hotel has 72 rooms on four floors. Lots of visiting parents, professors, and prominent guests of the nearby **John F. Kennedy School of Government** stay here. The hotel is privately owned and run and has no restaurant. ◆ 110 Mt. Auburn St (at Eliot St). 864.5200; fax 864.2409 ら

25 Casa Mexico ★★$$ This small basement shrine to fine Mexican cuisine is a secret treasure. Atmosphere it has in spades, plus some hard-to-find dishes like chicken *mole poblano* (with a rich garlic, onion, chili peppers, and chocolate sauce). After more than a quarter-century in business, this tiny restaurant does everything just right. ◆ Mexican ◆ Daily lunch and dinner. 75 Winthrop St (at JFK St). 491.4552

26 The Coffee Connection ★★$ Ensconced in **The Garage,** a complex of youth-oriented stores and restaurants, this cafe is the Square's premier rendezvous for potent fresh-roasted coffee, equally full-bodied conversation, and light meals. The food's okay, but the coffee's the thing here, all different kinds served all different ways. Most customers choose the super-strong "melior" brewing method; look around, and you'll likely see at least one frazzled student nursing a giant pot to cope with the course load. There's a coffee bar, but better still, sit at one of the tables on the upper level so you can watch who comes and goes, always an intriguing collection of characters. Weekday mornings and late afternoons are the cafe's quietest hours, but there's usually a line. You can also enter from Dunster Street, up a short flight of stairs and to the left. Be forewarned: There are no rest rooms on the premises! The retail operation sells 30 different award-winning coffees, excellent teas, and every kind of brewing paraphernalia imaginable. You can order by mail, too. ◆ Cafe ◆ Daily breakfast, lunch, and dinner. 36 JFK St (between Mt. Auburn St and Massachusetts Ave). 492.4881 ら

26 John Harvard's ★★$ What makes this spot so appealing are the eight brews created on the premises and chef Joseph Kubik's spirited, out-of-the-ordinary pub fare, which may include grilled sausages with fresh spaetzle and buttermilk fried chicken with spiced corn bread. Look for a series of Hogarthian panels conceived by muralists Josh Winer and John Devaney that depicts a semi-spurious (but hilarious) biography of John Harvard, the infamous brewmaster. ♦ American ♦ Daily lunch and dinner. 33 Dunster St (between Mt. Auburn St and Massachusetts Ave). 868.3585 &

26 La Flamme A classic eight-seater, this old-fashioned barber shop (women welcome) has shorn such heads as Henry Kissinger's. Prices are still holding steady at a reasonable $9 a clip. ♦ M-Sa. 21 Dunster St (between Mt. Auburn St and Massachusetts Ave). 354.8377 &

26 Herrell's Ice Cream
Steve Herrell is generally credited with starting the whole gourmet ice cream boom at his out-of-the-way Somerville shop back in  1972. He made a few million selling his first name and then started up again with his last. His hand-cranked product, in luscious flavors like moccacino and chocolate pudding, are still among the best, dense and intense, and the "back room" here—a former bank vault painted to resemble an underwater grotto—is the coolest place in Cambridge on a hot summer evening. ♦ Ice Cream ♦ Daily noon-midnight. 15 Dunster St (between Massachusetts Ave and Mt. Auburn St). 497.2179. Also at: 155 Brighton Ave (at Harvard St). 782.9599; 350 Longwood Ave (at Brookline Ave). 731.9599

27 Urban Outfitters All the chic-looking students and the general under-30 crowd shop here for the latest in men's and women's urban attire, fashion accessories, housewares, and a whole slew of trendy novelties. You'll find lots of popular name brands and the store's own label. A bargain basement sells vintage clothing, too. You can enter the store from Brattle Street, making this a convenient cut-through. ♦ Daily. 11 JFK St (between Massachusetts Ave and Mt. Auburn St). 864.0070. Also at: 361 Newbury St (at Massachusetts Ave), Back Bay. 236.0088

28 WordsWorth The Square's busiest bookshop discounts all but textbooks, publishes a newsletter, and sponsors an excellent reading series at the **Brattle Theatre** (readings are free, but tickets must be obtained in advance). This is a full-service general bookstore with a fully computerized inventory system, developed by the owner and adopted by other bookstores, tracking 60,000 to 100,000 titles in 95 subject areas. The fine children's section has its own staff, and there's also a bountiful selection of greeting cards, calendars, and wrapping papers. ♦ Daily. 30 Brattle St (between Eliot and Mt. Auburn Sts). 354.5201

29 Brattle Street Called Tory Row in the 1770s because its residents were loyal to King George, this glorious avenue still retains its share of magnificent summer homes (they were once country estates and their spacious lands spilled right to the river's edge). In the summer of 1775 the patriots under George Washington appropriated the homes. Today the thoroughfare is far more densely inhabited, but its sumptuous properties secure its reputation as one of the country's poshest streets.

Henry Hobson Richardson designed the **Stoughton House** at No. 90 in 1882. No. 159 is the **Hooper-Lee-Nichols House,** parts of which date back to the 1600s, now headquarters of the Cambridge Historical Society. The society is open to the public on some afternoons and offers tours (497.1630) of Tory Row and the **Old Burial Ground.** John Bartlett, the Harvard Square bookseller who compiled the famous *Bartlett's Familiar Quotations,* lived at No. 165; the house was erected for him in 1873. ♦ From Sparks St to Harvard St

29 Motto/MDF Side by side are two small shops with different wares, but the same distinctive esthetic. Both are owned and operated by Jude Silver, whose own art background influences her emphasis on modern, functional, and sophisticated creations.

Motto sells abstract avant-garde jewelry of striking materials, textures, compositions, and tones. They can suggest European élan, classical coolness, industrial efficiency, or southwestern warmth. **MDF (Modern Design Furnishings)** offers personal and home and office accessories, lamps, small furniture, and men's jewelry—all fabricated from nontraditional materials. Brides-to-be can register at this store, and both stores will gladly take special orders, pack, and ship all over the country. ♦ Daily. 17-19 Brattle St (between Eliot and Church Sts). Motto 868.8448, MDF 491.2789 & (Street level)

Harvard College was the only college in the Northern Hemisphere until 1693.

29 The Learning Store The brainchild of **WGBH,** Boston's public television station, this shop is a lively gallimaufry of media—books, tapes, software products, etc.—arranged under playful rubrics like "Brain Aerobics" (puzzles) and "Socrates' Sandbox" (preschool toys). It's a browser's—and hacker's—heaven. ◆ Daily. 25 Brattle St (between Eliot and Church Sts). 661.6008 ♿

30 Jasmine/Sola Moderately expensive women's clothing and accessories are featured here, as well as women's shoes (which range widely in price), including some hard-to-find brands. The couture ranges from casual to dressy, with an emphasis on unusual rich fabrics and striking styles. The jewelry is always fun, much of it produced by independent and emerging jewelry makers. Also here is "Sola Men," a modest selection of great-looking men's clothing and shoes, often European in style. The stunning window displays are the work of Kristin Lauer's Blue Potato Installations, whose main source is junkyards. ◆ Daily. 37 Brattle St (between Eliot and Church Sts). 354.6043 ♿

ᴛʜᴇBRATTLE THEATRE

31 The Brattle Theatre This more-than-a-century-old independent movie house extraordinaire has struggled to preserve its identity in the midst of increasingly commercial Harvard Square and in an era of movie-chain monopolies. Renovated from top to bottom, but retaining its rare rear-screen projection system, this is one of the country's oldest remaining repertory movie houses. If it doesn't look much like a movie house, that's because it opened as **Brattle Hall** in 1890, founded by the Cambridge Social Union as a place for literary, musical, and dramatic entertainments.

From 1948 to 1952 the **Brattle Theatre Company** put on nationally acclaimed performances from Shakespeare to Chekhov with many notable stars, including Jessica Tandy and Hume Cronyn. The theater made a policy of hiring actors blacklisted during the US government's political witch-hunts of the era, including Zero Mostel. Subsequent financial difficulties inspired **Harvard** grads Bryant Haliday and Cyrus Harvey Jr. (who brought the first films of Fellini, Antonioni, Bergman, and Olmi to America) to convert it to an art cinema in 1953.

A local Humphrey Bogart cult was born here in the 1950s, when owners Harvey and Haliday screened neglected "Bogie" movies during **Harvard** exam time, drawing college students and other fans in droves. As the revived Bogie mystique spread across the country, a weeklong Bogart series became an annual tradition. In a historic 1955 decision,

the Massachusetts Supreme Judicial Court broke the state censorship law and ruled that the state commissioner of public safety couldn't ban a movie on Sunday. The movie that caused all of the ruckus was the Swedish film *Miss Julie.*

The movie house has shared its quarters with a variety of retail businesses since the 1960s. Today a faithful following comes for classic Hollywood and foreign movies, independent filmmaking, new art films, staged readings, and music concerts. Operated since 1986 by the Running Arts company, the theater offers genre double features nearly every night. The general roster: Monday, film noir; Tuesday, author readings sponsored by nearby **WordsWorth** bookstore, independent filmmaking, or other arts activities; Wednesday, Friday, and Saturday, theme selections such as a particular director, style, or content; and Thursday, international films. Innumerable Cambridge-area movie lovers are drawn by the attractive lineup and two-shows-for-one-price admission. A free two-month calendar of events is available in front of the theater. ◆ Daily. 40 Brattle St (between Eliot and Story Sts). Recorded information 876.6837 ♿

Within The Brattle Theatre:

Algiers Cafe ★★$ Head upstairs to the domed hideaway to sip minted coffee and feast delicately on *baba ganooj* or tabbouleh. This cafe made out like a bandit in the **Brattle Theatre** rehab: once a grungy (if atmospheric) underground cafe, now it's airy and gorgeous, with balletic little tables and prize rugs on the walls. Best of all, you're still left in peace to converse or cogitate. ◆ Middle Eastern ◆ Daily. 492.1557 ♿

Casablanca ★★$$ Long the last word in student romance, this Bogie classic's namesake has graduated from mostly bar to full-scale restaurant—keeping its oversize rattan chairs-for-two and David Omar White's beloved movie-homage murals (even though it meant moving whole walls). The menu includes Moroccan specialties such as lamb tagine (with preserved lemons and dates), but there's also a smattering of pasta, seafood, and good old American burgers. ◆ Moroccan/American ◆ Daily lunch and dinner. 876.0999 ♿

The largest private library in the world is the Widener Library in Harvard Yard, boasting more than 12 million volumes.

Restaurants/Clubs: Red   **Hotels:** Blue
Shops/ 🌳 **Outdoors:** Green   **Sights/Culture:** Black

32 E.R. Sage Market When you're tired of eating at restaurants, or you have a beautiful day and nothing to do but lounge on the lawn at **Harvard Yard,** this gourmet-food market is the perfect place to pick up the makings of a picnic. Breads are baked fresh daily on the premises. The deli-counter slices cold cuts from Angus beef and the finest poultry, and offers barbecue chicken, pasta salads, and every other kind of prepared food or salad you can think of. For dessert, you can choose from numerous brands of imported cookies. But the fruits look so fresh and inviting, you may forgo the forbidden sweets for nature's own. Or you can do it the French way: pick up a bottle of wine and a chunk of brie, and thou will be all set. ◆ Daily. 60 Church St (at Brattle St). 876.2211 Also at: 60 Massachusetts Ave (at Commonwealth Ave), Back Bay. 536.5225

33 The Globe Corner Bookstore An outpost of the Boston original, this shop specializes in books, maps, and guides for New England and world travel, and also carries travel-oriented novelties, games, and accessories. ◆ Daily. 49 Palmer St (at Church St). 497.6277. Also at: 1 School St (at Washington St). 523.6658

33 Passim ★$ One of America's oldest and best-known coffeehouses is Bob and Rae Anne Donlin's below-street-level club, where they began featuring folk music around 1971. Latin for "here and there," the name is pronounced *Pass*-im, although just about everybody says Pass-*eem*. This is the only remaining commercial coffeehouse presenting live music in Boston and Cambridge. The Donlins have always been true-blue friends to local folk and bluegrass groups, and among those they helped boost to fame are Jackson Browne, Tracy Chapman, Suzanne Vega, Greg Brown, Nanci Griffith, Tom Waits, and Patty Larkin.

The stalwart club has weathered well, and continues to showcase contemporary acoustic music, some traditional, too. It's small (50-person capacity), very unpretentious, and has no liquor license. There's a light menu of soups, sandwiches, quiches, desserts, coffees, teas, and cider during the day when it is a combination cafe/gift shop. No smoking is permitted (except during the day, in one section). The admission prices are low; the club deserves lots of support. Weekends feature a headliner with an opening act, the latter usually new local talent. Seating is first-come, first-served. ◆ Cover. Restaurant: Tu-Sa lunch. Gift shop: Tu-Sa afternoons. Call for show times. 47 Palmer St (off Church St). 492.7679

34 First Parish Church and Old Burying Ground This wooden Gothic Revival church, the 1833 creation of **Isaiah Rogers,** was partly funded by **Harvard,** in return for pews for students' use. The adjacent cemetery, called "God's Acre," is where numerous Revolutionary War veterans—including two African-American slaves, Cato Stedman and Neptune Frost, who fought alongside their masters—and **Harvard**'s first eight presidents are buried. Many of the graves' metal markers were melted down for bullets. ◆ 3 Church St (at Massachusetts Ave)

Within the First Parish Church:

Nameless Coffeehouse The country's oldest free, volunteer-run coffeehouse is a neighborly venue where local folk musicians play. Tracy Chapman sang here during her days as a Harvard Square street performer. ◆ Free. Shows F-Sa. 3 Church St (at Massachusetts Ave). Recorded information 864.1630

35 Colonial Drug The name conjures old-fashioned images, but this tiny drugstore is quite sophisticated, with an award-winning selection of more than 900 fragrances, complete cosmetic and treatment lines, Kent brushes, and other European high-quality personal care items. Members of the family running this more-than-50-year-old local institution call themselves "people with absolutely no common scents." ◆ M-Sa. No credit cards accepted. 49 Brattle St (off Church St). 864.2222

36 Brattle House This 1727 frame house, on the National Register of Historic Places, belonged to William Brattle, a Tory who fled in 1774 and for whom the street is named. Margaret Fuller, the feminist editor of *The Dial,* lived here from 1840 to 1842. The house is headquarters for the Cambridge Center for Adult Education, which sponsors a heady array of courses, as well as a well-attended holiday season crafts fair. ◆ 42 Brattle St (between Eliot and Story Sts)

36 Charrette Catering to design professionals, the sleek inventory here includes top makers' and the store's own lines of great-looking fine art and office supplies, portfolios, framing and modeling supplies, drafting instruments, furniture, and desktop-publishing software. The shop is a magnet for the local architecture and design community, along with students from the **Harvard University Graduate School of Design.** (There's a small outlet at the school for emergencies.) This branch stocks more than 6,000 products, with 41,000 available at the warehouse. If you need something the store doesn't have, check out the thick catalog; your purchase can sometimes be sent from the warehouse that same day.

In addition, a spin-off enterprise called **Charrette Reprographics** specializes in the latest technologies for design professionals' presentations. ♦ Daily. 44 Brattle St (at Church St). 495.0200 ♿ (weekdays only). Also at: 777 Boylston St (between Fairfield and Exeter Sts), Back Bay. 267.2490. Charrette Reprographics also at: 1033 Massachusetts Ave (at Ellery St), Cambridge, 495.0235; and 184 South St (between Lincoln St and Atlantic Ave), Waterfront. 292.8820

36 Harvest Restaurant

★★★$$$ Restaurants come and go frequently in the Harvard Square area, but excellence flourishes. Architects and original owners **Jane** and **Ben Thompson** (of **Benjamin Thompson & Associates**), hid the restaurant from the street in a passageway alongside the **Crate & Barrel** store. It has earned its lofty place in the local dining circuit, though, with inventive seasonal entrées. The chef likes to experiment, creating all-original stocks and sauces, and the contemporary American cuisine spotlights wild game and exotic fish specialties; in fact, there's an annual international Wild Game Festival here every February. The pastry chefs bake wonderful breads and desserts on the premises all night. The dining room's evening menu changes to take advantage of fresh native ingredients.

More casual, the adjacent **Ben's Cafe** offers less expensive but delicious regional American dishes. (Both the cafe and main dining room offer the same menu at lunch.) A light bar menu is also served between lunch and dinner and after dinner hours. The regular clientele in both the restaurant and the cafe is a rich Cambridge mix: faculty and international scholars, deans and university presidents, college students and parents, writers, poets, and actors. On a summer night, it's delightful to dine in the courtyard, where you can order from either menu. The restaurant's bar is crowded in the evenings, especially Thursdays, with unattached singles who are seeking more of the same. ♦ American ♦ M-Sa lunch and dinner; Su brunch and dinner. Reservations recommended for the dining room. 44 Brattle St (between Eliot and Story Sts). 492.1115 ♿ (from Mt. Auburn St)

36 The Harvest Express ★★$ Located at the same address as **Harvest Restaurant,** this separate shop serves delicious food to go, or to eat on the spot (there's minimal seating). Try the pasta *fagioli* (with beans) soup, pasta salads, sandwiches, calzones, or hot entrées. Numerous nonmeat dishes are featured to please Cambridge's many vegetarians, and there are always tons of fabulous desserts to choose from—espresso brownies, ginger-oatmeal cookies, various cakes, and lots of other squares and bars. ♦ Italian/Takeout ♦ M-Sa. 44 Brattle St (between Eliot and Story Sts). 868.5569 ♿ (from Mt. Auburn St)

36 Design Research Building

Ben Thompson built this architectural equivalent of a giant glass showcase in 1969 for **Design Research,** the store he founded to introduce Americans to international modern design products for the home. The store was taken over by **Crate & Barrel** in the mid-1970s. Under the nationwide chain's auspices, **Thompson** has seen his notion spread all over the country and made more affordable, though less imaginative. He certainly knows how to display for interest, as a later project, **Faneuil Hall Marketplace,** attests. ♦ 48 Brattle St (at Story St)

37 Barillari Books This spacious full-range bookstore discounts all hardcovers and paperbacks except text editions, with an extensive fine arts, architecture, and photography department that includes history, monographs, and theory. The cookbook and children's book sections are also good. Pick up the morning paper (they also carry lots of journals and reviews) and sit at the small outdoor patio, where cappuccino, espresso, and imported Italian cookies and chocolates are served. Located off the beaten trail, this shop is never crowded and you can peruse quite peacefully. Just west of the store is a shortcut to Brattle Street. ♦ Daily. 1 Mifflin Pl (on Mt. Auburn St, between Eliot and Story Sts). 864.2400, 800/772.1448 ♿

38 Mandrake Book Store More than 40 years in business, this bookstore specializes in psychotherapy and art, architecture, and design; all the works are selected and arranged with fastidious expertise. It's located near Architects' Corner, where a number of architects built their own quarters in the early 1970s, architectural styles interacting quite amicably. ♦ M-Sa; closed Saturday July-August. No credit cards accepted. 8 Story St (between Brattle and Mt. Auburn Sts). 864.3088 ♿

39 Clothware Mix and match from carefully selected, uncommon women's attire made from natural fibers, especially cottons and silks, at this small, well-known shop. The designer lines, including a private label made by an original owner, focus on graceful, classic, and fun-to-wear styles. The lingerie selection here is especially tempting. Some accessories, including leggings, tights, scarves, hats, lots and lots of socks, jewelry, wallets, handbags, and more are carried here. The shop has regular sales, but this is not a place for a bargain-hunting excursion. ♦ Daily. 52 Brattle St (at Story St). 661.6441

39 Blacksmith House Bakery Cafe ★$

"Under a spreading chestnut tree/The village smithy stands/The smith a mighty man is he/With large and sinewy hands. . . " The smithy in Henry Wadsworth Longfellow's famous poem *The Village Blacksmith* lived in this old yellow house dating from 1811, the **Dexter Pratt House.** (A stone nearby commemorates the famous chestnut tree that once was.) For more than 45 years the resident bakery has concocted delicious Viennese-style pastries, linzertortes, coffee cakes, croissants, brioches, breads, and cookies. Special offerings, like the *bûche de Noël* (Yule log) are created for holidays. Buy treats from the bakery, or enjoy them at the cafe's outdoor patio or historic interior, with its quaint rooms and creaky floorboards. The cafe shares the bakery's kitchen and also serves soups, salads, sandwiches, and hot entrées. The house now belongs to the Cambridge Center for Adult Education, which offers courses, lectures, seminars, films, and cultural activities. ◆ Bakery/Cafe/Takeout ◆ Bakery: daily. Cafe: M-W breakfast and lunch until 5PM; Th-Sa breakfast, lunch, and dinner; Su lunch. 56 Brattle St (between Story and Hilliard Sts). 354.3036 &

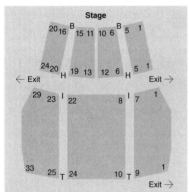

Stage

40 Loeb Drama Center/Harvard University

The center—built in 1959 by **Hugh Stubbins**—is home to the prestigious **American Repertory Theatre (ART),** a nonprofit professional company affiliated with the university that presents new American plays, neglected works from the past, and unconventional interpretations of classics. The student **Harvard-Radcliffe Dramatic Club** is also based here. The **ART** has premiered works by Jules Feiffer, Carlos Fuentes, Philip Glass, Marsha Norman, Milan Kundera, Larry Gelbart, and David Mamet. The "Mainstage" series runs year-round; the company's "New Stage Series" is presented at the **Hasty Pudding Theatre** on Holyoke Street.

The center's main stage (see the floor plan above) was the first fully flexible one in the country, easily converting into different stage styles. Frequent free student performances

are also held in the experimental theater; information is available at the box office. The theater seats 556 people. ◆ Daily. 64 Brattle St (at Hilliard St). 547.8300 & (infrared hearing amplifiers available on request)

41 Radcliffe Yard Stroll through **Radcliffe**'s pretty green centerpiece and notice the college's first building, **Fay House,** an 1806 Federal mansion. **Radcliffe College** was founded for women in 1879, named for **Harvard**'s first female benefactor, Ann Radcliffe. It was Harvard's sister school until they were united in 1975, when the administrations were merged and equal admission standards adopted for men and women. **Radcliffe** remains an independent corporation with its own president, but students share housing, classes, facilities, and degrees.

Radcliffe's buildings include the stately **Agassiz House,** where the **Harvard Gilbert and Sullivan Players** put on operettas. **The Arthur and Elizabeth Schlesinger Library** has the most extensive collection of books, photographs, oral histories, and other materials on women's history—including manuscripts and papers belonging to a number of famous women and organizations—in the country. The college's **Mary Ingraham Bunting Institute** is a highly regarded postdoctoral program for women scholars, writers, and artists. ◆ Bounded by Mason St and Appian Way, and Garden and Brattle Sts (enter from Brattle or Garden)

42 Christ Church America's first trained architect, **Peter Harrison,** designed this church as well as **King's Chapel** in Boston. The 1760 **Apthorp House,** still standing but surrounded by newer buildings just off Plympton Street, was built for the first rector, East Apthorp. Its extravagance so shocked Puritans that they dubbed the house "The Bishop's Palace," sparking a controversy so fierce that Apthorp quickly returned to England. Cambridge's oldest church, the former Tory place of worship served as barracks for Connecticut troops, who melted down the organ pipes for bullets during the Revolution. Theodore Roosevelt taught Sunday school here while at **Harvard.** Like the Boston chapel, the church's interior is simple and filled with light.

Cross the street to see **Cambridge Common,** the site of General Washington's main camp from 1775 to 1776, now only a tiny and scruffy traffic island. Continue to Dawes Island (in the middle of Garden Street heading toward Harvard Square) and look for the bronze horseshoes embedded in the sidewalk, marking William Dawes's ride through town on the way to warn the populace in Lexington with the famous cry "The British are coming!" The shoes were given to the city of Cambridge by his descendants as a Bicentennial gift. ◆ Garden St (between Appian Way and Massachusetts Ave)

43 Sheraton Commander $$ Near **Cambridge Common** and a short walk to the Square, this gracious old reliable has 176 understated but pleasant rooms on six floors, in which prominent political guests often stay. A complimentary *Wall Street Journal* is delivered to each room. Eight "executive king" rooms include a sitting area, a small dining area, a canopied bed, and a whirlpool bath. Hotel amenities include a fitness room, multilingual staff, a concierge, a business center, and complimentary valet parking. Rooms for people with disabilities and for nonsmokers are available. **The Brandywine** restaurant serves continental fare. ♦ 16 Garden St (between Berkeley and Mason Sts). 547.4800, 800/325.3535; fax 868.8322 ら

44 Longy School of Music Founded in 1915 and housed in the 1889 **Edwin Abbot Mansion** (listed in the National Register of Historic Places), this very active—and esteemed— music school hosts a wide array of notable concerts of every era and style, in intimate **Pickman Hall**. ♦ 1 Follen St (at Garden St). 876.0956 ら

45 Harvard College Observatory It's open to the public for Observatory Nights, when there's an hour-long lecture-film program geared toward teens (and up), followed by a chance to look through some nifty telescopes—weather permitting. For the "Sky Report," a recorded update of astronomical information, call 491.1497. The domed pavilion is the only surviving element of the original building, designed by **Isaiah Rogers** in 1851. It was built after the appearance of "the Great Comet" in 1843 sparked public interest in astronomy. ♦ Free. Third Thursday of every month. 60 Garden St (at Madison St), north of Harvard Square. 495.9059

46 Henry Wadsworth Longfellow House During the Siege of Boston from 1775 to 1776, George Washington moved his headquarters from **Wadsworth House** near **Harvard Yard** to this stately Georgian residence, built in 1759 by a wealthy Tory, John Vassall, who fled just before the Revolution. Longfellow (pictured above) rented a room here in 1837, then was given the house by his wealthy new father-in-law upon marrying heiress Frances Appleton in 1843. (She died here tragically years later, burned in a fire in the library.) Longfellow wrote many of his famous poems in this mansion, including *Hiawatha* and *Evangeline*. He lived here for 45 years, with prominent literary friends often gathered round. The house has been restored to the poet's period, with thousands of books from his library, plus many of his possessions. Vestiges of the spreading chestnut tree that inspired him were made into a carved armchair, on display, presented as a birthday gift from Cambridge schoolchildren. The home stayed in the Longfellow family until 1973, and is now operated by the National Park Service as a National Historic Site. Call to find out about special events, including children's programs, a celebration of Longfellow's birthday in February, and poetry readings and concerts held on the east lawn in the summer. Half-hour tours are given throughout the day; reserve in advance for groups. A bookstore offers most of the Longfellow books in print, plus books on his life, the literary profession, poetry, and more. Incidentally, the first poem to win national acclaim was Longfellow's *Song of Hiawatha,* published in Boston on 10 November 1855. ♦ Admission; free for those under 16 and over 62. Daily. 105 Brattle St (across from Longfellow Park). 876.4491 ら (staff will assist)

47 Mount Auburn Cemetery The cemetery is worth seeking out for a sunny afternoon stroll and picnic, and fine bird-watching. Now one of its illustrious residents, Henry Wadsworth Longfellow called Mount Auburn the "city of the dead." Founded in 1831, making it the first garden cemetery in America, its 170 acres are verdant with unusual native and rare foreign trees and flowering shrubs. Oliver Wendell Holmes, Isabella Stewart Gardner, Mary Baker Eddy, and Winslow Homer are among the more than 70,000 persons buried here. When it was founded, the cemetery introduced a new concept of interment in the US. Before, colonial burial grounds were rustic graveyards where the dead were buried in an erratic fashion. Grave markers were frequently moved about along with bodies, with the dead's remains even shuttled from one burial ground to another (Boston's cemeteries offer plenty of evidence of these casual practices). But with the creation of Mount Auburn, the idea of commemorating an individual with a permanent, unencroachable burial place was instituted. A ritual of memory took root in America, with personal gravesites becoming a new status symbol. Stop by the office and pick up maps for self-guided walks, either a horticultural tour of more than 3,000 trees, or a walking tour of the cemetery's notable memorials. The Friends of Mount Auburn offers special walks, talks, and other activities. ♦ 580 Mt. Auburn St (bounded by Grove St and Coolidge Ave). 547.7105 ら

Restaurants/Clubs: Red	**Hotels:** Blue
Shops/ 🌳 Outdoors: Green	**Sights/Culture:** Black

Kendall Square

The *Red Line* **Kendall Square T** stop is the closest to the **Massachusetts Institute of Technology (MIT).** Located in the station is a kinetic musical sculpture consisting of three pieces titled *Pythagoras, Kepler,* and *Galileo* by artist/inventor Paul Matisse, grandson of Henri. Commuters crank wall handles on either side of the subway tracks and set large teak hammers into motion, which strike 16 tuned tubular chimes and produce melodious bell-like music—that's *Pythagoras.* Pull another handle a number of times, and a triple-headed steel hammer strikes an aluminum ring, producing a low F-sharp note—that's *Kepler. Galileo's* mechanism makes rumbling, windlike music. In unison, the pleasing concert soothes impatient **T**-riders. The work is part of the **MBTA**'s "Arts on the Line" program, which has commissioned art for 23 Boston-area subway stations.

Massachusetts Institute of Technology was founded in 1861 on the Boston side of the river by William Barton Rogers, a natural scientist. **MIT**'s first president, Rogers envisioned a pragmatic institution fitted to the needs of an increasingly industrialized and mechanized America. The modest technological school, then called **Boston Tech,** moved to its current site in 1916, quite comfortable with its industrial surroundings. **MIT** has never aspired to **Harvard**'s picturesque Olympian aura, but rather has focused on scientific principles as the basis for advanced research and industrial applications. Appropriately, the school's motto is "Mens et Manus" (Mind and Hand). Often referred to as "the factory," the institute grew rapidly and played a significant role in scientific research with the onset of World War II. In hastily assembled laboratories, **Harvard** and **MIT** scientists developed the machinery of modern warfare. In peacetime the same labs have produced instrumentation and guidance devices for NASA and nuclear submarines.

The institute has an international identity, and graduates have founded local, national, and multinational high-tech companies. Today, it has schools of **Engineering, Sciences, Architecture and Planning, Management, Humanities, Health Sciences and Technology,** and **Social Science.**

For general information on **MIT** or to join one of the free student-guided campus tours, lasting just more than an hour and offered weekdays, stop by the **Information Center** (Rogers Building, 77 Massachusetts Ave, 253.4795), open Monday through Friday 9AM to 5PM. Arrange tours in advance if you're with a group.

If you decide to go on your own tour, take a chance on getting lost for a bit in the domed Neo-Classical **Rogers Building** (77 Massachusetts Ave) with its factorylike maze of hallways. Amble across the 150-acre campus weighted with monumental architecture. Despite the institute's well-deserved image as the temple of high-tech, it gives the arts elbow room, too, and has several excellent museums as well as some superb modern architecture and public art. The **MIT Museum** (265 Massachusetts Ave, 253.4444) houses photos, paintings, scientific instruments, and technological artifacts. **The Albert and Vera List Visual Arts Center**'s (Weisner Building, 20 Ames St, First floor, 253.4680) three galleries present challenging art and design in diverse media. If you're an old/young salt or trekking about with kids, visit the little **Hart Nautical Galleries**' (Rogers Building, 77 Massachusetts Ave, First floor, 253.5942) display of ships' models and plans representing vessels from all over the world. If you still have time to spare, walk through *Strobe Alley* (77 Massachusetts Ave, Fourth floor), a demonstration of high-speed stroboscopic equipment and photographs by the late Harold E. "Doc" Edgerton, class of 1927. Admission is free to all but the **MIT Museum.** Call for times; many of the galleries close during the summer.

Weisner Building
COURTESY OF PEI, COBB, FREED & PARTNERS

East Campus, on the east side of Massachusetts Avenue, has an impersonal, businesslike look, particularly since new office and research buildings have sprouted around Kendall Square since the early 1980s. In the last few years Main Street at Kendall Square has gotten a sprucing up, with the arrival of a major hotel and numerous cafes and restaurants. **MIT** has, fortunately, preserved a network of big green spaces, where fine outdoor art can be found. In Killian Court behind the **Rogers Building** is Henry Moore's *Three-Piece Reclining Figure* (erected in 1976). (Another Moore work, *Reclining Figure,* is located off Ames Street between **Whitaker College** and **I.M. Pei**'s **Weisner Building, Center for Arts & Media Technology**, pictured above). Michael Heizer's sculpture *Guennette* stands opposite.

Looming over Killian Court is the **Great Dome, MIT**'s architectural focus. From this grassy expanse, the view to the river and Boston beyond is magnificent. At McDermott Court, look for **I.M. Pei**'s **Green Building, Center for Earth Sciences** (constructed in 1964). In front is the giant black-steel sculpture *La Grande Voile* ("The Big Sail"), designed by Alexander Calder. Nearby is a 1975 black-steel sculpture by Louise Nevelson called *Transparent Horizon.* At the end of Main Street near the Longfellow Bridge is a small outdoor plaza adorned with a controversial creation called *Galaxy* by sculptor Joe Davis. The focal point is a meteoritelike stainless-steel globe encrusted with strange topographic textures and patterns, clouds of steam billowing from below. The mysterious globe is ringed by 12 smaller ones that cast unusual illuminations at night. Picasso's *Figure découpée* (completed in 1963) stands in front of the **Hermann Building** at the far east end of campus. A five-mile system of underground passages, the "infinite corridor," connects the **East Campus** buildings.

The **MIT Press Bookstore** (292 Main St, 253.5249) sells scholarly books and journals on engineering, computer science, architecture, philosophy, linguistics, economics, and more; and the **MIT Coop** (3 Cambridge Center, 499.3200) is the scion of the **Harvard Coop.** Boston's punk population—as well as the merely bargain-savvy—outfit themselves at the **Garment District** (200 Broadway, 876.5230), where vintage clothing mingles with Doc Martens.

For a variety of dining options, visit the **One Kendall Square** (Hampshire St, at Broadway) development, a handsomely renovated factory complex. It's home to **The Blue Room** (494.9034), a jazzy modernist boîte where the floor show consists of chef Stan Frankenthaler's boisterous world-beat cooking; **Goemon Japanese Noodle Restaurant** (577.9595), specializing in noodle dishes and tempura; the **Cambridge Brewing Company** (494.1994), a comfortable pub/restaurant where you can sample the company's own beers and ales.

Another chapter of the famous local **Legal Sea Foods** (5 Cambridge Center, 864.3400) empire is here. All kinds of fresh fish are served just about any way you could imagine in this crowded and noisy place. Accommodations can be had at the **Boston Marriott Cambridge** (2 Cambridge Center, 494.6600).

West Campus, west of Massachusetts Avenue, has a more residential and relaxed atmosphere. Look for **Kresge Auditorium,** designed in 1955 by **Eero Saarinen,** unmistakable with its curving roof, one-eighth of a sphere resting on three abutments and floating free of the auditorium structure beneath. Also by **Saarinen,** the exquisite interfaith **MIT Chapel** is illuminated by a skylight that focuses light on the altar and is surrounded by a small moat that casts reflections upward on the interior walls. Harry Bertoia designed the sculpture behind the altar. Sought after as a site for weddings, the cylindrical structure is topped by Theodore Roszak's aluminum belltower and bell.

Baker House
COURTESY OF THE MIT MUSEUM AND SAMUEL CHAMBERLA

Nearby is **Baker House** (pictured above), a 1949 dormitory designed by **Alvar Aalto,** whose serpentine form cleverly maximizes views of the Charles, and the **Miracle of Science** (321 Massachusetts Ave, 828.2866), a newfangled bar and grill modeled (loosely) on a chem lab.

East Cambridge

This multicultural community—predominantly Italian and Portuguese—was once a prosperous Yankee enclave. In the 19th century factories turning out glass, furniture, soap, boxes, woven hose, and other goods flourished along the Charles, and the "Quality Row" of fine town houses sprung up (now 83-95 Third St). Then, slowly, the riverside industries declined. After suffering through decades as a forgotten backwater, East Cambridge recently underwent major urban renewal and development. Look for the magnificently restored **Bulfinch Superior Courthouse Building,** original site of the Middlesex County court system, now occupied by the **Cambridge Multicultural Arts Center** (41 Second St, 577.1400) with its two galleries and theater.

A new addition to the neighborhood is the **Cambridgeside Galleria** (pictured above) on

First Street, where you'll find the **Lechmere** (491.2000) department store, a local institution that sells anything and everything for the home at bargain prices. **Filene's** (621.3800) and **Sears** (252.3500) are also here, along with many other shops, services, and **The Sports Museum of New England** (see the "Charles River Basin" chapter).

Nearby is pleasant **Lechmere Canal Park** with its lagoon and 50-foot geyser. Bostonians and Cantabrigians alike flock to **Michela's** (1 Atheneum St, 225.3366), loved for innovative Italian fare, including consistently marvelous pastas and sauces made fresh daily by chef Jody Adams.

Central Square/Riverside

Central Square is a sprawling area located straight down Massachusetts Avenue toward Boston. The section of Cambridge most resistant to gentrification, it also claims the greatest concentration of international restaurants and interesting clubs. Close to Harvard Square, and relatively upscale, **Cafe Sushi** (1105 Massachusetts Ave, 492.0434) offers a spectrum of sushi and sashimi. **Dolphin Seafood** (1105 Massachusetts Ave, 661.2937) is a friendly little family place serving good and reasonably priced seafood. **Roka** (1001 Massachusetts Ave, 661.0344) serves an extensive array of superior Japanese dishes and sushi. Located off Massachusetts Avenue, **Cremaldi's** (31 Putnam Ave, 354.7969) is a neighborhood grocery/cafe with European distinction. **Mimi's Oriental Grill** (950 Massachusetts Ave, 354.1665) serves spicy Szechuan specialties in an elegant modern setting. **Pampas** (928 Massachusetts Ave, 661.6613) has cornered the market on South American *churrasco*-style meat (spit-roasted over an open-fire, then carved tableside). In Central Square proper, **Middle East Restaurant** (472 Massachusetts Ave, 492.9181, 354.8238), a combination restaurant/nightclub, books some interesting eclectic acts. **Mary Chung** (447 Massachusetts Ave, 864.1991) is a modest-looking place with superb Mandarin and Szechuan specialties. Central Square has lots of noteworthy Indian restaurants, the best of which is **India Pavilion** (17 Central Sq, 547.7463). Stellar pastries—cafe fare, too—can be found at **Cézanne** (424 Massachusetts Ave, 547.9616).

Heading toward Boston down Main Street, off Massachusetts Avenue, is **Al's Lunch** (901 Main St, 661.5810), a whimsical little storefront luncheonette serving tasty breakfasts and lunches. Next door you'll find some of the best ice cream anywhere, at **Toscanini's** (899 Main St, 491.5877). For superb regional American cuisine, visit **Anago** (798 Main St, 876.8444). For home-style Italian cuisine, try **LaGroceria** (853 Main St,

547.9258). A little out of the way, but worth the effort, **Green Street Grill** (280 Green St, 876.1655) shares space with old-time **Charlie's Tap** and serves flamboyant dishes with Caribbean influence in a funky setting.

Evening entertainment in Central Square centers on music of all kinds, with clubs ranging from neighborhood-casual to somewhat chic. Starting off with the tiniest and rowdiest, stop in **The Plough and Stars** (912 Massachusetts Ave, 492.9653) an Irish pub with live Irish blues, country, and bluegrass music. You can hear local bands and dance the night away at the **Cantab Lounge** (738 Massachusetts Ave, 354.2685). **T.T. The Bear's Place** (10 Brookline St, 492.0082) is a homey rock 'n' roll club featuring local bands. An art-bar featuring progressive New Wave and rock dancing, **Manray** (21 Brookline St, 864.0400) connects to **Campus**, a predominantly gay jukebox joint. Six blocks off Massachusetts Avenue—don't walk it at night—is the **Western Front** (343 Western Ave, 492.7772), a long-lived club known for reggae, rasta, and more that's great for dancing. Cambridge's best-looking club, built expressly for music, is **Nightstage** (823 Main St, 497.8200), which books a wide variety of great bands.

Central Square has quite a few interesting shops, including two gold-mine record shops, **Cheapo Records** (645 Massachusetts Ave, 354.4455), and **Skippy White's** (555 Massachusetts Ave, 491.3345). Inexpensive (men-only) lodging is available at the **YMCA** (820 Massachusetts Ave, 661.9622). Accommodations are what you'd expect: tiny rooms, shared baths, recreational facilities, and some house regulations.

Inman Square

A 20-minute walk south on Cambridge Street from Harvard Square (or the same distance east on Prospect Street from Central Square), Inman Square is a quieter residential district with a surprising array of great restaurants, both ethnic and American, and an outstanding club or two. (It used to have many more.) The square is slowly being gentrified, shedding much of its character as a family neighborhood with a variety of ethnic populations. It's definitely worth making a dinnertime journey here. Although renovated beyond recognition, the **S&S Restaurant Deli** (1334 Cambridge St, 354.0777) is an Inman Square old-timer, serving traditional and gourmet deli-diner fare.

New Korea (1281 Cambridge St, 876.6182) is one of Greater Boston's best spots for authentic Korean cuisine. The nationally known and very popular **East Coast Grill** (1271 Cambridge St, 491.6568) will more than satisfy cravings for gourmet barbecue and great grilled fare. Next door is **Jake &**

Earl's Dixie BBQ (1273 Cambridge St, 491.7427), owned by **East Coast Grill,** which purveys simpler, cheaper, but also delicious barbecue and fixings to go. **Chez Vous** (1263 Cambridge St, 868.3161) features such Caribbean staples as conch and goat; everything's highly spiced. **Cafe China** (1245 Cambridge St, 868.4300) serves gourmet Chinese. For spicy cooking, try **Magnolia's** (1193 Cambridge St, 576.1971). Come with a ravenous group to homey family-run **Casa Portugal** (1200 Cambridge St, 491.8880) to enjoy heaping helpings of excellent Portuguese cuisine. **Daddy O's Bohemian Cafe** (134 Hampshire St, 354.8371) affects a beatnik decor but proffers bourgeois 1950s comfort food, along with contemporary cuisine. For after-dinner music, go to **Ryles** (212 Hampshire St, 876.9330), a casual and comfortable jazz club booking top local and national acts; or **Cantares** (15 Springfield St, 547.6300), a Latin-American restaurant that also features merengue and salsa dance music and blues jam sessions. For dessert, visit **Rosie's** (243 Hampshire St, 491.9488) for "chocolate orgasms" and other sinfully delicious treats.

North Cambridge

First, three pleasant dining prospects are worth a jog westward, toward Fresh Pond via Concord Avenue. **The Peacock** (5 Craigie Circle, 661.4073) offers marvelous French country cooking. **Chez Nous** (147 Huron Ave, 864.6670) demands a special trip for superb French cuisine. Come back the next day for brunch at folksy, well-worn **Pentimento** (344 Huron Ave, 661.3878).

Now head northward on Massachusetts Avenue toward Porter Square: **Chez Jean** (1 Shepherd St, 354.8980) offers tasty bistro-style French food. Stop in for enchiladas at **Mexican Cuisine** (1682 Massachusetts Ave, 661.1634) which shares space with a noisy bar. **Changsho** (1712 Massachusetts Ave, 547.6565) is magnificently decorated, offering a wide array of Chinese dishes. **Boca Grande** (1728 Massachusetts Ave, 354.7400) serves some of the tastiest Mexican fare anywhere. **Half Shell** (1760A Massachusetts Ave, 661.6580), a "modern diner," offers moderately priced pizzas. **Matsu-Ya** (1790 Massachusetts Ave, 491.5091) serves good Japanese and Korean dishes. The **Cottonwood Cafe** (661.7440) and its downscaled sidekick, **Snakebites Cantina** (354.6555), serve neo–Tex-Mex fare (both at 1815 Massachusetts Ave). **Christopher's** (1920 Massachusetts Ave, 876.9180) is popular with locals for its pubby atmosphere. For Lebanese and Greek cuisine and belly dancers, go to **Averof** (1924 Massachusetts Ave, 354.4500). **Tapas** (2067 Massachusetts Ave, 576.2240) offers

reasonably priced tasting portions of an international cuisine. And **Ristorante Marino** (2465 Massachusetts Ave, 868.5454) features cooking from the Abruzzi region of Italy, and uses all natural, organic products from local farms in its food preparation.

Massachusetts Avenue toward Porter Square also offers interesting shopping, including international clothing boutiques, shops purveying natural foods and products, and antiques. **Pepperweed** (1684 Massachusetts Ave, 547.7561) sells contemporary attire from American, Japanese, and European designers. Particularly numerous are vintage clothing and accessories stores, including **Red Dog Antiques** (1737 Massachusetts Ave, 354.9676); **Atalanta** (1766 Massachusetts Ave, 661.2673); and **Vintage Etc.** (1796 Massachusetts Ave, 497.1516). **Joie de Vivre** (1792 Massachusetts Ave, 864.8188) is a delightful shop selling unusual and artful trinkets and gifts. This stretch of Massachusetts Avenue includes several excellent children's stores, including **The Children's Workshop** (1963 Massachusetts Ave, at Porter Sq, 354.1633). **The Music Emporium** (2018 Massachusetts Ave, 661.2099) sells old and antique stringed instruments as well as acoustic and folk-related music and instruments. Keep on going until you get to **Kate's Mystery Books** (2211 Massachusetts Ave, 491.2660), an eccentric "Murder-Mystery Central" for all of New England.

For elegant digs, try **A Cambridge House Inn** (2218 Massachusetts Ave, 491.6300, 800/232.9989; fax 868.2848) bed-and-breakfast inn (pictured above), built in 1892 and listed on the National Register of Historic Places. Its 17 rooms (ten with private baths) are handsomely restored and decorated, and an elaborate breakfast is complimentary.

Thomas Brattle—the early Harvard College treasurer for whom Brattle Street was named—ensured himself a spirited send-off by bequeathing "a half crown bill to each of the students of Harvard College that shall come to my funeral."

Restaurants/Clubs: Red		**Hotels:** Blue
Shops/ ☂ Outdoors: Green		**Sights/Culture:** Black

Bests

Kristine Fayerman-Piatt
Owner/General Manager, **Cornucopia on the Wharf**

The **Isabella Stewart Gardner Museum**—particularly the interior courtyard—a visit to another era in Boston; every wall crammed with works of art.

The African tropical animal exhibit at the **Franklin Park Zoo**—very un-Boston; I especially like the pygmy hippo.

A stroll down **Hanover Street** in Boston's **North End** on a warm summer's evening—like being in Italy.

Jeffrey Twiss
Director of Public Relations, **Boston Celtics**

Fenway Park—unique pro-baseball stadium.

Museum of Science—terrific displays.

Mugar Theatre—great feature films.

Aquarium—always a treat for any age.

JFK Museum—something everyone must see.

Boston Common (summer)—**Swan Boats** and people watching!

Faneuil Hall—great stores and food!

Children's Museum—great hands-on stuff.

Top of **Prudential Tower**—outstanding views of Boston

Filene's Basement—great bargains on clothes!

Sports Museum—anything about New England sports is here!

Legal Sea Foods restaurant—the *best* in seafood!!

Bill Caruso
Environmental Consultant and Attorney/Greenthink Environmental Co.

Arnold Arboretum, Jamaica Plain—walking, biking, picnics.

Jamaica Pond—walking, sailing, rowing.

Commercial Wharf harbor cruises—whale watching, jazz cruise.

Isabella Stewart Gardner Museum—central courtyard, cafe, classical galleries.

McKim, Mead & White's **Boston Public Library,** Copley Square—superb.

Trinity Episcopal, Copley Square—an **H.H. Richardson** masterpiece.

Plaza Bar, Copley Square, **Copley Plaza Hotel**—good jazz (traditional).

Swan Boats, Boston Public Garden, Charles River Esplanade—biking, jogging, concerts (in season).

Newbury Street, Back Bay—window shopping.

Parker's Bar, Parker House Hotel—martinis.

The Last Hurrah! Parker House Hotel—tasteful swing music, good chowder.

Legal Sea Foods restaurants—several locations, good fresh fish.

Ellen E. Rooney
Chairman, Boston Licensing Board

A good introduction to the city is a view from the **John Hancock Tower** observation deck. On a clear day, the view is spectacular. It's a good way to get one's bearings.

Boston is a city of neighborhoods. In addition to the selection of restaurants downtown (the variety of Italian restaurants in the **North End,** Chinese and Vietnamese offerings in **Chinatown**), why not sample an Irish breakfast in the **Allston/Brighton** area, Dorchester, or South Boston, or try one of the Vietnamese restaurants on **Dorchester Avenue.**

As an avid reader, one of my favorite haunts is the **Avenue Victor Hugo** in Newbury Street. It's a secondhand bookstore that carries a careful selection of fiction, nonfiction, and classics, as well as a good stock of literary magazines. Another favorite is the **Boston Public Library** in **Copley Square.** I've always loved browsing there, and the **McKim Building** is a treasure.

I try to cut through the **Public Garden** on a regular basis. It's especially beautiful in spring, when the flowers are in bloom, but it's just as lovely in winter, after a snowfall.

The tree-edged terrace just outside the **Museum of Fine Arts Cafeteria** is a pleasant place to read the Sunday papers over a cup of coffee. It's conducive to solitude, but also convenient for families with young children.

In my neighborhood, the **Back Bay,** I recommend a stroll down **Marlborough Street** in summer, both for the architecture and the gardens. I like to walk down the **Commonwealth Avenue Mall** during all seasons. And, of course, there's the shopping and eating available on **Newbury Street,** a prime people-watching site, from the vantage point of a sidewalk cafe.

The *Mapparium,* in the **Christian Science Publishing Society,** is interesting for adults, as well as children. Although names of countries have changed through the decades, it's still fun to stand inside it and get a real sense of our placement in the world.

Those 45-minute harbor cruises are a good way to get the city into perspective. Seeing the skyline from the water shows the city in all its splendor.

Lydia Shire
Chef/Owner, Biba

Shopping on **Newbury Street.**

Swan Boat rides and feeding the swans in the Public Garden.

Cape Cod in August.

A late-night meal at **Moon Villa** in Chinatown.

Driving on **Memorial Drive** from Harvard Square to Boston, and out to Lincoln in the fall for pumpkins.

Mai tais at **Mr. Leung.**

Sipping cocktails at **Jasper's.**

Other Neighborhoods

Boston's outer neighborhoods are close-knit communities with distinctive personalities. And that makes sense, since most of them developed independently before being absorbed by Boston. Even more than landfilling, annexation increased the city's size. Boston was an overcrowded seaport in 1850, but by 1900 the metropolis had flung itself across a 10-mile radius and engulfed 31 cities and towns. Public transportation—horsecars, followed by electric trolleys—made it possible for people to live in "streetcar suburbs" within easy traveling distance to their workplaces. The expanding middle-class and immigrant families began moving beyond Old Boston, rapidly swelling the commuter ranks, so now these many Boston neighborhoods are largely residential, with a smattering of important historical, recreational, and cultural attractions.

Charlestown

The **North End** and this neighborhood stare at one another across the mouth of the **Charles River**. Now a small satellite that's rather tricky to get to—reached by crossing the **Charlestown Bridge** by car or on foot, departing by boat from **Long Wharf** in the summer, or riding an **MBTA** bus—Charlestown was actually settled one year before Boston, in 1629. Most of the harborside town was burned by the British during the Battle of Bunker Hill in 1775, then rapidly rebuilt as a flourishing port where wealthy captains and ship owners lived in grand mansions on the hillsides. The opening of the **Charlestown Navy Yard** brought jobs and prosperity from the 1800s to the early 1900s, attracting waves of European immigrants while well-to-do families moved out. Charlestown was annexed to Boston in 1874. Maritime activities began shrinking and the Great Depression increased the neighborhood's economic woes. Charlestown deteriorated faster as the **Navy Yard** dwindled and was finally shut down by the federal government in 1974. But the neighborhood has been rebounding steadily, with the beautifully sited **Navy Yard** transformed into residential, office, retail, and medical-research space. Many have recognized the charm of Charlestown's narrow colonial streets bordered by neat little residences. A predominantly white, Irish-American enclave since the turn of the century, Charlestown is still a family-oriented neighborhood entrenched in tradition. Young professionals have been moving in, however, and change is afoot that will further open up this insular spot. At press time, two parks (**Thompson Square** and **City Square Park**) were slated to be completed.

Ordinarily visible from Copp's Hill in the North End, the USS *Constitution* is the oldest commissioned ship in the US Navy, maintained to this day by Navy personnel. Launched 21 October 1797 in Boston, the ship (pictured at left) served in Thomas Jefferson's campaign against the Barbary pirates, and won 42

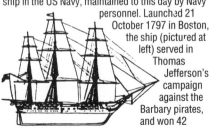

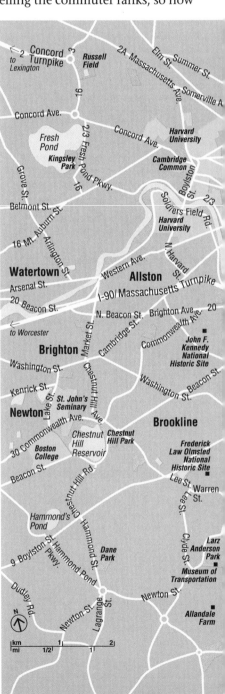

battles in the War of 1812, never losing once. Nicknamed "Old Ironsides" for its combat-proven wooden hull, not for any iron plating, the ship (except when under repair) is permanently moored at Constitution Wharf in the **Charlestown Navy Yard.** (It makes one tour—called the "turnaround"—of the harbor every Fourth of July, to remain a commissioned warship, and to face a different side of the ship to the sun and wind upon return.)

At press time, top-to-bottom tours—including the claustrophobic living quarters below deck—had been suspended for restorations to the ship, but tours of the berthing decks are still scheduled daily (call 242.5670 for more information). The **Constitution Museum** (Constitution Wharf, 426.1812) screens a film revealing more of the ship than the tours ever did, as well as all of "Old Ironsides's" history, to compensate.

The enormous **Charlestown Navy Yard** (242.5601) was founded in 1800 to build warships and evolved over 170 years to meet the Navy's changing requirements. A National Historic Park, the distinguished-looking navy yard is a physical record of American shipbuilding history. Among its 19th-century workshops, barracks, and other structures: the **Ropewalk**—the last in existence—designed by

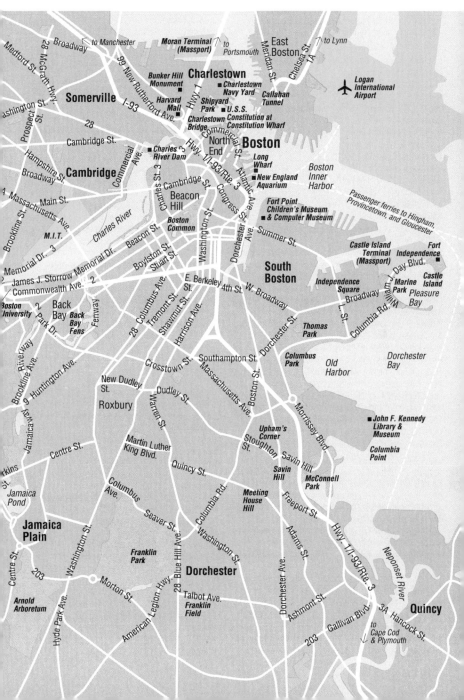

Other Neighborhoods

Alexander Parris in 1836 and nearly a quarter-mile long, where all rope for the navy was made for 135 years; **Dry Dock Number 1,** tied with a Virginia dry dock as the first in the US, and called Constitution Dock because "Old Ironsides" was the first ship to dock here; the ornate **Telephone Exchange Building,** completed in 1852; and the **Commandant's House,** an 1809 Georgian mansion. You can also board the USS *Cassin Young,* a World War II destroyer of the kind once built here. Originally a pumphouse, the **Constitution Museum** (242.1812) displays original documents and other important artifacts from the historic vessel; it is open daily, and there is an admission charge. Before leaving, visit **Shipyard Park** on the waterfront.

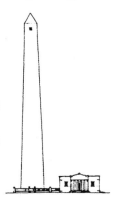

Every American schoolchild learns how the Battle of Bunker Hill was really fought on **Breed's Hill,** where **Solomon Willard**'s **Bunker Hill Monument** (242.5641) now points to the sky (pictured at right), visible from many Boston locations. The hill rises from the midst of formal **Monument Square** and its handsomely preserved 1840s town houses.

Climb the grassy slope to the monument, part of the **Boston National Historic Park.** The Marquis de Lafayette laid the cornerstone in 1825, visiting the US for the first time since his days as a dashing youthful hero. The monument was finally completed in 1843, and Daniel Webster orated at the dedication. The 220-foot-tall obelisk of Quincy granite rises from the area where, on 17 June 1775, Colonel William Prescott reportedly ordered his citizen's militia not to fire "until you see the whites of their eyes." The Redcoats ultimately seized the hill, but suffered more than 1,300 casualties, a devastating cost that boosted the colonists' morale. Climb the 295 steps to the monument observatory for fine views; back at the bottom, notice the dioramas portraying the battle. It's open daily, and there's no admission charge. Boston Park Rangers offer free talks in the summer.

Leave Monument Square and descend serene Monument Avenue to Main Street. If you visit the **Bunker Hill Monument** late in the afternoon and then dawdle, you can plan on enjoying a wonderful dinner at **Olives** (★★★$$; 10 City Sq, 242.1999). Olivia and Todd English's bistro-style restaurant is friendly, noisy, and known for such creatively rustic dishes as savory tarts, bouillabaisse, spit-roasted chicken, and butternut-squash raviolini; many of the specialties are cooked in a wood-burning brick oven. Reservations are accepted only for six or more, so get your name on the list very early—at least by 5:30PM. That likely means an early dinner, but it's the only way to ensure seating. As a fallback, there's always **Figs** (★$; 67 Main St, 242.2229), a plainer pizza-and-pasta offshoot with the same owners. Or bide some time at the circa-1780 **Warren Tavern**

(2 Pleasant St, 241.8142) nearby, with drinks and plenty of atmosphere. Named for the Revolutionary War hero General Joseph Warren, who died in the Battle of Bunker Hill, the tavern also serves dinner. You could then continue your sight-seeing on **Main Street** up **Town Hill** to **Harvard Mall** (on the National Register of Historic Places); the young minister John Harvard and his family lived near here. When Harvard died at 31, he bequeathed half of his fortune and all of his library to the college in Cambridge that adopted his name in thanks. At the mall's edge is charming **Harvard Square**—not to be confused with the famous square in Cambridge—and its modest mid-19th century dwellings. Leaving Charlestown, visit the **Charles River Dam Visitors' Information Center** (250 Warren Ave, City Sq, 727.0059) on the river, for a 12-minute multimedia presentation explaining the Charles River Dam's operations: flood control, fish ladders, and boat locks. You can also take guided tours of the dam, which has one of the mightiest pumping stations in the country.

South Boston

Expanded by landfill since the 18th century, South Boston ("Southie") is now a peninsula of approximately four square miles, with broad beaches and parks. Founded in 1630 as part of Dorchester, it was largely undeveloped until annexed to Boston in 1804, with the first bridge to Boston built the next year. Then real-estate speculators arrived, and Yankee gentry built handsome wooden houses along **East Broadway** and around **Thomas Park** on **Telegraph Hill.** With the building of bridges to Boston, railways, and growth of industry, the arrival of great numbers of Irish-Americans at century's end established the tight-knit neighborhood known as "Southie" today. Lithuanians, Poles, and Italians also settled here. The wealthy merchants moved out as immigrants moved in and Back Bay became the latest magnet for fashion seekers. Like Charlestown and East Boston, South Boston is a white enclave with a family focus and few minority residents. More than half the neighborhood population is of Irish ancestry, and a major local event is the annual St. Patrick's Day parade and festivities. Drive in for great views of the harbor and islands from **Day Boulevard** and **Castle Island** at **Marine Park.** On the island (actually no longer an island), visit star-shaped **Fort Independence** (727.5290). It's open afternoons from Memorial Day to Labor Day, and free tours are offered. Then walk along **Pleasure Bay,** designed by Frederick Law Olmsted. Near the fort is a statue of Donald McKay, who designed Boston clipper ships, including the famous *Flying Cloud.* Southie abuts the **Fort Point Artists' Community,** formerly an industrial and wool-processing area where the **Children's Museum** and the **Computer Museum** are now grand attractions (see the "Waterfront/Fort Point Channel" chapter). A popular Irish bar complete with priests is near the **Broadway T** station. **Amrhein's** (★$; 80 West Broadway St, 268.6189) is family owned and run. A century old, it has the oldest beer-pump system in Boston, and the oldest hand-carved wooden bar in the country. People come from all over for great meat-and-potatoes meals, fabulous onion rings, and of course, beer.

Dorchester

If it weren't part of Boston, racially, ethnically, and economically diverse Dorchester would be an important Massachusetts city in its own right. Originally, it was even larger and included South Boston and Hyde Park. Dorchester is an area of intimate neighborhoods, like the close-knit **Polish Triangle,** or **Dudley,** home to Hispanic and Cape Verdean families. **Dorchester Avenue,** nicknamed "Dot Ave," is the community's spine, with lots of ethnic and family-owned businesses: Irish pubs and bakeries are alongside Southeast Asian markets alongside West Indian grocers selling curries and spices. In 1630 the Puritans landed at Mattapannock, today called **Columbia Point,** and, fearing Indian attacks, established homesteads near a fort atop **Savin Hill. Upham's Corner** was once known as **Burying Place Corner** because of the cemetery founded there in 1633, the **Dorchester North Burying Ground.** Nearby is Boston's oldest standing house, the 1648 **Blake House** (735 Columbia Rd); both the burying ground and house are on the National Register of Historic Places. Atop **Meeting House Hill** is the **Mather School** (1 Parish St, 635.8757), the oldest elementary school in the nation, founded in 1639 as a one-room schoolhouse.

From **Dorchester Heights,** patriots commanded a clear view of the Redcoats during the Siege of Boston in 1776. Here George Washington and his men set up cannons, heroically hauled through the wilderness for three months by Boston bookseller-turned-general Henry Knox. The guns were trained on the British, powerful persuasion that convinced them to flee for good. It is now a National Historic Site, with a monument, located in **Thomas Park** (off Telegraph St, near G St, 242.5642). At press time the monument was closed for restoration; call before going, unless you only want to view it from the outside. The park is open daily.

Dorchester was an agricultural community well into the 1800s. Gradually, rich Bostonians built country estates and summer residences on its southern hilltops. In the early 1800s commercial villages grew up along the **Neponset River** and the waterfront. With the electric tram's inauguration in 1857, Dorchester became a suburb of Boston, annexed in 1869. Lovely Victorians are sprinkled throughout this neighborhood, but the best-known architectural style in Dorchester is its distinctive three-family houses called "three-deckers," which became the rage in the early 1900s. But after World War II the suburban ideal of single-family homes and shopping malls emerged, and Dorchester suffered from flight and neglect. Though still not a safe place to wander, attempts are being made to upgrade its image. One sign of the neighborhood's vitality is the rejuvenation of the 1918 **Strand Theater** (Upham's Corner, 282.8000), a former movie palace restored as a grand venue for performing arts and community events.

Make an appointment for a free tour explaining how a major metropolitan daily gets printed every day, as *The Boston Globe* (135 Morrissey Blvd, 929.2653)

has been for more than 120 years. The hourlong tours are scheduled Tuesday and Thursday, with a 15-minute film included.

The **John F. Kennedy Library and Museum** (Columbia Pt, 929.4500. ☐), a 1979 design of **I.M. Pei & Partners,** couldn't find a home in Cambridge and landed out on Columbia Point—inconvenient for tourists but a dramatic site with glorious unobstructed views of the ocean. The stark, magnificent library is the official repository of JFK's presidential papers and many personal belongings. The library archives contain all of his papers, classified and declassified, all of his speeches on film and video, and also Robert F. Kennedy's senatorial papers. The museum displays seven exhibitions on JFK and two on RFK, with tapes and videos. The library also possesses 95 percent of Ernest Hemingway's works. Admission is charged to the museum; there are discounts for senior citizens and children under 16. Children under six are free. Also in the neighborhood is the **Bayside Exposition Center** (200 Mt. Vernon St, 825.5151), where trade shows and events are held.

Jamaica Plain

Originally part of neighboring Roxbury, Jamaica Plain ("JP" to Bostonians) was once fertile farmland. In the late 1800s it became a summer resort for wealthy Back Bay and Beacon Hill residents, who drove their carriages along the tree-shaded Jamaicaway to pass the season at splendid estates surrounding Jamaica Pond—"The Pond." On the other side of town, thousands of factory workers labored in JP's 17 breweries, all of which eventually closed. (Boston Beer Company, maker of the multi-award-winning Samuel Adams Lager Beer, took up the torch of tradition in 1984.) In the 1830s railroads began bringing well-to-do commuters who built Greek Revival, Italianate, and mansard residences; in the 1870s streetcars brought the growing middle class. Today JP is one of Boston's most integrated neighborhoods, its three square miles filled mostly with families.

Centre Street developed early as JP's main artery and retains its small-town character. Along its bumpy, narrow length are good, cheap ethnic restaurants, bodegas, Irish pubs, mom-and-pop stores, and a slowly growing number of upscale establishments. Boston has few vegetarian restaurants, and one of its very good ones is macrobiotic **Five Seasons** (★$; 669A Centre St, 524.9016), offering simply prepared, innovative international dishes. Read the paper over coffee and a treat at spacious and spare **Today's Bread** (★$; 701 Centre St, 522.6458), with its big windows on the street, wonderful croissants—try the poppy seed-and-cheese–muffins, desserts, quiches, salads, and sandwiches.

One of Boston's best Irish bars and a local institution is **Doyle's Cafe** (★★$; 3483 Washington St, 524.2345), with its famous clock logo. In a cavernous vintage setting full of memorabilia, try fine Irish coffee and Bloody Marys, abundant brunches, basic delicious food, and a variety of beers on tap.

Some of the loveliest sections of Frederick Law Olmsted's **Emerald Necklace** are in or border Jamaica Plain: Jamaica Pond, the **Arnold Arboretum,** (see page 151) and **Franklin Park** (see page 152). The city's last working farm is likewise in JP: **Allandale Farm** (259 Allandale Rd, 524.1531), open from May to Christmas Day. As spring turns to summer turns to fall, you can buy plants, fruits, vegetables, apples, pumpkins, cider pressed on the premises, and Christmas trees and wreaths. The farm has been operating on the old **Brandegee Estate** for more than 125 years.

Brookline

Actually, Brookline isn't part of Boston—although not for lack of Boston's trying. When the cramped city began busily annexing towns to solve its land crunch, independent-minded Brookline refused to be swallowed. It is home to an increasingly diverse ethnic population, and is a somewhat expensive place to live.

Coolidge Corner (pictured above), where Harvard and Beacon Streets meet, is a mini-Harvard Square with old-fashioned and new-fashioned establishments. The **Coolidge Corner Theatre** (290 Harvard St, 734.2500), was saved from the development scourge by movie lovers, and offers interesting, intelligent vintage and contemporary films. A few blocks from the theater is John F. Kennedy's birthplace (29 May 1917). Open daily (there's an admission charge except for senior citizens and children under 12), it is now called the **John F. Kennedy National Historic Site** (83 Beals St, 566.7937). The Kennedys lived here until 1921.

An undiscovered gem in Brookline is the **Frederick Law Olmsted National Historic Site,** (99 Warren St, 566.1689) the rambling home and office named "Fairsted" by its owner, who was America's first landscape architect and founder of the profession in this country. Olmsted's successor firm practiced here until 1980, and the site archives are now open to the public Friday through Sunday or by appointment other days. On display here are valuable plans, photographs, and other documentation of the firm's work. No admission is charged.

If you're hungry, try one of the excellent local delis, like **B & D Deli** (★$; 1653 Beacon St, 232.3727); or

kosher **Rubin's** ($; 500 Harvard St, 731.8787) on the Allston border. Have a casual, delicious dinner at the **Tam O'Shanter** (★$$; 1648 Beacon St, 277.0982), nicknamed "The Tam," which doubles as a club. Also casual, the **Harvard Street Grill** (★★$$$; 398 Harvard St, 734.9834) offers a calmer, more refined setting and elegant American cuisine like lobster terrine and watercress, grilled rack of lamb, and pork loin with pistachios. Parking, by the way, is limited to two hours during the day and notoriously impossible overnight, when all visitors' cars on the street between 2AM and 6AM are subject to ticketing.

The **Museum of Transportation** (Carriage House, Larz Anderson Park, 15 Newton St, 522.6140) is also in Brookline and explores the cultural and sociological impact of the automobile on American society. Open Wednesday through Sunday, special exhibitions on other transportation topics, such as German aviation are shown here as well. Admission is charged.

Allston-Brighton

Polyglot Allston-Brighton is Boston's most integrated district, where Irish, Italians, Greeks, and Russians are joined by growing numbers of Asians, African-Americans, and Hispanics. Most Bostonians associate this neighborhood with students from the local universities, large numbers of whom live here. An agricultural community founded in 1635, the neighborhood later was the locale for huge stockyards, slaughterhouses, and meat-packing operations serving the region, then became industrialized. Since World War II there has been dramatic change led by the construction of the Massachusetts Turnpike, which further split Allston from Brighton, already divided by railroad tracks. Allston-Brighton has developed in a haphazard way that makes it confusing to navigate, but it has many pleasant streets with nice old homes, apartment buildings, and a cozy feel. The neighborhoods have innumerable ethnic restaurants and markets, pubs, interesting shops, and antiques stores. A popular hangout is **Harper's Ferry** (156 Brighton Ave, 254.9743), an established blues club; also, **The Sunset Grill and Tap** (130 Brighton Ave, 254.1331) is known for its international array of beers.

Somerville

Once primarily a working-class suburb, Somerville has grown increasingly popular with students and yuppies crowded—or priced—out of Cambridge. There's a steadily growing restaurant/club scene. Try **Dali** (★★★$$; 415 Washington St, 661.3254), an authentic and lively Spanish restaurant with irresistible tapas—great for satisfying multiple urges or for groups that are into sharing. **Redbones** (★★$; 55 Chester St, 628.2200) stands out for its authentic southern barbecue. The **Elephant Walk** (★★$$; 70 Union Sq, 623.9939) is a Cambodian-French venue guaranteed to intrigue the most jaded palate. Catch some rock at **Johnny D's Uptown** (17 Holland St, 776.2004); or for music of a more improvisational nature, stroll into the **Willow Jazz Club** (699 Broadway, 623.9874).

Child's Play

With its participatory museums and ubiquitous parks, Boston is a city custom-designed for family sightseeing—provided you don't hard-sell too many of the educational aspects (a temptation to anyone who tends to romanticize such historical events as the midnight ride of Paul Revere and the Boston Tea Party).

Start the minute you hit town. The best way to approach the "Hub" (as Boston is often called) from the airport is not by land, but by sea—specifically, on the **Airport Water Shuttle** (recorded information 439.3131, 330.8680), which heads straight for the imposing **Boston Harbor Hotel** ($$$$; 70 Rowes Wharf, 439.7000, 800/752.7077). Other hotels are only a short ride via cab or subway. But if you want to start right on the sight-seeing, and aren't too heavily loaded with luggage, you can check your bags at the **Children's Museum** (300 Congress St, at Museum Wharf, 426.8855), a short harborside stroll away. Plan to devote a few hours to this rehabbed warehouse packed with lively interactive exhibits. School-age children will enjoy the neighboring **Computer Museum** (300 Congress St, at Museum Wharf, 426.2800), especially the mammoth "Walk-Through Computer," a discolike cave of flashing floor lights and rainbow-colored spaghetti wiring.

Refreshment awaits outside on the wharf, where a snack stand shaped like a giant **Milk Bottle** (300 Congress St, at Museum Wharf, 426.7074) serves sandwiches, salads, and ice-cream treats. Also moored out front is **Lightships** (310 Congress St, at Museum Wharf, 350.6001), a barge-turned-restaurant that features generous hamburgers. **Jimbo's Fish Shanty** (245 Northern Ave, at Fish Pier, 542.5600) has train sets that delight kids and may serve as the perfect testing ground if they've never sampled seafood.

If your children happen to be historically inclined, or at least not totally averse, try them out on a stretch of the **Freedom Trail** (242.5642). Or better yet, sign up for a "Boston by Little Feet" tour (367.2345), which is offered on weekends. If you prefer just a customized sampling of the Freedom Trail, board one of the trolleys that ply the circuit; you can get off at particular stops to prowl around, or just stay put. The guides' patter is entertaining, and best of all, this option is easy on the feet. If you're strong enough to withstand cries of "Oh Mommy, can't I have that $1,000 teddy bear?" there's **FAO Schwarz** (440 Boylston St, at Berkeley St, 262.5900). Every toy you or your child could imagine is showcased tantalizingly at this fun, albeit high-priced store. Other kid-pleasers include the **New England Aquarium** (Central Wharf, between Milk and Atlantic Sts, 973.5200); **Faneuil Hall** (Faneuil Hall Sq, between Congress St and Merchants Row), where you can stop for a snack; and the **Public Garden** (between Charles St S and Arlington St, Beacon Hill), where a very tame **Swan Boat** ride or, in winter, a brief spin on ice skates is a must, plus a visit to the knee-high brass statues commemorating the *Make Way for Ducklings* children's book.

For one last, dizzying look at all you've seen, zoom up the glass-sheathed **Hancock Tower Observatory** (200 Clarendon St, between St. James Ave and Trinity Pl, 572.6420). You'll go 60 floors in 30 seconds flat. Take in the staggering views, as well as a nifty little diorama that re-creates Paul Revere's famous ride.

Bests

Marisa Lago
Chief Economic Development Officer, City of Boston

Boston, best known as a Yankee haven, the land of the bean and the cod, also moves to a Latin rhythm. When it comes to dining, the whole range of Hispanic gastronomy can be found in Boston and its surrounding suburbs.

Typical Spanish tapas (exotic appetizers; three or four make a great meal) are found in an unexpected locale—Somerville—at **Dali** (415 Washington St, 661.3254). Salvador himself would be proud of the surreal decor and superb food.

Moving south of the border (gastronomically) and into Boston's neighborhoods (geographically), **Buteco II** in the South End (57 West Dedham St, 247.9249) offers delicious—and filling—Brazilian food, including the national specialty, *feijoada*.

Pampas in Cambridge (928 Massachusetts Ave, 661.6613) is a meat-eater's paradise. Waiters walk around with huge spears laden with every type of grilled meat—chorizo, goat, rabbit, and more standard fare (chicken, lamb, sirloin). It's prepared Argentinian style *(parillada)* over an open flame, and it's all-you-can-eat.

William B. Ketter
Editor, *The Patriot Ledger*

Durgin Park near **Faneuil Hall Marketplace** as a bit of old Boston with Irish pols and Yankee Clam Chowder.

Hamersley's Bistro in the South End. The menu is pricey but worthwhile—especially the squab (baby pigeon) in a red wine sauce. Eating this helps keep Boston clean. And don't pass on the Fenway Park sausage sandwich. It's better than being there.

The *Dictionary of Place Names* suggests that the Jamaica Plain suburb originated with a tribe named the Jamaco or Jameco (Algonquin for "beaver"); in addition, a booklet issued by the City of Boston for the Bicentennial notes that many prominent local families made their fortunes off Jamaica rum. Another apocryphal legend tells of an English woman whose husband told her he was heading for Jamaica; on her way to track him down, she found him, quite by chance, in the Boston suburb.

Day Trips

Boston is a wonderful place to explore, yet when you've had your fill of city life, it's easy to leave town for some stimulating day—or weekend—trips. In just a few hours, public transportation or a car can take you to the rocky beaches of **Cape Ann** or the dunes of **Cape Cod;** the green hills of the **Berkshires;** the beckoning mountains, lakes, and fall colors of New Hampshire and Vermont; or Maine's coastal villages and idyllic islands. And if Boston begins to seem too large an urban center, in only one hour you can escape to **Providence, Rhode Island;** if that's too small for you, in four hours you can be in New York City. Many New England spots have seasonal attractions, but don't let the off-season keep you away—it's often their nicest, quietest time. Cape Cod and the islands in winter, for example, have their own compelling moods. A great source for guidebooks on day trips and travel throughout New England—or the world, for that matter—is **The Globe Corner Bookstore** (3 School St, 523.6658; 49 Palmer St, Cambridge, 497.6277). Also, get a wealth of free information on what to see and do in Massachusetts by calling or writing the **Massachusetts Office of Travel and Tourism** (100 Cambridge St, 13th floor, Boston 02202, 727.3201, 800/447.6277). The following are destination ideas rather than itineraries; arm yourself with information on hours and prices before you go—or just head out with a good map or two and a spirit of exploration.

North to the North Shore

Head north of Boston for the best clams in the world. While on the quest, there's plenty more to see. The infamous **Saugus Strip** along Route 1, for instance, is an eyesore to some and beloved by others for its Miracle Mile–style roadside signs and attendant establishments, vintage kitsch inspired by America's love affair with the auto. This stretch of Route 1 is home base for several of America's biggest, gaudiest restaurants. A giant cactus sign and herd of life-size cattle heralds **Hilltop Steak House,** affectionately called "The Hilltop" (Southbound Rte 1, 233.7700), home of red meat, potatoes, and overeating. A Polynesian theme reigns at **Kowloon** (Northbound Rte 1, 233.9719), located across from **The Hilltop;** and for Chinese food in Disneylike ambience, there's gargantuan **Weylu's** (Northbound Route 1, 233.1632). As you ride along, keep an eye out for a miniature golf course with a towering tyrannosaurus rex, a ship-shaped restaurant, the **Prince Restaurant** (517 Broadway, 233.9950)—a pizza place shaped like the Leaning Tower of Pisa—and other quirky sights.

For a different historical slant, take the Main Street exit off Route 1 to the **Saugus Iron Works National Historic Site** (244 Central St, 233.0050), a reconstruction of the first integrated iron works in North America (created in 1646). The site includes a furnace, a forge, seven water-powered wheels, and a rolling and slitting mill. A well-kept Saugus secret is the **Breakheart Reservation** (177 Forest St, 233.0834), a park with 600 acres of oak, hemlock, pine-covered hills, two freshwater lakes, 10 miles of trails, and lots of birds.

Take Route 1A north from Boston to Route 129 to **Marblehead,** a picture-postcard New England seaside town with early New World flavor and historical attractions, splendid views of the ocean, plus boutiques and good seafood restaurants. It's a perfect place for a leisurely day of walking and poking around. The **Old Town** predates the American Revolution and boasts Federal-style sea captains' homes and neat cottages. For more information, contact the **Marblehead Chamber of Commerce** (62 Pleasant St, 631.2868).

Salem, "the witch city," is a short drive west from Marblehead on Route 114 to Route 1A. The notorious witchcraft trials of 1692, one of the colony's most troubled chapters, caused 19 people to be hanged before the hysterical Puritan populace regained reason. Pick up self-guided walking tour maps (and any other tourist information you may need) from the **Salem Chamber of Commerce** (Old Town Hall, Front St, 508/744.0004).

Don't miss the **Salem Maritime National Historic Site** (174 Derby St, 508/744.4323), where American maritime history is enshrined in the **Custom House, Derby House/Wharf, Bonded Warehouse, West India Goods Store,** and lighthouse. Explore three centuries of historic Salem at the **Essex Institute Museum Neighborhood,** comprising a library, museum (132 Essex St, 508/744.3390), and seven period houses. Less critical to see, but beloved by kids, is the **Salem Witch Museum** (19½ Washington Sq N, 508/744.1692). Visit the inspiration for Nathaniel Hawthorne's novel, *The House of the Seven Gables* (54 Turner St, 508/744.0991); and the **Peabody Museum** (161 Essex St, 508/745.9500), for its collections of maritime history, ethnology, natural history, and Asian export. If you don't want to direct your own steps, take the **Salem Trolley Tour,** run by **Hawthorne Tours** (508/744.5463); it departs from Museum Place.

Continue north on Route 1A to **Beverly** for an afternoon of vaudeville-esque *Marco the Magi's Production of Le Grand David and His Own Spectacular Magic Company* at the 750-seat **Cabot Street Theatre** (286 Cabot St, 508/927.3677) for the Sunday show or at the more intimate 450-seat **Larcom Theatre** (13 Wallis St, 508/922.6313) for the Saturday show. Or catch a Broadway musical (often with Broadway stars) or celebrity concert at the **North Shore Music Theatre** (162 Dunham Rd, 508/922.8500).

En route northeast from Beverly to **Gloucester** is **Manchester-by-the-Sea,** the first North Shore summer resort, serving "Proper Bostonians" in the 1840s. The pretty-as-a-picture **Singing Beach** is a favorite for Boston day-trippers. To avoid the parking hassle, rise early and take a morning beach train on the **Rockport Line Commuter Rail** from **North Station** (722.3200). When you've had enough sunning, swimming, and clambering over rocks, it's a short, pleasant walk into town for a bite to eat before the train ride back.

To drive Cape Ann's rugged shore, continue north on Route 127 to Gloucester. You can also travel here via ferry from Rowes Wharf in Boston on **Mass Bay Lines** (542.8000). The largest town on the North Shore, Gloucester was settled as a fishing colony in 1623 and is still an important port. Its famous landmark is Leonard Craske's statue, the *Gloucester Fisherman,* honoring the intrepid fishers who have died at sea. The fishing fleet is blessed annually, with attendant colorful festivities in late June. Whale-watching excursions leave from here.

A favorite pastime is eating fresh lobster. Two local restaurants that are especially good are **Bistro** (2 Main St, 508/281.8055) and **White Rainbow** (65 Main St, 508/281.0017). Or spend an illuminating evening at the **Gloucester Stage Company** (267 E Main St, 508/281.4099), housed in a rehabbed fish factory. The plays of patron/resident playwright Israel Horovitz often deal with the local way of life.

By day, visit the **Cape Ann Historical Association** (27 Pleasant St, 508/283.0455) to see the stunning collection of 19th-century American painter Fitz Hugh Lane's luminous views of Gloucester Harbor and islands. Perched on rocks overlooking the harbor is "Beauport," the **Sleeper-McCann House** (75 Eastern Point Blvd, 508/283.0800). Beauport was built in the early 1900s by architect/interior designer **Henry Davis Sleeper,** who greatly influenced contemporary tastes and stylesetters, including Isabella Stewart Gardner. The second owner of the mansion, Charles McCann, lived there with his wife, Helena Woolworth, of the five-and-dime empire. Within are 18th- and 19th-century decorative arts and furnishings.

Then move on to the **Hammond Castle Museum** (80 Hesperus Ave, 508/283.2080, 800/283.1643). The medieval-style castle was the humble home of inventor Dr. John Hays Hammond Jr., whose brainstorms included shaving cream, the car starter, electrified toy trains, the forerunner of stereophonic sound, and the precursor to remote control—more than 437 patented inventions. Hammond's resplendent digs contain medieval furnishings, paintings, and sculpture. Monthly organ concerts are played on the 8,600-pipe organ, the largest in a private American home. Tours are given year-round.

A short drive up Cape Ann from Gloucester is tiny **Rockport,** a fishing-community-turned-artists' colony that can be happily meandered in a day. (It's a dry town, by the way.) Parking can be difficult in the center of town unless you arrive as early as the birds, so take the commuter train from **North Station** (722.3200) in Boston if you can—it's a very pretty ride. Rockport's light is particularly beautiful at day's end and in early spring and late fall. The **Toad Hall Book Store** (51 Main St, 508/546.7323) is wonderful for old-time friendliness and service and has a large selection on local geography, history, and lore. The more touristy restaurants and shops are densely clustered on **Bearskin Neck** (closed to cars); for more interesting galleries and restaurants, walk along **Main Street** (where, incidentally, the movie *Mermaids* was filmed). Just beyond town is a windswept haven and public park, the 68-acre **Halibut Point State Park and Reservation** (off Gott Ave, 508/546.2997). An acclaimed annual event held Thursday through Sunday evenings throughout June that's worth coming out for is the Rockport Chamber Music Festival (508/546.7391).

Heading inland on Route 133 from Gloucester is **Essex,** with a staggering concentration of antiques shops in a single-mile stretch. Stop for sustenance at super-casual, rambling **Woodman's** (Main St, 508/768.6451), a North Shore favorite, where Lawrence Woodman first dipped clams in batter and deep-fried them in 1916. Come early or late to avoid huge family crowds, but if you can't, the steamers, lobsters, clams, scallops, chowder, etc., are worth a wait. Nearby **Ipswich,** also prized for its clams and perhaps more so for its beautiful beaches, has more 17th-century houses than any other town in America. On Ipswich Bay, the **Crane Memorial Reservation** includes four miles of shoreline and excellent sandy beaches. In the old Crane residence, the **Great House** (290 Artilla Rd. 508/356.4351), there are weekend concerts and art lectures during the summer, complemented by gorgeous Italianate gardens with sea views.

Near the northeastern tip of Massachusetts, via Route 1A North, is **Newburyport,** once a shipbuilding center and birthplace of the US Coast Guard. Stroll along the waterfront park, promenade, and through the restored commercial district, an enclave of three-story, brick-and-granite buildings. For many, the town has gone overboard gussying itself up for tourists, but it's a nice place to while away a few hours if you're in the mood for shopping, eating, or strolling.

One of Massachusetts's treasures is the **Parker River National and State Wildlife Refuge** on **Plum Island** (508/465.5753), which offers unsullied beauty, refreshing sea air, and glimpses of wildlife. From Newburyport, head north on Route 1A to Route 113 to Newbury and watch carefully for signs to Plum Island and the wildlife refuge. Headquartered at the old Coast Guard lighthouse at the island's northern end, the 4,662-acre refuge has six miles of sandy beaches, hiking trails, observation towers for spotting more than 300 bird species, saltwater and freshwater marshes, sand dunes, surf fishing, nature-study hikes, cross-country skiing, beach plum and cranberry picking, waterfowl hunting, and clamming. Come early on summer weekends because the refuge closes when its quota of 240 cars is reached, often by 9AM. It then reopens at 3PM, so if you're shut out early, spend the day in Newburyport and try again later. In late summer and autumn the marshland takes on rich, soft coloring and the sunsets are breathtaking. The island really empties out after the summer.

Northwest of Boston is **Lowell,** America's first successful planned industrial complex and now a National and State Historical Park (Visitors' Center, 246 Market St, 508/459.1000). Located at the confluence of the Concord and Merrimack Rivers, Lowell was transformed from a sleepy agricultural village into an industrial powerhouse in 1822 by Boston merchant Francis Cabot Lowell and fellow investors. Lowell's Boston Manufacturing Company had already successfully developed a textile mass-production system driven by water-powered looms in Waltham. Though Lowell (the town) first played a pioneering role in the American industrial revolution, it gradually became a squalid environment where women mill workers and immigrants were exploited. Now revitalized by high-tech industries, its fascinating past has been preserved. Today you can tour the mill complexes, operating gatehouses, workers' housing, and a five-and-a-half-mile canal system. Self-guided tour maps are available at the visitors' center, including one for Jack Kerouac's Lowell. Guided interpretive mill and canal tours are offered numerous times daily during the summer; reservations are required. The **Lowell Heritage State Park** *Waterpower Exhibit* (25 Shattuck St, 508/453.1950) is open daily. The town is also the birthplace of James Abbott McNeill Whistler. **The Whistler House Museum of Art** (243 Worthen St, 508/452.7641) displays 19th- and 20th-century American art, including works by Whistler.

Bostonians and visitors alike go beyond Massachusetts's northern border for fall foliage splendor, hiking, cross-country and downhill skiing, rock climbing, canoeing, shopping at factory outlet stores, tranquillity, and natural beauty. To determine which places and recreational activities appeal to you most, contact the **New Hampshire Office of Travel and Tourism** (603/271.2666); **Vermont Travel and Tourism** (802/828.3239); or the **Maine Publicity Bureau** (207/582.9300).

Near Northwest

A few miles northwest of Cambridge on Route 2A are **Lexington** and **Concord,** historic towns where the first military encounters of the American Revolution took place. Concord grapes were first cultivated here, as were the ideas of Louisa May Alcott, Ralph Waldo Emerson, Nathaniel Hawthorne, and Henry David Thoreau. The most notable among the many historic sites are the **Lexington Battle Green**—or **Common** (Visitors' Center, 1875 Massachusetts Ave, 862.1450). Here the first skirmish of the Revolutionary War broke out on 19 April 1775 between the Concord-bound British troops and Colonial Minutemen, alerted earlier by messengers on horseback of the Redcoats' approach. (A reenactment of the Battle of Lexington is staged annually.) The second battle of the day was fought in neighboring Concord, where the citizen militia attacked and drove the British soldiers from North Bridge. Daniel Chester French's famous *Minuteman* statue now stands guard over the bridge.

Minute Man National Historical Park encompasses 750 acres in Concord, Lexington, and **Lincoln,** commemorating the start of the colonies' War for Independence. The park is a narrow strip running on either side of Battle Road (a portion of Route 2A). It begins beyond **Lexington Center** with the **Battle Road Visitor Center** (862.7753) located at one end, off Route 2A on Airport Road in Lexington; and the **North Bridge Visitor Center** (508/369.6993) on the other end, west of Monument Street on Liberty Street in Concord. Though interpretive films and information are on hand, you'll need a bit of imagination to conjure scenes of strife in this bucolic setting. For sophisticated Provençal sustenance, stop in at **Aigo Bistro** (84 Thoreau St, 508/371.1333), the latest venture of Moncef Meddeb, whose greatest hits to date include **L'Espalier** (see page 129) and the **Harvard Book Store Cafe** (see page 181).

Concord's most precious asset—although sometimes not treated that way—is the **Walden Pond Reservation** (Rte 126, 508/369.3254), open daily from 5AM to dusk. The quiet pond is 62 glimmering acres nestled in 333 woody ones. The transcendentalist and free-thinking Thoreau lived and wrote alongside the pond from 1845 to 1847, in a 10-by-15-foot hand-hewn cabin. Visitors to the reservation will find woods and pathways descending to smooth water, where sandbars slope to hundred-foot depths. Bostonians delight in this gentle place, so it gets overcrowded and overworked as summer progresses, but slowly recovers during fall and winter—the best time for waterside contemplation.

Architecture enthusiasts inevitably make the trek to the **Gropius House** (68 Baker Bridge Rd, Lincoln, 227.3956). Follow Route 2 West to Route 126 South, and watch for Baker Bridge Road. German architect **Walter Gropius** built the house in 1938, the year after he came to America. His iconoclastic modern residence introduced the Bauhaus principles of function and simplicity to this country. The house's industrial quality is derived from its commercial components, a revolutionary architectural approach at the time. **Gropius's** residence includes furniture designed by him, Marcel Breuer, and others, and creates an extraordinary quality of place. The house is part of the historic homes collection of the **Society for the Preservation of New England Antiquities (SPNEA),** which offers excellent guided tours. Nearby, and also located in Lincoln, is the **DeCordova and Dana Museum and Sculpture Park** (Sandy Pond Rd, 259.8355). The castlelike museum shows work by mostly New England contemporary artists in its galleries and 35-acre sculpture park. July and August feature outdoor concerts in a shady grove. This is a gorgeous spot for a picnic and stroll any time of year.

Heading back toward Boston, in **Waltham,** take in a dazzling show at the **Rose Art Museum** (736.3434) at **Brandeis University;** also check what's on stage at the college's **Spingold Theatre** (736.3400). The best restaurant in this area—it's up there in the Boston pantheon—is the **Tuscan Grill** (361 Moody St, 891.5486).

West to the Berkshires

Take either the Massachusetts Turnpike (I-90) west from Boston all the way to New York State, or the more northerly and scenic Route 2, which also traverses the state. A popular destination west of Boston is **Old Sturbridge Village** (US 20, off I-84, 508/347.5383), perfect for a family outing. Encompassing more than 200 acres, the historic museum re-creates an early 19th-century New England agricultural community, and features some participatory activities. Its vintage displays include a clock gallery, folk art and portraiture, firearms and militia accoutrements, a working farm, blacksmith, shoemaker, potter, and cooper, and gardens of culinary and medicinal herbs.

The Berkshires refers to the westernmost part of Massachusetts, a verdant region dappled with rivers, lakes, and gentle hills. It's a romantic and serene area with twin legacies: culture and leisure. For information, call or write the **Berkshire Visitor's Bureau** (The Berkshire Common, Pittsfield, MA 01201, 413/443.9186, 800/237.5747). From March to early April you can see tree-tapping, watch sap reduce into real maple syrup, and savor the precious end product. Nestled within mountains, the Berkshires offers hiking, camping, biking, fishing, canoeing, fall foliage, skiing—and welcoming country inns to retire to after the day's activities. Head for the town of **Becket,** off Route 2, the summer home of **Jacob's Pillow** Dance Festival (413/243.0745), the oldest dance festival in the country, where you can see performances by some of the world's most exciting companies. Picnic under the trees before a performance. Stay and/or dine nearby at the **Federal House** (102 Main St, Lee, 413/243.1824). Visit famous **Tanglewood** (Rte 183, Lenox, 413/637.1600, 266.1492 in Boston), summer home to the **Boston Symphony Orchestra.** The lush 200-acre estate is a popular destination for a one-day trip from Boston. Many listeners forgo seats in favor of a picnic on the grass while taking in the symphony. The world-renowned Tanglewood Music Festival is held here annually from July through August, and other events include the Popular Artists Series (throughout the summer) and Labor Day Weekend Jazz Festival.

Not far from **Lee** and **Lenox** in the Berkshires is **Stockbridge,** a perfectly cast New England town known for its **Norman Rockwell Museum** (Main St, 413/298.3822); and for the landmark **Red Lion Inn** (Main St, 413/298.5545), which has been there since its beginnings as a hostelry in 1773. The well-preserved inn provides rural charm year-round with a lobby fireplace, a cat or two, music from the grand piano, and rockers along the front porch ideal for reading the Sunday paper.

Just beyond Stockbridge is **Chesterwood** (4 Williamsville Rd, off Rte 183, 413/298.3579), the former studio and summer residence of the prolific sculptor Daniel Chester French, who created Abraham Lincoln's famous image in the Washington, DC, memorial and the *Minuteman* statue in Concord, not to mention many works around Boston. Casts, models, tools, drawings, books, and French's personal belongings are displayed here. There's a garden and nature trail, too.

North from here on Route 7/20 is **Williamstown,** home of **Williams College** and the **Sterling and Francine Clark Art Institute** (225 South St, 413/458.9545). The institute houses a wonderful collection of 15th- to 19th-century paintings, drawings, prints, and antique silver. The Williamstown Theatre Festival (1000 Main St, between Rte 7 and Park St, 413/597.3400) is like a summer camp for well-known stars of stage and screen. By day, detour on Route 20 to the **Hancock Shaker Village** (413/443.0188), a restoration of the Shaker community founded here in 1790. Twenty buildings have been restored, including a remarkable round stone barn. Shakers lived here until 1960.

South to the South Shore

Before opting to leave Boston for more distant destinations, spend an afternoon island-hopping along the lovely local chain of **Boston Harbor Islands** (see "Sojourns to the Sea: The Boston Harbor Islands" on page 64 for more information). Bostonians often lose sight of them, just beyond what was once the city's front door, and yet the islands offer bird watching, hiking, walking, picnicking, and all sorts of other recreational activities. Enjoy cooling sea breezes on the boat rides to and from the islands, even on the sultriest summer days.

For an unusual architectural tour, from Boston take I-93 South to Route 138 South, heading southwest inland to **North Easton**. Oliver Ames (see **Oliver Ames Mansion,** page 123), manufacturer of the common shovel that helped to build America—as well as a railroad tycoon and Massachusetts governor from 1887 to 1890—chose **Henry Hobson Richardson** to design numerous public buildings for North Easton, manufacturing home of the Ames shovel.

In the course of nine years, **Richardson** built a library, train station, civic center, and other buildings in his characteristic Romanesque rugged masonry style, with other major artisans playing important roles. (**Richardson**'s friend and occasional collaborator, Frederick Law Olmsted, designed the complementary **North Easton Common**.) The result: a sampler of late 19th-century civic architecture that vividly portrays **Richardson**'s ideas.

Head for gentle surf on the South Shore. Motor down I-93 South to Route 3A, the winding shore road to **Hingham** with its graceful town center, home of the **Old Ship Meetinghouse** (Main St, 749.1679). This is the oldest wooden church in continuous use in America, built in 1681, with pulpit, pews, and galleries dating from 1755. Visit a rare pastoral setting made by human design: **World's End Reservation** (Martin's La, 749.8956), a 250-acre part of a harborside estate designed by Frederick Law Olmsted and one of the Trustees of Reservations' beautiful park holdings. Forget about Boston's proximity until you reach the park's edge on the water, where you'll find unusual urban views. Then take a peek at **Boston Light,** the oldest operating lighthouse in America, easily viewed from

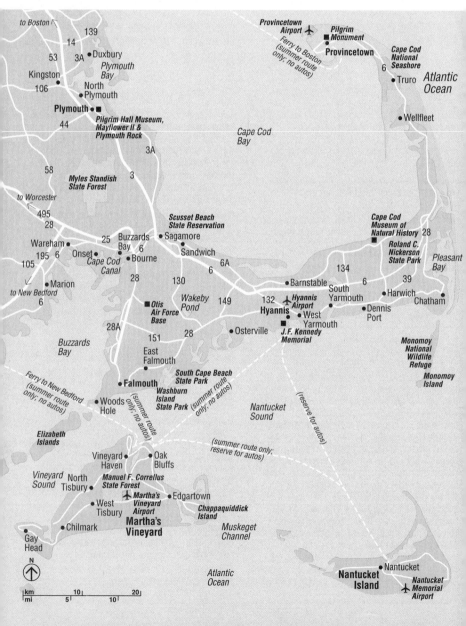

Nantasket Beach on Route 22 in **Hull,** a teeny town at the end of a peninsula stretching north of Hingham into Boston Harbor. Nantasket Beach is a two-mile stretch of beach with a bathhouse, a playground, a promenade, a 1928 carousel, and the **Hull Lifesaving Museum** (1117 Nantasket Ave, 925.5433). The beach is also accessible by **Bay State Cruises**' ferry (723.7800) from Long Wharf on Boston's waterfront. Continue south on Route 3A to **Duxbury** and **Duxbury Beach,** one of the finest barrier beaches on the eastern shore and a paradise for birders and walkers year-round.

On the way to Cape Cod, take Route 3 South to exit 4 and visit **Plimoth Plantation** (137 Warren Ave, 508/746.6544) in Plymouth, a "living museum" of 17th-century Plymouth. The famed rock, as well as a replica of the *Mayflower,* are located at the center of town. Also in Plymouth is **Cranberry World** (255 Water St, 508/747.2350), with two outdoor working bogs—quite a sight, and you can buy the tart, delicious berry made into all sorts of treats.

Once a prosperous fishing and whaling center, Cape Cod is shaped like a large fishhook curving 75 miles into the Atlantic and gleaming with hundreds of freshwater ponds and lakes. Bordering **Cape Cod Bay** and the ocean are resort communities with beaches, clam shacks, summer theater, etc., extending all the way to **Provincetown** at the tip, where the Pilgrims first landed. Much of the cape has been intensely developed, causing erosion to whittle away some lovely land, but fortunately residents are forcing the pace to slow. One of the state's great treasures is the **Cape Cod National Seashore,** a protected 30-mile-long system of pristine beaches, woodlands, and marshes, culminating in the magnificent Provincetown sand dunes (headquarters: Marconi Station area, South Wellfleet, 508/349.3785). For more on Cape Cod, including campsites, contact the **Cape Cod Chamber of Commerce** (Mid-Cape Hwy, Hyannis, MA 02601, 508/362.3225). By car take I-93 South to 3 South, and cross the **Sagamore Bridge** onto the Cape to Route 6 East (and get a good look at the imposing **Cape Cod Canal**). Or ride the ferry from Commonwealth Pier on Boston's waterfront (**Bay State Cruises,** 723.7800). You can go round-trip in one day to Provincetown, although the best plan is to stay at least one night.

At **Falmouth** (South on Route 28 from 3 South) visit the **Ashumet Holly Reservation and Wildlife Sanctuary** (286 Ashumet Rd, 508/563.6390), open year-round, to see a small, unusual sanctuary with many holly varieties. Enjoy the Cape Cod natural environment at the Massachusetts Audubon Society's **Wellfleet Bay Wildlife Sanctuary** (Rte 6, Wellfleet, 508/349.2615), one of Cape Cod's loveliest places.

But the most special place to be—the timing depends on your tastes—is Provincetown. An artists' and Portuguese fishing community that welcomes everyone, Provincetown's population swells from 3,800 in the off-season to 25,000 people in summer. It's a gay haven, with a sensuous atmosphere and active tourist life from Memorial Day weekend until summer's end, but it has a quiet side also. No matter what time of year, it feels comfortable and safe here; return in winter when "P-town" has shrunk and you'll feel as if you have the town and an ocean to yourself. Endowed with the loveliest National Seashore stretch, the town's outskirts are wonderful for bicycling and jogging. For a sweeping view of the tiny town and its ocean setting, climb the **Pilgrim Monument** (High Pole Hill, 508/487.1310, 800/247.1620). The tallest granite structure in the US, the tower hovers high on the village skyline. Visit the funky, fascinating **Heritage Museum** (356 Commercial St, at Center St, 508/487.7098), open mid-June through October only. **Commercial Street** is indeed the Main Street of P-town, where the greatest concentration of restaurants, shops, and lodgings converge. The easiest way to find good accommodations and cuisine, including special off-season listings, is to call or write the very helpful **Provincetown Chamber of Commerce** office in advance (Box 1017, Provincetown, MA 02657, 508/487.3424). The office is located at 307 Commercial Street, MacMillan Wharf.

Martha's Vineyard, an island off Cape Cod southeast of Boston, is another well-loved vacation spot; ferry reservations for cars are often sold out for summer weekends by Christmas. The "Vineyard" has wonderful beaches, sunsets, sailing, walking, picnicking, and bicycling. Its population balloons from 12,000 to 100,000 in the summer. Down-island—on the eastern side—are **Vineyard Haven, Oak Bluffs,** and **Edgartown.** The latter is the most popular with tourists and has rich architectural styles from saltbox to Greek Revival. Up-island—on the western side—are **Tisbury, Chilmark,** and **Gay Head,** which is known for its varicolored clay cliffs. Like Cape Cod and **Nantucket,** the Vineyard is just as wonderful—or more so—out of season. To get there, you and your car can ride the ferry from **Woods Hole** (**Steamship Authority,** 508/540.2022); or without a car you can leave from **New Bedford** (**Cape Island Express Lines,** 508/997.1688). New Bedford is a historic and still-important seaport, where you'll find the excellent **New Bedford Whaling Museum** (18 Johnny Cake Hill, 508/997.0046) and discount shopping, too. Seasonal, passengers-only ferries also leave for the Vineyard from Hyannis (508/775.7185) and Falmouth (508/548.4800). You can also fly into **Martha's Vineyard Airport** (508/325.5300).

For information on Vineyard events, places, and accommodations, call or write the **Martha's Vineyard Chamber of Commerce** (PO Box 1698, Vineyard Haven, MA 02568, 508/693.0085). The office is located on Beach Road. Eat fresh and delicious fish at the elegant, expensive **L'Etoile** (Edgartown, 508/627.5187); en route to Menemsha at the **Beach Plum Inn** (off North Road, 508/645.9454); or at **Oyster Bar** (Oak Bluffs, 508/693.3300). In Oak Bluffs, wander among the **Carpenter Gothic Cottages,** a Methodist revival campground of Victorian Gothic cottages from the late 1800s, oddly ornate with filigree trim.

Located 30 miles southeast off the mainland of Cape Cod, Nantucket is a historic whaling island known as the "Gray Lady of the Sea" for its gently weathering clapboards, and for the clothes worn by its Quaker settlers. Nowadays, the island is a summer playground for the unflashy, monied crowd (keep an eye out for the famous Nantucket-red pants). When it's sweltering in Boston, the sea breezes keep Nantucket cool and its serene weathered beauty is restorative, with gray-shingled houses and rose-covered cottages, moors of heather, cranberry bogs, and gnarled pines. There's absolutely no need for a car here because you can walk, bicycle, or ride a moped from one end of the island to the other. Arrive via ferry from either Hyannis, Martha's Vineyard, or Woods Hole. You can also fly to **Nantucket Memorial Airport** (508/325.5300). For tourist information, call or write the **Nantucket Island Chamber of Commerce** (Main St, Nantucket, MA 02554, 508/228.1700).

The town of **Nantucket** is the exceedingly picturesque and quaint center of activity, and is packed with interesting shops and restaurants. The deli-style **Expresso Cafe** (40 Main St, 508/228.6930) is easy on the budget; **21 Federal** (21 Federal St, 508/228.2121) and the **Boarding House** (12 Federal St, 508/228.9622) aren't, but they're worth every penny. For the ultimate in laid-back (if top-dollar) charm, plan a stay at the **Wauwinet** (120 Wauwinet Rd, 508/228.8768), a historic inn surrounded by beaches at the very edge of civilization. All of the island's beaches are dazzling and easily accessible; as long as you reserve well ahead, you'll fare well at any of the island's reasonably priced bed-and-breakfasts.

Beyond the commonwealth's southern border, yet within a one- to two-hour ride, are Providence and **Newport**, Rhode Island. Providence is the capital of the "Ocean State" and its industrial and commercial center, as well as a major port. The city was founded by Roger Williams, who was banished from Boston by the single-minded and often intolerant Puritans. A city guide and map of landmarks is available at the **Greater Providence Convention and Visitor's Bureau** (30 Exchange Terrace, Providence, RI 02903, 401/274.1636). It's worth a special trip to one of George Germon and Johanne Killeen's renowned restaurants: **Al Forno** or **Lucky's** (both at 577 S Main St, 401/273.9760). **Al Forno** offers rustic Italian-style decor and food, the latter mainly grilled over hardwood or roasted in a brick oven; **Lucky's** tends toward French provincial in decor, but the cuisine is similar to **Al Forno**, with large portions at moderate prices. For an evening out, the **Trinity Repertory Company**, (201 Washington St, 401/351.4242) is nationally renowned; try going round-trip by train from **South Station** in Boston.

South of Providence is Newport, which still echoes its origins as a colonial seaport. The town has always been associated with opulence and the sea: yachts, the navy, competitive sailing, and seaside palaces of the rich. Annual celebrations include the star-studded Newport Jazz Festival, the country's oldest. The **Cliff Walk** is Newport's other most popular attraction, a three-and-a-half-mile shoreline path and a National Historic Walking Trail, with the Atlantic Ocean on one side and the famous summer mansions on the other.

Seen on Screen

Boston and **Cambridge** offer plenty of movie houses for first-run films, but listed below are a number of places to go for more unusual and international offerings. Check the "Calendar" section of the *Boston Globe* on Thursday and the *Boston Phoenix* on Friday for special, foreign, and revival films and series.

Boston Film-Video Foundation (1126 Boylston St, at Hemenway St, 536.1540) screens local, national, and international works by independent filmmakers.

Boston Public Library (Rabb Lecture Hall, Dartmouth St, at Copley Sq, 536.5400) is a great place to satiate an urge to see all of Katherine Hepburn's or Cary Grant's classics or to see Eugene O'Neill's plays brought to the screen, or other ever-popular greats. Their free movie series in a comfortable theater attracts the entire spectrum of Bostonians.

Brattle Theatre (40 Brattle St, between Eliot and Story Sts, Harvard Sq, 876.6837) is a highly regarded independent repertory movie house in Cambridge offering classic new art films, staged readings, and other performances. Special categories of double features are presented most nights.

Ciné Club at the French Library (53 Marlborough St, at Berkeley St, 266.4351) offers a popular ongoing series of recent and classic French films in a lovely setting.

Coolidge Corner Theatre (290 Harvard St, at Beacon St, Coolidge Ct, 734.2500) headlines an innovative program of classic and contemporary local, national, and international films in a great old **Brookline** theater that was once rescued from the specter of gentrification. Animation and cartoon festivals and other special events are held here too.

Harvard-Epworth Series (Harvard-Epworth Church, 1555 Massachusetts Ave, across from Cambridge Common, 354.0837) features everything from silent movies with piano accompaniment to more recent art films (no films are shown June-September).

Harvard Film Archive (24 Quincy St, between Massachusetts Ave and Broadway, 495.4700) screens repertory and contemporary international cinema in the **Carpenter Center for the Visual Arts** in Cambridge.

Institute of Contemporary Art (955 Boylston St, at Hereford St, 266.5152) offers wonderful movies in this very pleasant auditorium, including Palestinian and Israeli films and an Argentinian film series.

Museum of Fine Arts (465 Huntington Ave, at Museum Rd, 267.9300 ext 454) regularly screens interesting alternative films from foreign and ethnic to documentary and avant-garde in its **Remis Auditorium**. Japanese or Italian films might be shown, or the Ingrid Bergman movies made in Sweden before she became a Hollywood star. Many films receive their first US screening here.

The Wang Center for the Performing Arts (268 Tremont St, at Stuart St, 482.9393) offers live jazz in the lobby before its Classic Film Series, which features old and not-so-old favorites shown on this former movie palace's fabulous big screen.

Bests

Patrick Bowe
Owner, **rocco's,** Boston and **Harvard Restaurant,** Harvard Square

Compiled with input from savvy waiters, bartenders, managers, and a dashing lady wine steward:

Coffee: Any **Coffee Connection,** on the run; **Sonsie** on upper **Newbury** to sit and ponder.

Knocking around: **Gardner Museum,** museum-heaven on a small scale; main and side streets of **Harvard Square; North End** streets, markets, joints; **Esplanade** (watch for movies and concerts in the summer); **Beacon Hill.**

Tea, wine, relaxation any time of day or night: **Bristol Lounge, Four Seasons Hotel.**

Cocktails: **Capital Grille; Marais** (great long bar); **Biba** bar (good snacks, wine selections).

Panorama: The **Spinnaker Bar** at the **Hyatt Cambridge** (great Boston views, a stop on first date with my wife); **Top of the Hub** in Back Bay (view is the draw).

Important Eating: **Hamersley's, Jasper's.**

Less Obvious: **Hungry I** (romantic); **Dali** (Spanish, tapas); **Elephant Walk** (French and Cambodian).

Most Obvious: **Harvest.**

Music: **Regattabar.**

Offbeat to very casual . . .

Drinking: **Miracle of Science** (young, happening bar); **Commonwealth Brewery** (Brew Pub); **Doyle's** (great old neighnorhood bar in Jamaica Plain).

Good Eating: **East Coast Grill** (small, wood-fired, fun); **Pomodoro** (tiny, North End); **Figs** (pizza and pastas at original **Olive's** site); **Redbones** (BBQ).

Music: **Johnny D's**

Caroline Knapp
Styles Editor, *The Boston Phoenix*

A burger and Bass draft at the **Miracle of Science,** a bar and grill/neighborhood hangout/essence-of-cool spot near the **Massachusetts Institute of Technology (MIT),** where the food is great and they use petri dishes as ashtrays.

The **Charles River,** especially on calm days. I'm a rower, and the Charles is one of the finest sculling spots in the country. If you don't row, sit on the banks some sunny morning and watch: rowing is strength and elegance in action, and it's one activity that makes Boston stand out as a city.

Martinis at the bar of the **Ritz-Carlton Hotel,** especially if it's snowing outside. Find a window seat overlooking the **Public Garden** (the complimentary bowl of nuts happens to have an exceptionally high number of cashews).

An early morning *caffè latte* on **Hanover Street** in the **North End.** Go on a weekday morning, not over the weekend, when it's too crowded with tourists. Bring the *New York Times* crossword puzzle, and eavesdrop on old Italian men.

The **John Hancock Tower** at twilight is best seen from across the river, in Cambridge, when the tower reflects the sunset and the river reflects the tower and surrounding lights.

Roasted chicken (or just about anything else) at **Hamersley's Bistro,** and a glass of wine at the bar of **Biba** on a Saturday afternoon, before it's crowded. Anything seafood-related at **Jasper's** restaurant. Dinner with another food lover at **The Blue Room,** or **The East Coast Grill.**

Clara Wainwright
Artist/Founder of the Great Boston Kite Festival

Chinatown—with its Chinese and Vietnamese restaurants—where stir-fried octopus, beefsteak soup, baby octopus, and quail eggs are available on a 24-hour basis. Also take advantage of the great fabric stores here.

Jamaica Pond is stocked with trout, and at any time of day there are people fishing, boating, and parading.

Culture Shock on Newbury Street has great, stylish clothing from London and Boston designers at affordable prices. Just down the street, heading downtown, is **Nomad,** a fabulous marketplace of ethnic clothing and jewelry. Be sure to check out the Ken Born and Mexican T-shirts at **Nomad.**

Patrick Lyons
Entertainment Impresario, Lyons Group Management

A visit to Harvard Square, home to a unique mixture of people who are educated, radical, bohemian, and just plain "out there." Buskers and street musicians there today evoke memories of Bob Dylan in the 1960s. Incidentally, it is also the home of **Harvard University.**

Every other day **Ristorante Toscano** on Charles Street imports fresh mushrooms from Milan. As an appetizer, they are near a religious experience.

Stroll past **Louisburg Square** on Beacon Hill and capture the essence of Boston Brahmin existence.

Walk along the **Charles River,** from the **Harvard Bridge** (opposite **MIT**) down **Memorial Drive** for the undisputed best view of Boston day or night.

Take a Sunday afternoon drive north to **Woodman's Lobster in the Rough** in Essex; they invented the fried clam in 1902.

A twilight cruise of Boston Harbor with a special stop beneath one of **Logan Airport's** flight paths. Listening to the 747s scream overhead is a thrill.

See the city nightlife on **Lansdowne Street** (in the shadow of **Fenway Park**)—rave, R&B, techno, industrial, reggae, world beat, disco, soul, ska, rock, and about every underground fashion statement known to Boston. There are five nightclubs, and no waiting! (Note: We should know—we operate them.)

Index

A

Index

Index

Index

Restaurants

Only restaurants with star ratings are listed below and at right. All restaurants are listed alphabetically in the main (preceding) index. Always call in advance to ensure a restaurant has not closed, changed its hours, or booked its tables for a private party. The restaurant price ratings are based on the average cost of an entrée for one person, excluding tax and tip.

★★★★ An Extraordinary Experience

★★★ Excellent

★★ Very Good

★ Good

$$$$ Big Bucks ($20 and up)

$$$ Expensive ($15-$20)

$$ Reasonable (10-$15)

$ The Price Is Right (less than $10)

Hotels

The hotels listed below and at right are grouped according to their price ratings; they are also listed in the main index. The hotel price ratings reflect the base price of a standard room for two people for one night during the peak season.

Credits

Writer and Researcher
Peter Tietjen

Writers and Researchers
(Previous Editions)
Julia Collins
Sandy MacDonald
Nancy Robins

ACCESS®PRESS

Editorial Director
Lois Spritzer

Managing Editor
Laura L. Brengelman

Senior Editor
Beth Schlau

Associate Editors
Kathryn Clark
Kathleen Kent

Contributing Editors
Gwynn Press
Susan Cutter Snyder

Map Editor
Karen Decker

Assistant Map Editor
Susan Charles

Manager of Design and Production
Cherylonda Fitzgerald

Senior Designer
Claudia Goulette

Designers
Michael Blum

Map Designers
Michael Blum
Patricia Keelin

Manager, Electronic Publishing
John R. Day

Cover Design
William McCoy
Rainbow

Special Thanks
Jim Andrews
Philip Bergen,
Bostonian Society
Boston Architectural
Center
Metropolitan District
Commission
Jerry Stanton
Ron Warren

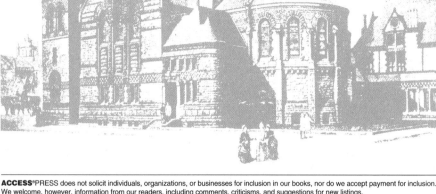

Trinity Church

ACCESS® Guides

Order by phone, toll-free: 1-800-331-3761

Travel: Promo # RØØ111
WSJ: Promo # RØØ211

Name _____ Phone _____

Address _____

City _____ State _____ Zip _____

Please send me the following **ACCESS**® Guides:

☐ **BARCELONA**ACCESS® $17.00
0-06-277000-4

☐ **BOSTON**ACCESS® $18.00
0-06-277049-7

☐ **BUDGET EUROPE**ACCESS® $18.00
0-06-277120-5

☐ **CAPE COD**ACCESS® $18.00
0-06-277123-X

☐ **CARIBBEAN**ACCESS® $18.00
0-06-277128-0

☐ **CHICAGO**ACCESS® $18.00
0-06-277048-9

☐ **FLORENCE/VENICE/MILAN**ACCESS®
$17.00
0-06-277081-0

☐ **HAWAII**ACCESS® $18.00
0-06-277068-3

☐ **LAS VEGAS**ACCESS® $18.00
0-06-277055-1

☐ **LONDON**ACCESS® $18.00
0-06-277129-9

☐ **LOS ANGELES**ACCESS® $18.00
0-06-277131-0

☐ **MEXICO**ACCESS® $18.00
0-06-277127-2

☐ **MIAMI & SOUTH FLORIDA**ACCESS®
$18.00
0-06-277070-5

☐ **MONTREAL & QUEBEC CITY**ACCESS® $18.00
0-06-277079-9

☐ **NEW ORLEANS**ACCESS® $18.00
0-06-277118-3

☐ **NEW YORK CITY**ACCESS® $18.00
0-06-277124-8

☐ **ORLANDO & CENTRAL FLORIDA**ACCESS® $18.00
0-06-277069-1

☐ **PARIS**ACCESS® $18.00
0-06-277132-9

☐ **PHILADELPHIA**ACCESS® $18.00
0-06-277065-9

☐ **ROME**ACCESS® $18.00
0-06-277053-5

☐ **SAN DIEGO**ACCESS® $18.00
0-06-277004-7

☐ **SAN FRANCISCO**ACCESS® $18.00
0-06-277121-3

☐ **SANTA FE/TAOS/ ALBUQUERQUE**ACCESS® $18.00
0-06-277054-3

☐ **SEATTLE**ACCESS® $18.00
0-06-277050-0

☐ **SKI COUNTRY**ACCESS®
Eastern United States $18.00
0-06-277125-6

☐ **SKI COUNTRY**ACCESS®
Western United States $18.00
0-06-277066-7

☐ **THE WALL STREET JOURNAL**
Guide to Understanding Money & Markets
$13.95
0-06-772516-3

☐ **WASHINGTON DC**ACCESS® $18.00
0-06-277077-2

☐ **WINE COUNTRY**ACCESS®
Northern California $18.00
0-06-277122-1

Prices subject to change without notice.

Total for **ACCESS**® Guides:	$
Please add applicable sales tax:	
Add $4.00 for first book S&H, $1.00 per additional book:	
Total payment:	$

☐ Check or Money Order enclosed. Offer valid in the United States only.
Please make payable to HarperCollins*Publishers*.

☐ Charge my credit card   ☐ American Express   ☐ Visa   ☐ MasterCard

Card no. _____ Exp. date _____

Signature _____

Send orders to:
HarperCollins*Publishers*
P.O. Box 588
Dunmore, PA 18512-0588

Send correspondence to:
ACCESS®PRESS
10 East 53rd Street,18th Floor
New York, NY 10022